THE STORY OF THE

Pall Mall Gazette

FREDERICK GREENWOOD when he became Editor of the *Pall Mall Gazette*

From a portrait by an unknown artist, in the possession of the Author

THE STORY OF THE

Pall Mall Gazette

of its first editor

FREDERICK GREENWOOD

and of its founder

GEORGE MURRAY SMITH

J. W. ROBERTSON SCOTT, C.H.

Hon. M.A. (Oxon.)

The backward glance that enheartens the pilgrim

GREENWOOD PRESS, PUBLISHERS

WESTPORT, CONNECTICUT

Originally published in 1950
by Oxford University Press, London, New York & Toronto

Reprinted with the permission
of Oxford University Press, Inc., New York

First Greenwood Reprinting 1971

Library of Congress Catalogue Card Number 73-141266

SBN 8371-5826-5

Printed in the United States of America

To the precious memory
of all the Editors
who gave up their posts and salaries
for their opinions

CONTENTS

If I doe borrow anything you shall finde mee to acknowledge it and to thank him that lighted me a candle.—*Donne*

For permission to print copyright letters or portions of letters from Sir James Barrie, Lord Morley, and Mr. Bernard Shaw I am indebted to Lady Cynthia Asquith, Mr. Guy Morley, and Mr. Shaw respectively.

J. W. R. S.

ILLUSTRATIONS

PREFATORY

CHAPTER I

Why it was worth while attempting this Book

THACKERAY'S 'PALL MALL GAZETTE'[1] — THE EDITOR WHO BROUGHT GREAT BRITAIN £1,500,000 A YEAR — JOHN MORLEY AND W. T. STEAD — A PEAK IN JOURNALISTIC HISTORY — A PUBLISHER WHO MADE A FORTUNE AND GAVE THE NATION THE 'DICTIONARY OF NATIONAL BIOGRAPHY'

To seek out truth, above all things, and to present to readers, not such things as statecraft would wish them to know, but the truth, as near as they can attain to it.—*The Times*, 1852
Is not every able editor a ruler of the world, being a persuader of it?—*Carlyle*

As I have put aside several publishers' proposals for books in order to write this one, and as, in my eighty-fourth year, the time I have left gets shorter, there must seem to me special reasons for setting about it.

There are three.

The book is a work of piety in memory of the first editor of the newspaper on which it was the distinction of my young manhood to serve, a record of his outstanding work and worth, which someone ought to have written long before this.

It is an act of devotion to ideals of journalism which I have urged for sixty years,[2] and helped to maintain in the *Pall Mall*

[1] For American readers: Pall Mall, pronounced *Pell Mell*, was the name of the street developed from one of the alleys in which the game of *pall mall* was played. A hard, wooden ball was driven through an iron ring. The *Oxford English Dictionary* explains: French *pallemaille*; Italian, *palla* variety of *balla*, a ball; Latin *malleus* hammer. A mell court in Hampstead, damaged in the War, was re-opened by the American Minister in London, Mr. J. C. Holmes, in July last year.

[2] In 1888 I wrote with zest an article in praise of 'The New Journalism', in

Gazette, the *Westminster Gazette*, and the *Daily Chronicle*, in the *New East* which I started in Tokyo, and in the *Countryman* which I founded in the Cotswolds, and edited, the *New East* for three and the *Countryman* for twenty years—as told in my *Faith and Works in Fleet Street.*[1]

It is a modest contribution to literary, journalistic, social, and political history because it offers new facts and incidents, new points of character, and new curiosities of experience in relation to all sorts of people from Queen Victoria downwards.

Founded in 1865, fourteen months before I was born, the *Pall Mall Gazette* was named, as every reader of Thackeray knows, after the most distinguished newspaper in fiction, the journal which he provided for Arthur Pendennis. In character his *Pall Mall Gazette* was as far removed as it could well be from that other *Gazette*, of Eatanswill, imagined by Dickens two years before in the *Pickwick Papers*, which Thackeray had desired to illustrate. It was to be 'written by gentlemen for gentlemen'.

The paper in *Pendennis*, its author asserted, 'had its offices in Catherine Street, Strand'. The actual *Pall Mall Gazette*, created by Frederick Greenwood, which was never to hear the end of 'written by gentlemen for gentlemen', saw the light not many yards distant, in a Strand side street, Salisbury Street, now swept away. The paper was afterwards produced, and continued to be produced when I was on it, in the now rebuilt Northumberland Street, in the Strand also, a little farther west. Northumberland Street is the narrow street opposite the South Africa building, on the site of which stood, in my time, Morley's impeccable hotel, a post-office, and the shop of the bootmakers who showed in their window a letter from Carlyle testifying to the satisfaction they had given in Cheyne Row.

I am the only survivor of the office staff of the *Pall Mall*

Matthew Arnold's sense, a proof of which was approved by W. T. Stead. Arnold coined the phrase in the *Nineteenth Century*, May 1887, the reference being to Stead's *Pall Mall Gazette*. See *Literary Recollections* by Sir Edward Cook (Macmillan).

[1] Hodder & Stoughton, 1947.

Gazette under W. T. Stead and his successor Sir E. T. Cook.[1] They were the third and fourth—the second was John (afterwards Viscount) Morley—of the half-dozen remarkable editors of a remarkable journal. I sub-edited for six years in that poky office in Northumberland Street, in which, when it was Hartshorn Lane, Ben Jonson lodged and, it has been thought, Richard Savage had an adventure.

The paper which began life with Greenwood as initiator and editor, and George Smith, of the famous publishing firm of Smith & Elder, as proprietor, was new in plan and appearance, and distinctive in spirit and quality. Whether edited by Greenwood, Morley, Stead, Cook, Harry Cust, or J. L. Garvin, it had an influence out of all proportion to the number of copies sold, and more than once it made history.

It was Greenwood who suggested to the Foreign Secretary of the time (Lord Derby) the buying of the Suez Canal shares for Great Britain,[2] and—amazing behaviour in the eyes of a modern news editor!—when the transaction was promptly carried out, within a few weeks, was above saying anything about it in his paper! To-day these shares, bought for less than five millions, including commission, bring in to the Chancellor of the Exchequer a million and a half a year. Queen Victoria spoke of the purchase as 'a great and important event', Disraeli as 'not the least important event of our generation'.

Greenwood's journalistic career is also to be remembered because, on points of principle, he resigned the editorship not only of the *Pall Mall Gazette*, but of his second journal, the *St. James's Gazette*.

Greenwood has the further credit of having refused the Piggott forgeries, the cost of the legal proceedings following the publica-

[1] Sir Edward Tyas Cook is not to be confounded with Sir Edward Cook, C.S.I., E. T. Cook, the musician, E. T. Cook (Mrs. E. Thornton Cook), author of *Her Majesty* and other volumes, or E. T. Cook who wrote so many acceptable gardening books.

[2] A condensation of Chapter XVIII, 'Who Got Us the Suez Canal Shares?', and Chapter XIX, 'Dizzy, Lady Bradford and the Faery', appeared in the *Quarterly Review*, July 1949.

tion of which in *The Times* discredited our honoured journal, reduced it almost to insolvency, and placed it in the hands of Northcliffe.

The stand which Greenwood made, as a Conservative, against the Boer War was also noteworthy. There is in these pages new information about both Chamberlain and Rhodes.

In raising my memorial to a master of journalism who did uncommon service in political and social exposition, exhortation, criticism, and leadership, and fostered the work of men who became famous, I am not, in Carlyle's phrase, 'currying dead dog'. It is exactly forty years since Greenwood died, but what he stood for, in his profession and in public life, was never of greater national importance than it is to-day, and has never had the sympathy of a larger number of instructed people.

Greenwood is not in the National Portrait Gallery. The only portrait of him is the one in my possession, reproduced as the frontispiece of this book, and there is no bust of him anywhere. Only a few years ago Lady Oxford and Asquith assured me that she had 'never heard of Frederick Greenwood'. Although he is known to have been at Hatfield, Lord Salisbury tells me that no letters are to be found there of the man who did more for his father and Lord Beaconsfield in their contentions with Gladstone than any of their supporters in the Press. The late Lord Derby, with whose father Greenwood was engaged in the momentous purchase of the Suez Canal shares, knew of no papers at Knowsley. The hundred pages of index to the able five-volume *History of Modern England* by Herbert Paul, a fellow journalist, who wrote in Greenwood's lifetime, do not disclose a single reference to the *Pall Mall Gazette*, except a small footnote, until the editorship of John Morley.

But Greenwood described himself truly when he said that, as editor of that paper, he occupied 'a place of power, at least equal to half a dozen seats in Parliament'. Always excepting Delane, editors and politicians did not in his time, however, as Lord Quickswood once wrote to me, 'mingle nearly so freely as they do to-day'. 'It is now a common thing', as an historian of the Press notes, 'to write biographies of journalists',[1] but no one

[1] BOOKS ABOUT EDITORS. Delane's life has been written in one volume by E. T. Cook and in two volumes by A. L. Dasent, and there are the fullest details about him in the engrossing *History of 'The Times'*. Derek Hudson and Harold Child are the authors of *Thomas Barnes of 'The Times'*. Among biographies of editors we have the lives of W. T. Stead by his daughter and by F. A. Whyte, Saxon Mills's *Sir Edward Cook*, J. L. Hammond's *C. P. Scott*, also *The Making of the 'Manchester Guardian'*, Wilson Harris's *J. A. Spender*, H. J. Massingham's *H. W. M.*, Hamilton Fyfe's *T. P. O'Connor*, H. A. Taylor's *Robert Donald*, Russell Stannard's *Dictators of Fleet Street*, Lord Cockburn's and Greig's *Francis Jeffrey* of the *Edinburgh Review*, Sprigge's *Life and Times of Thomas Wakley* of the *Lancet*, Sir William Beach Thomas's *Story of the 'Spectator'*, and Amy Strachey's *St. Loe Strachey, His Life and His Papers*—Hutton and Townsend desired that no memoir should be written of them—G. S. Layard's *Shirley Brooks* of *Punch*; Kennedy Williamson's *W. E. Henley*, Philip Mairet's *A. R. Orage*, E. T. Cook's *Edmund Garrett*, T. H. Darlow's *Robertson Nicoll*, Kathleen Garvin's *J. L. Garvin*, Algar Thorold's *Henry Labouchere*, Hesketh Pearson's *Labby*, F. W. Maitland's *Life and Letters of Leslie Stephen*, R. S. Lambert's *Cobbett of the West*, and Alice Head's *It Never Could Have Happened.*

Lives of editor-proprietors include the books of Tom Clarke, Hamilton Fyfe, Max Pemberton, Louise Owen, and R. M. Wilson on *Northcliffe*, F. A. Mackenzie's *Lord Beaverbrook*, Sidney Dark's *Sir Arthur Pearson*, and Hulda Friedrichs's *Sir George Newnes.*

Among autobiographies there are Sir John Robinson's *Fifty Years in Fleet Street*, Wickham Steed's *Through Thirty Years*, J. St. Loe Strachey's *River of Life* and *Adventure of Living*, J. A. Spender's *Life, Journalism and Politics*, the *Papers of Sir William Hardman*, R. D. Blumenfeld's *R. D. B.'s Diary*, *In My Time*, and *R. D. B.'s Procession*, Hamilton Fyfe's *My Seven Selves*, *My Memories*, and *Sixty Years in Fleet Street*, Eric Parker's *Memory Looks Forward*, H. J. Higginbottom's *Vivid Life*, Edmund Yates's *Recollections*, Catling's *Life's Pilgrimage*, *Editor's Retrospect* by Charles A. Cooper of the *Scotsman*, Sir Francis Burnand's *Records and Reminiscences*, and C. K. Shorter's *Autobiography.*

Books by or about journalists who were not or for only a short time editors include H. W. Nevinson's *Between the Acts*, *Essays in Freedom*, *Changes and Chances*, *In the Dark Backward*, *Running Accompaniments*, *Films of Time*, and *Visions and Memories*, in all of which there is autobiographical matter, Sir Henry Lucy's *Diaries*, *W. T. Arnold* by Mrs. Humphry Ward and C. E. Montague, *E. L. Blanchard* by Clement Scott and Cecil Howard, Oliver Elton's *C. E. Montague*, the *Memories of W. H. Helm*, the *Life and Adventures of George Augustus Sala*, Sir Philip Gibbs's *Adventure in Journalism*, *Sixty Years Ago and After* by Sir Max Pemberton, *Victorians, Edwardians and Georgians* by John Boon of the Exchange Telegraph Company, James Milne's *Window in Fleet Street*, C. E. Fayle's *Harold Wright*, and Sir John Hammerton's *Books and Myself.*

There are various books by C. E. Montague, H. M. Hyndman, James Milne, and Sir Alexander Mackintosh, Alfred Robbins's *The Press*, G. B. Dibblee's

has written a life of Greenwood. Sir William Robertson Nicoll, who often tried to persuade him to autobiography, said that 'unless Sir James Barrie can be induced to take up his pen there is small hope that any worthy account of him will ever appear; those who might have written it are nearly all passed away'. To-day, as the editor of *Notes and Queries* adapts to me from the sixteenth century, 'All his friends are lapped in lead.' The distance his life went back is shown by the fact that Thackeray and Dickens had both been in his house.

Journalism is under marked obligations not only to Greenwood but to the men who worked on the *Pall Mall Gazette*. Twice over, staff and chief contributors—and a journalist who has been editor of two London daily papers does not go beyond the fact when he says 'no paper had so many interesting people connected with it'[1]—had the backbone to walk out with their editor. One staff did it when, on a change of proprietor, the paper turned Liberal. A second staff followed their example when, after Greenwood's time, it became Conservative again.

Nowadays, most people who recall the *Pall Mall Gazette*, think of it in its last days, either when it was the property of the first Lord Astor, or was passing, through various hands, at a moderate standard of quality, to extinction. But after Green-

The Newspaper, Wilson Harris's *Daily Press*, Kingsley Martin's *The Press the Public Wants*, Francis Williams's *Press, Parliament and People*, Stanley Morison's *The English Newspaper*, Derek Hudson's *Journalists and Newspapers*, Tom Clarke's *Journalism*, Kennedy Jones's *Fleet Street and Downing Street*, Wilfrid Hindley's *Morning Post*, Comyns Beaumont's *Rebel in Fleet Street*, A. E. Wilson's *Playgoer's Pilgrimage*, *T's* (James Thorpe's) *Friends and Adventures*, Robert Sinclair's *Fifty Years of Newspaper Life*, books on *Moberly Bell* by Kitchin and Moberly Bell, and *Anywhere for a News Story*, to which Nevinson and a dozen other journalists contribute; and histories of journalism such as those by Knight Hunt, Andrews, Grant, Pebody, Fox Bourne, and J. D. Symon, and the Reports by the Royal Commission and by P.E.P.

Among the most recent autobiographies of American editors may be mentioned *The Happy Profession* and *Atlantic Harvest* of Ellery Sedgwick, *The Autobiography* of William Allen White, and *The Disappearing Daily* of Oswald Garrison Villard. Of an earlier date are the writings of Walter H. Page, and Hendrick's memoir of him, the *Fifty Years a Journalist* by Melville S. Stone and Edward Bok's autobiography, *The Americanisation of Edward Bok*.

[1] *Press Parade*, Hamilton Fyfe (Watts).

wood's editorship of fifteen years, which ended in 1880, it had for a period (the Astor sale was in 1892[1]) a noteworthy history of which I hope one day to record my memories.

John Morley's service for a short time as editor of the *Pall Mall Gazette*, and, for a longer span, as the intrepid conductor of the *Fortnightly Review*[2] and the author of books of no ordinary significance in his day, has almost slipped from our memories.

The man who followed him contrasted as remarkably with Morley as with Greenwood. But there was no question about his prowess and his powers. It was Stead—last year was his centenary—of whom his faithful friend, Lord Esher, the *fidus Achates* of our King's grandfather, said that the editor of the *Pall Mall Gazette*, the confidant and backer of pro-Consuls, 'came nearer to ruling the British Empire than any living man'; and Esher, the editor of the *Spectator* once declared, 'knew more about the Commonwealth and talked more sense than most men'.[3] What is certain is that 'that great journalist and earnest Puritan', as E. C. Bentley[4] justly calls him, was the true inventor and pioneer of the New Journalism in its worthy aspects, and an honest man. Like the rest of us, he had his foibles and made mistakes, but he forced the House of Commons to pass the Criminal Law Amendment Act which raised from 13 to 16 the 'age of consent' of girls to their seduction, sent General Gordon to the Sudan, gained by his 'Truth about the Navy' the enduring affection of the puissant Admiral Fisher, and by his physical and moral courage, the purity of his character, his national spirit, and his unceasing activity won the regard and indulgence of some of the truest men and women of his time. To-

[1] It was on the purchase by Lord Astor that I retired from it.

[2] After Morley's retirement it was for short periods in the hands of T. H. S. Escott and Frank Harris before W. L. Courtney took over in 1894. He was editor until his death. The *Fortnightly* was then bought by a Canadian called Hammond, who was titular editor from 1929 until 1937. Until 1939 it was edited by W. Horsfall Carter; from that date it has been conducted by John Armitage.

[3] See *Journals and Letters of Reginald Viscount Esher* (Nicholson & Watson) and *Cloud Capp'd Towers* (Murray).

[4] Author of *Trent's Last Case*.

day he is either confounded with my friend and neighbour, Wickham Steed (the distinguished foreign correspondent and former editor of *The Times*, and sometime editor, in succession to Stead, of the *Review of Reviews*), or is forgotten.

Only what another editor, H. W. Massingham, called 'the ungainly adjective, "influential" ', describes the *Pall Mall Gazette*. In turning over its pages one thinks of a phrase once applied to the defunct *Saturday Review*, 'It is difficult for the present generation to understand the influence it exercised.'

In the history of the *Pall Mall Gazette*, account has also to be taken of Greenwood's secessionist *St. James's Gazette*, not to speak of his *Anti-Jacobin*.

There is, further, the last of what were called 'the Gazetteers', the green *Westminster Gazette*, started by Cook and 'Mr. Newnes of *Titbits*'[1] when the *Pall Mall Gazette* was sold to the father of Lord Astor. After Cook, for a quarter of a century, J. A. Spender, in the closest touch with the leaders of the Liberal party, carried on the traditions of the journal. Finally, came the decrepit stage as a morning paper, and ultimate submergence in the *Daily News*, and Bouverie Street's own affiliation with Whitefriars Street in the *News Chronicle*.

Some years ago I came to feel it to be a duty to add to my own recollections all I could gather about a newspaper with which, at its best, British journalism unquestionably reached one of its peaks. Such an effort might be of service, I thought, in strengthening the purpose of young men and women who have a vocation for journalism and are minded to sustain it in honour.

I hoped, also, that the book might appeal to the 'general reader' interested in the ways of writing men and women, whether filling the columns of newspapers or producing books. I have written indeed, as Lord Goschen said in his two-volume life of his publisher-grandfather, primarily 'for the general public rather than for experts'.

The falling-away of a section of the Press of recent years, of

[1] Afterwards Sir George Newnes. The phrase was Henry Yates Thompson's. See Chapter XX.

which, in my *Faith and Works in Fleet Street*, I tried to make neither too much nor too little—'I am', I said, 'a believing, not a desponding oldster'[1]—does not hinder the intelligent public from appreciating the immense service which newspapers of the first quality render to the social, national, and international advance. Nor does it lessen interest in the method of their production and in the animated relations of their editors with their readers and proprietors. In the following pages I throw some light on these matters, and offer insight into the way in which movements of importance are aided by disinterested journalistic endeavour, and editors merit praise and achieve honest distinction.

The book has also its timeliness following the Report of the Royal Commission on the Press, and when there is 'a new wave of interest in Victorianism' not only in this country but, as there is constant evidence, in the United States.

This volume is not only about a famous editor but about a famous publisher. I am glad that a plenitude of new unpublished material, from several sources, enables me to give, along with my portrait of Greenwood, a fuller account than has yet been available of George Murray Smith. A man of countless literary friendships and generosities, the cleverness with which, outside his publishing sphere, he took to ship-owning, and gained an honest million and a half out of Apollinaris would have delighted Samuel Smiles. The *Pall Mall Gazette* could not have held on as it did, could not have made the mark it did without the *bonhomie* and stalwart proprietorship of the courageous publisher to whom we are indebted for the twenty-one, now twenty-five, volumes of the *Dictionary of National Biography*.

I picture the setting of Greenwood and Smith in journalistic and literary conditions and relationships unfamiliar to this

[1] When Mrs. Humphry Ward said to Mr. Gladstone that 'more was made of scandals nowadays by the newspapers', the old man would not have it. 'When I was a boy', he said—he left Eton in 1827—'there were two papers, the *Age* and the *Satirist*, which were worse than anything that exists now.'—*Faith and Works in Fleet Street* (Hodder & Stoughton).

generation. No effective presentation of the *Pall Mall Gazette* could be made without some account of the social fabric and temper eighty years ago, in which this eminent newspaper came into being. As Greenwood was to write in 1901, the journal was 'more original than is apparent now'.

Exceptional technical and social experience had been acquired by Smith as a publisher, for many years, of books of the first quality, as founder of *Cornhill*—as much a 'new departure' in periodicals as the *Pall Mall Gazette* was in newspapers—as a colleague with Thackeray in its direction, and as a man of considerable commercial interests. Greenwood was in association with *Cornhill* and for a year or two its editor. In conducting it, Smith and Greenwood gained the acquaintance and friendship of some of the chief writers of their time.

So Thackeray, who not only invented the name of the newspaper, but was the first editor of *Cornhill*, and the honoured firm of Smith & Elder come into the story. Concerning their authors, including Thackeray, Browning, Charlotte Brontë, Ruskin, and Trollope, the reader will find some fresh illustrations of character and temperament.

The mass of information I have gathered has made it imperative that the present book should not go beyond the *Pall Mall Gazette* under Greenwood, his work on its offshoot, the *St. James's Gazette*, and his labours in his last years. Greenwood himself said that 'a memoir of the *P.M.G.* during the fifteen years it was in my hands' would, by itself, 'fill a book'.

I have had the advantage of having in my hands no fewer than 500 unpublished letters from 'the statesman of the leading article', as George Meredith called Greenwood. There will also be found in these pages some unpublished letters from Carlyle, John Morley, J. M. Barrie, Richard Jefferies, General Gordon, Lady Dorothy Nevill, W. E. Henley, and Bernard Shaw, and a new story or two of Queen Victoria.

Mr. Asquith once remarked that 'the biographer is not a judge'. 'How little we learn', wrote Augustine Birrell, 'of the character of a dead man we have never seen.' Deliberately, this book is not a 'study'. It is a narrative, from every source available to me, of what Greenwood and Smith did, an account of the conditions in which they worked, and of what those who knew them and read what they wrote and published thought of them. As well as Greenwood's letters I am able to reproduce many characteristic notes by Smith. From all this, I feel, my readers may form an unforced impression of, in Carlyle's phrase, 'genuine bits of thoroughly human stuff'.

Greenwood, a man of peculiar personal distinction, 'with a backbone', said *The Times*, 'almost too stiff for this world', went neither to public school nor university—he began life as a printer's apprentice—but taught those who did. Somewhat greater educational advantages came the way of Smith, but he, too, never saw a university. He shaped his own career. I have found the time I have had the opportunity of spending with these two unusual men well spent. 'As the memory of the just is blessed', wrote William Penn, 'so there seems to be a blessing upon those that have a right remembrance of them.' 'I esteem biography', said Johnson, 'as giving us what comes near to ourselves, what we can turn to use.'

But in biography there are constant dangers. One is the danger of what Lloyd George called 'drowning a man's life in the story of his times'. I have made determined endeavours to avoid this, but am glad to have had the privilege of salving a good deal of interesting information about the well-known people whom Greenwood and Smith knew.

Another difficulty is that feelingly stated, on the basis of some experience, by the author of *A Publisher and his Friends*. 'In my work dealing with a large number of transactions, which, though carried on concurrently, are allied to one another by nothing save their accidental association with one individual, the difficulties of maintaining the even consecutive current of the narrative are obviously so great as to be almost unsurmountable.'[1] Here I can only say that I have done my best.

[1] Samuel Smiles (Murray).

I have attended to the demand lately made by a well-known publicist who says that 'a biographer is less than fair to himself when he provides too few trivialities of speech and act; they may reveal character with point and brilliance'. In that work of patience and devotion, the four large volumes of his engrossing *Letters and Private Papers of Thackeray*,[1] Dr. Ray writes sensibly that 'the re-creation of any personality is made possible by the accumulation of many kinds of *petits faits vrais*'. I have preserved odds and ends which interested me, and will, I trust, interest 'general readers' as well as fellow journalists. It is one of the daughters of the imaginer of the *Pall Mall Gazette* who writes that 'it is the by-the-way things that are most vivid'.[2] We must acknowledge what Henry James called 'the contributive value of accessory facts'. There is, as John Aubrey says, 'trueth and usefulness to be picked out of them'.

My publisher has paid me the compliment of saying that this is 'a leisurely book'. At times, no doubt, I have in Stendhal's phrase, 'dawdled down the road'. But as Sterne said, 'digressions incontestably are the sunshine, the life, the soul of reading; take them out—you might as well take the book with them'. I seek comfort in Fulke Greville, 'Trifles are often read with curiosity later, even though the collector may be an ordinary person like myself.' But some of the things I have had the fortune to come by are not 'trifles'. What a help to an all-round estimate of Coventry Patmore is, for instance, Kate Greenwood's account—even though it be the account of a neurasthenic—of her visit to his house in Chapter XXXIV!

Sir Max Beerbohm has suggested that there is always something rather absurd about the past. In Greenwood and Smith we salute the shades of Britons who were notably of their period. Among our publicists and men of wealth to-day there is no one of just their Victorian-Edwardian make-up. There is a gap between their time and ours. It was different in its beards and whiskers, in its clothes, in the way it talked and wrote, in eco-

1 Oxford University Press.

2 *Letters of Anne Thackeray Ritchie* (Murray).

nomics and politics, in range of view on every subject, in the number of readers of newspapers and books, in transport of every kind, in the whole apparatus of life, in the acquaintance that one class had with another, in notions of the possibilities of social betterment and community action, in impressions of other countries (especially of the United States), and in the character, demeanour, and action of the Houses of Parliament, the Army, Navy, Diplomacy, and the Public Offices.

In Greenwood's girt-up, individual writing we find integrity, courage, manliness, and faithful patriotism. We find also, along with some wise and timely forecasts, unfulfilled prophecies and needless forebodings. The posture of public affairs as Greenwood saw it, the condition of the British people and other peoples, and their potentialities as he knew them, personal trials, wifelessness, uncertain health, and the debility of advancing years brought this 'Able Editor' dejected moments. But he was ever plucky and honest, without self-seeking, a man who, when, in our view to-day, he was sadly wrong in the conclusions he drew and the counsel he gave, had thought out for himself the course he would have his fellow countrymen follow. What he knew and believed he had taught himself. At no time had he a soft life, and he was content to take his way as he could. In all he wrote he is a faithful reflector of his time. One watches him with sympathy facing his public and family trials. When he made mistakes he tried to repair them. Whatsoever things, in his sight, were honest, just, and of good report one finds him honouring.

It is wholesome for us to look into pits from which we have brought ourselves. As we come on forebodings that events did not justify, we may doubt the validity of easy, sour judgements in our own time. In the endeavours we make, Frederick Greenwood often clears our minds and deepens our purpose.

The author of a recent life of a Prime Minister has said that 'to preserve a slight bias in favour of the subject is the most attractive kind of biography'. 'To write with authority about a man', R. L. S. felt, 'we must have at least some common ground of experience and fellow feeling.' I have 'some common ground of experience' with Greenwood, and 'fellow feeling' is not an excessive phrase for my sentiment about him. At first he was but one of the historical characters of my old newspaper, 'one of the legendary characters of Fleet Street', as R. J. Cruikshank wrote to me. But as, in his letters and articles his life laid itself open, as his achievement and public rectitude proclaimed themselves, my regard grew for this man I never saw, this editor, with many of whose party and international opinions and social attitudes I am at variance.[1] He was, in the phrase that Ruskin used about his own father, 'an entirely honest man', worthy of a painstaking if imperfect attempt to commemorate him. He would have been pleased to know that his life was eventually to be written, however inadequately, by a former member of the staff of the paper he created.

Similarly, one cannot follow the course of George Smith's life without feeling that here was a man, outstanding in his calling and his time, whose career and character are worthy of remembrance.

Charles Cowden Clarke, writing in appreciation of his wife's labours on *The Complete Concordance to Shakespeare*, testifies that she went through her manuscript seven times. If the value of the present book were to be estimated by the number of times I have gone through it I might have greater credit! But we all know from an authority already quoted, if not from personal experience, that 'to adjust the minute events of literary history is tedious and troublesome'. 'It requires indeed', he adds, abashing one, 'no great force of understanding.' It may be so, but, as the best of biographers says, 'were I to detail the number of books I have consulted and the inquiries I have found it necessary to make, by various channels, I should probably be thought ridiculously ostentatious'.[2] In the words of a sixteenth-century writer,

[1] 'My grandfather I scarcely knew', wrote Lord Goschen in his life of his grandfather, 'I have made his acquaintance as I progressed with my task, reading countless letters and learning how he was judged by his contemporaries, but in large measure allowing him to gain my affection by what he wrote, did, and suffered.'

[2] Boswell.

I can only 'hope the well meaning shall bee accepted although the merite maye justly be condemned'.

In a book in which there has been such a handling, rehandling, and handling yet again of a mass of material, over a period of several years, during which the work has often had to be completely put aside, there must be slips. I have been at all the pains I could, and exercised all the care I could, and, like Celia Fiennes, 'where I have been mistaken I easily submitt to correction'. I shall be grateful for corrections, references, or offers of letters or scraps of reminiscence with which I can at least better my private copy of the book if a new edition be never asked for.

I have tried to add to the usefulness of the volume by taking some trouble over the index.

By gracious permission of His Majesty the King, and the helpfulness of Sir Owen Morshead, I have had the advantage of copying and utilizing certain documents in the library at Windsor Castle. Her Majesty Queen Mary has also honoured me with information. I am further under obligation to a busy Prime Minister, always interested in literary effort, and to an old friend, the Chancellor of the Exchequer, for kindly having inquiries made on two occasions on my behalf.

I have particularly to thank the famous Edinburgh publishers, Messrs. William Blackwood & Sons, for directing me to a large collection of Greenwood letters chiefly addressed to the late John Blackwood, for allowing me to have further correspondence in their own possession copied, for permitting me to quote from Greenwood's work in *Blackwood*, and for the readiness with which they have answered the many questions I have addressed to them.

Messrs. Macmillan have, also, as will be seen, kindly lent me letters. They, too, have answered a number of questions.

Mrs. Reginald Smith, daughter of George Smith, could not have been kinder in many conversations, in the numerous letters I have caused her to write replying to points on which I needed trustworthy particulars, and in lending me material, books, and illustrations.

Mr. W. H. Robinson, a grand-nephew of Greenwood, went to no end of trouble in interrogating his alert, considerate, and interested centenarian mother, with whom I had the pleasure of a chat the year before she died, and in piecing together bits of family history. A nearer relative, Mr. W. T. Allen, a nephew, has also aided me.

The late Mr. Davenport Jones, the solicitor to the Greenwood family, now extinct, felt he could properly entrust to me a large box full of letters from Greenwood to his daughters and their letters to each other. From four women who knew Kate and Jessy Greenwood—the late Mrs. Hill-Reid, Mrs. Triggs, Miss Pain, and Mrs. Lusted—I have had much readily given help.

Lieut.-Colonel A. C. Oppenheim has helped me greatly with particulars of his father's friendship with Greenwood. Mr. Derek Patmore was good enough to send me copies of letters from his great-grandfather Coventry Patmore, Greenwood's friend. Over a considerable period, Mr. Andrew Stewart, of the Press Club, has spared no effort to be of use, and I am also much indebted to the Club for the facilities it has generously given me and for the papers and books it has lent. I have special obligations to Mr. Frederick Page and I have to thank Mr. Hamilton Fyfe for various items of information.

Mr. Charles Drew of the Record Office, Mr. A. T. Ellis, lately Deputy Keeper at the British Museum, Mr. T. C. Skeat of the MSS. Department, Mr. H. J. Aldridge, Assistant Keeper, the Director of the Newspaper Branch at Colindale, and Dr. Meikle, Mr. W. R. Dobie, and Mr. William Park of the ScottishNational Library have been most obliging.

I also wish to thank the Marquess of Salisbury, the Marquess of Zetland, Viscount Cecil, the Hon. Oliver Stanley, M.P., Sir John Murray, Mr. F. Ashton-Gwatkin, C.M.G., Mr. James Bone, C.H., Major Desmond Chapman-Houston, and Captain G. W. L. Meredith. Mr. W. F. Casey, editor of *The Times*, with Mr. Stanley Morison, Mr. Derek Hudson, and Mr. J. S. Maygood of our leading paper, have been very good in verifying statements and clearing up difficulties. I have had useful data from Lady Hamilton, the Hon. Mrs. Kenneth Campbell, Miss Phyllis Bentley, Miss E. M. Bigg-Wither, Mrs. Hester Thackeray Fuller, Miss Florence B. Low, Miss Stanley Smith, Miss Stead, and Mrs. Wyatt-Smith.

I have also pleasure in acknowledging my obligations to Messrs. G. Bell & Sons, Mr. R. Brooke-Caws of Messrs. Coutts, Mr. V. Bulkeley-Johnson of Messrs. Rothschild, Messrs. Richard Clay & Co., Mr. R. H. Code-Holland, Mr. Eric Constable, Mr. A. W. Coates, Mr. R. J. Cruikshank, the editor, and the librarian of the *News Chronicle*, Mr. Geoffrey Cumberlege, Mr. Paul H. Emden, Mr. W. H. Hadley, Mr. F. Harding, Mr. R. Hodder-Williams, Mr. Gerard Hopkins, Mr. William Kent, Mr. James Milne, Mr. Reginald Horrox, Mr. A. J. Leach, Mr. Samuel J. Looker, Mr. J. A. Masterman, Mr. C. F. Osborn, Mr. Arthur Rogers, Mr. A. H. Spencer, Mr. J. L. Stevens, two of the London representatives of the Suez Canal Company, Mr. Emlyn Thomas, Mr. C. L. Wayper, Mr. Frank Whitaker, and Mr. C. D. Williams. Five obliging correspondents, the lamented Mr. Robert Barrington-Ward, editor of *The Times*, the Earl of Derby, Mr. J. L. Hammond, Sir Alexander Mackintosh, and Mr. W. M. Crook, have passed away.

I have particularly to thank my wife who has assiduously read typescripts and proofs and offered useful criticism, and has secured in some places greater clarity of expression.

For very kindly reading the proofs and often making useful suggestions I am indebted to a friend and colleague of long standing, Mr. Eric Parker, formerly of the *St. James's Gazette* and the *Spectator*, and, later, editor of the *County Gentleman*, and then of the *Field*, and himself the author or editor of three dozen or more widely appreciated books.

J. W. ROBERTSON SCOTT

IDBURY MANOR,
KINGHAM, OXFORD,
Autumn 1949.

The Pall Mall Gazette.

Thackeray's sketch, in *The History of Pendennis*, of Captain Shandon writing, in the Fleet Prison for debtors, the prospectus of the *Pall Mall Gazette* while the publisher Bungay, the more convincing figure, waits.

CHAPTER II

The Imaginary 'Pall Mall Gazette' in Thackeray's 'Pendennis' and 'Philip'

CONCEIVED IN FLEET PRISON — 'WRITTEN BY GENTLEMEN FOR GENTLEMEN' — MR. BLUDYER, MR. FINUCANE, AND MR. MUGFORD — 'EDITED BY A SNOB FOR A VULGARIAN'

THE *Pall Mall Gazette* is first heard of in the thirty-second chapter of *The History of Pendennis* which Thackeray published in 1849–50. In the preceding chapter we have been introduced to Mr. Doolan's *Dawn* and Mr. Hoolan's *Day*, and to Mr. Archer, who complains of being kept four hours at the Palace 'with nothing but yesterday's *Times*, which I knew by heart, as I wrote three of the leading articles myself'!

The *Pall Mall Gazette* is mentioned in a letter to George Warrington from Captain Shandon, in the Fleet Prison. We read that a publisher, Bungay, wants from Shandon—the original was 'the brilliant reckless Maginn'[1]—a genuine West End article, 'dashing, trenchant and d..... aristocratic'. 'We've two lords,' Bungay says, 'but the less they do the better. We must have you. We'll give you your own terms, and we'll make a hit with the *Gazette*.' The paper was to be published 'as a counterpoise to the *Whitehall Review*'.[2] George Warrington and Arthur Pendennis saw Shandon finish the prospectus of the *Pall Mall Gazette*.

[1] *Maginn*, 1793–1842. Poet, journalist, and miscellaneous writer, thus described by Lockhart:

> Here early to bed, lies kind William Maginn,
> Barring drink and the girls, I ne'er heard a sin;
> Many worse, better few, than bright, broken Maginn.

Maginn was once called 'the ablest journalist who ever lived, in the sense that he could state his case with a clearness and persuasiveness which carried the reader away'. He is stated somewhere to have stood 6 ft. 8 in.

[2] A *Whitehall Gazette* was to come out in 1876.

Our imprisoned Captain announced . . . that the time had come . . . when it was necessary for the gentlemen of England to band together in defence of their common rights and their glorious order, menaced on all sides by foreign revolutions, by intestine radicalism, by the artful calumnies of mill-owners and cotton lords, and the stupid hostility of the masses. . . . The ancient monarchy was insulted, the Church was deserted by envious dissent and undermined by stealthy infidelity. The good institutions which had made our country glorious and the name of English Gentlemen the proudest in the world, were exposed to assault and contumely from men to whom . . . no history was venerable and no law binding. It was because the people of England believed in their gentlemen that this country overcame the greatest enemy a nation ever met. The gentlemen of England must be their own champions; they must not be belied and misrepresented by hireling advocates.

The prospectus went on to say that some gentlemen whose names were not brought before the public—they were the needy Shandon, the old hand Warrington, and young Pendennis—had determined to bring forward a journal of which the principles—but here are Shandon's words:

We number influential friends in both Houses of the Senate and have secured allies in every diplomatic circle in Europe. Our sources of intelligence are such as no other journal could acquire. The very earliest information connected with the movement of English and Continental politics will be found only in the columns of the *Pall Mall Gazette*. The Statesman and the Capitalist, the Country Gentleman and the Divine will be amongst our readers because our writers are amongst them. We address ourselves to the higher circles of society—the *Pall Mall Gazette* is written by gentlemen for gentlemen, its conductors speak to the classes in which they live and were born. The field-preacher has his journal, the radical freethinker has his journal; why should the gentlemen of England be unrepresented in the Press?

The literary and fashionable departments of the *Pall Mall Gazette* were to be 'conducted by gentlemen of acknowledged reputation; men famous at the universities, known at the Clubs and of the Society which they described'. To advertisers, Shandon 'pointed out delicately that there would be no such medium as the *Pall Mall Gazette* for giving publicity to their sales; and he eloquently called upon the nobility of England, the baronetage of England, the revered clergy of England, the bar of England, the matrons, the daughters, the homes and hearths of England to rally round the good old cause'.

For writing the prospectus, Bungay gave a five-pound note to Shandon, who went off with it to the prison tavern as soon as his visitors left.

The last sentence of the chapter tells of the receipt by Pendennis of a parcel of 'new, neat, calico-bound books, travels and novels and poems, for review for the *Pall Mall Gazette*'. A friend of Shandon's, John Finucane, was to be sub-editor, and, from a remark of his, 'Won't we send the *Pall Mall Gazette* up to ten thousand a week', we see that the journal was not to be, like the newspaper of its name which was to come into being in the future, a daily.

At a dinner given by the publisher (Chapter XXXIV) a guest asks, '*Pall Mall Gazette*, *Pall Mall Gazette*?', and Shandon, now out of prison, replies, 'Because the editor was born in Dublin, the sub-editor at Cork, because the proprietor lives in Paternoster Row and the paper is published in Catherine Street, Strand'.

Chapter XXXV is headed 'The *Pall Mall Gazette*', and gives an account of the start.

> Considerable success attended it. Great names were cited amongst the contributors. But an article on foreign policy, which was generally attributed to a noble lord whose concern with the Foreign Office is very well known, was composed by Captain Shandon in the Bear and Staff public house. A series of papers on finance, universally supposed to be written by a great Statesman, were composed by Mr. George Warrington. In the political department Mr. Pendennis did not take any share, but he was a most active literary contributor. Mr. Jack Finucane, the sub-editor, compiled with paste and scissors. He scanned all the paragraphs of all the newspapers. He didn't let a death or a dinner-party of the aristocracy pass

without having the event recorded, and from the most recondite provincial prints and distant Scotch and Irish newspapers he fished out astonishing intelligence regarding the upper classes. It was a touching sight to see Jack Finucane, with a plate of meat from the cookshop and a glass of porter from the public-house, recounting the feasts of the great, and in tattered trousers and dingy shirt sleeves cheerfully describing most brilliant *fêtes*. You would have imagined that he dined with ambassadors, and that his common lounge was the bow-window of White's. Pendennis took a good deal of pains with his reviews. And what was the astonishment and delight of our friend Major Pendennis on walking into one of his clubs, where some gentlemen of good reputation were assembled, to hear them talking over a number of the *Pall Mall Gazette* and of an article making some bitter fun of a book recently published by the wife of a celebrated member of the Opposition party. The book was a 'Book of Travels by the Countess of Muffborough', in which it was difficult to say which was the most wonderful, the French or the English.

Later, we learn how,

the *Pall Mall Gazette* being duly established and Arthur Pendennis's merits recognised, he worked away hard every week preparing reviews, with flippancy certainly, but with honesty and to the best of his power. It might be that a historian of threescore, who had spent a quarter of a century in composing a work of a couple of days' reading in the British Museum, was not altogether fairly treated by such a facile critic. The actors at the theatres complained of him woefully too. But there was not so much harm done after all. Those who got a little whipping got what in the main was good for them. Mr. Arthur Pendennis gained the sum of four pounds four shillings weekly, and with no small pains and labour.

We are told, also, about the *Pall Mall Gazette* office. Shandon and Finucane would be scribbling at either end of a table, and Mr. Bludyer 'would impound books at the counter in spite of the remonstrances of Mr. Midge, the publisher, and after looking through the volumes, would sell them at his accustomed book-stall, and, having drunken and dined in a tavern upon the produce of the sale, would call for ink and paper and proceed to "smash" the author of his dinner and the novel'.

And then we are suddenly informed that Bludyer and Shandon are dead. Nothing is said about Finucane. And we hear no more of the *Pall Mall Gazette* in the *History of Pendennis*.

Thackeray returned to the *Pall Mall Gazette*—he had a wide experience of the Press—in *The Adventures of Philip* (1862). Halfway through the first volume, we come on 'Finucane, now editor of the *Pall Mall Gazette*; he married the widow of the late eccentric and gifted Captain Shandon'. On the next page we read that 'since those early days of the *Pall Mall Gazette*' it 'had passed through several hands'. The proprietor is now one Frederick Mugford, who, in its pages, 'committed a systematic literary murder once a week'. 'He came of the old school of the press. He had risen from the ranks and retained some of the manners and oddities of the private soldier. He knew that his young men laughed at his peculiarities and did not care a fig. He used bad language with great freedom (to hear him bullying a printing office was a wonder of eloquence).' But 'when he went to the Under-Secretary's office he was never kept waiting. Mugford had a curious knowledge of what was going on in the world and of the affairs of countless people.' Thackeray had evidently in mind Cook of the *Saturday Review*, on whom we shall have a word in the next chapter. Incidentally, Mrs. Mugford appears; 'when the Mugfords purchased the *Gazette*, Mrs. Mugford used to drop bills from her pony chaise and distribute placards setting forth the excellence of the journal'. In the second volume one Bickerton is editor and Philip has become Paris correspondent. But we have soon an account of his doings as sub-editor. Then he adds to his work the correspondentship of a New York paper. Later, he is the sub-editor of a *European Review*, which dies in its sixth number, and is back 'on his sub-editorial stool at the *Pall Mall Gazette*'. Before the book closes there enters 'an able reporter', one Phipps of the *Daily Intelligence*. As for the *Pall Mall Gazette*, as conducted by Bickerton for Mugford, Sir Edward Cook describes it correctly as 'edited by a snob for a vulgarian'.

CHAPTER III

To the Real One

BUT, IN ORDER TO SHOW SOMETHING OF WHAT JOURNALISTIC CONDITIONS HAD BEEN, BY WAY OF DICKENS'S SEVENTEEN NIGHTS' EDITING OF THE 'DAILY NEWS', AND THE UNRULY J. D. COOK'S 'SATURDAY REVIEW'

THE *Pall Mall Gazette* with which we are concerned, an evening paper established in 1865, owed little more than its name to the imaginary journal with the contents of which Thackeray had entertained the readers of *The History of Pendennis* fifteen years before,[1] in 1849–50, and *The Adventures of Philip*, in 1861–2. It was mainly indebted to the *Saturday Review*, which was started in 1855, and to *Cornhill*, which came out in 1860. In several ways they were something new in weekly and monthly journalism; and a number of writers contributed to all three publications, the weekly, and monthly, and the new daily.

Cornhill is of particular interest. A member of its staff, and for some time its editor, Frederick Greenwood, was the initiator and first editor of the *Pall Mall Gazette*. Then the proprietor of *Cornhill*, George Smith,[2] not only furnished the capital and business guidance for the new paper, but, as a book publisher of repute and long experience, the head of Smith, Elder & Co., one of the four leading firms of book producers, brought to the new journal a considerable acquaintance with the writing men and women of the period. In Greenwood's and Smith's varied experience we see the laying of the foundations of the *Pall Mall Gazette*.

Of the stodginess of which the daily journalism of the time immediately before the *Saturday* and *Cornhill* was capable, one gets some notion in turning over the early numbers of the *Daily News*, edited for seventeen nights by Dickens in 1846. A paper

[1] 1850 is the date in my copy of the first edition, but the story was published in parts during the previous year.

[2] George Murray Smith, later in life. See page 30.

conducted by a novelist, who had had years of experience as a reporter in the country and the Press Gallery of the House of Commons, commends itself to the public in No. 1 with three leading articles all on Free Trade. The space left on the editorial page is alluringly devoted to the Money Market and City News. The page opposite keeps it in countenance with nothing but railway company meetings and other railway news.[1] Page two, not to be outdone, is occupied by reports of two Free Trade meetings, three columns of which consist of a speech by Cobden which is printed verbatim without a single 'break'. On the paper's two remaining pages—there are three pages of advertising—general news has a losing fight of it with two columns and a half of *London Gazette*, dull reports of lawsuits, a poem—on Free Trade—two and a quarter columns headed simply 'Music' and a column and a half from Ireland. The best 'copy' in the issue is the first chapter of a series, 'Travelling Letters, Written on the Road, By Charles Dickens', two columns. But this is put away at the back of the paper, along with a lively account, in the Dickensian manner, in half a column of the smallest type, of two cases at Bow Street. There are no foreign telegrams, for 'our express from Paris had not arrived'.

The circulation was 4,000 and the price fivepence. When the sales rose to 22,000, *The Times*, at sevenpence, claimed 'at least 25,000'. Every newspaper at this period had to bear a red penny stamp, and there was also a duty on advertisements and on paper.

Dickens had his fears lest he should be compromising his reputation with the readers of his novels by editing the *Daily News*. When the *Pall Mall Gazette* of the *History of Pendennis* was supposed to be published, periodical literature, let alone newspaper editing, was, as Leslie Stephen notes, 'hardly considered to give fitting employment to a gentleman'. Warrington is imagined as writing for the best papers of the day, but he tells Pendennis that he is ashamed of writing for money. Lockhart

[1] It was the time of the railway mania; the railways editor had indeed the same salary as Dickens, £2,000. Salaries of London morning-paper editors may now run up to £10,000.

was troubled in 1819 by the thought of 'losing caste in Society' if he entertained the proposal of Disraeli to edit John Murray's daily *Representative*, and Jeffrey had been 'at first afraid to let it be known that he was editing the *Edinburgh Review*' (founded in 1802). As late as *The Egoist*, one of Meredith's characters says, 'Papa will not like your serving with your pen in London: he will say you are worth too much for that.'

An indication of the change which took place in public opinion was seen in the kind of men who contributed to the success of the *Saturday Review*. Its proprietor was Beresford Hope (1820–87), the M.P. who called Disraeli an 'Asian Mystery', and brought upon himself a retort reflecting on his 'Batavian graces'—he had Dutch blood and was stout. I came on a photograph of this curious-looking person in Harry Furniss's *Paradise in Piccadilly*.[1] 'A very amiable cultivated man,' says Leslie Stephen,[2] 'he professed an Anglicanism of the type that suits the refined country gentleman. He converted the remains of an old monastery into a missionary college. He built churches supposed to represent the high-water mark of the ecclesiastical revival of the time, and he was a fitting representative in Parliament of the University of Cambridge, where the country clergy had then the predominant interest.'

The editor of the *Saturday*, J. D. Cook, 1808–68, Stephen goes on, 'was an amusing contrast'. 'The details of his career as narrated by himself were supposed to owe something to his creative imagination. He seemed to know little of literature outside the newspapers. His manners rather suggested that he was a survivor of the old Shandon or Maginn race. He was a successful and meritorious editor. He had a keen scent for promising talent.' And someone adds, 'often made very judicious corrections in the work of men immeasurably superior to himself in ability and acquirements'. But Beresford Hope is supposed to have said that, but for his own control, the paper would have been given to 'radicalism and unchurch'.

[1] John Lane.

[2] *Life of Sir James Fitzjames Stephen*, Leslie Stephen (Smith, Elder).

However that may be, there were among the contributors Fitzjames Stephen (afterwards a judge), Leslie Stephen himself, Lord Robert Cecil (afterwards, as the Marquis of Salisbury, Prime Minister), John Morley, Sir William Harcourt, E. A. Freeman, Froude, Sir Henry Maine (who suggested the name of the paper), Goldwin Smith, Walter Bagehot, Owen Sandars who had 'a peculiar skill in stating the case for the other side with absolute fairness and then showing with deadly moderation that there was nothing in it', the Duke of Newcastle, the Rev. William Scott of the *Christian Remembrancer*, and G. S. Venables, who is said to have done two or three leaders a week. He was the man who broke Thackeray's nose at Charterhouse. 'One of his fancies', Stephen goes on, 'was a prejudice against the editorial "we". His remarks would take the form of a series of political aphorisms not so much expressing personal sentiment as emanating from wisdom in the abstract. They seemed to be judicial utterances from the loftiest regions of culture, balanced, dignified, and authoritative, though of course edged by a sufficient infusion of scorn for the charlatan or the demagogue.'[1] 'As memoirs are published', writes F. W. Maitland, 'it becomes always more evident that anyone who never wrote for the *Saturday Review* was no one.' Greenwood, as will be seen later, was a contributor towards the end of his life. The *Saturday*'s pay is said to have been £2 or £3 an article. To-day, articles in a weekly review may be eight to ten guineas, special articles twelve or fifteen, or, in particular cases, twenty-one or twenty-five. A difference is customarily made between amateurs and professionals.

To return to the editor: John Douglas Cook came from Aberdeen, and had been a reporter and afterwards a leader-writer on *The Times*. Then, with Beresford Hope as proprietor, he edited the *Morning Chronicle*,[2] which died under him. The *Saturday Review* was started with some of the *Chronicle* staff, 'to

[1] See page 26.

[2] Started in 1769 by 'Memory Woodfall', who reported the House of Commons without shorthand. There were associated with the *Chronicle* the poets Campbell, Coleridge, and Moore, the essayists Hazlitt and Lamb, the author of *The School for Scandal* and *The Rivals*, and Dickens.

attack the influence of *The Times* under Delane', and was 'the first weekly to drop news as one of its principal features'. (An odd volume of the *Illustrated London News* of 1846 I chance to have is largely news.) It is said to have bought, for a time at any rate, the books it reviewed. The *Spectator*, so long its rival, had been begun, twenty-seven years before,[1] by R. S. Rintoul, who conducted it until 1858, three years after the appearance of the *Saturday*. Two years later it was bought from one Scott by Meredith Townsend, who took into partnership Richard Holt Hutton.[2] Cook of the *Saturday*, who was without hair on his face or his head, is described by one observer as 'bearing the traces of a very hard and dissipated life in early years', and by another as 'a stout, square, bull-necked, red-faced, apoplectic-looking man, in the prime of life with the taste of an epicure'. The memory of his hot temper survives in a story that, for a typographical blunder, he once threw the printer of the *Chronicle* on the fire, and in what Mrs. Lynn Linton (the author of *The True Story of Joshua Davidson* and *The Girl of the Period*) wrote: 'A Napoleon among editors indeed, but, mercy on us! what a temper. Has he not sworn at me? Yes, and actually hit me, if he thought I had not carried out properly any of his commands in the smallest detail.' The office of the paper was until 1893 in Albany.[3] Cook had been succeeded by Philip Harwood, who was followed by Walter Pollock. Before the *Saturday* came to an end the notorious Frank Harris controlled it.

[1] The *Spectator* of Addison and Steele, started in 1711, ran until 1714.

[2] St. Loe Strachey became editor in 1898, but Townsend contributed until 1908.

[3] Usually written 'the Albany', but the oldest member assures me that the correct name is 'Albany'.

THE PROPRIETOR AND HIS FRIENDS

CHAPTER IV

Two Young Men from the North

THE BEGINNINGS OF A PUBLISHING FIRM — AN OLD TIME SCHOOLING — THE OVERLAND ROUTE — A STORY OF 'OLD MORALITY' — MACAULAY — BULWER LYTTON

THE eminent publisher, George Smith, of Smith, Elder & Co., a man of character, enterprise, and achievement,[1] was very much his father's and his mother's son. First about his father. A year before Waterloo two young men, one of them his father (also called George Smith), born on a farm, and the other Alexander Elder, both in the bookselling line, and both Scotsmen, like the founders of the firms of Macmillan and John Murray—Smith was from Elgin,[2] Elder from Banff—set up business as booksellers and stationers in London, in Fenchurch Street. On the day Smith landed at a Thames wharf, with his bundle on his back and very little in his pocket, hooligans bantered him with 'Any old

[1] Some of the story of George Smith is told in a book printed for private circulation. It contains four entertaining chapters of personal experience which Smith contributed to *Cornhill*. I have been informed that it was written 'with meticulous care; you can take it that all descriptions of events in it are accurate'. After these chapters there is a reproduction of the informing account with which Sir Sidney Lee, in 1901, prefaced the first Supplement to the *Dictionary of National Biography*. Then comes the appreciation which Sir Leslie Stephen wrote in *Cornhill*. I have also a copy of *The House of Smith Elder*, which the late Dr. Leonard Huxley, who succeeded Reginald Smith in the direction of *Cornhill*, published in 1923. With this material, with articles by Thackeray's daughter, Lady Ritchie, with others in *Cornhill*, and with incidents from other sources, I was equipped to piece together a narrative of some interest. Good fortune brought me, however, unpublished information of equal, if not, in some directions, of more value than all this. I am therefore able to offer many new facts and much fresh colour in relation to a memorable development not only of journalism but of publishing.

[2] The father of Mr. C. J. Chancellor, general manager of Reuters, has a book bearing the imprint of Smith's shop in Elgin.

clothes to sell?' and it was after a successful set-to with them that he got through the Mint district.

He secured a job with Rivington, a publisher who told a clerk who asked for an increase of wages that he himself was content with one roll at breakfast and there was no need for him to have two. Smith bettered himself with Byron's John Murray, who recognized his character for standing no nonsense, and had him by his side at after-dinner coffee-house sales to the booksellers. Sent one day with a message to Byron, he was to see the poet dancing with joy at news of the success of one of his books.

Two years after the starting of Smith, Elder & Co., Smith married a girl from his own country named Murray,[1] unrelated to the famous John. She was of 'quite exceptional shrewdness and strength of mind, and of extraordinary courage, never downcast'. Her son, our George Smith, was in middle life to give her name to all his children and to sign himself George Murray Smith, or more commonly George M. Smith. But he remained 'George Smith' to his friends.[2] He was born on March 19, 1824, over the shop in Fenchurch Street at a time when many merchants, there and in Mark Lane and Mincing Lane, were living over their premises.

We get some impression of the grave young fellows his father and his father's partner were from the fact that, on the opening page of their first day-book, Smith penned a prayer for the right conduct of the business, and that in 1817 he is writing home about a sermon he has heard Chalmers deliver in London. 'The breathlessness of expectation', he relates, 'permitted not the beating of a heart to agitate the stillness.' And the first book

1 Elizabeth Murray's father, who had prospered as a glassware manufacturer, had retired to the coast of Kent.

2 '"George Smith", as she always familiarly called him', writes Mrs. Humphry Ward. In Scotland, where the legal position of women was for a long time higher than in England, it is still the custom, in documents, in legal proceedings, and on tombstones, to describe a married woman not only by her husband's name but by her own, thus Jean Mackay or Campbell, and the adoption of a mother's name is not uncommon. For instance, on my father's death, in my youth, I assumed my mother's name of Robertson.

published by the young firm—they were booksellers and stationers—was a collection of the sermons of a Scottish minister in London.

In the year of young George's birth, Smith & Elder removed to 65 Cornhill and took into partnership one Mackintosh, who had a connexion with India. This led to the development of an Indian agency that gained a position of importance. It was to have a branch not only in India but in Java and on the West Coast of Africa. On one occasion, when challenged as to the range of goods it could supply, it provided several skeletons. While the firm was young a great Indian firm failed and Smith and Elder were advised that, by counter claims, they might legally escape a large part of their liability. Smith prevailed on his partners not to adopt this course, and years afterwards the firm was offered important facilities by an Indian house because 'we know Mr. Smith to be an honest man'.

The child growing up in Cornhill remembered the ancient watchmen with their watch-boxes, and the advent of the modern policeman or 'peeler'. His mother was amused at the embarrassment of a maiden sister who had never seen one, and, on her arrival on a visit, was perturbed because 'a gentleman in uniform was walking up and down in front of the house'. When the Reform Bill was passed, the boy heard the rejoicing crowd sweeping through the streets shouting 'Light up or you'll have your windows broken!' But candles had already been placed in position.

George Smith described himself as 'troublesome' as a schoolboy.

I cannot accuse myself of any disgraceful act. I was not idle or dull. I was always first or second in my classes. Had I been fortunate enough to fall into the hands of a wise teacher I might have made a respectable scholar. But I had an impish humour, and was credited with being the most warlike of my school world. By the time I was sixteen I was six feet high but so thin that I could make the middle fingers and thumbs of my two hands meet round my waist. I had no real love of fighting but I found myself engaged in incessant combats. My housemaster at Blackheath had no sense of humour but a plentiful supply of that element of unreality and cant which boys so quickly detect and resent. We found delight in making his life a burden. When I crept under a table and tied a cracker to his shoestring my punishment was to write out the 119th Psalm [of 176 verses] thrice during a half-holiday.

George was secretary of a 'Row Society' which recorded in minutes all the mischief it had done or intended to do. The number of rows in which each boy was involved was put to his credit. If he relapsed into a discreditable state of good behaviour he was remonstrated with at a special meeting. As often happened at boarding establishments of the period, 'hunger was almost a constant experience'. Alas, the minutes of the Row Society in Smith's handwriting came into the hands of authority, and his parents were invited to withdraw him from the school and advised to send him to sea. Yet 'on the whole', Smith said, 'I did not do ill. I was a glutton for work, had a quick memory and a delight in some branches of study, such as Euclid.' When, later, at Merchant Taylors School he had, as a holiday imposition, the Latin prosody in the Eton grammar, he was able to repeat it with no more than three mistakes.[1] When he left he 'knew thoroughly four books of Euclid, had a smattering of French, a pretty good knowledge of Horace, and could read a few chapters in Xenophon'.

The firm of Smith & Elder was now prospering. Young Smith came into the business at fourteen, a year after the accession of Queen Victoria, as an apprentice with indentures for seven years and no wages. His hours were half past seven in the morning until eight at night, with an hour and three quarters in all for meals. As he did not get his breakfast until nine, and had little to do in the early morning, he improved the time by reading the Bible from end to end, including the genealogical chapters of the Old Testament. He was fond of Job, and, with the tena-

[1] Three pages of rhyming verse, *de Syllabarum Quantitate*, devoted to prosody, in Kennedy's public school Latin primer, long since out of use. Eton boys had to learn it. Winston Churchill mastered it at his prep. school.

cious memory of a boy, remembered much of it. Many years afterwards he was at a dinner party at which the Dean of Westminster was his neighbour. Someone having quoted the phrase about being 'saved by the skin of his teeth', one of the guests exclaimed, 'What wonderful phrases these Americans do invent!' There was discussion as to the origin of the phrase, and Smith turned to the Dean, who had written a commentary on Job, and said, 'You and I at least know where it comes from'. Next day the Dean sent him a copy of his book.

Smith's father 'delighted in thoroughness', so the youth had to learn to do up parcels, was sent to a pen-maker to learn how to mend quills, got an insight into both book-binding and book-keeping, and gained some familiarity with printing. One of his tasks was copying overseas letters into a letter-book, 'copying presses being as yet unknown'.

The leisurely route taken by correspondence for India via the Cape, was, with its 'almost intolerable delays, a great handicap to business', and Lieutenant Waghorn's scheme for a shorter route across the Isthmus of Suez and through the Red Sea was welcomed. Meadows Taylor tells Henry Reeve that the time for mails was reduced to two months instead of six. As the Government was chilly to the Waghorn plan, merchants joined to bear the cost of the experimental trips. Letters were brought to Smith & Elder to be stamped for the express to Marseilles, where they were received by Waghorn and carried to Bombay, whence he brought a packet to England. The 'postage' was high. Waghorn, 'a sailor-like man, short and broad', was 'excitable in a high degree and of tremendous energy'. Once when he was unable to get a messenger to his satisfaction, he trotted himself, 'travel stained and dirty', all the way from Cornhill to the Foreign Office, in order to secure the prompt delivery of a dispatch. Unfortunately he was quarrelsome, and 'the greatness of his feat in opening a new and shorter route between East and West was'—like another stroke for the public good in the Near East of which we shall hear later—'never properly recognized'.

George as he grew up devoted his 'dinner hour and the

allowance my father made me for a chop' to learning to ride, 'an accomplishment which has prolonged the term and added enormously to the working vigour of my life. I had outgrown my strength: I was singularly lanky with no promise of a vigorous manhood. But I came to delight in horse exercise and it had the most extraordinary effect on my health. I have always accustomed myself, even when most pressed by business, to a certain amount of horse exercise.' Towards the end of his life he believed himself to have been riding in Rotten Row for more years than anyone else.[1] 'It is more than forty years since I used first to take my ride in the Park before breakfast. My sister rode with me at one period, and every morning, Mr. W. H. Smith, afterwards Leader of the House of Commons ['Old Morality'] fell in by my side. He usually went off saying "Now I must go home to lunch". Lunch at 8 a.m. seems odd and my sister said to me, "How strange that he mistakes lunch for breakfast so persistently". "No", I said, "he means lunch. He breakfasts every morning at four, is in the Strand at his business by half past four, lunches at 9 and dines at 3."' So Sir Stafford Cripps is not the only Front Bencher to make four o'clock his time for getting out of bed.

Among the authors in those 'annuals' of the period which Smith & Elder produced—*Friendship's Offering* sold 10,000 copies at twelve shillings—may be found Ruskin, Coleridge, Mrs. Norton, Miss Mitford, Miss Strickland, Alfred and Frederick Tennyson, Southey, Macaulay, the Ettrick Shepherd—in company with the peasant poet, the ill-fated John Clare, who was to gather most of his fame after his death—and Mrs. Hemans. Other publications were *The Diadem, a Book for the Boudoir*, at a guinea and a half, and *The Comic Offering, or Lady's Mélange of Literary Mirth*. *The Times* urged the *Diadem* as 'a constant com-

[1] A friend of mine, a well-known rider, the nonagenarian William Stone, of Albany—the crest on his paper is a careering horse—tells me that he recalls George Smith and that he (Stone) rode in the Row from 1869 for sixty years. 'I well remember the old brigade', he writes to me, 'Burnand, Linley Sambourne, the Prince of Wales, Lord Lonsdale, Lady Brooke, Mrs. Langtry, Maude Millet, Tree, Henry Arthur Jones, Adrian Jones, and many more.'

panion of fashionable life' and found its 'thirteen embellishments truly beautiful'. A *Coast Scenery* had forty engravings by Clarkson Stanfield, R.A., and a *Byron Gallery* thirty-six. Fifteen volumes of *A Library of Romance* at six shillings each, were 'to reduce the price of fiction'—novels were then in three volumes —'more nearly to that of other books'. But this effort, described as 'one of the boldest strokes to which the enterprise of age has given birth', was before its time. The price of the guinea and a half three-volumer did not come down to six shillings for half a century. *Random Recollections of the House of Commons*, by a Bohemian reporter of the *Morning Advertiser* called Grant, brought to the shop a protesting brewer M.P., known by his fellow legislators as 'Brown Stout', who 'standing before the counter, stormed against the book, its writer, and its publishers'.

In another department of literature the firm published Sir Humphry Davy in nine volumes and Darwin's *Zoology of the Voyage of the 'Beagle'*, a costly work in large quarto volumes, towards which the Government made a grant of £1,000. 'Of all the famous men with whom I have had relations', said George Smith, 'very few were at all comparable with Darwin in charm of manner, suavity, gentleness, and a consideration for others which was the expression of a genuine kindliness of nature. I was very young and the sweetness of his temper took my heart captive.' Towards the expenses of Dr. Andrew Smith's five-volume *Zoology of South Africa* the Government grant was £1,500. The Duke of Northumberland gave £1,000 to help the publication of a work by Sir John Herschel in royal quarto.

Following the association of the firm with Lieutenant Waghorn of the Overland Route, Layard and Mitford were sent on an overland journey to Asia to get material for a travel book, but 'the two gentlemen were in a state of violent quarrel'. However, they eventually repaid the travelling expenses advanced to them. Alas, of another pair of authors, dispatched to France to prepare an historical work, it is recorded that 'after a very short time' these gentlemen also fell out. When one of the pair was asked what the trouble was about he would say no more than 'That man!'

On a youthful holiday Smith and his sister noticed, on a Caledonian Canal boat, a man whom they thought might be, perhaps, 'a brick merchant in Tooley Street'. He was Macaulay. 'I never saw a man read so rapidly', Smith noted. 'He turned over page after page with lightning speed, I supposed to see if there was anything new in them. I was mistaken; this was his ordinary fashion of reading.' On getting ashore, Smith's sister and Lady Trevelyan shared a fly, and Macaulay walked with the young publisher. 'He talked all the time.' He had been to Glencoe to study the scenery for the famous chapter in his History.

Not long afterwards young Smith had an interview with Bulwer Lytton over a book which was never published.

> He received me in an old, greasy dressing gown, the mouthpiece of a long hookah betwixt his lips. While he talked the hookah constantly went out. Whereupon Lytton would light it again with a tallow candle in the fireplace. Late that day I passed in the Park a gentleman with high-heeled boots, luxuriant locks, a pinched-in waist, and a swaggering walk. It was Lytton, looking twenty years younger. His affectations brought much ridicule on him. I remember Mulready, who was painting his portrait, complaining that he found him unreasonable. 'I never could satisfy him about his eyes, and sometimes I was inclined to use street language about them. He was constantly urging me to throw into them what he called "a melancholy expression, looking into space, etc."' When Mr. Grant Duff rented Knebworth, Lytton's seat, I was a visitor and was amazed to find what a make-believe the whole place was—sham names all over the place, 'Queen Elizabeth's retiring room', 'Queen Elizabeth's something else'. By the lake were the remains of a theatrical looking summerhouse built for the purpose of writing *The Last Days of Pompeii.*

In later years Bulwer Lytton's wife used to come to see Smith. 'She was a most formidable person, a handsome woman with fine eyes; but if I ventured to differ from her at all, her face took on an aspect so menacing that I was never quite sure what was to happen next.' In view of Smith's future relationship with

Frederick Greenwood, one's attention is caught, in the present Lord Lytton's life of his grandfather, by a note of his progenitor having been to dinner where the guests were 'chiefly literary coves', among them 'my enemy the editor of the *Pall Mall Gazette* with whom I had the hypocrisy to shake hands'. No doubt the paper had been inappreciative of Lytton's writing.

CHAPTER V

Adventure with £1,500

'ORION' HORNE — LEIGH HUNT — BROWNING — MARRIAGE — THE RUSKINS — THE DEFAULTING PARTNER — WIT AT THE MUSEUM CLUB

As for affairs at Cornhill, Elder does not seem to have been a very capable publisher, and two managers were successively sent away. So it came about that young Smith, at the age of nineteen, his mother abetting, induced his father, who persuaded his partners, to set apart, unfettered by conditions, £1,500 with which he could make, as Scots say, 'a kirk or a mill' of the publishing department of the Anglo-Indian or Scoto-Indian business. He 'was not to be questioned or interfered with'.

The energetic youngster's first venture was to get a book from that odd but forceful and industrious literary worker, 'Orion' Horne. He was the man who had had the first, second, and third editions of the epic from which he got his nickname issued at a farthing—the fourth and fifth were a shilling and half a crown.[1] John Drinkwater once said that *Orion* would be 'a suitable ground for the anthologist of the flattest lines of poetry'. A line occasionally seen quoted is ''Tis always morning somewhere in the world', and a motto from the epic appears on the front page of Meredith's *Poems* of 1851. The work, one chapter of which

[1] Richard Henry (afterwards Hengist) Horne, 1803–84. Before *Orion, an Epic Poem in Ten Books*, he had issued *Exposition of the False Medium and Barriers excluding Men of Genius from the Public*, *Spirit of Peers and People: A National Tragi-Comedy*, *The Death of Marlowe*, *The Russian Catechism, with Explanatory Notes*, *Letters of Elizabeth Barrett Browning* addressed to himself, *Schlegel's Lectures on Dramatic Art and Literature*, *Essay on Tragic Influence*, and a *History of Napoleon*. It was on the basis of Horne's report, as commissioner on the employment of children and young people in mines that Mrs. Browning wrote her 'Cry of the Children'. Horne went to the Australian gold-fields, where he became a magistrate, and on his return wrote more books. He received a Civil List pension, the amount of which was increased by Lord Beaconsfield, and made Buxton Forman his literary executor.

Smith had persuaded Horne to burn as an injudicious personal attack, was reviewed by Thackeray in the *Morning Chronicle*. A novel by the eccentric author, in which one of the characters had committed murder by means of a wooden leg which was really an airgun, Smith would not have, but he undertook *The New Spirit of the Age*—just when is there not a new spirit and a new age? Somebody's *Queen of the Stage* Smith also published, with a satisfactory financial return, and a book of poems by a girl whose mother said, 'I want my daughter to marry and it is a good thing for a girl to have a literary reputation'.

After that, George Smith advanced to an original of a different quality from Horne, Leigh Hunt, whom he managed with equal address. The aspiring publisher, who had lent his aid one day when he found the poet-essayist uncertain about the subtraction of 13*s.* 9*d.* from £1, delighted him with £100 for *Imagination and Fancy*—'You young Prince', he cried—and explained to the unpractical author what a cheque was, and gave him notes in exchange for it. Then, when Mrs. Hunt unwittingly put in the fire the envelope containing these notes, he took him—'carrying a naked Psyche in his hand'—to the Bank of England to get the mischance repaired. There he heard Hunt's famous speech to one of the clerks: 'And this is the Bank of England! And do you sit here all day and never see the green woods and the trees and the flowers and the charming country? Are you contented with such a life?' 'All the time he was holding the little naked Psyche in one hand, and, with his long hair and flashing eyes, made a surprising figure.' Smith describes Hunt as 'of tall stature, with a sallow not to say yellow complexion and long hair. His mouth lacked refinement and firmness, but he had large expressive eyes. His manner, however, had such a fascination that, after he had spoken for five minutes, one forgot how he looked.' Smith was frequently invited to supper by Hunt, and delighted in his stories of Shelley and Byron, whom the essayist called 'Birron'. At the home of a member of the publishing house of Chapman, Smith met Browning who gave him copies of all his early books.

How many people now remember G. P. R. James? Smith & Elder were to pay him £600 to £700 for the first edition of each of the novels he wrote. At the high price at which fiction was then published, the editions varied from 1,000 to 3,000. James was diligent, and Smith had soon on hand the manuscripts of three or four novels. So, after a rumpus, during which Harrison Ainsworth, like Tony Weller's friends, came with James one day 'to see fair play', the supply had to slacken down. Smith described Ainsworth as a kind of copy of Count d'Orsay, 'brilliant with pins and rings and long oiled locks', and his work as 'tame and commonplace'. The circulation of his books gradually fell because, G. H. Lewes declared, doctors had ceased to recommend them, with a milk diet, as unexciting reading for patients recovering from fever.

Shortly after Smith came of age, ill health compelled his father to retire to Box Hill, where, on a few acres, he went back to the farming of his youth, and, by spade culture and 'a lavish use of manure', grew crops of cereals and roots surprising to neighbouring agriculturists.

Elder also retired, and George had the whole weight of the publishing business on his shoulders, for the remaining partner confined himself to the overseas department. The young publisher was then twenty-three, the age at which John Murray the First became his own master; John Murray the Second succeeded at twenty-four. Smith, who was 'in lodgings in one part of London or another', began his day early and 'seldom left business till ten o'clock at night'. When his father died his mother left Box Hill for Westbourne Place, Bayswater, 'at that time consisting of private houses only', and her son lived with her.

All seemed to be going well with the business when Smith discovered that his partner, 'a man of brilliant social gifts, moving in the best circles, a fine talker and writer', had been for a long time robbing the firm. It is evidence of the progress it had been making that the defalcations came to 'more than £30,000'. Smith & Elder's capital included all the funds of his mother and of Elder, and sums deposited by other persons. So, sustained by his mother's 'serene courage and clear intelligence'—'if the worst came', she would say, she and his sister would open a berlin wool shop—Smith, who, under the strain, he writes, 'often could not lie down in my bed', rejected the expedient of bankruptcy and undertook to meet all the obligations of the house within a term of years.

He did it 'in much less time than had been agreed upon'. But, because he had to avoid transactions involving risk, he was compelled to decline the publication of books he would have liked to have had on his list. Among these were Browning's. In later years the poet, whom he had 'always liked', brought him *The Ring and the Book*, and, after that, all he wrote. For *The Ring and the Book* he had £400 for an edition, a larger sum than Browning had received from any of his books. Later, the whole of them and the works of Mrs. Browning were transferred to Smith & Elder. 'Our relations grew very intimate, and for many years, and up to the time of Browning's death, he was on terms of closest friendship, not only with me but with my family. We all admired and loved him, and he evidently found our household congenial.' Smith said he never met any other man of letters who was also so thoroughly a man of affairs. Yet in manuscript 'Red Cotton Nightcap Country' was 'full of libels'. They were eliminated on the advice of a friend of the poet, Mr. Justice Coleridge.

Reference has frequently been made to Browning's affection for his son. Smith described it as 'almost painful in its intensity and absorption'. The poet's charm and manner and force of intellect won him, as we know, a large circle of friends. 'His intimate friendships were not many, but they were of the closest character.' During the long illness of Barry Cornwall, Browning used to sit with him for hours every Sunday, and after his death he continued with his widow the faithful Sunday visit.

The news of Browning's own decease reached Smith in a telegram from Venice shortly after midnight. The shock was so great that he could not go to bed. It was a snowy night but he decided to take the news to Buckle of *The Times*, with whom he was on friendly terms, and the news was published exclusively in that paper. All the arrangements for the funeral in the Abbey were made by Smith, who was one of the pall-bearers.

The burden on the young publisher about this time was heavy. 'He not infrequently fainted', and 'had difficulty in insuring for a large amount as security for his mother.' It is evidence of his strength of character that he had retained, for his technical abilities, the defaulting partner in the service of the firm. The man had the allowance that he had been accustomed to draw under the partnership agreement but had no longer the opportunity of handling remittances. This leniency had not, however, the hoped-for result. He relapsed and finally went to India. The day before his departure he married a Frenchwoman who lived under his protection, and showed his confidence in the friendship of the partner he had wronged by leaving him the task of paying her a monthly allowance and writing a few lines periodically about her welfare.

Another stumbler from the narrow path, with whom Smith was brought into contact, lived in Queen's Bench prison. 'The life there was what would now seem very strange. Many of the inmates were gentlemen in dress and manner, such as you would see on the shady side of Pall Mall during the season. The style of living was good and racquets were always going on.'

Smith, not only publisher but India merchant, worked as few men work. We have to think what a business man's correspondence alone involved in the days before shorthand typists. Smith dictated to two clerks—sometimes, before mail days, till four in the morning—'while two other clerks were copying'. Is it surprising that business men of the period made so much of good handwriting, and saw to it that schoolmasters esteemed it? In later years he wondered whether he should have done so much himself. 'Business methods have improved', he said, 'and heads of firms have learned to delegate. The perfection of business is never to do anything with your own hand that other people can do as well, or nearly as well.' He continued to slog till after he was married and was about twenty-nine or thirty. The progress he made with the business was noteworthy. The firm had 200 clerks—although Smith was a generous employer, one cannot help wondering what clerks' pay was at that time—and the amounts which passed through the banking account in the years 1846–66 were £48,088, £57,506, £175,989, £405,163, £627,129. The volume of the business done was to 'increase fifteenfold in twenty years'.

Smith attributed his success from his young days to 'more than ordinary fitness for business. I was keenly interested in business affairs and quick to see everything that could affect business. I had a certain faculty for reading men and a capacity for clear and quick decision.' This, he said, is 'a mental habit which makes business easy'. He would repeat the lines:

> Action should follow thought
> Quick as the thunder's clap
> Upon the lightning's flash.

'But although I had this faculty of swift and courageous decision I was afflicted with great shyness. I often suffered greatly from what is called funk before making a speech or doing anything important.' On the other hand, he was 'essentially practical'. 'My first question in any crisis was, "What can we do?" Regrets are idle, speculation a waste of energy. The sole question for a sensible man is, "What is to be done?"'

As he grew older he smiled at 'the eager audacity with which he plunged into the great world of business'. He was to make not a little money outside publishing. He 'tried many experiments, some ingenious, all more or less original'. He remembered what he had read as a boy about 'large profits being sometimes extracted from transactions minute in themselves but great in their aggregate'. Once, as a young fellow, he happened to learn through a friend the kind of brown papers which were used in Manchester and the fact that supplies were paid for quarterly. He procured samples and cash prices and then walked round the leading warehouses and picked up orders for a good deal of paper to be paid for monthly. His mother was accustomed, when he had a new enterprise in view, to speak of 'George's brown paper schemes'.

At an early stage of his commercial life, he added to the profits of the firm by arranging that it should do some of its own insurance on its overseas business. He recognized that, at that time, on consignments for the East, there was less risk between London and Hongkong than between Hongkong and Shanghai.

But in his busy years, though he had little time for recreation he did sometimes indulge himself. Like Browning, he was an admirer of Helen Faucit, afterwards the wife of Sir Theodore Martin, the biographer of the Prince Consort. As a youth he had sometimes gone to see her 'as often as four evenings a week'. Later in life, as we shall find, she became one of the best friends of his wife and himself. To his theatre-going he added membership of the Museum Club, where G. H. Lewes, Douglas Jerrold, and 'Father Prout', 'an elderly man with a grave face',[1] made the fun. Lewes shone as an impersonator; Jerrold, 'a little man with a broad bent back', in wit, repartee, and of course, puns. Mahony's humour was 'more subtle and refined'. One night Smith did kind offices for Jerrold when he found him drunk in the hands of a policeman. The Club came to an end from 'lack of funds to pay the tradesmen'. The wit displayed there, Smith thought, 'would no doubt be counted too personal for these days; taste and manners have undergone a change'. In his opinion Lord Houghton, though he had gifts as a wit and conversationalist, did not reach Museum Club level. Abraham Hayward was, he thought, the last survivor of the great talkers he knew.

Smith testified that more wine was drunk at dinner than became customary later. His mother told him that in her younger days the men, on joining the ladies, were 'not exactly tipsy but unpleasantly familiar'. His father told a story of being at some house where wine was boisterously urged upon him, and of the door being locked when he tried to escape from the room. On jumping out of the window into the garden he was

[1] F. S. Mahony, 1804–66. 'Oliver Yorke' in *Fraser's*.

pursued. Our George Smith thought 'the cigar has replaced the wine glass as a vehicle of after-dinner hospitality'. In his earlier days 'men smoked very little; a gentleman seen with a cigar in Piccadilly would instantly have lost caste'.

All of us who read in bed have our little dodges. Smith made a point of not putting a marker in a book to show where he had stopped reading before falling asleep. The last page or two, he considered, might have been read in a half-drowsy state, so, noble fellow, he 'began reading the next night at the point at which my memory of the book held good'.

He thought that a man, in order to be a successful publisher, must not only have 'an expert knowledge of all the forms of business but a taste for speculation and a high degree of courage in taking risks. Many able and cultured men fail just at this point.' When he once told his eldest son that he was determined to take a certain risk the young man said, 'Oh, father, you will never be so old as I am'. A publisher requires, Smith was sure, not only these qualifications but 'a measure of tact and sympathy. A broker who acts as middleman between a cotton plantation and a cotton mill has no need of sympathy. It is all a matter of hard business. But a writer, a man of genius stands in a different category. His publisher's relations with him ought to be considerate and sympathetic. In the relations of publisher and author there is possible an element of friendship and trust to a degree which can hardly be found in any other business relationship.'

In his publishing, Smith was also helped by the fact that the financial position he attained enabled him 'not to look too anxiously to the question of whether a book meant profit or loss. I could afford to take risks for the gratification of my own tastes, and to pay prices to authors I liked and for work which I personally admired that a publisher whose livelihood depended wholly on his profits could not afford.'

Smith freely acknowledged that he had been aided in his literary friendships by his wife. 'Our house, especially in our early married life, was attractive to an interesting circle of eminent men, literary and artistic.' He met his wife, a Miss

Blakeway, at a ball on April 5, 1853. It was on an Indian mail day and he had been hard at work from four o'clock in the morning until half-past seven in the evening. The story of his idyll is characteristic.

> It was, with me, a case of love at first sight. My mother, who got up early, had the habit of coming into my room almost every morning, for a little talk, and I had no secrets from her. Few sons and mothers have ever been on terms of closer confidence. The morning after the memorable ball I said to her, 'I have seen the woman I am going to marry'. 'That is all very well', my mother replied, 'but we have yet to know what the lady will say.' My habits of quick decision, joined with warmth of feeling, made delay intolerable. I rode over to the house where the ball had been given, but Miss Blakeway had gone home. I secured the assistance of my sisters and had one or two brief opportunities of seeing her.

The joyous man was married within four months. During his engagement he bought a horse to ride over to see his fiancée—she lived at Clapton—'nearly every morning before breakfast, eight miles, and then on from Clapton to the City'.

After the marriage ceremony—'marriage', he wrote, 'has given me lifelong satisfaction'—he took his bride to Tunbridge Wells and Paris for the honeymoon. But 'the strain of business was such that a stream of correspondence followed him'. In Paris, 'to copy the letters in reply I had a press but no screw. I had to secure copies by sitting on the press.' During the honeymoon the gold discoveries in Australia were reported. Smith sent instructions to London to buy a large number of revolvers and consign them to Melbourne. 'I felt sure that, where there was so much gold, revolvers would be needed.' The consignment sold at a good price.

Later, he took a contract for supplies to the hospitals in the Crimea, and the army doctors, who were to go out, used to come to Cornhill. 'Their uniforms, for some reason, included spurs, and occasionally they were worn upside down.' The firm also sent large quantities of scientific instruments to India and what Smith believed to be the first telegraphic equipment. Smith &

Elder posted an enormous number of newspapers to all parts of the world. In order to avoid dishonesty by the lads who dispatched them, Smith and the well-known publisher of the *Athenaeum*, Francis, put to the authorities a scheme for wrappers being stamped with firms' names. The plan was adopted by W. H. Smith & Sons and other large newsvendors.

In the year of his marriage Smith arranged for H. S. King, who had a bookseller's shop at Brighton, which still exists, to take over a quarter share of the business. But, though, he said, he 'got some relief from work, partnerships have their disadvantages'. Three years later, however, the Indian Mutiny reduced the volume of non-publishing business. Smith used to say that the Mutiny cost him a fortune. The firm was supplying officers with all sorts of equipment besides books and papers. 'We bought for them on commission, always securing the best goods at the lowest rates, and charging them a commission on the actual cost.' But 'so many of our debtors were killed that a large amount was lost to us'. Then the East India Company disappeared, and the Government supplied itself with the stores which the firm had been shipping.

In 1855 Smith had made his first venture with newspaper ownership. He had started the *Overland Mail* (news of India for Great Britain) and the *Homeward Mail* (news of Great Britain for India). During the last war, they were amalgamated in the *Indiaman*, a publication now defunct.

Mention has been made of the fact that Ruskin was a contributor to one of Smith & Elder's annuals. He was represented by drawings and poems, afterwards collected in an edition of forty copies for private circulation. Smith was no more than twenty-one when he first met Ruskin's father. Ruskin senior came to Cornhill with a story of having been with a book of his son's, *Modern Painters*, to John Murray, to whom he had proposed publication at the author's expense. Murray, he declared, had refused to read it until it was in type. George Smith accepted the book, and, for a time, the firm published all Ruskin's works, including *The Stones of Venice*, *The Crown of Wild Olive*, and

Sesame and Lilies. There was to be 'thirty years' close personal connexion'.

15, Waterloo Place. S.W.

Dec 22nd. 1886

Dearest Isabel

Please see if we have a copy of Ruskin's Lectures on Architecture at home, and if this note arrives in time bring it with you — if you have one. I only want to refer to something in it.

Yours affectionately

GS

Handwriting of George Murray Smith in a letter to Mrs. Reginald Smith. He commonly signed 'G.S.'

At parties at the Ruskins', Smith met, among others, Burne-Jones, Millais, and George Richmond. His recollections of the parents have special interest since the publication of *The Order of Release* by Admiral Sir William James. Ruskin *père*, 'a shrewd and clever man' had 'a good deal of humour', Mrs. Ruskin was 'devoid of the faintest sense of it. She would interrupt her brilliant son in talk which held us spell-bound, by a correction with some trivial and perfectly irrelevant detail. She was pugnaciously Protestant, and I remember winning a bet that, before the evening was over, she would call the Virgin Mary "a creature". John, to his father and mother, was little less than a demi-god.'

As for the unhappy marriage with Effie Gray, Smith says that, when he dined with Ruskin shortly after it took place, 'it was easy to see that wedded life was not for them all happiness. Ruskin was absorbed in his studies of art, and after dinner, when his wife sat alone in the drawing-room, we used to be carried all over the house to see his new purchases. My wife and I were engaged to dine with Ruskin on the very day his wife left him, and the father came to tell me what had happened and to prevent us keeping our engagement.'

At one of John's birthday parties, when Smith proposed his health—after a glass of the Nelson sherry, part of Domecq and Co.'s pre-Trafalgar stock—the speech was received 'with indignation' by the person praised. 'I had said the kindest things, much more than he deserved, in respect of his writings on art and the influence of those writings, but I had left out the only thing he had done worth mentioning, his contributions to the science of political economy.'

Smith found Ruskin 'a man of surprises'. One evening he 'volunteered to sing a nigger song, and sang it with great energy'. When, in later life, Smith drew his author's attention to the flowers on the carpet at Waterloo Place, to which the firm had removed from Cornhill, Ruskin said, 'Flowers! Pickled cabbage, you mean.' One thinks of Herbert Spencer's carpet, the colours of which, when they faded, the man of science touched up.

After the death of Ruskin's father men-servants were abolished at Denmark Hill. 'The guests were waited on by three or four parlour maids, all of them pretty. Throughout the dinner a constant conversation went on between Ruskin and one of these damsels. One night he discussed his plan, partially carried into effect, of establishing shops for the sale of good tea. "Then", he said, "I should put a nice young girl, neatly dressed and with clean hands, to serve the tea faithfully. That would suit you, Mary

Ann, would it not?" and Mary Ann, with a bob, answered "Yes sir".'

Smith and his wife were among the observers of Ruskin's roadmaking by Oxford undergraduates. One of the supervisors proved to be an old Denmark Hill gardener, who, in reply to an inquiry by Smith said, 'There isn't one worth a shilling a day and dear at that.'

In 1873 Ruskin transferred the publication of his books to George Allen, after what E. T. Cook, his editor, with Alexander Wedderburn, in thirty-nine volumes,[1] calls 'a curious correspondence'. Smith and Ruskin had corresponded on a 'My dear Ruskin' and 'My dear Smith' basis. The business relationship was broken off by a lawyer's letter to Smith & Elder.[2] But the day came when Ruskin was to write, in discussing the joys and sorrows of life: 'For my part, what I should like best to do at the present moment would be to be sitting at one side of the table and my old publisher at the other, with a bottle of my father's sherry and a plate of walnuts between us, listening to some of his good stories.' And when Cook was assistant editor and then editor of George Smith's and Greenwood's *Pall Mall Gazette*, and George Smith had long ceased to be proprietor, Cook used to have, I know, many amiable letters from Ruskin.

[1] E. T. C. also wrote, *The Life of John Ruskin* in two volumes (Allen).

[2] For several pages on the conditions in the book trade in which Ruskin became his own publisher see the Cook-Wedderburn *Works of Ruskin*, XXVII. I, xxxiii *et seq*. (Allen).

CHAPTER VI

Charlotte Brontë and Thackeray and their Publisher

'ALL HER FAME TO BE BEAUTIFUL' — G. H. LEWES — NEW LETTERS — THE CHARACTER OF THACKERAY

WE all know the story of how there came to Smith & Elder a packet of manuscript (*The Professor*) from 'Currer Bell', how they declined it but expressed high appreciation of the author's talent, and, shortly afterwards received *Jane Eyre*, and, though convinced that the author was a woman, corresponded with 'Currer Bell, Esq.'. But I have some particulars about the firm's relations with the novelist, and the number of books about Charlotte Brontë and her sisters which have been published since I first set to work on the present pages suggests that they will be of interest.

First, about the Currer Bell parcel. The guilelessness of the sisters is shown by the fact that the addresses of other publishers to whom it had been previously sent had been left on the wrapper. And a day or two after the receipt of the package there came a stamp because an 'experienced friend' of Currer Bell had stated that publishers refrained from answering communications unless postage was enclosed. Mr. W. Smith Williams, who wrote to the aspirant, was 'a most agreeable and most intelligent man' whom George Smith had discovered doing book-keeping as his day's work, and writing for the *Spectator* of an evening. He suffered, however, from the 'chilly temperament' of Rintoul, the editor, who used to assure him that 'the *Spectator* is not enthusiastic and cannot be'. Smith started on the *Jane Eyre* manuscript after breakfast one Sunday, was so engrossed that he lunched on a sandwich and took very little dinner, and finished the story before he went to bed. He bought the copyright for £100, and, in all, paid the author £500, 'an amount not then so inadequate as would appear at the present day'.

A third-rate publisher called Newby advertised a book 'by the author of *Jane Eyre* under her other *nom de plume* of Acton Bell'. So Charlotte and her sister Anne came to London to furnish Smith & Elder with 'ocular proof that there are at least two of us'. The 'two rather quaintly dressed little ladies, pale-faced and anxious-looking'—'Currer Bell' in spectacles—were announced without giving their names, and identified themselves with a Smith & Elder envelope addressed to 'Currer Bell, Esq.'.

Charlotte Brontë speaks of Smith as 'a practical man', 'a firm intelligent man of business, though so young'. His conduct was 'kind and upright', his house's 'performance always better than their promise'. In Mrs. Trevelyan's *Life of Mrs. Humphry Ward*[1] Charlotte is quoted as saying that she 'never had a truer or wiser counsellor'. Smith found her 'quick and clear intelligence delightful', but her personal appearance 'interesting rather than attractive. She was very small and her head was certainly too large for her body. She had fine eyes, but her face was marred by the mouth and complexion. There was little feminine charm about her, and of this fact she was uneasily and perpetually conscious. I believe she would have given all her genius and fame to have been beautiful. Perhaps no woman ever existed who was more anxious to be pretty than she. She had a pretty little foot, of which she was rather vain, and she had too small a waist. I have little doubt that tight-lacing shortened her life.' Anne Brontë was 'a gentle, quiet, rather subdued person, by no means pretty, yet of a pleasing appearance. Her manner was curiously expressive of a wish for protection and encouragement, a kind of constant appeal which invited sympathy.'

Smith and his mother did their best to show the sisters what would interest them in London. Charlotte, who 'stayed with us several times' for weeks, visited *The Times* office, the Bank, Newgate, Bedlam, the Crystal Palace several times, and Fleet Street, lighted up at night. She was given opportunities of seeing

[1] Constable.

the Duke of Wellington for whom, with her father, she had a particular admiration, and Cardinal Wiseman and Macready—neither of whom she approved of—met the Carlyles, Rogers, Monckton Milnes, Mrs. Crowe (*The Night Side of Nature*), and the Procters, and was taken to a Quaker meeting. But the parson's daughter, Smith assures us, found in a form of worship different from that of her own Church, 'more amusement than edification', which is somewhat surprising in view of the acquaintance of the Brontë family with the Methodists, who, in the conduct of their services, also diverged considerably from Church of England practice. Smith and Charlotte even went, 'as Mr. and Miss Fraser', to a phrenologist.

Generally, Charlotte was 'self-absorbed and gave the impression that she was always observing and analysing the people she met'. In a letter to Smith she noted in him 'an undercurrent of quiet raillery, an irresistible laugh to yourself; a not unkindly but somewhat subtle playing on your compassion, in short a shy touch of Mephistopheles, with the fiend extracted'. Miss Thackeray has described the visit of Smith and Charlotte to her home. Mrs. Brookfield said she was the most difficult woman to talk to she had ever met.

Smith describes the occasion on which, in his house, Charlotte, in mittens, assailed Thackeray for having committed the *gaucherie*, after one of his lectures, of introducing her to Mrs. Smith in a loud voice as *Jane Eyre*. 'With head thrown back and face white with anger, and hardly reaching to Thackeray's elbow [he was 6 ft. 3 in.], she said, "What would you have thought if I had introduced you before a mixed company as 'Mr. Warrington'?"' Smith also tells of G. H. Lewes catching it for having said to her, 'There ought to be a bond of sympathy between us, Miss Brontë, for we have both written naughty books'. But did not Lady Herschel once say to Smith's mother, when, in her drawing-room, she saw a copy of *Jane Eyre*, 'Do you have such a book as this about, at the risk of your daughters reading it?' I myself remember being told when a small boy that the novel was 'unsuitable reading at your age'. And Lady Eastlake's observation in her review of the book in the *Quarterly* is not forgotten, 'If written by a woman, it must be one who has forfeited the right to the society of her sex'.

Smith stated that the conflagration in *Jane Eyre* had its foundation in an incident when Charlotte Brontë and his sister were with him at a dramatic performance at Dickens's house and the scenery caught fire.

Thackeray and Charlotte did not get on because 'her heroics roused his sense of humour. Miss Brontë wanted to persuade him that he was a great man with a mission, and Thackeray, with many wicked jests, declined to recognize the mission. The affectation with which he discussed his books, very much as clerks in a bank would discuss the ledgers they had to keep for a salary, was provoked by what he considered Charlotte Brontë's high falutin'. Thackeray was one of the few famous men I have known who did not care for adulation. He was not fond of the society of what are called clever women, that is women whom he felt to be critical. In repartee a clever woman easily had the better of him. He liked the type in whose society he could unbend and be at ease. He was not greedy of compliment.' But while Charlotte scolded Thackeray, she 'recognised his greatness and once said he was "a Titanian mind" '. On seeing his portrait by Laurence her remark was, 'There came up a lion out of Judah'. It was to him that she dedicated the second edition of *Jane Eyre*.

To step forward nearly a century—towards the end of August 1946—some readers probably heard on the wireless, 'The Brontës, by Alfred Sangster, adapted for broadcasting by Peggy Wells, produced by Howard Rose'. I sent an extract which essayed a description of the meeting between Currer and Acton Bell with Smith, Thackeray, and Lewes, to Mrs. Reginald Smith. She wrote to me: 'It is a complete travesty of events as they are known to have taken place. I hope you will correct it. The standard of conversation put into the meeting between Thackeray, Lewes and my father is low. I never saw Thackeray or Lewes, but my father never talked in that way.'

Richmond's well-known portrait of Charlotte Brontë was commissioned by Smith. He also got Thackeray to sit for the Laurence portrait, so that—a typically kind thought—his daughters might have a portrait of their father while he was in the United States.

Mrs. Trevelyan in her *Life of Mrs. Humphry Ward* has this letter from Smith to Mrs. Humphry Ward dated August 18, 1898, about his feelings for Charlotte:

I was amused at your questions. No, I never was in the least in love with Charlotte Brontë. I am afraid that the confession will not raise me in your opinion. But the truth is, I never could have loved any woman who had not some charm or grace of person and Charlotte Brontë had none. I liked her and was interested by her, and I admired her—especially when she was in Yorkshire and I was in London. I never was coxcomb enough to suppose that she was in love with me. But I believe that my mother was at one time rather alarmed.

Mrs. Reginald Smith assures me that this statement 'represents the facts precisely. I do not think the relations between my father and Miss Brontë were ever sentimental. He regarded her from his youthful twenties as quite old, and besides he was a great admirer of beauty.' Smith was twenty-three when he brought out *Jane Eyre* and Charlotte thirty-one.

But one may be excused, perhaps, for recording what Sir William Robertson Nicoll thought he had to go upon as far as Charlotte was concerned. The novelist's early references to Smith have been quoted. She also wrote: 'George'—George, not Mr. Smith[1]—'is a very fine specimen of a young Englishman of business. So I regard him, and I am proud to be one of his props.' In 1850 Smith asked Charlotte to pay a visit to his sister and himself in Edinburgh.

I concluded he was joking, laughed and declined: however it seems he was in earnest. The thing appearing to me perfectly out of the question, I still refused. Mrs. Smith did not favour it; you may easily fancy how she helped me to sustain my opposition, but her worthy

[1] But in their correspondence she never got farther than 'My dear Sir'.

son only waxed more determined. His mother is master of the house, but he is master of his mother. This morning she came and entreated me to go. 'George wished it so much'; he had begged her to use her influence, etc., etc. Now, I believe that George and I understand each other very well, and respect each other very sincerely. We both know the breach time has made between us; we don't embarrass each other, or very rarely; my six or eight years' seniority, to say nothing of the lack of all pretension to beauty, etc. are a perfect safeguard. I should not in the least fear to go with him to China. I like to see him pleased, I greatly *dislike* to ruffle and disappoint him, so he shall have his wish; and if all be well I mean to join him in Edinburgh after I shall have spent a few days with you.

The journey was made, and the visitor, in writing of Smith, compares him, to his advantage, with Sir J. Kay-Shuttleworth, for whose work, as the founder of our system of popular education, Matthew Arnold said he 'will have a statue'. He received a baronetcy.

Her description of 'Dr. John' in *Villette*, the original of whom was Smith—his mother was 'Mrs. Bretton'—may be recalled. Some of the proofs were corrected at the Smiths' home.

Dr. John *could* think, and think well (she wrote in *Villette*) but he was rather a man of action than of thought; he *could* feel, and feel vividly in his way, but his heart had no chord for enthusiasm. To bright, soft, sweet influences his eyes and lips gave bright, soft, sweet welcome, beautiful to see as dyes of rose and silver, pearl and purple, imbuing summer clouds; for what belonged to storm, what was wild and intense, dangerous, sudden and flaming, he had no sympathy, and held with it no communion. . . . Reader, I see him yet, with his look of comely courage and cordial calm. . . . Lucy must not marry Dr. John; he is far too youthful, handsome, bright-spirited and sweet-tempered.

Then we have this letter (Jan. 20, 1851) from Charlotte herself to a confidante:

You draw great conclusions from small inferences. Those 'fixed intentions' you fancy—are imaginary. The 'undercurrent' amounts simply to this—a kind of natural liking and sense of something congenial. Were there no vast barrier of age, fortune, etc., there is perhaps enough personal regard to make things possible which now are impossible. If men and women married because they like each other's temper, look, conversation, nature and so on—and if besides, years were more nearly equal—the chance you allude to might be admitted as a chance—but other reasons regulate matrimony—reasons of convenience, of connection, of money. Meantime I am content to have him as a friend.—and pray God to continue to me the common sense to look on one so young, so rising and so hopeful in no other light.[1]

At this time Charlotte was nearly thirty-five and Smith twenty-seven. There was an occasion when Smith talked of a trip up the Rhine, but nothing came of it. She wrote to her gossip: 'I am not made of stone; what is mere excitement to him is fever to me.'

There were passages with a member of the Smith & Elder staff, one Taylor. He came on the firm's business to Haworth. He was a little red-haired man, described by her as 'horribly intelligent, quick, searching, sagacious with a memory of relentless tenacity'; and he made some impression. Farewells were said when he went for five years to Bombay to be Smith & Elder's representative.

Smith sent Charlotte an early copy of *Esmond*, which she called a 'relentless dissection of diseased subjects'. When in 1853 he told her of his engagement to be married her reply was brief: 'In great happiness, as in great grief, words of sympathy should be few. Accept my meed of congratulations and believe me sincerely yours, Charlotte Brontë.' Her letter to him announcing her approaching marriage—they married in the same year, 1854—was more than 500 words long. In the course of it she said:

I thank you for your congratulations and good wishes; if these last are realized but in part I shall be very thankful. It gave me also sincere pleasure to be assured of your happiness. Though of that I never doubted. I have faith also in its permanent character—provided Mrs. George Smith is what it pleases me to fancy her to be. You never told me any particulars about her, though I should have liked them much, but did not like to ask questions.

[1] *Shakespeare Head Brontë Life and Letters* (Blackwell).

As for the step she herself was taking, it was 'no hasty one; on the gentleman's side at least; it has been meditated for many years, and I hope that in at last acceding to it, I am acting right; it is what I earnestly wish to do'. As to her feelings towards Nicholls she could not

deny that my own feelings have been much impressed and changed by the nature and strength of the qualities brought out in the course of his long attachment. I fear I must accuse myself of having formerly done him less than justice. I mean to try to make him a good wife. There has been heavy anxiety—but I begin to hope all will end for the best. My expectations are, however, very subdued—very different, I daresay, to what yours were before you were married. Care and Fear stand so close to Hope. I sometimes scarcely even see her for the shadows they cast. And yet I am thankful, too, and the doubtful future may be left to Providence.

The links of communication with London, she added, in a final passsage 'have waxed very frail and few. It must be so in this world. All things considered, I don't wish it otherwise.'

Smith and Charlotte corresponded until her death in 1855. Leslie Stephen, in the *Dictionary of National Biography*, mentions the offer of marriage 'made to her in 1851 by a man of business in a good position' who had her father's favour. Charlotte had refused Nicholls in 1852 at her parent's dictation.

When Mrs. Gaskell was collecting materials for her life of Charlotte, Smith gave her the pleasure of drives, in his wife's barouche with 'a very fast pair of horses', to places the novelist had visited in London. He noted Mrs. Gaskell's 'quick interest in social questions'. In Manchester he and his wife found her much occupied in a scheme for cheap dinners, and lunched with her at one of the coffee houses which had been started, 'having as fellow guests a postman and a sweep'. Hers was 'a most charming personality', but in the biography she had a passage about Branwell which gave Smith trouble and made it necessary to suppress the first edition. Sir James Stephen (the father of Fitzjames Stephen), who had espoused the cousin of the lady supposed to be libelled, wrote to Smith when all was settled that he had shown 'how to encounter loss, vexation and disappointment with the temper of a gentleman and the spirit of a Christian'. Out of friendship for Smith, Mrs. Gaskell, when in Paris, once sat up all night to make for him a copy of a pamphlet which he urgently wanted for the *Pall Mall Gazette* and a friend had lent her. Also she introduced him to Madame de Peyronnet who was in the secrets of the Orleanists and was to write for the paper. The circumstances of Mrs. Gaskell's death were tragic. She had gone to the country to supervise some alterations in a house which, unknown to her husband, she had bought out of her literary earnings as a refuge for them both, and died there suddenly; and her husband first knew of her death when he saw it announced on a newspaper placard.

Lady Ritchie's anecdote of her father and Smith is well known. 'There's a young fellow just come', Thackeray said to the family, 'he has brought £1,000 in his pocket. He has made an offer for my book. It is the most spirited, handsome offer. I scarcely like to take him at his word; he's hardly more than a boy. His name is George Smith. He's waiting there now, and I must go back.' The book, *Esmond*, was so successful that £250 was added to the £1,000. It was with a copy of this novel in his hand that Thackeray said to his American friend, Fields, 'Here is the very best I can do. I am willing to leave it when I go, with my card.'

Before *Esmond*, 'long before you were famous', as Smith once said to Thackeray, he had sent him a message through Williams, who had some acquaintance with him, that if ever he were in need of a publisher Smith & Elder would be glad to serve him. But *Vanity Fair* went past them. Their first dealings with Thackeray were over *The Kickleburys on the Rhine*—I see a first edition advertised for thirty shillings—for which Chapman & Hall, owing to the non-success of *Rebecca and Rowena* in their hands, would not give him his price. Smith, invited to see him on the subject, at once wrote out a cheque, and, though *The Times* severely criticized the book, it sold sufficiently well.

Thackeray might be dilatory with 'copy' but he was punctilious in money matters. In one instance he brought back a sum paid on account, £500 or so, because he had not furnished his instalment in time. And after his death a slip of paper was found bearing the words, 'I.O. S E and Co 35 pp'. The friendship between Smith and Thackeray had become 'very close and unrestrained'. The novelist was not a good manager of his affairs and used to confide his difficulties to Smith, who would say, 'Well, you know a bank whereon the wild thyme grows'. Thackeray's mode of suggesting that a cheque would be convenient was to walk into Smith's room with his trouser pockets turned inside out. His publisher used to take out his cheque-book and look at him inquiringly and the sum needed would be mentioned.

We are only nowadays getting near a complete picture of Thackeray. Frederick Greenwood, who had opportunities of knowing him closely, writes on a later page that 'we have no accurate picture of the great "Thack"'. Smith agreed that his character was 'very complex'. But 'regard and affection grew ever higher' as the intimacy between them became closer. 'His nature', he said, 'belonged to a very noble type, while his faults were comparatively trivial. He no doubt suffered in the estimation of many of his acquaintances—though not in the esteem of those who knew him well—from the fact that he had lived a Bohemian life. The traces survived. And his domestic life was broken up by a tragedy which entitled him to the tenderest and most forbearing sympathy. He was self-indulgent to a degree in minor matters, and no doubt offended many of his friends in consequence.' For example, 'he thought nothing of fabricating an excuse for throwing over an engagement if it suited the convenience of the moment'.

As for his 'cynicism', it was 'of the brains not of the heart'. 'No sketch of him does justice to his kindness and sensibility. His life overflowed with kindly deeds. He took to a poor and sick friend in Paris a pill-box carefully sealed which proved to be full of Napoleons.' Thackeray's manner with children was 'simply beautiful. My wife, when he was staying with us once brought out to him our eldest son, then a baby, and asked him to give the infant his blessing. He put his hand on the child and blessed it with a tenderness which brought tears not only into its mother's eyes but into mine. As he read aloud his Roundabout paper written on the death of Macaulay and Washington Irving he broke down. "Yet people say I have no heart, Douglas Jerrold said so to me, and Charles Dickens has often said so to others."'

About a year and three-quarters before he died he wrote the following consecration of his new house in Palace Gate: 'I pray Almighty God that the words I write in this house may be pure and honest, that they may be dictated by no personal spite, unworthy motive or unjust greed of gain, that they may tell the truth as far as I know it and tend to promote love and peace amongst men for the sake of Christ our Lord.'

'Yet the truth has to be told', Smith said, 'that he often quarrelled, and the quarrel normally arose from some indiscretion or carelessness of speech in himself. He was careless of reticence and slow in repartee.'

Several persons have testified that, like so many other writing men, he was not a good speaker. Yet Smith notes that 'he prepared his speeches with great industry, and his secretary generally, and sometimes myself, would hear him rehearse them, saying "Hear, Hear" at appropriate intervals. But no amount of preparation saved him from being a curiously bad speaker and one very easily disconcerted. He spoke in a way that was very difficult to follow. His speeches were too terse.'

That Thackeray was an idle man Smith would not agree. 'He had a great natural tendency to indolence. It was with difficulty he brought himself to work. He worked with energy and effectiveness—and wrote sometimes with extraordinary rapidity—when he was once excited. But he was easily thrown off the line. He would take odd and fanciful precautions against himself.' At one time he thought that if he had chambers in which to do his writing, 'an atmosphere of diligence would be created'. The experiment lasted a fortnight. At another time he tried driving round and round Wimbledon Common, but without effect. One recalls how when Charles Lamb's sister got him some quiet little room (at three shillings a week) to write in, he found he could not endure its solitariness. Nor was he better off when Mary fitted him up with a table and chair in a Temple garret and bade him 'write away as if he were in a lodging in Salisbury Plain'. Charles could not write without Mary's presence in the same room. Thackeray once complained to Smith that his secretary 'would look at him, and so put him off; and, not long after that, he looked away'. As for this secretary, he is said to have had a gift for losing manuscripts hardly less remarkable than Thackeray's. The novelist was 'careless, not to say slovenly, about his papers, would thrust them in anywhere and forget the place.' Yet he wrote an exceedingly clear hand, indeed two hands, one for 'copy' and one for correspondence. He once said that if all else failed, he could earn sixpence by writing the Lord's Prayer in a circle of the dimensions of the coin.

Thackeray was markedly loyal to his friends. Once, in reply to the letter of an editor, Smith had written, as he recognized, rather intemperately. The correspondence was sent to Thackeray, who said he would stand by him although he had 'ridden too hard.' 'With all my experience of men', said Thackeray, 'you are the man who is fondest of having his own way.'

Thackeray 'pretended to believe that he had a great many enemies and kept up the fiction with diligence and humour. His humour was often of a grim kind, and he did like humbugging people.' But the words about the Prince Consort's death that Thackeray added to the Roundabout paper, 'On Letts's Diary'[1] seemed to Smith so 'exquisite in their felicity of form and grace of sentiment' that he had them framed, and they hung in his study.

[1] See Oxford Thackeray, *The Wolves and the Lamb*, &c., p. 675.

GEORGE MURRAY SMITH in 1865, the year in which the *Pall Mall Gazette* was started, five years after the starting of *Cornhill* in 1860

CHAPTER VII

The Starting of 'Cornhill' with Thackeray as Editor

THE AUTHOR OF 'TOM BROWN'S SCHOOLDAYS' — 'GOOD MANNERS, GOOD EDUCATION AND GOOD ENGLISH' — TRAITS OF GEORGE ELIOT — A MAGAZINE 'LAVISH TO RECKLESSNESS'

THE sketch of Thackeray in some of his relationships with George Smith and others has been carried forward in order to give an impression of the character and temperament of the two men who, on the starting of *Cornhill*, were to have one of their closest periods of co-operation. Early in 1859 Charlotte Brontë's 'firm, intelligent man of business' had a plan for a monthly magazine to be well written and well illustrated and sold for a shilling. It was to have the best qualities of the reviews and also of the periodicals which published novels—'it is hard', wrote Leonard Huxley, 'to measure by present standards the popularity of the serial two or three generations ago'. Above all, it was to publish instalments of a novel by Thackeray. The idea of this 'flashed suddenly', Smith writes, 'as did most of the ideas which have in the course of my life led to successful operations'.[1]

To Thackeray, three of whose books Smith & Elder had published, Smith betook himself with a slip of paper which many of us have read, but which, for its perspicacity, is worth reading again. On the paper was written:

Smith, Elder, & Co., have it in contemplation to commence the publication of a Monthly Magazine on January 1st, 1860. They are desirous of inducing Mr. Thackeray to contribute to their periodical,

[1] A humbler scheme produced to Smith before he had his plan for *Cornhill* had come from W. H. G. Kingston, the boys' author of my juvenile days, who wanted to start a boys' magazine 'containing tales of a high character and sound Protestant principles showing the youth of England the dangers of Popery'.

and they make the following proposal to Mr. Thackeray: 1. That he shall write either one or two novels of the ordinary size for publication in the Magazine—one-twelfth portion of each novel (estimated to be about equal to one number of a serial) to appear in each number of the Magazine. 2. That Mr. Thackeray shall assign to Smith, Elder, & Co., the right to publish the novels in their Magazine and in a separate form afterwards, and to all sums to be received for the work from American and Continental Publishers. 3. That Smith, Elder, & Co., shall pay Mr. Thackeray 350*l* each month. 4. That the profits of all editions of the novels published at a lower price than the first edition shall be equally divided between Mr. Thackeray and Smith, Elder, & Co., 65 Cornhill: February 19, 1859.

'I wonder whether you will consider it', said Smith to Thackeray, 'or will at once consign it to the waste paper basket.' The novelist, 'with characteristic absence of guile, allowed me to see that he regarded the terms as phenomenal. . . . He said "I am not going to put such a document as this into my waste-paper-basket"'. He was agreeable to the proposal.

But who was to be editor? The author of *Tom Brown's School Days*, Tom Hughes, was invited, but could not serve; he had thrown in his lot with Macmillans.[1] Although 'other names

[1] THE CHARACTER OF THOMAS HUGHES. George Smith thought highly of Hughes's literary judgement and abilities, had a real friendship with him, and appreciated 'his manly character and original, unselfish and courageous efforts for the masses', but did not agree with his methods. 'At a gathering of artisans Hughes would say, "Let us take off our coats and smoke a pipe in our shirt sleeves." He aimed to come down to the manners of his company: it would have been better if he had kept his natural manners. When I had to preside at any meeting of the kind or to attend one I always put on my best frockcoat and provided myself with a cigar instead of a pipe. Hughes held frequent arguments with me on the subject, but neither convinced the other. I told him my wife consulted me as to what kind of dress she should wear when she went to teach a girls' class at the Working Men's Club. I advised her to put on her prettiest dress, with her very latest Parisian bonnet. Hughes would have had her borrow a dress from her maid.

'Hughes's social schemes were meritorious from the point of good intentions, but unfortunately he was no man of business. He did not know how to translate a good idea into effective practice. As a result, his schemes often failed and involved their author in disaster. His colony in Tennessee, "Rugby", intended to evolve a new and finer type of social life, ended in absolute

were under consideration, none seemed exactly suitable'. After one of Smith's before-breakfast gallops the idea came, 'Why not Mr. Thackeray, and you yourself do what is necessary to supplement any deficiencies on his part as a man of business? Think of the writers who would be proud to contribute under his editorship?' So there was another interview with Thackeray, who accepted a salary of £1,000 a year. Later, he wrote: 'As I think of the editor business I like it, but the magazine must bear my cachet'—with a thought, no doubt, on some namby-pamby periodicals of the time—'be a man of the world magazine'.

It may be mentioned that Thackeray, who at the university had been a contributor to three magazines—one was called the *Chimera* and another the *Snob*—was not an editor for the first time. In *Lovel the Widower*, the novel which appeared in *Cornhill*, one of his characters speaks of getting possession of 'that neat little literary paper, *The Museum*, and giving himself airs as editor'. The periodical with which Thackeray himself had had to do with was the *National Standard and Journal of Literature, Science, Music, Theatricals and the Fine Arts*. When he took over from a somewhat notorious character called 'Alphabet Bayley' (from his string of initials) he wrote in it:

> Under the heading of this *National Standard* of ours there originally appeared, 'Edited by F. W. N. Bayley, assisted by the most eminent men of the day'. Now we have *changé tout cela*—no, not exactly *tout cela*, for we still retain the assistance of a host of literary talent, but Frederick William Naylor Bayley has gone. We have got free of the Old Bailey, and Changed the Governor.

failure. Hughes came to me in great distress one Sunday morning for advice and help. I took the burden off his shoulders and pulled the tangled concern straight, for which Hughes was to the end very grateful. Whether I shall ever see any of the money I put in is highly conjectural.

'Hughes was not successful as a politician, though of course popular with his constituents. His high and noble character added a grace to the office of county court judge which he held, though I am afraid he considered natural justice more important than a strict adherence to legal procedure. Mrs. Hughes, while the most devoted and affectionate of wives, was a staunch Conservative, while he was an advanced Radical. Hughes certainly changed his political opinions considerably before his death.'

But, as Henry Vizetelly says, 'neither Thackeray's caricature portraits, his verses, his letters from Paris, nor the temporary transformation of the paper into a purely literary organ achieved success for it, and, after being carried on by its new editor for some months, with a slight change in its title and an addition to its price, it succumbed early in its second year of existence'.

Between the ages of thirty and thirty-five, Thackeray had been writing book-reviews and art-criticism at three guineas a week, and, before he became editor of *Cornhill*, had been associated with all sorts of papers from *The Times* downwards, and in all sorts of capacities. He reviewed Carlyle's *French Revolution* and *John Sterling* in *The Times* (Aug. 3, 1837 and Nov. 1, 1851) and he was art critic for the *Morning Chronicle* when Dickens was one of its Parliamentary reporters. He applied indeed for the editorship of the *Chronicle* evening edition, a post which was given to Charles Mackay, Marie Corelli's father. In 1836 Thackeray's stepfather had been chairman of a company which launched the *Constitutional and Public Ledger*, with Joseph Hume and Grote among its backers; it gave the future novelist a salary of £400 as Paris correspondent. The career of this journal was as short as the *National Standard*'s.

In 1840 he is saying to his mother that he is bringing out, on his own account, 'a weekly paper, the *Foolscap Library*', changed on publication to the odd title of *The Whitey-Brown Paper Magazine*. In what must be one of the most sanguine letters a founder of a periodical ever wrote, he says:

> I think it will take: and the profits of it are so enormous if successful that I don't like to share them with a bookseller: there is no reason why I should not make a big lump of money. I don't know that I shan't have to borrow from Father:—the thing is a fortune but wants about £50 to start it. Why shouldn't I sell 5,000, 10,000 copies?—they will pay me 40 or 80 a week; so a week is 400 a year of which I would put by 3 at the very least per an: see Alnascher in the 'Arabian Nights'.[1]

I do not remember reading anywhere what came of the

[1] *Letters of Anne Thackeray Ritchie*, Hester Ritchie (Murray).

Whitey-Brown. Neither the British Museum nor the Bodleian has a copy.

In 1844 he is writing to Bradbury and Evans:[1]

> Will you put me at the head of a slashing, brilliant, gentlemanlike, sixpenny, aristocratic, literary paper containing each week good reviews of a book or two, not notices; good novels in series: good theatrical articles, etc. a paper that—should not look for a large but a gentlemanlike circulation: and have a decided air of white kid gloves. Have the papers signed and by good men, Buller, Carlyle, Forster, Milnes, [Fitz]Gerald and a University man or two. I would take the Fine Arts, light literature and the theatre under my charge with the dinner-giving (all except *me* paying part) and I know no man in Europe who would handle it better.

But Barkis was not willin'.

Cornhill, the name of the Smith-Thackeray magazine, was sniffed at. Fancy the *Leadenhall Market Magazine*, exclaimed one wiseacre, who had forgotten that Fielding had a *Covent Garden Journal*.[2] It was also hidden from this critic that there would be a *Temple Bar*, a *Belgravia*, a *St. Paul's*, even a *Strand*—not to speak of a *Pall Mall* and a *St. James's*. The name *Cornhill*, wrote Thackeray in the advertisement of the periodical—in the form of a letter to G. H. Lewes—was 'from its place of publication'. In this new magazine, it was explained—and here something of the character of the *Pall Mall Gazette* is forecast—people were 'to tell what they know, pretty briefly and good humouredly', and not 'in a manner too obviously didactic', and there would be expected from them 'good manners, good education and good English', and 'we shall suppose the ladies and children always present'. Thackeray said to Trollope, 'One of our chief objects is getting out of novel-spinning, and back into the world'. 'We agreed', he wrote to Smith, 'that both of us should have a veto on articles.' 'This relation between publisher and editor would have worked ill in the case of some men', said Smith, 'but

[1] In a hitherto unpublished letter in Gordon Ray's *Letters and Private Papers of William Makepeace Thackeray* (Oxford University Press).

[2] Austin Dobson wrote '*The* "Covent Garden Journal", *being a hitherto unwritten Chapter in the Life of Henry Fielding*'.

Thackeray's nature was generous, and my regard for him was so sincere that no misunderstanding ever occurred.'

The cover of *Cornhill*—'What a happy design!' cried Thackeray—showed a sower; but we have all admired it on our copies of the magazine. The original is at the Victoria and Albert. Smith acknowledged that the sower was using his left hand only, whereas a sower sows with right and left hand alternately. The artist was Frederick Walker.

When making-up day came, the editor would not claim the first place for his own novel in his pages. He gave precedence to Trollope's *Framley Parsonage*—'exactly as a host would invite a guest to walk into a room before himself', wrote George Smith admiringly.

Trollope, a future contributor to the *Pall Mall Gazette*, had been surprised not only by *Cornhill* offering him £1,000, 'more than double I had yet received' for a three-volume novel, but 'by the suddenness of the call'. Copy had to be 'in the printer's hands within six weeks'. The explanation 'must be found', he says, 'in the habits of procrastination which had at that time grown upon the editor'.

Smith 'wanted a tale of English life, with a clerical flavour'. The business-like Trollope was ready to supply it, and, as he had to return to Ireland on his Post Office work, 'wrote the first few pages in the railway carriage'. He bore in mind, he says, that for serial publication 'the author should not allow himself to be tedious in any single part.... Who can imagine the first half of the first volume of *Waverley* coming out in shilling numbers?' He made such speed that by the time he had half-finished *Framley Parsonage* he went back to another story he had in hand, *Castle Richmond*, and 'this did not create either difficulty or confusion'.

Until Trollope attended 'a sumptuous dinner' given by Smith to his contributors, he had never met Thackeray. 'One of the most tender-hearted human beings I ever knew' was how he was to describe him. They became fast friends. A fellow guest was Millais, who illustrated *Framley Parsonage*, and gratified its author by the pains he took to understand his characters, for when Trollope carried some of them on into other books he had 'his early ideas impressed indelibly on his memory by the excellence of the delineations'. The author adds that during the writing of *Framley Parsonage*, the fourth novel of 'the new shire I had added to the English counties, I made a map of the dear county'.

The Small House at Allington was another novel that Trollope contributed to *Cornhill*, after disappointing the proprietor with an inferior *Brown, Jones and Robinson* for which he had paid £600. For the last novel he wrote for the magazine, *The Claverings*, he received 'the highest rate of pay that was ever accorded to me', £2,800, paid in a single cheque.

Siegfried Sassoon notes that Meredith's *Adventures of Harry Richmond* appeared, with illustrations by Millais, at a time 'when to be serialised in *Cornhill* meant success for a novelist'.

Although *Cornhill* had been forestalled by two months by *Macmillan's*,[1] the sale of the first number, January 1860—128 pages with a few wood engravings—was 110,000. No more than 80,000 had been ordered. Such a sale was 'without precedent in English periodical literature'. The magazine, Monckton Milnes said, was 'almost too good'; he could not see how the contributors, the publishers, and Thackeray 'are to be paid out of it'. But he enters into the enterprising spirit of George Smith and Thackeray by suggesting an article by 'the old Premier', Palmerston. 'An unprecedented shillingsworth—limited to the inoffensive' was Leslie Stephen's honest judgement. In an opening ode 'Father Prout' wrote:

> With Fudge and Blarney, or the Thames on Fire
> Treat not your buyer:
> But proffer good material
> A genuine cereal,
> Value for twelve pence and not dear at twenty.

The success attained was so remarkable that the editor had an experience uncommon to editors with their first number. His

[1] Which it had been proposed to call the *Round Table* 'for the encouragement of all that is manly and elevating'. An American is writing a history of it (1859–1907).

proprietor doubled his salary. One who met Thackeray in Paris found him 'wild with exultation and full of enthusiasm for excellent George Smith'. But there was a fly in the ointment of the happy publisher. A rate of five guineas per page had been fixed for advertisements, but the business department had omitted to raise it as the printing grew. For the second number Smith made it twenty guineas.

As for the rates of pay to contributors, 'our terms', wrote Smith, 'were lavish to recklessness; no pains and no cash were spared to make the magazine the best'. Thackeray, apart from his remuneration for his serial, had twelve guineas a page for articles; and Tennyson was offered a large sum if he would supply another 'Idyll'. He did contribute 'Tithonus'.

For *Romola*, in sixteen instalments, Smith offered a 'sum without precedent', £10,000 'with certain limited rights of publication afterwards'. But George Eliot preferred not to extend the book beyond a dozen instalments, and accepted £7,500. Alas, the sale of the magazine was not increased by the story. After its publication the author sent to *Cornhill* 'a very remarkable story', *Cousin Jacob*, which she insisted should be regarded as a present. Later, Smith was offered *Felix Holt* for £5,000 and read it to his wife, but did not think it would be a profitable venture.

When George Eliot read aloud the first part of *Romola*, Smith noted that her voice was 'clear, sweet and soft'. Her face, as we have all read, and seen in the portraits, was not feminine. It had a curious resemblance, as has been said, to the face of Savonarola. Her dress was in 'put-your-things-on-any-way style'. 'But the impression she made was lost when you listened to her.' Smith and du Maurier agreed that, owing to her power of drawing out the people with whom she spoke, they never conversed with her 'without feeling that they were cleverer fellows than when they entered her house'.

Owing to George Eliot's relations with Lewes, the excellent Madame Bodichon (Barbara Leigh Smith)[1] was for some time

[1] 'I am one of the cracked people of the world and I like to herd with the cracked, queer Americans, democrats, socialists, artists, poor devils, or angels,

the only woman at her 'at homes'. Even Smith, who attended frequently, did not introduce his wife and children, though he once took his eldest son. 'She was undoubtedly a sad woman, but she had a genuine affection for Lewes.' When it was rumoured that they had married on the Continent—though, as Lewes's wife was still alive, the ceremony would not count in England—'many ladies hastened to call on her'. Some of them continued to do so when the rumour proved to be baseless. Gradually the social ban was lifted, and George Eliot and Lewes stayed with Jowett, Lady Stanley of Alderley, and the biographer of the Prince Consort, Sir Theodore Martin, and his wife.

Before meeting George Eliot, Smith knew Lewes, and found in him sometimes 'a repellent strain of coarseness'.[1] 'He could say very coarse things in a soft and gracious voice' and, at the Sunday parties, might display 'unintellectual boisterousness'. Smith knew his pretty wife and 'how she came to leave her husband for a man like Thornton Hunt[2] was not easy to understand'. But Lewes 'always preached a we-may-do-as-we-like morality, and, unless report maligned him, did very much as he liked'. 'He was fond of boasting of his successes and I once gravely asked him to what he attributed it. He was a very ugly man to begin with, and his face and body were pitted with smallpox. He fixed upon the only feature he possessed which was likely to excite admiration. He put his finger to his eye and said "It is my eye".'

George Eliot came to lean on him. She was slow in coming to a decision; he was decisive in judgement. She had a great affection for Lewes's children by his first wife and left her money to them. Cross's *Life and Letters* gives the impression of a perfect companionship. The correspondence was abridged but we shall have it in full before very long.

George Eliot's marriage with Cross took place within eighteen

and I am never happy in genteel family life.'—*Barbara Bodichon*, Hester Burton (Murray).

[1] Mrs. Humphry Ward writes that she took 'a prompt and active dislike' to Lewes. Carlyle saw no reason why his wife should not call.

[2] Leigh Hunt's son.

months of Lewes's death. One day she wrote to Smith asking him to call and suggested a day. It proved to be the day on which she died.

The interest of the *Cornhill* authors was maintained not only by their pay but by a quarterly dinner at their proprietor's house. The following, arranged alphabetically, are the names of some of them (excluding the editors themselves) from the start until—if the regrettable event may be anticipated—the cessation of regular monthly publication. The asterisks mark contributors to the first six numbers, a remarkable indication of the quality of the early issues:

Matthew Arnold
A. C. Benson
E. F. Benson
George E. Birmingham
Sir John Bowring
Charlotte Brontë*
Emily Brontë*
Mrs. Browning*
Sir John Burgoyne
Boyd Cable
Frances Power Cobbe
Wilkie Collins
E. T. Cook
Edward Dowden
Dr. W. H. Fitchett
Mrs. Gaskell
George Gissing
Frederick Greenwood
Rider Haggard
Thomas Hardy
M. J. Higgins ('Jacob Omnium')
James Hinton
Dean Hole
John Hollingshead
Thomas Hood*
Anthony Hope
E. W. Hornung
Thornton Hunt
Washington Irving*
Sir John Kaye
Andrew Lang
Charles Lever*
G. H. Lewes
Mrs. Lynn Linton
Frederick Locker
Lord Lytton*
George MacDonald*
Sir Henry Maine
'Lucas Malet'
A. E. W. Mason
George Meredith
Herman Merivale
Monckton Milnes*
Laurence Oliphant*
James Payn
Adelaide Procter
R. A. Proctor
'Father Prout'
Charles Reade
John Ruskin*
George Augustus Sala
Albert Smith

Fitzjames Stephen*
R. L. Stevenson
John Addington Symonds
Alfred Tennyson*
Miss Thackeray
Sir Henry Thompson
Anthony Trollope*
H. A. Vachell
Stanley Weyman

The artists, while illustrations continued to be used, included Millais,* Leighton,* Doyle, Walker, George du Maurier, Noel Paton, Charles Keene, Luke Fildes, Herkomer, G. D. Leslie, Marcus Stone, Mrs. Allingham, and F. B. Dicksee.

The payments for contributions during the first four years came to £32,280, in addition to £4,376 for illustrations, and between 1860 and 1879 'purely literary work' cost £84,675.

Smith & Elder, after having had a branch office in Pall Mall—it was No. 45, almost opposite Marlborough House—finally left the City and established themselves in the familiar colonnaded quarters, 15 Waterloo Place. As one passes it one sometimes remembers that Matthew Arnold occasionally slept in a prophet's chamber there when it became too late for him to catch his train. His four lectures on Celtic Literature were published in successive numbers of *Cornhill.*

CHAPTER VIII

Thackeray and Trollope, with George Smith at their Elbows

COUNSELS TO CONTRIBUTORS — EDITORIAL SHORTCOMINGS AND MERITS — 'MY SQUEAMISH PUBLIC' — THACKERAY'S LAST DAYS

WHAT are called, in the offices of the Press to-day, 'good names' did not represent all the writers who came into or tried to come into *Cornhill*. The periodical to provide 'amusement, instruction, knowledge, pleasure, poetry, pathos and fun' was 'open to all comers'. While Thackeray wanted 'twelve good articles or twelve good books', besought the Brownings for 'a short poem from one or both of you', and solicited, unsuccessfully, a contribution from Longfellow, he was, he said, 'conductor of a concert' and spent hours of his days attending to the unknown or the well-enough known, but, in respect of their particular offerings, unsuitable.

Tom Hood's son was told that he could do better than 'A Remarkable Dream'. 'Twenty-five pages of ghost story' were returned to a Mr. Cupples with the sound counsel, 'Cast about in your mind whether there is anything you know or have seen'. 'Clever Verses' went back to the writer of them because the editor was 'too old-fashioned' for such rhyming as 'wrath' with 'north'! To one correspondent Thackeray wrote, 'I shall be glad to look at short, readable and suggestive articles from the manufacturing districts'; and he helped with cash—he was frequently lending money—Ernest Jones the Chartist, and inquired if he 'could do a Chartist article'. 'Tears bedimmed' the editorial spectacles on reading somebody's 'very tender and pathetic verses', one reads in a letter printed for the first time in that remarkable collection, the *Letters and Private Papers of Thackeray*, in Gordon Ray's four stout volumes.[1] But 'they

[1] Oxford University Press.

ought to be better. Why not polish them more and more and make them as bright as they possibly can be? Indeed, they are worth the trouble.' And the kind editor not only says he hopes 'to have them back at an early day' but takes the trouble to suggest a number of alternative readings. Another contributor gets this note: 'The article is very lively, well written and pleasant, but won't, I think, do for us. So I return with many thanks and not a little regret to send back such a merry little paper.' Although Trollope defends himself, in respect of what he had offered, by citing Effie Deans and Hetty Sorrel, he tells his editor that he feels 'no annoyance at the rejection of my story; an impartial editor must do his duty'. To a contribution about *séances*, 'Stranger than Fiction', which was printed, Thackeray appended the note:

> As editor of the magazine I can vouch for the good faith and honourable character of our correspondent, a friend of twenty-five years' standing; but as the writer of the astounding narrative owns that he would refuse to believe such things on the evidence of other peoples' eyes, his readers are therefore free to give 'or withhold their belief'.

Cornhill's historic rejection, after many remonstrances had been received, not only by Thackeray but by Smith, was the stopping, after three instalments, of Ruskin's *Unto this Last*. It is described by the best authority on his works as 'the most widely dispersed, and perhaps the most influential of all his writings'—the author believed it to be his best book, 'most pregnant in ideas and most successful in style'. Ruskin's writing was denounced in the Press as eruptions of 'windy hysterics' and 'utter imbecility', the 'intolerable twaddle' of a 'whiner and sniveller' screaming like 'a mad governess—a perfect paragon of blubbering'. The writing is elsewhere described as 'too deeply tainted with socialistic hurry'—the year was 1860 and the 'S' still a small one. The actual decision not to publish further papers was taken, it is said, by Smith. Ruskin describes Thackeray as writing to him 'with great discomfort to himself and many apologies to me'. As is well known, the publication of the essays, when transferred to *Fraser's*, was again interrupted in deference to protests. In *Fraser's* the papers reached a fourth instalment (1863). 'Froude had not wholly lost courage, but the publisher indignantly interfered.'

'The sacred arcana of *Cornhill*', writes E. T. Cook, 'consist of a series of leather cases, each containing half a dozen little ledgers. In these Mr. Smith entered, month by month, in his own minute and pleasant hand, the subjects of all the articles and illustrations, the prices paid to every author and artist, the number of copies sold of each number and of each volume.'[1]

Smith writes that he cannot truly say that Thackeray, to whose house he used to drive round every morning, 'to discuss manuscripts and subjects', was a good editor. He was 'uncertain and wayward, far too tender-hearted—could not say "No" to a contributor'. And in 'judging an article', Leslie Stephen has said, what everyone who has been an editor knows, that 'first thoughts are as likely to be right as second or third. It is best to decide at once and put your contributor out of pain.'

Thackeray suffered not only from indecision but from the 'incorrigible habit of loitering' which Trollope noted. 'I know perfectly well', says Vizetelly, in reference to *Vanity Fair*, that 'much of the work was written under pressure from the printer'. He declares that, when arrangements were made with Bradbury & Evans for the publication, no more than the first monthly part was in existence. As for 'much of the remainder, not infrequently the final instalment of copy needed to fill the customary thirty-two pages, was penned while the printer's boy was waiting in the hall'.[2] 'This was a common occurrence with much of Mr. Thackeray's monthly work', he adds, 'and the strange thing is that, produced under such disadvantageous conditions as these, it should have been so uniformly and thoroughly good.' Smith says that, in making-up *Cornhill*, space had frequently to be left for the completion of Thackeray's novel. Once, with *Philip*, he was a page short. The publisher went to his house—Thackeray

[1] *Literary Recreations*, E. T. Cook (Macmillan).

[2] Thackeray in *Pendennis* has a drawing of such a messenger asleep.

was in bed from one of the attacks to which reference is made on page 80—and additional manuscript was out of the question. He said that there were some verses about somewhere, and Smith, under his direction, hunted through drawers until he found 'Martin Luther's Song'.

Smith had his troubles also with some of his editor's contributors. One day, for instance, he had to go to the chambers of George Augustus Sala—for it was in the bargain that the publisher should help Thackeray all he could—and wait till the renowned word-spinner of the *Daily Telegraph* finished his article. When that paper was just beginning to make a success, largely through Sala's leading articles, Smith met the proprietor at Sala's house. Next day Levy Lawson called to ask whether he could give him an order for printing ink. After the death of Sala his widow brought Smith a book in which her husband, in his minute hand, had made, for use in his articles, a surprising collection of odd facts, clever sayings, and fragmentary information of all sorts.

But if Thackeray was, as Trollope, with his ultra-methodical habits of work, regarded him, 'an indifferent editor' in some respects, he was quite journalistically eager in his pursuit of 'good copy'. 'He was not even afraid'—I again quote Sir Edward Cook, who, when he wrote, had had his own experience at the *Pall Mall Gazette*—'of what might be called sensational journalism', the sensational journalism, however, of which I remember Matthew Arnold writing that he, for one, was not afraid. Thackeray understood, as do all good editors, that everybody, whatever his calling, 'may be able to tell something about it'. 'So I want you', he wrote to Sir Henry Thompson, the eminent physician and early advocate of cremation, 'to describe the cutting off of a leg'. 'And do it', he went on, 'so that, by reading your description, a ship's captain at sea would be able to take a sailor's leg off.' What Thackeray expected, it is difficult to conceive, but the description, when it came, proved to be too instructive; it had to be 'wrapped up', and appeared mildly as 'Under Chloroform'.

And against what Smith and Trollope have written, Thackeray had the merit as editor that he could handle a difficult situation with a contributor. Read, for example, his letter to 'My dear kind Mrs. Browning' returning 'Lord Walter's Wife', despite its 'pure doctrine and real modesty and pure ethics'. It was hard for him, he told her, 'to have to say "No" to my betters'. But he said it so agreeably that Mrs. Browning replied with a letter as winning as his own, and sent him a poem more suitable for what her editor called 'my squeamish public'. 'He says', she reports, that in England 'plain words permitted on Sundays must not be spoken on Mondays.'[1]

We have seen that the limitations of the public of the eighteen-sixties brought *Unto this Last* to a close, and that when Ruskin transferred himself to *Fraser's*, he was soon suspended there also—'the outcry', he writes, 'became too strong for any editor to subdue'. But the editor of *Cornhill* was prepared to take some chances, for he tried to get a contribution from Carlyle, who 'amid Prussian rubbish'—he was in the toils of *Frederick the Great*—tells 'dear Thackeray' that he does 'not quite give the matter up'. It may have been at another time that Carlyle thought he might do 'plenty of things' for *Cornhill*. But none materialized.

Thackeray had also that without which an editor is short of the essential equipment of his calling, the firmness to cut and amend contributors' manuscripts according to his requirements or the writers' shortcomings. He even wrote bits in, and, at times, made additions. There was reproduced in facsimile in *Cornhill*, some years back, three proof pages of a story on which Thackeray had operated. In this instance, he not only altered in several places but crossed out the last page and provided a new conclusion. One thinks of Dickens as editor of *Household Words*. 'When once he got the proof of someone's story on his desk he

[1] Anne Thackeray Ritchie to Mrs. Douglas Freshfield in 1891: 'Do you think the British public would allow me to quote the fact of the Dame du Palais, the Princesse des Ursins, escorting the King to bed, carrying a sword, a lamp and a *pot de chambre*? I am afraid not!'

thought nothing of playing with it until it was practically rewritten.' I remember a copy of the *Westminster Gazette* at the office in which Ruskin had completely blacked out or had inked 'blottesquely'—the word he used—condensed or expanded every single news item in the paper according to his notions of what was good for our public.

Modern editors will note with some surprise that the corrections by Thackeray were not done in the 'copy' but, in a costly way, in proof, and not in galley proof but still more expensively in page proof. And, in making the corrections, he took no pains, apparently, to mitigate cost by saving 'over-running'. But the charges for composition were lower then.[1] And the editors had the excuse that the contributions offered to them were not in typescript, as they would be to-day, but handwritten, and it was difficult and a strain on the eyes to read them closely in manuscript.

What of the compositors? The copy of few prospective contributors to *Cornhill* can have been anything like as clear as Thackeray's own, to the end of his days a marvel of distinct and pleasing calligraphy. No wonder that, as we have seen, Smith, who as a publisher had to read so many manuscripts, put among the virtues 'a good handwriting'. 'Next to the necessity of carefully considering the general policy of the newspaper to which an amateur determines to lay siege', said one of whom we shall hear later, Adelaide Drummond, 'the principal factor of success is the possession of clear and readable handwriting.'

It is not surprising, all things considered, that two years' editing (1860–2) sufficed Thackeray, as 'this noble man of genius' himself explained in one of his *Roundabout Papers* entitled 'Thorns in a Cushion'. Of those *Roundabout Papers* Leslie Stephen, an acknowledged judge, wrote that they were 'models of the essay which, without aiming at profundity, give the charm of the graceful and tender conversation of a great writer'. More notable contributions by Thackeray to *Cornhill* were his *Four Georges*.

[1] Carlyle almost rewrote his *Miscellanies* in proof.

Although, as an editor, Thackeray lasted longer than Dickens, and used to see as many people and get about as much as 'Boz' did, he was no sounder in health. (Forster said that Dickens's 'habits were robust but not his health'.) The year after the starting of *Cornhill* Thackeray mentions that he has a bladder stricture, and he had frequently to lie up for a day or two. In 1861, his second year, he writes of 'one of my attacks of illness which are now so frequent. I'm so weak and nervous from illness (and other circumstances) which become immensely annoying when the *corpus* isn't quite *sanum*'. In May 1862 he says, 'I am constantly ill, and I grow awfully nervous'. 'De Finibus' appeared in *Cornhill* in August.

Thackeray had moved into his 'fine new house at Palace Green, Kensington, opposite the old Palace', on the last day of March. In 1860 he had written, 'My dear relatives are furious at my arrogance, extravagance and presumption.' And there is a subject to which he recurs, 'No one has come to marry my dear girls.' Also, he adds, 'I am free-handed, have to keep my wife', who was insane,[1] 'to help my parents, and to give—in fact my expenses are very large'. He says that he is making about £5,000 a year (income tax was only 10*d*. in the £!). But all through the *Cornhill* period his letters dwell on the few years he has to live. In 1861 he is writing, 'the terminus cannot be far off'; he died in 1863.

His letter of resignation to 'My dear Smith' had been sent two years before. 'I have been thinking over our conversation of yesterday', he writes. 'Today I have taken my friend Sir Charles Taylor into my confidence and his opinion coincides with mine, that I should withdraw from the magazine.' 'Before ever the magazine appeared', he added, 'I was, as I have told you, on the point of writing such a letter as this'—which recalls Dickens's perturbations of spirit before undertaking the editorship of the

[1] Her illness began four years after marriage when Thackeray was twenty-nine. Eleven years before his death he wrote, 'Though my marriage was a wreck I would do it over again, for love is the crown and completion of all earthly good.' 'Dear Mama', writes Anne Thackeray Ritchie, 'so silent, so undemanding, so loving, so contented.'

Daily News. Two days later he says in a letter to Smith: 'I daresay your night, like mine, has been a little disturbed. I had this pocket pistol in my breast yesterday, but hesitated to pull the trigger at an old friend. My daughters are for compromise. They say "It is all very fine for Sir Charles Taylor telling you to do so-and-so. Mr. Smith has proved himself your friend always"'—Anne Thackeray writes in 1864 'our kind friend Mr. Smith'. '*Bien*', he goes on, 'It is because I wish him to remain so that I and the magazine had better part company. So goodbye, and God bless you and all yours.' Smith records that Thackeray in consulting 'his own comfort and peace of mind, came to a wise decision in resigning the editorship'.

In turning over *Cornhill* one comes on pleasing evidence that the relations of Thackeray and Dickens were not always those of estrangement. 'Boz' tells of a day when Thackeray 'unexpectedly presented himself, announcing that some passage in a certain book had made him cry and that he had come to dinner because he couldn't help it and must talk a passage over'. When, two years after resigning the editorship of *Cornhill*, Thackeray died in his sleep on Christmas Eve, 1863, Dickens refused payment for the kindly memorial article he contributed. Carlyle's tribute was that Thackeray had 'no guile or malice against any mortal'. It will be remembered that when Macaulay was found dead in his chair, Thackeray's *Lovel the Widower* was lying on the table beside him.

Smith was scrupulous in refusing to negotiate with Thackeray's daughters on his copyrights and in recommending them to be represented by two or three friends. Fitzjames Stephen, Herman Merivale, and Henry Cole acted. Thackeray had only a half interest in most of his books, the other half being owned by Bradbury & Evans and Chapman & Hall. Smith paid £5,000 to the daughters and a smaller sum to these two publishers, and had a cordial letter of appreciation from Thackeray's mother, then Mrs. Carmichael-Smyth.

CHAPTER IX

Harriet Martineau, Mrs. Humphry Ward, and Mrs. John Ruskin

WILKIE COLLINS — BLANK CHEQUES — DU MAURIER — JOHN LEECH AND CRUIKSHANK — MILLAIS — NEW CARLYLE LETTERS

THAT vigorous personality Harriet Martineau had an admirer in George Smith. Her early brochures on political economy had been read aloud by his father to the family circle when he was a child. Smith & Elder bought some of her copyrights and ultimately published her autobiography, 1,500 copies of which were kept in a locked room at the printer's for some years before she died. Smith was entrusted with the secret of Harriet Martineau's novel. In order to hide the authorship, proofs of it were to be sent to Charlotte Brontë. The novel was concerned with England a hundred years later, and the time is now up. The scanty inhabitants of the open country lived in huts made of the boughs of trees and were hunted like wild beasts by the townspeople! The book was never published. As we know, the friendship of the author and Charlotte Brontë came to an end when Harriet Martineau in her downright fashion slated *Villette* in the *Daily News*.

Smith & Elder were the successful publishers of a more modern author, Mrs. Humphry Ward. (They had declined a story of hers when she was eighteen.) Macmillan's had rejected *Robert Elsmere* on the ground that the subject was not likely to appeal to the public, but Smith, though the author says, 'I am certain he had no faith in the book's success', accepted it at once, with an advance of £200. About half a million copies were sold in the United States within a year of the book's publication.[1]

[1] An edition of 5,000 copies a fortnight was the rule, after the one-volume edition appeared. Hundreds of thousands have been circulated in the sixpenny and sevenpenny editions. It has been translated into most foreign tongues.—*A Writer's Recollections*, Mrs. Humphry Ward (Collins).

GEORGE MURRAY SMITH in the last year of his life, 1901
Painted by John Collier
By kind permission of the National Portrait Gallery

Apart from its subject, which now seems so out of date—Mr. Gladstone, it will be remembered, revelled in it in a review, and undoubtedly did the book a good turn; but the three volumes were already in a third edition.[1] It may be noted that the work was at first too long even for a three-volume novel. Condensation, which the author thought she could manage in a fortnight, took a year, and the novel, when published, was 'closely printed' and 'twice the length of an ordinary novel'. Of Smith, Mrs. Ward wrote to his son, 'his position as a publisher was very remarkable'. 'He was the friend of his authors, their counsellor, banker and domestic providence often—as Murray was to Byron. But nobody would ever have dared to take the liberties with him that Byron did with Murray.' Smith gave her for her work after *Robert Elsmere* 'larger sums than any other novelist received from him'. For *Sir George Tressady* he paid £10,000. He also made what she described as 'princely terms' in the United States, where some rogue produced a faked volume called *Robert Elsmere's Daughter, A Companion Story to 'Robert Elsmere' by Mrs. Humphry Ward.* A characteristic passage between the author and her publisher occurred in relation to *Marcella.* Mrs. Trevelyan says that Smith had 'sent her, according to promise, a considerable sum in advance of royalty, setting forth at the same time, with his habitual candour, the exact sum which his firm expected to make from the same number of copies. Mrs. Ward thought the profit not enough, and wrote at once to propose a decrease of royalty on the first 2,000 copies.'

Among Smith's novelist friends was Wilkie Collins, introduced to him by Ruskin. *Armadale* was published in *Cornhill.* Collins so firmly believed in the possibilities of low-priced editions that, in disagreement with Smith on the subject, he transferred his publishing in 1874 to Chatto & Windus. He wanted sixpenny editions. In 1866 and 1867 Smith had brought out *The Last Chronicle of Barset* in sixpenny monthly numbers, a very different thing. Chatto & Windus kindly inform me that,

[1] There are two pages of Gladstone's conversation in Mrs. Trevelyan's *Life of Mrs. Humphry Ward* (Constable).

with fourteen of Collins's books, they did not get lower than six shillings, and afterwards in 'illustrated boards', two shillings. Collins was 'a little man with a strangely-shaped head; above each brow was a bulge'. He had social gifts and shone at men's parties, and endured with 'serene patience' gout, rheumatism, and other ailments which had some relation, perhaps, to the merry meetings in which he had taken part. His brother married a daughter of Dickens. With Dickens, I always remember, Collins visited the small market-town in which I was born, Wigton in Cumberland.

Another contributor to *Cornhill* was the burly, pugnacious, methodical Bohemian, Charles Reade. His book was *Put Yourself in his Place*.

When Smith was staying with Trollope he found that, on mornings when he did not hunt he dragged about a garden roller at what might be called a canter. He was a very loud talker and so was Reade, and once, when they were in conversation at the Garrick, Thackeray heard their voices in the street. They were then about fifty. 'What must they have been at eighteen', Thackeray ejaculated.

Smith and his wife were acquainted with Dean Stanley and Lady Augusta, described by him as 'one of the most perfect women of the world, rich in every social gift'. The Dean once sat up with him until two in the morning talking about his travels in Russia. As to his infamous handwriting, Lord Houghton's ran it hard for unintelligibility; indeed Smith had more than once to return notes of his for transliteration. It was with the Dean, Matthew Arnold, and Tom Hughes, that Smith paid a visit to his old school, Rugby, on Dr. Temple's last day as head.

Smith paid £1,000 for Arthur Helps's *Friends in Council*. The author (with Sir Theodore Martin) lost money in a pottery enterprise which was to utilize the clay on his estate. Smith had to forgo an opportunity of visiting him when the Prince of Wales was to be the only other guest. The publisher had a troublesome time over the Queen's *Leaves from the Journal of our Life in the Highlands*, on which Helps continually sought his counsel on trifling points. The book was first set up in secrecy by the manager and one compositor at Smith & Elder's printing office—formerly the house of Goldsmith—and an edition of forty copies for private circulation was prepared. Then the Queen agreed to a public edition. Smith noted that the words 'Author's Proofs', on the galleys were in the handwriting of Her Majesty, who enjoyed her authorship. The publisher received a copy inscribed by his sovereign.[1] Smith & Elder also published General Grey's *Early Years of Prince Albert*, which brought the author several thousand pounds. But a cheap edition, which the Queen favoured, left a balance against the estate when Grey died. A dispute with the executors ended in Farquhar, the banker, offering Smith a blank cheque and saying, 'You are a gentleman.' But, though George Smith was 'startled and touched' by a banker committing the sin of giving a blank cheque, he said: 'This will never do. If you will give me a cheque for so much'—naming a sum less than the amount claimed—'I shall be quite content.' After the stock was sold there was not much loss. Sir Theodore Martin's *Life of the Prince Consort* had an enormous sale. It has been mentioned that Smith and his wife were close friends of Sir Theodore and Lady Martin. He said that he had 'never seen a more tragic figure' than the husband at Lady Martin's funeral.

A series of articles about Eton in *Cornhill* by 'Jacob Omnium' (Matthew James Higgins)—his first book had been called *Jacob Omnium, the Merchant Prince*—made a sensation and led to reforms. Smith once spoke of the 'amazing power and humour' of Higgins's articles in *The Times* which anyone with a sense of style could identify even when signed 'Belgravia Mother', 'Paterfamilias', or 'Mother of Six'. 'He came into my room in Pall Mall one day and found me in the agonies of composition. "Are you writing an epic poem?" he asked. "Worse than that", I replied, "I am writing a letter to *The Times*." He asked why and I told him my grievance—what it was I have forgotten now —and Higgins looked at what I had written. "Do you mind my

[1] Further particulars will be found on page 99.

giving you a little help?" he asked. "Mind!" I said, "I shall be grateful to my dying day." He took my attempt over to the Oxford and Cambridge Club opposite, and in a very brief time, brought me a letter putting my case so clearly that, for at least twenty-four hours, all my natural conceit disappeared.'

When Trollope's *Framley Parsonage* was to appear in *Cornhill*, Smith went to see Millais in his lodgings in Bryanston Place in order to ask him to illustrate it. 'His wife was in the room with him with one or two children. When I had last seen her she was Mrs. John Ruskin, and it was somewhat odd to see her bearing another name and in another relation. On a later visit she happened to open the door to me, and when I went into the studio to Millais, I clumsily said, "How well Mrs. Ruskin is looking". I could have bitten off my tongue with vexation. But Millais set me at my ease at once. "Yes, my dear fellow", he said, with a frank laugh, "you can't get rid of the old name, can you?" He was one of the handsomest of men, and to see him walking betwixt his two fair daughters was delightful.'

Among the stories Smith told of Millais was one about a visit paid him by an American who wanted his portrait painted. Millais said he would try to fit him in for a sitting shortly. 'But I have my passage for New York for next week', said the visitor, 'can't you begin at once?' Millais was amused and got out a canvas and set to work. The portrait was finished in four days and the sitter was so pleased that he invited the painter to visit him at his home where, he mentioned, he had horses which came up to the window to receive lumps of sugar. 'You know, sir,' he said, 'that portrait is so like me that when I get home the horses will go to it for lumps of sugar instead of coming to me.'

Romola was illustrated by Frederic, successively Sir Frederic and Lord Leighton. He took great pains with the sketches and the drawings on wood—a kind of work new to him—but 'it was characteristic of Leighton to bestow pains upon everything he did. He was one of the most accomplished men of his time, spoke German, French and Italian and never said an unkind word in any language to anyone'. As an illustration of his courtesy, his secretary, an old colleague of mine on the *Pall Mall*, told me that a frequent beginning of the letters he dictated, which the secretary wrote in longhand from a shorthand note—it was before the days of typewriters—was 'Pardon my addressing you by the hand of my secretary'.

Leighton's next-door neighbour was Val Prinsep, 'a tall, robust, massive-limbed man who could bend a poker. He affected a certain amount of roughness and contempt for artistic effeminacy'. On an old lady, given to gushing, saying to him one Show Sunday, 'Where did you get that wonderful sky from? Oh, it is too beautiful', he replied, 'Yes, madam, I thought I had got in a rummy effect.'

When the stock of du Maurier's originals for his drawings on wood became numerous, Smith and his wife constituted themselves, with Mrs. du Maurier, a committee to dispose of them, and within a year the artist received twelve hundred guineas. This acceptable addition to his income had the important result that, 'from that time du Maurier's sole remaining eye recovered rapidly and he was able to make good use of it until his death'. When he used to talk to Smith about the possible loss of his sight, he was consoled by the assurance that he had another way of earning a good living. Smith had seen some verse of his, and had in mind also the terse and clever sentences he attached to his *Punch* drawings. He was persuaded that du Maurier could profitably turn novelist, as in due course he did.

Once Smith found du Maurier and Henry James sitting together on a Hampstead stile. When he said he had to go home and suggested that they might walk together, du Maurier said, 'We can't; we have agreed to sit here until we can give a satisfactory reason to each other for the success of *Trilby*.' Well', Smith replied, 'I will call on Mrs. du Maurier and tell her not to be anxious if she doesn't see her husband till this day week.'

If I may recall my own impression of the *Trilby* period, I should say that a slight air of impropriety, which the present generation is unable to comprehend, had something to do with the success of the story. The probability that I am not far wrong is borne out by Smith's story of the dramatic version of the novel at the Haymarket—at which, by the way, he and his wife thought that 'du Maurier with his handsome wife and children was prouder of his family than of his play'. The Prince of Wales sent for du Maurier and complimented him, and, later in the evening presented him to the Princess. Her Royal Highness did not like Dorothea Baird's bare feet ('or at all events, feet which appeared quite naked', Smith actually added). 'I hope', said du Maurier, addressing the Prince, 'you do not object, Sir.' 'Oh dear no,' said the Prince, 'I like them.' At the *Pall Mall Gazette* we were particularly interested in *Trilby* because the heroine was the sister-in-law of Edward, afterwards Sir Edward Cook who succeeded W. T. Stead as editor. I seem to recall some discussion, not dissimilar from that over Trilby's feet, when the American actress Mary Anderson appeared as Galatea. Indeed it was believed, if my recollection serves me, that that actress, who later on, as Madame de Navarro, was my neighbour in the Cotswolds, and a reader of the *Countryman*, was not herself completely at ease about her stage appearances. To return to du Maurier, he began life as a mining engineer and was sent to a supposed copper mine in Cornwall, an enterprise from which he saw cause promptly to disengage himself.

When at Brighton, Smith and his wife had meetings with John Leech and his family. He was 'a simple, unaffected, amiable man with no enemies and many friends, and an almost absurdly vigilant watch for subjects for *Punch*. He was fond of hunting, and the fine hunters he drew make a good rider's mouth water. In conversation he was quiet and gentle. No gleam of wit stole into his talk. His humour all ran to the point of his pencil.'

Frederick Walker, who, in dissatisfaction with his work, had slashed to pieces with a carving knife a portrait of Mrs. Smith and her three children, died at thirty-five.

Smith had 'a far off and dim recollection' of Cruikshank[1] as a 'short, quaint-looking figure, with keen, alert eyes, sharp nose, and a quick, jerky way of speaking'.

[1] See page 113.

Of 'the high-strung sensitiveness' of Frederick (afterwards Sir Frederick) Burton, Smith had experience. He had often asked him to 'paint something' for him, but without result until one day, at Sir Theodore Martin's, the artist volunteered to make a drawing of Mrs. Smith. She 'probably sat a hundred times' and it was three years before it was finished! Burton spoke of it as his *magnum opus*. When the work was done Smith wrote to Burton telling him the drawing was beyond value to him and enclosing a blank cheque with the request not to hold his hand in filling it up. Burton filled it up for five hundred guineas. 'When the cheque came through my bank account I wrote to Burton saying he had been unjust to himself, that I had discovered from the stamp who his bankers were, and should take the freedom of supplementing the price with another five hundred guineas. Burton replied in a letter of great stiffness, the effect of which was that if I took the liberty of interfering with his banking account it would alter the friendly relations between us.'

To the Farquhar and Burton blank cheque stories may be added a third. One day Smith betook himself with his wife to the studio of Alexander Munro—the sculptor who did the fountain in Berkeley Square—with a view to giving him a commission for a marble figure of their eldest daughter, then an interesting child of four. Munro drew him behind a large piece of sculpture and said, 'I will do your beautiful child with pleasure but how I should like to make a portrait of your wife.' He executed 'a very pretty profile portrait in *alto relievo*, perfect but for a streak of colour in the marble which came right across the nose. Munro did another, and again he was unfortunate; a streak of colour showed beneath an eye. A third portrait was a very beautiful piece of work. I sent him a blank cheque and said that in filling it up he had to remember that he had executed three portraits. Months passed by, the cheque failed to appear in my banking account and I had almost dismissed the matter from my mind. Late one evening I received a letter from the manager of my bank to say that he thought there must be some error but my account was overdrawn by £3,200! I went to the bank early next morning and found that, by some mistake, a large sum of money had gone to the credit of another Mr. Smith. My mind had flown, however, to the blank cheque in Munro's possession and I saw him and said, "You must fill up that blank cheque of mine." "Oh", he said, "I am keeping that as a nest egg." This was somewhat disconcerting but I said he must really make use of the cheque and close the transaction. He then filled it up, but for what I thought was an unreasonably moderate sum. After this I gave no more blank cheques, even to artists.'

Some time afterwards Munro asked Smith if he minded his using the spoilt marbles for fancy subjects. He was perfectly willing, provided the likeness were destroyed. One marble became an ideal face, 'Sabrina', and was bought as a present to the headmaster of Eton on his retirement. The other was sold to a Dr. Franks in France. But this was not the end of the matter. Franks lent his marble to an artist who reproduced it in terra-cotta, and the replica was nearly if not quite as good as the successful marble. Indeed Smith bought several of these replicas for presents to his daughters and friends. Munro, who retained his Inverness accent, owed the opportunity of an artistic career to the Duchess of Sutherland who had been impressed by some carvings he did as a boy in slate.

The witty widow of 'Barry Cornwall' (Bryan Waller Procter) used to have on her writing table four portraits, one of Robert Browning, one of James Russell Lowell, one of Henry James, and one of George Smith, and the four men affected jealousy over the respective positions of the pictures. Lowell wrote lines to Mrs. Procter beginning, 'I know a girl—they say she's eighty'. When Smith once asked Mrs. Procter why a certain man was so popular with women when he never made love to them, she replied, 'No, but we always think he is just going to.' One of her canons of social conduct was 'Never refuse an invitation without giving the actual reason.' Another was, 'Whenever in doubt as to whether to write or not, write.' Smith was one of her executors.

Mrs. Procter was a stepdaughter of Basil Montagu,[1] and he and her mother were kind to Carlyle when he came to their house in 1824. Samuel Laurence's portrait, in the possession of the Carlyle House Memorial Trust, gives us some impression of what he was like at this period. She printed letters he had written to the Montagus, and the first copy was given to Smith. One letter said, 'You had faith enough in human nature to believe that, under the vinegar surface of an atrabiliar character, there might lurk some touch of principle and affection. There are moments when the thoughts of these things make me ten years younger.' He referred to Miss Welsh as 'this young lady, an ardent, generous, gifted being, banished to the pettiness of a country town; loving, adoring the excellent in all its phases but without models, advisers or sympathy'. Later, he speaks of being 'wedded to the best of wives, with all the elements of enjoyment richly ministered to me, and health rather worse than it was wont to be'. In another letter he says 'my wife exceeds all my hopes and is in truth amongst the best women the world contains. She loves me with her whole soul. Good Jane! She is sitting by me knitting you a purse.' On an early publisher —of *Sartor* probably—he had the sentence, 'His one true God being Mammon, he does worship him with an edifying devoutness.' He speaks of 'the persuasion of people that, whatever becomes of others, they are entitled of right to be entirely fortunate. All their days they continue to believe that in their lot in life they are unjustly treated, and stand in amazement that they should be disappointed, so very strangely, so unfairly.' 'One day,' he declares—he is writing from Edinburgh—'I shall surely speak out these things that are lying in me, and giving me no sleep until they are spoken. One day I hope to give you one of the most surprising books you have met with lately.' Of Jeffrey he says, 'There is a glance in the eyes of the man which almost prompts you to take him in your arms.' Of Leigh Hunt and the life of Byron he writes, 'Was it not a thousand pities Hunt had

[1] A natural son of the Earl of Sandwich. A writer on legal and other subjects. Died 1851.

borrowed money of the man he was to disinhume and behead in the course of duty afterwards? Poor Hunt? He has a strain of music in him, but poverty and vanity have smote too rudely over the strings.[1] Today I saw de Quincey; alas poor Yorick!' This is his reference to Goethe, 'He tells me yesterday to write soon "for days and weeks are growing more and more precious to him".'

Once in the Spanish Ambassador's chapel a lady sitting next to Smith gave him a book. As she turned he was struck by her gaunt and haggard countenance. It was Adelaide Procter, the poet, daughter of 'Barry Cornwall' and his wife, with whose 'interesting and spirituelle face' he had been charmed at a party of Thackeray's. Thackeray had invited him to dinner to meet the original of 'Amelia'. Smith in accepting said he would go a thousand miles to meet 'Becky Sharp'. Thackeray replied, 'I can't ask you to meet her. She is three women made into one, and not one of the three could be asked to enter a decent house.' At the dinner Smith sat next Mrs. Brookfield, 'the handsomest woman I have ever seen'. The talk of her husband, the Rev. W. H. Brookfield, was 'a sort of intellectual champagne'.

[1] James Hannay, to whom there will be reference later, is said in Hare's *Story of My Life*, to have once noticed, on visiting Carlyle, two sovereigns lying on his mantelpiece. As he and Carlyle were good friends, he asked him the reason. Carlyle did not give any definite answer, and Hannay said, 'Neither you nor I are quite in a position to play ducks and drakes with sovereigns'. On which Carlyle replied, 'Well the fact is Leigh Hunt likes better to find them there than that I should give them to him'.

CHAPTER X

'Cornhill' under Eight Editors

GREENWOOD, LESLIE STEPHEN, JAMES PAYN, ST. LOE STRACHEY, REGINALD SMITH, LEONARD HUXLEY, LORD GORELL, AND PETER QUENNELL — THE QUEEN AND HER PROOFS

BECAUSE *Cornhill* was associated with the *Pall Mall Gazette* in so many ways, it is worth while to halt for a few more pages the story of that newspaper's beginnings, and to complete the account of the periodical into which Smith and his editors put so much of themselves. 'Can a magazine which is professedly a miscellany, which brings together articles on all subjects, have a soul?' asked Sir Edward Cook in the jubilee issue of *Cornhill.* The same question may be asked about a newspaper. It is a question the answer to which is known to every true worker in responsible journalism, journalism at the height of its powers, journalism in the stress of which it is worth forgoing a good deal in life, journalism among the callings to which men and women may give with modest satisfaction their strength, their thought, and their effective years. The sure affirmative answer comes out of the experience not only of true journalists but of their faithful readers, for whom they have provided information, enlightenment, refreshment, and encouragement. These men and women know which journals have been mainly trading ventures, 'printer's ink on paper', and which other journals, in many countries, in our time and in the years before us, have served their day with vigour and conviction. In 'the hundred volumes' of *Cornhill*, Sir Edward Cook declared, 'the soul is the spirit of humane culture. This spirit was most practically expressed in the essay, not necessarily the literary essay, but the essay which, whatever its subject, treats it in the temper of humane letters.'

On the retirement of Thackeray in 1862 the magazine was conducted by a triumvirate. For two years this triumvirate consisted of Smith, Frederick Greenwood—who had been a frequent contributor from the second number, and had helped Thackeray as sub-editor[1]—and that 'wonder of versatile talents', George Eliot's G. H. Lewes. When Lewes gave up (1864) Greenwood became editor for four years, Sir Sidney Lee says. This would mean that Greenwood continued for three years after the starting of the *Pall Mall Gazette*, which seems strange. Later, the magazine was in the hands of Smith and Dutton Cook. On Dutton Cook's retirement[2] (1871) the indomitable Leslie Stephen, who had made his way from holy orders to agnosticism, and had written for the magazine since 1866, took charge, and held on until he became editor of the *Dictionary of National Biography* (1882). As to the share which Smith took in the direction of the periodical, Sir Edward Cook has the judicious observation, in his *Literary Recreations*, that 'in the land of *Cornhill* there was a succession of Prime Ministers, but the sovereign remained the same, and his influence, though exercised with unostentatious tact, was, I suspect, great and constant'.

In general, Leslie Stephen was firmer with contributors than his father-in-law, Thackeray, had been. 'More than once', W. E. Norris says, 'he made me re-write whole chapters, and he would scrawl all over one's tidy manuscript.' There were also excisions, with apologies—'very likely you are right and I am wrong, but I must use my own judgement'. His editorial tastes were wide; Cook notes that in looking down the 'Contents' list of *Cornhill* one might pass from 'The Great God Pan' to 'Parrots I have Known'. In Stephen's time, John Morley was editing the *Fortnightly Review*, and making a courageous and influential publication of it.

Like Thackeray, Stephen had to give a thought to Mrs. Grundy. *Far from the Madding Crowd* was printed only 'with gingerly treatment'—'three respectable ladies had protested'—

[1] When, after the novelist's death, a furniture dealer found in an old desk which had stood in Thackeray's bedroom a drawer full of letters sent by him as a boy to his mother, and copies of letters he had written as a man to persons of some note, Greenwood was instrumental in getting the collection into the hands of the family.

[2] Dramatist and novelist. Did the theatres for the *Pall Mall Gazette*, 1867–75.

and *The Return of the Native* was declined. 'Such were noses in the mid-Victorian age', writes Stephen. But he printed some of W. E. Henley's *Hospital Verses*, and part of Matthew Arnold's *Literature and Dogma*—the present generation cannot realize how outrageous that book seemed. Arnold said of one of his lectures that it should appear in *Cornhill* because it 'pays best and has much the largest circle of readers'. With regard to his own contributions, Stephen wrote so freely that he would sometimes put to them other initials than his own. Cook, himself the author of essays which are supreme in their kind, is interesting to read[1] on the essays of 'L. S.' They 'were in many respects unlike Thackeray's; they were more strenuous, connected, and direct; perhaps the sap was a little drier, for Stephen was no sentimentalist; but they had a very pleasant flavour of their own, and a refreshing common sense, which is not so common as it might be in the modern essay'. 'The only sting in it', said Meredith of Stephen's *Cornhill* style, 'was an inoffensive humorous irony that now and then stole out for a roll over, like a furry cub, or the occasional ripple on a lake in grey weather.' Another 'L. S.' in *Cornhill* was 'R. L. S.' *Virginibus Puerisque* and *Familiar Studies of Men and Books* appeared in its pages, but the paper on Raeburn was declined by Stephen and some other editors. John Addington Symonds's *Greek Poets* and *Sketches and Studies in Italy* ran through the magazine, and Henry James also wrote for it. Many contributions were unsigned. Trollope's novel in the first number did not bear his name—indeed, a young woman in the west of England posed to her relatives and friends as the authoress of *Framley Parsonage*. Lever was anonymous, and so at first was George MacDonald.

With his editing Stephen, as we know, combined mountaineering. Meredith said that he 'walked from Alp to Alp like a pair of one-inch compasses on a large-sized map'. Sir George Trevelyan spoke of the mountaineer's nature: 'he never seemed to think an ignoble, a feeble or a timid thought.' Greenwood said: 'Love is a word which certain rugged but intelligible preju-

[1] *Literary Recreations* and *More Literary Recreations* (Macmillan).

dices are always at hand to suppress when men speak of men, but none of his friends were able to stop at friendship for him.'

When Leslie Stephen retired (1882), *Cornhill* had once more a novelist editor, James Payn. Stephen had received the editorship when the circulation was 'not a fifth of that of the initial number', and gave up when it was no more than 12,000. The fall in sales was held to be due to the waning of the public taste for serials, to what Payn termed 'the failure of the literary and especially the classical essay to attract the public', to the competition of periodicals conceived on more popular lines, and, no doubt, to the increasing readableness of the daily and weekly press, and to the increased sale of books. The experiment was tried of reducing the price to sixpence.

Payn, whose handwriting, owing to arthritis, rivalled in vileness that of Dean Stanley—both were successfully challenged to read their own script—had directed *Chambers's Journal* for seventeen years, and his *Lost Sir Massingberd* had increased its circulation by 20,000. He was editor of *Cornhill* from 1883 to 1896, and made a feature of short stories. Although his advice to Stanley Weyman was to 'give a year to a book' he was himself the author of sixty-nine volumes. He told that novelist that his plan was to have two large cards before him, one containing the plot and the other the dramatis personae of his story. He was Smith & Elder's reader, and brought in notable writers; but Smith said he 'lacked intellectual courage; I don't know how many times I made him almost jump out of his chair by mentioning sums I proposed to pay for books'. To the regret of the firm, Payn refused *John Inglesant*, but Smith himself failed to see the possibilities of *The Woman in White*. *Cornhill* sales fell 'substantially' during the editorship of Payn, though he had undertaken to make the magazine 'readable from cover to cover'; and illustrations (wood engravings) were gradually abandoned (1886).

Smith found Payn 'upright, sincere and kind, a man to be admired and liked'. He was a model of industry. 'He wrote novels, reviewed books, contributed leading articles to *The Times*, "Notes of the Week" to the *Illustrated London News*, and letters of literary and social gossip to half a hundred newspapers.' Smith did not know the total income he made, but on one occasion, when Smith & Elder sent in their honest income tax returns, the income tax people 'could not understand how the profits were no larger when we paid one employé, Payn, £3,000 a year'. On the question whether he would not have done better to have written less, Payn said to Smith: 'I should not get so much for one first-rate book as I do for three second-rate ones'. He was the father-in-law of G. E. Buckle, editor of *The Times*, from whom we shall be quoting in a later chapter.

The successor of the kindly Payn—someone spoke of his 'singularly bright geniality'—was the ardent and public-spirited St. Loe Strachey, afterwards editor of the *Spectator*, and proprietor of the *County Gentleman*—to which for seven years I contributed a page—and father of the Food Minister. During Strachey's editorship the price of the magazine went back to a shilling, and *Cornhill*, as Cook put it, was 'more consciously patriotic'. E. V. Lucas was among Strachey's finds. But 'the circulation fell lower, and *Cornhill* became "unremunerative" '. 'Indirectly, however, its literary excellence was not only among the imponderables which gave prestige to the firm but possessed a more ponderable value in attracting good authors to Waterloo Place.' *Longman's, Macmillan's, Murray's,* and *Temple Bar*, which were also kept in existence for the same reason, no doubt, after their revenues had ceased to meet their expenditures, 'went down under the same stress'.

Then followed, for more than seventeen years, Reginald Smith, K.C., whose gift for friendship has often been acknowledged. George Smith had died in 1901. Reginald Smith—not his son but his son-in-law—saw a rise in circulation during the War of 1914, and printed many first-rate articles and much outstanding fiction. The price of the magazine was changed from '1*s*. ordinary to 1*s*. net'—one almost forgets that there was a time when magazines and reviews as well as books were sold at a discount. For January 1910 there was a jubilee number of particular excellence and historical interest—it contained accounts of all the editors of *Cornhill* and a contribution by Mrs. George Smith. Reginald Smith, who died in 1916, had been head of Smith & Elder for some time. Few men have left behind them a memory of greater kindness, ability, and industry. A contributor said that to have known him was 'a liberal education in human kindliness, in thoughtful courtesy and in love of letters'. Many of his authors dedicated their books to him. One called him an 'inexhaustible fount of kindness'. Mrs. Humphry Ward said he had been 'shelter and comfort, advice and help, through many years'.

I have felt it to be a privilege to know Mrs. Reginald Smith. In her eighty-sixth year she is alert, erect, and distinguished, and always kind, helpful, and busy.

Here I may include an interesting inscription by Reginald Smith which, by the courtesy of Sir Owen Morshead, I have read in the Royal Library at Windsor Castle, and, by the gracious permission of the King, I am permitted to reproduce with some unpublished notes by Queen Victoria. The inscription, signed 'Reginald John Smith, one of His Majesty's Counsel, Nov., 1908', is in an interleaved quarto copy of Her late Majesty's *Leaves from the Journal of Our Life in the Highlands*, printed by Smith, Elder & Co., and reads:

Seven volumes which formerly belonged to the late Frederick Enoch, one of the staff of Messrs. Smith, Elder & Co., 13 Waterloo Place.

At the time when that firm printed, at first privately, and later for publication, Her late Majesty Queen Victoria's *Leaves from the Journal of Our Life in the Highlands, from 1848 to 1861*, Enoch served in the capacity of private secretary to the late Sir Arthur Helps, Clerk to the Privy Council, who edited the book for Queen Victoria; and it was during that employment that Enoch collected various proofs corrected by the Queen either for the private edition or for the published edition, with the sketches from her hand and letters which are to be found in this volume.

The four octavo volumes contain proofs, some of which are corrected by the Queen, of the two private editions of the book and in different stages. The remaining two volumes are copies of the two private editions of the book presented to Enoch at his request by the Queen and by her inscribed.

Shortly after the publication of the work in 1868 Enoch left the house of Messrs. Smith, Elder & Co., his leaving being unexplained. Later, falling on evil days and poverty, he retired to Ringmeer, in Sussex, where he was befriended by a blacksmith named Charles Painter; to this charitable man he bequeathed on his death [7 Jan., 1905] his only possession, these seven volumes, having always enjoined that they should not be sold in the lifetime of Sir Arthur Helps [who died in 1875].

The books were in May 1908 entrusted to a firm of auctioneers in London for sale, and knowledge of them came alike to His Majesty the King and to me. The King was anxious that the books should not be sold publicly and that they should find their appropriate home—in the Royal Library at Windsor Castle, and I was able to fulfil these His Majesty's wishes, conveyed to me by Lord Esher. Having purchased the volumes, I was privileged to present them to His Majesty at a private audience with which I was honoured at Windsor Castle on 18th Nov. 1908. The King evinced great interest in the volumes, particularly in the illustrations, and was pleased to express his cordial thanks for the gift, while he charged that the books should be bestowed in the Royal Library and there carefully safeguarded, being considered as of confidential character. In the Royal Library they will now remain with this record of their story.

There is pasted in this interleaved copy a card with 'Victoria, R and I' on it, written by the Queen in appreciation of the services rendered by Enoch. He notes that 'the first proof of all was set up from excerpts taken, irrespective of dates, from the original diary'.

The manuscript notes and corrections are generally in the autograph of the Queen, but there are a few in another hand, no doubt that of Sir Arthur Helps. A letter of his runs: 'My dear Enoch, What answer am I to give the Queen to her last letter? Yours very truly, A. H.' Her Majesty uses note-paper with black edges in three grades of black, the deepest about an inch wide! The dedication is corrected by the Queen in pencil. In the following reference to John Brown—'His attention, care, and faithfulness cannot be exceeded; and the state of my health, which of late years has been very sorely tried and weakened, render such qualifications most valuable and indeed most needful in a constant attendant upon all occasions'—'permanent' had been originally written for 'constant'. Four pages in Her Majesty's writing are on the news of the death of the Duke of Wellington; another nine provide the passage beginning, 'We drove into Dublin'. In one place 'very fine' is substituted for 'so fine'; in another 'great effect' for 'pretty effect'. In the phrase 'after eating really a very hearty luncheon' the words 'really a very hearty' are struck out. So is this sentence: 'In running after him [Prince Albert, who had just shot a deer] which I did very fast, I got such a tumble my whole length on the heather, and I think on a stone, for I hurt my knee a good deal.'

With Reginald Smith's death the publishing business of Smith, Elder & Co. passed from Waterloo Place to Albemarle Street, to the firm of John Murray, for which, it will be remembered, the father of George Smith worked before he joined Alexander Elder in starting Smith & Elder.[1] At Albemarle Street Dr. Leonard Huxley, who had been Stephen's helper for some years with *Cornhill*, became its editor, and served until his death in 1933. His successor was Lord Gorell, who is known as a novelist and a poet. He held office until the beginning of the 1939 War, when, as Sir John Murray told me, 'circumstances became too difficult' for the magazine. In 1944 it was possible to revive *Cornhill* for three numbers under the editorship of Mr. Peter Quennell, and there was a single issue in 1945. Up to the date of temporary suspension, 960 numbers—160 volumes—had been published. It is now a pleasure to find the magazine in regular publication again—as a half-crown quarterly—under Mr. Quennell's editorship. The old yellow cover has become light blue, and the design on it has been a little modified, but it has its old distinction.

[1] 'The firm of Smith, Elder, when we took it over', Sir John Murray writes to me in reply to my inquiry, 'was officially Smith, Elder & Co. and not Smith & Elder. As far as I know, the latter form had not been used for many years.'

CHAPTER XI

The Making of a Fortune

FROM PUBLISHER TO SHIPOWNER AND MINERAL WATER PURVEYOR — ENTER STEINKOPF — THE HUMOURS OF CHEAP HOUSING — PANTOMIME AND THE GOODWIN SANDS

ALTHOUGH the partnership of H. S. King in Smith & Elder came to an end by effluxion of time in 1868, three years after the starting of the *Pall Mall Gazette*, and the India and export departments became a separate business under his care, it is convenient to complete in this chapter the narrative of George Smith's life into the eighteen-seventies. He retained the publishing branch 'more as a luxury', he said, 'than as a profit-making business'. Although only forty-five he felt tired of hard work, and thought 'how agreeable it would be to rest, while keeping an interest in business which did not require constant office attendance'. But slackening off had the same effect on him as on many other active spirits before and since. He became ill. It was even thought that he might not recover. In search of health he went abroad, but travel did nothing for him. A prudent friend saw what was wrong. Smith's active brain was like 'millstones with no corn to grind; it is chafing itself into ruin'. This counsellor induced him to go into a partnership with a friend of his who was a shipowner. To the office of the new firm, Smith, Bilbrough & Co. in the City, Smith then betook himself in the mornings, and in the afternoons went to Smith, Elder & Co. in the West End. On his entrance into the shipping world he bought 'a commanding interest' in a dozen or more sailing ships. Next he built one of his own which, to the disgust of its captain, he named after Miss Thackeray's *Old Kensington*. It carried the largest cargo of wool ever shipped from Melbourne. He was greatly interested in the yarns of the captains he invited to dinner, and only wished he could get their experiences into *Cornhill*; but was hard put to hide from the men of the sea his ignorance of maritime practice. He once recalled the fact that a ship of his completely cut through a small craft laden with butter, and came out of the collision with her sides well buttered. The shipping business included sudden calls to quick decisions, which Smith said 'just suited me'. But as steam superseded canvas the trade grew less profitable, and he sold out the greater part of his interest and gave up the business, but was still part-owner of the *Old Kensington*. During his career as shipowner he became an underwriter, and was the last man to be received at Lloyd's without security.

Dr. G. M. Trevelyan, in his great *Social History*, makes a slip when he says that Smith 'made his money by selling valuable books to a serious-minded public'. He certainly was a most successful publisher, but his main fortune was gained outside the publishing world. His most conspicuous venture apart from his publishing—he was concerned with Sir Henry Thompson in the Aylesbury Dairy Company—was with Apollinaris. He made a million and a half out of it! As a business success it must be, in its class, almost a record. In 1872 he happened to drink some of the water at the house of Ernest Hart, who was editor of the *British Medical Journal*. Later he procured a private supply, and some time afterwards told his wife he thought he would go over to Germany and buy the spring. 'As if', she said, 'you have not enough irons in the fire already.' He was indeed a publisher, a shipowner and, by this time, proprietor of the *Pall Mall Gazette*. He was pondering the matter when he met a German Jew from Glasgow called Steinkopf—of whom more will be heard later—asked him if he knew anything of Apollinaris, and said he was inclined to buy it if the matter were not too troublesome. Steinkopf, who was going to Germany, promised to make inquiries, and reported that the owners were willing to negotiate. One Anton Kreuzberg came to London and said with some pride that they sold nearly 200,000 bottles in England. Smith inquired if he would sell him 10 million bottles, to be delivered at the rate of not less than a million a year, and give him the monopoly in the English market. Kreuzberg and Steinkopf (who was in a bad way financially and must have called a meeting of his creditors before the year was out) were taken aback by the size of the proposed transaction. But next day Kreuzberg agreed, and Steinkopf's alarms were disposed of by the retention of liberty to abandon the contract at any time on payment of a fine of two or three thousand pounds. During the first year more than a million bottles were sold.

The shares had been equally divided between Smith and Steinkopf. How Steinkopf got his share of the capital does not appear. Ernest Hart was offered a third share but could not find the money. He was therefore made 'scientific adviser'. This supporter of many good causes did not have the opportunity of doing much advising, but helped with the advertising; the phrase 'Queen of Table Waters' was his.

When the sales rose, Smith and his daughter went to Germany to see the proprietors of the spring, and had colloquies, full of humour, with the family. When he proposed that the yearly supply should be raised to 6 million bottles the Kreuzbergs became so excited that they said they could do no more business for the day. They must 'calm themselves' by going off for a long drive. The Smiths went with them. For later negotiations Steinkopf did not carry enough weight with the Kreuzbergs, who were worried, for one thing, by fear of the price of bottles rising. So Smith came on the scene again himself, agreed to buy bottles, arranged for powers of supervision of the bottling, and, as the price of bottles did not rise, but, as might have been expected, fell, made an incidental profit of £30,000. The total amount out of his own pocket invested by Smith in the whole Apollinaris transaction, from first to last—he sold it to a company in 1898—was £3,000 only.

At the time when the holders of the first half of his shares were anxious to buy the other half he happened to be in bed. He wrote on a slip of paper the price he required, and, to his surprise, a formal agreement was brought to him within twenty-four hours. He said to the man who represented the would-be buyer, 'You have been very quick over this. How have you managed it?' 'Well, you see,' he said, 'I said you were advanced in years and in bed, and if he wanted your signature he had better not be long about it.' 'I'm hanged if I'll stand for this', said Smith, 'take him back his agreement and say I shall be skipping about in a week. Then he can send it to me if he likes. I won't be a party to false pretences.'

At first the bottles used to be packed in hampers and sent to Rotterdam, whence they were shipped to London. This meant many handlings, and the breakages were enormous. Smith hit on the plan of having a small vessel that could go up the Rhine to the very place the beverage came from, and of the 'binning', with springs, of the hampers in the vessel's hold. The plan saved the company thousands of pounds. Economies which ran into more thousands were also made by paying employés a bonus on reduced breakages. Before long a spring was purchased to provide another mineral water named Apenta.

Smith's mother, who had meant so much to him, died in 1877. When, two years later, his eldest sister passed away, he suggested to the Rev. Samuel Barnett, rector of St. Jude's, Whitechapel, afterwards a Canon, that the next sister might be of some service to him in his work. Barnett proposed the collection of rents for some benevolent persons who had bought houses in order to let rooms at reasonable rates to the poor. Smith, in going with his sister on one of her rounds, discovered wretched conditions. Bringing his 'business judgement to bear on the problem', he proposed to 'build a tenement which could be let at low rents and yet yield an adequate if modest interest of 5 per cent. on the outlay'. He built a house to lodge forty families, but decent sanitary arrangements, planning for the washing and drying of clothes on the roof, provision for hanging boxes for flowers at the windows—hanging so as not to keep out the light—and a general instinct for thoroughness, cost more than was anticipated, and the yield was 3 per cent.

When tenants were in difficulty, the collector always happened to know an anonymous friend—Smith, of course—who might help. Smith also tried, in co-operation with a coal-owner of his acquaintance, to provide coal cheaper and of better quality than that the tenants were able to buy. But they thought he was making a profit out of them, and felt he was taking the bread out of the mouth of the coal-dealer round the corner. Although they suspected this man of giving them short weight and even of blackening stones to put in their coals, he was one of themselves, and Smith's benevolent attempt came to an end.

There was, however, a successful country jaunt or picnic once or twice a year, and sometimes a Christmas party at Toynbee Hall. At one of the picnics two working girls from the tenement—they made a living in their room by sewing sacks—expressed their thanks to Miss Isabel (Mrs. Reginald Smith) for allowing them to pick 'live strawberries and live gooseberries'. 'Ah, Miss', one of them said, 'I shall envy you in this beautiful garden when I am working in our little room to-morrow.' 'No', she added after a pause, 'I won't envy you; that would be downright mean.' In the course of a conversation between Smith and a tenant about prejudice the woman said, 'Prejudice there is; perhaps you, sir, don't care for whelks.'

Once, when Smith's sister was no longer collector, her successor told him of a situation which social legislation has made impossible nowadays. A woman tenant of a single room had, in consequence of old age, unfortunately lost her job. 'She was reduced to complete indigence, had neither food nor money, and could not even comfort herself with the light of a candle. Mrs. Hood had tried to persuade her to go to the workhouse, but her only answer was to throw herself on the floor and scream. I decided that the first thing to do was to get the woman into better physical condition, and the caretaker was instructed that she was to have a good dinner with him every day. At the end of a fortnight Mrs. Hood was to tell her that, if she would promise to go to the workhouse in case she got no employment, there was a gentleman who would help her for a month. The woman promised, was kept in decency for the month and then went peaceably to the workhouse.' To-day even the name of workhouse has been abolished,[1] and such a woman would have been able to live in her room on her old age pension and local allowance. One of Smith's tenants had to be sent away owing to the annoyance caused by the screaming of his wife when he beat her. The man said as he left that he 'didn't want to stay in a bloody house where he might not knock his bloody wife about as he bloody well liked'.

One of Smith's benevolences was to engage the whole of the dress circle at Covent Garden for ninety children to see the pantomime. They had a special playbill, refreshments between the acts, and a visit to the stage after the performance. Smith's idea was to have the whole dress circle an unbroken curve of happy faces. Unfortunately, by some miscalculation, the box office had reserved seats in the first row for 'two gentlemen, strangers to him'. The manager offered them a private box, but they would not budge. Smith felt that the whole effect of his party was going to be spoiled. 'You have carpenters?' he said to the manager. Yes, he had. 'Then', said Smith, 'turn the two seats those gentlemen occupy into a private box'. 'The obstinately discourteous pair were built round and the children got up and joined in an excellent shout.' Some time later Smith proposed to have his child friends at a party between tides on Goodwin Sands. But so many fearful mothers objected that the plan had to be abandoned.

Smith bought a house in Oakhill Park at Hampstead and made large additions. The view from it extended to Windsor Castle. He also had a house at Brighton. At later dates he lived in South Kensington and, finally, in Park Lane, in a house which had been the Duke of Somerset's. He also took a house at Weybridge. His clubs were the Reform—for which his seconder had been Thackeray—and the Garrick. While Hampstead was his home he and his wife had, on Fridays, an informal cold dinner available for relays of guests. On a Friday following two wet ones a large number of visitors was expected, and the butler was

[1] And Poor Law Institution after it.

told to get some small tables. Next day he was asked where he got them. 'Those were not tables, sir,' he replied; 'they were coffin tops; I borrowed them from the undertaker.' Among the strangers who were brought to these Friday dinners was Turgenieff.

ENTER THE EDITOR

CHAPTER XII

Greenwood's Way Up

AS A CENTENARIAN KNEW HIM — THACKERAY, DICKENS, AND MRS. BEETON — MRS. GREENWOOD — FIRST STEPS IN AUTHORSHIP

I AM able to add a good deal of interest to what has been known about the early days of Frederick Greenwood, the first editor of the *Pall Mall Gazette*. He was the eldest of the eleven children of James Caer Greenwood and his wife, formerly Mary Fish; his full name was Frederick Francis and he was born on March 25, 1830, in London. His father is described in the *Dictionary of National Biography* as 'a coach builder in Kensington'; and in Frederick Greenwood's own marriage certificate, which is lying before me, the father's description is also 'coach builder'. But, by the kindness of Mr. W. H. Robinson, I gleaned some new information from his mother, Mrs. Maria Robinson, a niece of Greenwood—a wonderful old lady whose remarkable memory and intellect were little impaired at the great age of a hundred and three.[1] Mrs. Robinson, until she was eleven or twelve, had 'the run of Frederick Greenwood's house', and she insisted that his father was but a coach trimmer, a term still used in the trade for a carriage upholsterer, and that his employers were 'the Quintons in the City Road, Clerkenwell'.

Frederick's mother was described by Mrs. Robinson as 'very dark, like a gipsy'. Frederick's brother James, 'The Amateur

[1] She recalled her father holding her up to see Sayers and Heenan, probably on the occasion, Mr. Robinson says, when the police stopped the championship fight. She said Heenan was 'such a great tall man' and Sayers comparatively small. She saw Garibaldi, and also the arrival in London of Queen Alexandra as a bride. She remembered that her grandmother, who lived to be over ninety, could obtain a light with a tinder-box as quickly as a smoker gets one with a petrol-lighter. To go still farther back, this grandmother's brother served in the galleys of the Moors.

Casual',[1] was also dark, but Frederick was fair and his hair red. Greenwood himself speaks of his maternal grandmother, in a

A Message from Mrs. Robinson at one hundred and three.

letter quoted on a later page, as Ann-ap-Rhys, of Carmarthenshire, 'with a memory alive with tradition of old, old murderous wars, and a keener relish for them than might have been expected'. Greenwood's temperament and character awaken interest in his regional origins, but the inquiries I made in Carmarthenshire were without result. In the letter referred to, I see Greenwood has written 'maternal' and subsequently changed the 'm' into 'p'.

Mrs. Robinson's recollection of his parents is that 'they

[1] See Chapter XVI.

were Londoners'. According to information which Mr. W. T. Allen, a nephew of Greenwood who remembers seeing him, has been good enough to give me, one of his forbears on his mother's side seems to have belonged to Wapping. There is a tradition of this man having won Doggett's coat and badge,[1] which he frequently donned. He had a liking for beer, so much so that 'when he was beyond the usual time of getting home, one of his children was sent to get the badge and bring it home for safety'.

On Greenwood's paternal side it would appear from some letters I have that, although Caer, in his father's name, suggests a Welsh origin—it means a fortified place, an earlier word than castle[2]—his roots, through his father, were in Yorkshire, a county in which, we shall see, he chose to spend many holidays.[3] I took the trouble, it will be noted in the interesting extracts from letters summarized in a footnote, to write to a number of well-known Greenwoods to ask them in what part of the country Greenwoods were most numerous, and their verdict, in their obliging letters, is overwhelmingly for Yorkshire and the West Riding.[4]

[1] Founded by an Irish actor in 1715 to celebrate the accession of George I.

[2] *Caer-dydd*, now Cardiff; *Caer-marthen*, Carmarthen.

[3] See Chapter XXXI.

[4] WHERE GREENWOODS ARE 'THICK ON THE GROUND'. The late *Viscount Greenwood* (who reminded me of what I had forgotten, that about 1907 he called on me in the *Westminster Gazette* office, and decided to take advice I gave him to 'stick to your law and politics, and you have a great chance of doing some good') wrote that all he could contribute to the history of 'that most enjoyable and patriotic editor, Frederick Greenwood' is that 'it is generally accepted that the Greenwoods originated in Yorkshire'. *Mr. Arthur Greenwood, M.P.*, who did such good service as Minister of Health, and was born in Yorkshire, told me that the medieval Greenwoods—one of them a baker who received some favour from Henry II—'seem to have sprung from a small area in the West Riding round about Hebden Bridge, Halifax, and Todmorden. The most frequent names in that district are Greenwood and Sutcliffe. If Frederick Greenwood was born in London, then I should think his father or his forebears came from the provinces'. *Miss Phyllis Bentley*, the novelist, declared that 'there are scores, nay hundreds of Greenwoods in and around Halifax'. *Mr. Robert Greenwood*, the short-story writer, said that the name is common in the Keighley and Skipton district. *Mr. J. F. Greenwood*, the engraver and water-

What was the London like into which Greenwood was born? 'It was worth while being born in the early 'thirties', Greenwood said in an article in the *Star*, towards the end of his life, in order 'to feel every day a difference so much to the good.'

It is a difference in nothing so great as in the bettered conditions, the fuller opportunities, the wider admission of poor men to the comforts and minor luxuries of life of every kind.

Nowadays, when the artisan's cupboard is full—that is to say, when he is earning fair average wages—there are half a dozen good things in it which were never seen there in those times, if even the names of them had ever been heard. I know of a clever village car-

colourist, reported that there is a Johannes de Grenewod in the poll tax list from Keighley, that one of that name fought at Flodden, and that to-day Greenwoods are 'almost as common as sparrows in the West Riding. I know of no place where they are so thick on the ground as round Hebden Bridge, which is some six or eight miles south of Haworth and ten or twelve from Keighley'. The Harley Street surgeon, *Mr. H. H. Greenwood*, a Halifax man, also stated that the West Riding is the region in which to find Greenwoods. Some light is thrown on the name by the following statement of his: 'My great-grandfather was a woodsman, and my grandfather a maker of wooden clog soles, but he also returned to the woods.'

As to Frederick Greenwood's connexion with Wales through his father, the late *Professor Greenwood, F.R.S.*, Emeritus Professor of Epidemiology and Vital Statistics, was good enough to refer me to his son, *Mr. George Greenwood*, an amateur of genealogy, who said Greenwoods were not numerous in Wales until the middle of the last century. 'In fact the only Welsh Greenwoods I ever heard of belong to Lord Greenwood's family. His grandfather, William, belongs to Radnorshire. This Greenwood would be a contemporary of Frederick's parents, and there might possibly be some connexion, though it is a long shot. The Hebden Bridge area is the home ground for Greenwoods. They teem in hundreds. In the West Riding one can trace the spread into Lancashire [*Walter Greenwood*, the novelist and dramatist, is a Lancashire man], Lincolnshire, Norfolk, and Oxford. The London Greenwoods are rather complicated and I have only delved into our branch, which started in Bethnal Green about 1618. None of my items link up with Frederick. Most of my particular ancestors were undertakers, cordwainers, bellows-makers, and the like.'

Mrs. Blomfield, Secretary of the Society of Genealogists, reported 'a very long pedigree of Greenwood of Yorkshire, shewing two Fredericks'. In Cardiff in 1872 there was a justice of the peace called Frederick Greenwood. There is also mention of a 'Frederick Greenwood, of Islington, armiger 1879, aged eighteen'. *Captain A. A. Greenwood* tells me that in his family (from Oxfordshire) 'Frederick is a family name', but he knows of no relationship with our Frederick.

penter who, at twenty-four, fifty years ago or less, smelt roast beef for the first time in his life (and to his great curiosity) while he was hanging pictures in the manor house near his dwelling; and this happened, too, in one of the home counties.

At about the same time, it was no startling sight to see grown lads of the labouring class walking the streets shoeless—and that within a mile of the Bank of England.

There was no penny weekly paper; you borrowed a newspaper now and then from a neighbouring public-house, or you joined with a friend or two to take in the *Weekly Dispatch*, price sixpence.

Highgate and Hornsey were as green and rural as most parts of Hertfordshire today. Westward anywhere beyond the toll gate at Kensington Gore was country: Hammersmith a hamlet. I have seen wheat growing within five minutes of Holland House, and taken nests, and lain deep in buttercups, and been greedy in orchards within thrice that distance from the railway station in Kensington High Street.

We have only to turn to the Hammonds' *Bleak Age* to find that in Greenwood's early days—in the eighteen-thirties—there were 4,000 non-resident parsons; more than 40 per cent. of the people who signed the married register made a mark; an archbishop was alive of whom it was told that when asked to hold a confirmation for the industrial districts of the West Riding, he replied that it must be held at Wakefield, for that was as far into the industrial area as a gentleman could be expected to go; and the Bill providing for a ten hours' working day had been passed, with Peel and Cobden declaring that it meant industrial disaster.

In the circumstances of the time Frederick Greenwood, as a member of a carriage upholsterer's family of eleven, went neither to public school nor university. According to Sir William Robertson Nicoll, who knew him as an elderly man, he started out in life as a printer's devil. He was actually apprenticed as a compositor to a firm which printed some of Carlyle's books, became a corrector of the press, and bound up for himself several of the sage's proofs.[1]

[1] I find that three of Carlyle's early books, published by James Fraser, 215

Among his fellow compositors Frederick Greenwood was known as, I am told, 'rather quick tempered and domineering'—his nickname among them was 'Gentle Joseph'. His brother James, a compositor along with him, called 'Bill'—his full name was William James—knew Dickens and, Mrs. Robinson says, lodged with a landlady called Mrs. Bardell. Frederick lived with Mrs. Robinson's father, Thomas Nobes,[1] in Wynward Street, off Goswell Road, and shared a bedroom with Mr. Robinson's uncle for six months for nothing. A fellow apprentice with him

Regent Street, were printed by Levey, Robson, and Franklyn, 46 St. Martin's Lane. Later, in 1843, this firm printed another Carlyle work for Chapman and Hall, and on its title-page they appear as Robson, Levey, and Franklyn, Great New Street, Fetter Lane.

[1] LINKS WITH JOHN CASSELL, CRUIKSHANK, AND FRANCIS PLACE. Mr. Robinson's uncle, Thomas Nobes—Nobes is a North Wales name—was also apprenticed to Wade [see next page], was father of the *Lancet* chapel, had a library of 4,000 books, could read in three languages, and did a page from the French for the *Court Journal*. His father, Thomas Nobes senior, as a young fellow walked to London from Gosport, and became associated with John Cassell (1817–65) founder of the well-known publishing firm, and known as an ardent total abstainer. He began life in London as a retail coalman. This grandfather remembered that at the door of Cassell's first shop it was necessary to go down one step.

Besides teetotalism, Nobes was interested in music, and, with his brother, played and sang in a Hampshire village church, like the characters in *Under the Greenwood Tree*. He was one of the crowd which pulled down the Hyde Park railings. But he was also a member of the Havelock or 48th Middlesex Rifle Corps, all total abstainers, of which the teetotal Cruikshank was Lieutenant-Colonel. Cruikshank had formerly been a private in the Loyal North British Volunteers. Mr. Robinson tells me that Cruikshank gave a copy of his *Worship of Bacchus* to the corps. It is related in William Bates's *George Cruikshank* (Houghton & Hammond, 1879) that the artist continued to hold his colonelcy in spite of the expressed opinion of his officers that he was, at his age, incompetent for the duties of the position. A memorial on the subject was sent to the Lord Lieutenant, and by him forwarded to the War Office. The result was an order, in 1869, to cashier every one of the fourteen officers who had signed the document. Then the regiment was left with three or four officers only, an octogenarian commander, and the rest mere lads. His own resignation followed. Returning to Nobes, he conducted several brass bands. In old age he became blind, but his grandson has 'seen him take his violin to pieces and glue it up again without assistance'. Mr. Robinson has another scrap of family history. His grandmother was in domestic service in the house of the Radical reformer, Francis Place (1771–1854) until she left to be married from the house of a Mr. Lambert who had been wounded at Waterloo.

was James Wade who afterwards became the printer or proprietor of *Sporting Life* and the *Court Journal*, published a book on shorthand, had his imprint on Beeton's *Englishwoman's Domestic Magazine*, and lived in Covent Garden. A brother of Frederick's, Walter Greenwood, who was a compositor at Wade's, dropped dead at his case. Robert Greenwood, who became the sporting writer of the *Daily Telegraph*, Hotspur, was no relative. Neither was Thomas Greenwood, the promoter of public libraries.

From the printing office at which Greenwood worked he managed to get some sort of footing in the Press—'from the age of sixteen, he supported himself'—and Mrs. Robinson recollected that Greenwood's mother 'did not approve of his going into such a risky business as journalism'. But even a journalist may not be the best counsellor to the future journalist. In Dilnot's *Romance of the Amalgamated Press* it is stated that 'G. A. Sala solemnly warned Alfred Harmsworth against adopting journalism as a career'! Mrs. Robinson recalled that there was a time when Greenwood subscribed to *The Times* and had the reading of it from 9 a.m. to 10 a.m., when it was passed to someone else. He often 'worked sixteen hours a day', and was associated with *La Belle Assemblée and Court Magazine*, a monthly, edited in 1832 by the Hon. Mrs. Norton.[1] James Laver, the authority on the history of women's dress, says it was one of the best fashion magazines ever published. It had one or two hand-coloured engravings and in the text several wood engravings. The publisher was named Bell, and it has been suggested to me that it would be in accord with the fashion of the time in humour if there was a punning reference to him in the title, *La Belle Assemblée*. (*Bell's Life in London*, now absorbed in *Sporting Life* was a survivor of *Bell's Messenger*.)

Greenwood contrived to marry at twenty (on July 14, 1850)—as a 'collector (*sic*) of the press', I read in the marriage certificate in my possession—a Catherine Darby. She is stated by the *Dictionary of National Biography* to have 'belonged to a landed family

[1] *Caroline Norton*, Alice Acland (Constable).

of Quaker connexions in Hampshire', but according to the certificate she was the daughter of 'John Darby, coppersmith'.[1] She had a brother, a yacht's captain at Gosport, and a sister who married a compositor on the *Lancet*.

Like Dickens and Thackeray, his two fellow editors whose journalistic careers have been outlined, Greenwood does not seem to have had a happy married life. I have been told that Mrs. Greenwood was 'eccentric' and left her husband when their daughter Kate, of whom we shall hear, was fourteen. There was another daughter, Jessy, and a son, Edgar, who as an adult was killed in a street accident.[2] Three other children, Frank, Edward, and Nelly, died young.

My centenarian informant, Mrs. Robinson, remembered the youngster Frank being set on the table to recite 'Little Billee' to a company at Greenwood's home which included Thackeray. She also saw Dickens there, two writers of boys' books, popular in their time, W. B. Rands and J. G. Edgar—Greenwood's boy Edgar was named after him—Bell, the proprietor of *Bell's Life in London*, and Mr. and Mrs. Beeton, of the famous cookery book. Mrs. Beeton (who died in the year the *Pall Mall Gazette* was started) she described as 'a good practical cook, very lively and chatty, and something of a practical joker. The wives of some of her friends complained that their husbands came home and said, "Why can't you cook like Mrs. Beeton?" so, at the next gathering at the house of Mrs. Beeton, she dished up a shocking meal in order to teach men not to criticise their wives.' Mr. Beeton, who started the *Queen*, was 'a very nice gentleman'.

[1] Mrs. Robinson was definite that she saw Darby's name in the family bible and that it was John Henry. 'Apparently', her son writes to me, 'he was a man of some substance, and had at one time three shops in Gosport, where the name of Darby is a common one. My mother's father, T. Nobes senior, who married Mrs. Frederick Greenwood's sister, was a shoemaker and his father a silversmith in Gosport, the mayor of which at present is a Nobes. One of my mother's stories is that a rector took some church plate work away from her grandfather and gave it to a churchman who botched it, and it was brought back to the dissenting craftsman.'

[2] See for particulars about Kate, Jessy, and Edgar, Chapters XXX–XXXV and XXXIX.

Dickens, as seen through the eyes of a little girl, was 'a very smart gentleman with curly hair and a velvet waistcoat, who talked an awful lot'; she 'didn't like him very much'. But Thackeray, 'a very big man, was a very nice gentleman'.

Frederick Greenwood and his wife seem to have first met at the house of Mr. W. H. Robinson's grandfather, Thomas Nobes, and to have begun their married life in lodgings in Gloucester Terrace, Exmouth Street. They then went to Albert Terrace, Copenhagen Street.

Mrs. Robinson was clear that Greenwood, when his wife left him, made her some allowance. 'She went to live with a Mrs. Williams—whose daughter married a son of Frank Vizetelly'—and 'was ill some time before her death'. In one quarter I have heard it suggested that she sought comfort in stimulants, but Mrs. Robinson said that 'although not a teetotaller, she was quite steady'. As to her oddity, 'when some friends visited her', says Mrs. Robinson, 'she didn't want to give them tea, so she hid all her cups under a chair cushion.' Again, 'when she was living with Mrs. Williams, my sister and I called on her and she stopped the clock, so that we didn't know the time and finally had to walk home, arriving in the early morning.' Another informant of mine, Mrs. Lusted, wrote to me: 'Mrs. Greenwood, when she went away, told her family that they could now get on without her. That was why Mr. Greenwood was in lodgings and hotels while the children finished their education. I think she was always expected back. Her name was never mentioned.' Mrs. Greenwood died on October 28, 1900, at the age of seventy-seven and is buried with her children, Frank and Edward (1863 and 1868) and her husband (1909) at Highgate Cemetery.

Mrs. Robinson stressed what others have been reported as saying of Greenwood, that he was 'very kind to children'. She remembers being at his house when he lent her his glasses to 'see the great comet', and she was 'so frightened that she dropped them on the grass'. This was at 'a large house with a triangular space in front in Rotherfield Street, near Downham Road, Islington', at which she saw Dickens and Thackeray. When we come to Greenwood's letters to his daughters Kate and Jessy we can be in no doubt as to his liking for children and particular concern for their welfare. Mrs. Robinson recalls that his young people were 'always allowed to see any visitors'.

Greenwood, who had celebrated his twenty-first birthday by having some part in the printing of the first English edition of Mrs. Beecher Stowe's *Uncle Tom's Cabin*, produced later *Louis Napoleon Bonaparte*—part of *The Napoleon Dynasty*, published the same year—and a *Life of Napoleon III*. In the introduction to his volume on Napoleon le Petit he owned to 'little knowledge of politics and less care', which, in view of the influence he was later to exert in the political world, is yet one more illustration of the limited accuracy with which most of us are able to forecast our future. A quotation from Macaulay was accompanied by the remark that 'history, when we look at it in small portions, may be so construed as to mean anything'. In 1854 Greenwood was the author of *The Loves of an Apothecary*.

Greenwood is heard of in connexion with the *Illustrated Times*, which was in no way associated with *The Times*. The idea of it was taken by David Bogue to Henry Vizetelly ten years after the starting of the *Illustrated London News*. This *Illustrated Times*, which was to appeal at twopence to a public for which the *Illustrated London News* at sixpence was too dear, was later absorbed by the *Penny Illustrated Paper*, which was ultimately taken over by the *News*. The *Illustrated Times* had some well-known contributors, and, just before the abolition of the stamp duties, dared to come out unstamped. It reached a circulation of 100,000 and, finally, of double that. Greenwood is described by T. H. S. Escott[1] as 'occasionally doing some editorial supervision', and by T. L. Stevens as the successor of Macrae Moir in the editorship. 'I remember him as a spruce young fellow with rather a supercilious air and a black knitted necktie', writes to me someone whose name I greatly regret I have mislaid: 'A disastrous change in the circumstances of the poor compositors came about when Mr. Greenwood took control of the copy. It may not have

[1] *Masters of Journalism* (Unwin).

been his fault, but we did not know whose else it could be. The change had come with the change of editors. Our lives were made miserable. We had to be at our cases every morning and all day afterwards lest work should come and others be put in our places. But day after day it happened that work did not come till it was just upon time to go home; and then we had to stand at our cases till every scrap of copy was set—always till midnight, often to four or five o'clock in the morning—with the result that next day we had nothing to do again till the editor condescended to send round a great batch of copy in the evening, when the same dreary process had to be repeated. The only consolation that the unhappy compositors had as they crawled homeward was in "nailing" (which does not mean blessing) the authors of their misery.'

This reflection on Greenwood, though it throws light on the unhappy conditions in which compositors then worked, does not accord with many testimonies to his kindness and consideration. Mr. David Williamson assures me, in a letter, that compositors had no reason at any rate to complain of Greenwood's proofs, for they 'had few alterations'. And, as a former 'reader', Greenwood had been in the closest association with 'comps'. But in the *Illustrated Times* period, industrial conditions were undoubtedly hard. At a later date I find H. J. Higginbottom, whom I knew—he was one of the later editors of the *Pall Mall Gazette*—writing of his printer father-in-law Neville's experience of Greenwood. He 'always spoke in terms of enthusiasm of the uniform consideration he extended to his printers, and of his zeal in superintending the smallest matters of detail in the making-up of the proofs. In this way Greenwood was an ideal editor from the printer's point of view.'

Greenwood showed ability in the discussion of public affairs as the first editor of the *Queen*. He had previously been its dramatic critic. When the paper was started it was not devoted to subjects of special interest to women. My centenarian informant, Mrs. Robinson, who must have been a sharp little girl, remembers going somewhere on a *Queen* Press ticket that 'Uncle

Fred' had provided. She was scolded by her aunt for mistaking a handsome lady-in-waiting for Queen Victoria, who did not impress her at all. Both Mr. and Mrs. Beeton were on the staff of the paper. On its being combined with the *Lady's Newspaper*, Greenwood lost the first of the succession of editorial chairs he was to abandon.

He had a contribution of some quality, 'An Essay without an End', in the second number of *Cornhill*, and his best story, *Margaret Denzil's History*, appeared during Thackeray's editorship. When it came out as a book (1864) one critic expressed dissatisfaction. The novel, he said, 'is clever with a sort of cleverness which one sometimes encounters in conversation which does not bore you but you instinctively dislike, talk which leaves an unpleasant taste behind it, in which conclusions have been jumped at apparently beyond contradiction, but which at the same time one knows to be hollow. The book is unpleasant, and apparently designedly so.' Towards the end of his life Greenwood considered rewriting *Margaret Denzil*, which, Robertson Nicoll says, 'was actually attributed by some sapient person to Queen Victoria'!

Before this story, Greenwood had published, in 1860, *The Path of Roses*, in gilt edges, illustrated by, among others, John Leech, Birket Foster, and Harrison Weir. 'This story', he explained, 'was printed in *Tait's Magazine* when, perhaps, the Author was juvenile of conception and less steady of hand than at present. But all authors are vain, and some are poor; and this one readily enough consented to revise his work for an *édition de luxe*. He has revised it accordingly, and is led to hope that, upon the whole, it will not look amiss on the drawing-room table.' In the same year he had produced, in collaboration with his brother James (of whom we shall hear), *Under a Cloud*—the Bodleian copy is uncut. *Looking Back* appeared in a periodical with the amiable title of *The Welcome Guest*. I have before me a copy (1859) containing chapter 19, headed in the manner of Thackeray, 'Containing matter which must appear absurd to every reasonable mind.' The story opens the magazine and is headed by a sentimental half-page 'engraving on wood'. Greenwood's later books were *The Lover's Lexicon*, and *Imagination in Dreams*, to which reference is made in due course.

When Elizabeth Haldane, in *Mrs. Gaskell and her Friends*, notes that Mrs. Gaskell's *Wives and Daughters* was never finished, she says: 'However this does not matter so much as seemed, for the end is evident, and Mr. Frederick Greenwood has put it into words. The work was admirably carried out.' His aid was also given to George Smith when Thackeray left *Denis Duval* unfinished. The conclusion written by Greenwood, *The Times* said in its obituary of him, was 'a remarkable feat, not unworthy of the master'. Another claim to distinction by Greenwood, by way of association, may be based on his having contributed to *Tait's Magazine* an article which appeared next one of de Quincey's essays.

It was to *Cornhill* that Greenwood contributed a poem, 'Good Night', of which two friends have sent me copies. I notice that Robertson Nicoll included it in his volume, *Songs of Rest*.[1] It is of the period:

Destroyer! what do you here—here by my poor little nest?
What have I done that your shadow lies on my brightest and best?
If 'twas my sin that smirched the cross on the door, O Death,
Blood of mine should efface it, and not this Innocent's passing breath.

O cruel to drench the fleece of my one little lamb with thy dew!
O sightless to quench the light in eyes so guileless and true!
O heartless and brainless to still the life in this hand that glows
And the love and the thought that breed in these wide, grey-fading brows!

The sweet, unflattering voice!—'Papa, do you think I shall die?'
'Die, my dear? All 's in God's hands, but I think—so think not I
You will live to be a big man; and when I am old and grey,
You shall take me by the arm and guide me along the way.

[1] Hodder & Stoughton.

'But if it should be death, do you know what it is, little one?'
It is only a falling asleep, and you wake and the darkness is gone.
And mamma and papa will sleep too; and when that the day is come,
We shall all meet together in heaven—in heaven instead of home.

'Don't you know that asleep in your bed, an hour like a moment seems?
Be not afraid of that! it is past in a night without dreams.
We are only apart, dear child, 'twixt the evening and morning light.'
'Good night, then, papa, and God bless you!' 'My darling, my darling, good night!'

With regard to Greenwood's novels and poetic efforts, it is of interest, in view of his future career, that, as a young man, he had gone into journalism, like many another aspirant, for 'only a little while'—his own words—and 'as a makeshift'. He wanted to be a novelist and to write poetry. But 'never as a boy or man', he was to say years after, 'have I been a grumbler, but only as a journalist and in the performance of the natural duties of journalism'. 'It would be ungrateful', he went on, 'to repine at a "perversion" which carried the pervert into so many pleasures and advantages and even to a place of power, at least equal to half a dozen seats in Parliament.'

CHAPTER XIII

'A Power and a Glory'

THE FADED 'ANTI-JACOBIN' — GREENWOOD'S NOTIONS OF A REAL 'PALL MALL GAZETTE' — CARLYLE'S SUGGESTION — 'A TURNING POINT IN JOURNALISM' — THE WORLD OF 1865

GREENWOOD's place in journalistic history and in the history of his own time was determined on the day he took home a volume he had picked up in Holborn Bars. It was a complete set of the *Anti-Jacobin*, to which, for a year, 1797–8, Canning, whose Roman figure keeps a blind eye on the House of Commons from Parliament Square, was 'one of the most active and certainly the most witty contributor'. Great Britain has had many 'anti' periods in its time, and this weekly, one reads in the *Encyclopaedia Britannica*, was 'started to ridicule the frothy, philanthropic and eleutheromaniac rant of the French Republicans and to denounce their brutal rapacity and cruelty'. The *Anti-Jacobin* has been declared to be 'perhaps the most brilliant success of its kind on record'.[1] Greenwood was taken by its originality, incisiveness, wit, literary character and appearance, and, to some extent, no doubt, by its political principles. In the journalistic world of his time, in which the daily papers were pompous and dull, packed with *clichés*, and forbidding in their typography, how fresh and pleasing seemed not only the high spirits and downrightness but the type and headlines, the wide double

[1] The *Anti-Jacobin* was intended to make its appearance every Monday morning when Parliament was sitting, and it lasted from November 1797 to July 1798. Its editor was William Gifford. Pitt contributed five articles. Canning's rhymes in it included the well-known

> Give me the avowed, the erect, the manly foe!
> Bold I can meet, perhaps may turn the blow;
> But of all plagues, good Heaven, Thy wrath may send,
> Save, save O save me from the candid friend!

It attacked Coleridge, Southey, Lamb, and Godwin.

columns and the easily-held size of page of the *Anti-Jacobin*! 'As I turned over its faded leaves,' Greenwood wrote years later, 'thoughts of the *Saturday Review* intruded (that journal was then at the topmost height of its reputation) and thereupon came this idea. Make as good a combination of the two as the current supply of mind allows, throw in a scrap or two of novel feature, mix with an eye to the needs and demands of the hour, publish every day, and you will have a new thing that ought to be a power and a glory.'

According to Escott, Greenwood was also struck 'by the place existing for a journal whose publishing hour should be luncheon rather than breakfast'. As he had been in close touch with George Smith, first as a writer for *Cornhill*, and then, for a short period, as its editor, it is likely enough that he knew that Thackeray had thought of a daily *Spectator* or *Tatler*.

Greenwood took his idea to the 'acting proprietor' of a publishing firm in the Strand which owned *Fraser's Magazine* and had its name on not a few of the books which were on our fathers' shelves. Young Parker was impressed, and Greenwood, while he does not seem to have proposed himself as editor, thought out the scheme a little more. There was correspondence to collect contributors—Arthur (afterwards Sir Arthur) Helps, Kingsley, and Froude were to write—and Gladstone, little knowing what he was to undergo from Greenwood's pen in a few years, was among the notabilities who warmly approved, at some length it is said by those who have seen his letter. But Parker's father was 'an infirm old man, with only a little time to live, it was thought', Greenwood says, 'and the risk of the undertaking fretted him'. The project was put aside. It was Parker junior, however, who died first.

That might have been the end of the *Evening Review*, the name Greenwood had in his mind, but for George Smith, who once said, 'What is called newspaper enterprise always had a strong attraction for me.' H. R. Fox Bourne asserts indeed—I have been unable to obtain any confirmation of the statement—that he was at one time a shareholder in the *Daily News*. However this may be, he was not attracted by G. H. Lewes's proposal that he should buy the *Leader* he had edited—it cost its proprietor his fortune. But in 1855 he started, as has been noted, the *Overland* and the *Homeward Mails*, and in 1860 he established *Cornhill* with, as we have learnt, 'a good fortune that may be fairly described as phenomenal'. In 1865, he said, he was 'ripe for some new publishing enterprise'. Some years before he had tried to induce Thackeray to edit, or Thackeray had suggested to him, 'a little daily sheet, something after the style of the *Spectator* and the *Tatler* of the days of Addison and Steele'. 'We got far enough to invent a title, *Fairplay*, since appropriated. Thackeray at last, however, abandoned the idea. His working energy seemed to fail him.' Unfortunately 'a characteristic letter', in which he conveyed his decision, cannot be found. Smith thought it possible that their talk about the kind of articles which should appear in *Fairplay* may have put the notion of the *Cornhill* 'Roundabout Papers' in Thackeray's head.

The paper Greenwood brought to Smith was to be non-political, or, as he properly corrected himself, non-partisan: 'it was to try all parties and policies by the test of honesty and sound sense, and it was to carry that spirit into the realms of literature and criticism. There was at that time much jobbery in literary criticism, as well as in politics, and we proposed to wage relentless war upon it.' And in the *Saturday Review* there was 'too much gall'. For instance, 'it could never review Trollope or Mrs Gaskell fairly'—was she not a Nonconformist minister's wife? As for 'the jobbery in literary criticism', some reviews were little more than publishers' puffs. It is curious that, during my time on the *Pall Mall Gazette*, when Churton Collins and others gibbeted Andrew Lang, Saintsbury, and Edmund Gosse for their log-rolling, no one remembered the early interest of the paper in honest criticism.

The idea of *Fairplay* faded when Thackeray proved indifferent, but the time Smith had given to the scheme made him willing to listen to Greenwood's proposal for 'an honest and courageous daily journal'. Thackeray had provided Arthur Pendennis, in the *Pall Mall Gazette*, with a journal 'written by gentlemen for gentlemen'. Why not a real *Pall Mall Gazette* somewhat on Thackeray's and the *Anti-Jacobin* model? In Greenwood's words, in recounting his interview with Smith, 'the charm worked'. Years afterwards, indeed, Smith was not sure that he had not himself suggested the name *Pall Mall Gazette*. For a time he had been in favour of the old name *Fair-play*, but 'came at last to feel that this was somewhat too bumptious; it would not do to proclaim the virtue of the paper in every issue.' The *Pall Mall Gazette* title was settled when he tried it on Annie Thackeray in his house at Brighton. 'O how pleased Papa will be', she cried, for 'though Thackeray had been dead two years, his daughter cherished the idea most vividly that her father kept his interest in all that happened here'. But when some of Smith's friends heard of the title they were incredulous. 'It is not a joke then?' they would say; 'you really do mean to have that name?' Greenwood himself thought *Pall Mall Gazette* 'trivial'. He feared it would be 'chaffed'—he puts the word in quotation marks—and felt that 'a meaning of snobbishness clung to it'. He still favoured *English Review*, which was tame, if explanatory. W. T. Stead has recorded that Greenwood urged that the paper was not to be published in Pall Mall, that the name 'needlessly narrowed its scope', and that 'it was not descriptive'—which was very much the kind of criticism passed on the name of *Cornhill*. Stead—and I remember how we at first thought the title of his own *Review of Reviews* cumbrous—remarks that 'objections can be taken to any and every title that is new, all of which seem formidable enough before the new paper has caught on, but seem idle after the public has been familiarized with the name'.

Certainly the *Pall Mall Gazette* was never to hear the last of 'written by gentlemen for gentlemen'. One reads about it long afterwards in Charles Pebody's *English Journalism* (1882):[1]

> The proprietor and editor have always repudiated the suggestion that the paper was published upon the lines of Thackeray's *Pall Mall*

[1] Cassell.

Gazette as a 'paper written by gentlemen for gentlemen', but the associations and even the style of the paper have been too much for them. The proprietor was Thackeray's publisher. The editor was Thackeray's associate in the conduct of *Cornhill*. They christened the paper with Thackeray's title. The conclusion was irresistible. The *Pall Mall Gazette* must be the ideal journal written by gentlemen for gentlemen, and that the public have persisted in counting it from the first day of publication.

And [if we may anticipate] the paper has strengthened the public in their belief. Its tone has from the first been aristocratic, the tone of the club window, of the smoking room, of the House of Commons and of the drawing room. You read your column or column and a half of the vigorous polished matter, read it with relish. It is keen, scholarly and trenchant. You feel you are reading the work of a man who knows all the ins and outs of the question he is handling, that he is a man with a cool head, a strong intellect, and a powerful pen, that he is a man who has cleared his mind of all cant, and that, with strong common sense, he possesses wit, a calm and perhaps cynical temper which sees and hears everything and sees through everything.

Smith had been candid about it. 'We had not only borrowed the name of the journal "written by gentlemen for gentlemen"', he said; 'to a very unusual extent our contributors were not professional writers in the ordinary sense and were in a higher social class than most newspaper men.' I wonder, however, whether Thackeray's 'by gentlemen for gentlemen' (1849) was absolutely original. I notice that Francis Jeffrey wrote of his own *Edinburgh Review* (started 1802) that that periodical was 'in the highest degree respectable as there are none but gentlemen connected with it'. Smith was impressed by Greenwood—who some time before had proposed to him the purchase of the under-capitalized *Queen*—'a man full of ideas and energy', he said. Greenwood's plan was for 'a small evening paper of about twelve pages' and he produced 'an elaborate and careful estimate of the cost'—of only £32 per issue! Like so many estimates of the kind it was not to correspond with experience. 'I did not rush into the enterprise', Smith said. 'It was under discussion for more than two years; Mr. Greenwood and I had frequent meetings which sometimes ran into the small hours. We invited friends to come to our aid and little committees often sat in my room for hours together.'

One difficulty was that Smith was in partnership with H. S. King, and, under the partnership agreement, could not enter upon the contemplated enterprise by himself. King, after much consideration, agreed that the paper should be published on the firm's account, that Smith should have the whole control and management, and that King should have the power at any moment to request him to discontinue the paper or to buy his interest in it at a valuation. A stipulation that Smith was to be at liberty to establish other newspapers, giving the not too hopeful King the option of being interested in them on the same terms, may be noted. It may have been a lure or it may have pointed to the vigorous Smith having a hazy notion of a many-paper ownership which, if it had come about, might have anticipated some developments of the last half-century in Fleet Street.

It is curious that Greenwood had, for a time at any rate, no thought of undertaking the editorship himself. The editor he proposed, and he pressed his suggestion hard, was Richard Holt Hutton, Meredith Townsend's colleague at the *Spectator*.[1] Carlyle was consulted, and thought of 'one Scott of Manchester, principal of some college in Cottonopolis', of whose sentences the *Pall Mall Gazette* was one day to write that they 'went tottering on, bent double under their weight of thought'. This was not, of course, a later Scott, C. P. S. of the *Manchester Guardian*, but Dr. A. J. Scott, the gifted head of Owen's College. There was a Dr. Caleb Scott, a leading Congregationalist, who was chief of the Lancashire Independent College and had a daughter who became a mathematician. It is a coincidence that this Scott was educated at Silcoates, the same school as W. T.

[1] I recall Townsend, after the death of Hutton, scaring me as a young student of foreign affairs, by giving me an article to do on the future of Constantinople. I was to discuss—and did discuss—the rival claims of Turkey, Russia, Bulgaria, and Greece, and the article duly appeared.

Stead, a future editor of the *Pall Mall Gazette*. Another thought of Carlyle's, Greenwood remembered, was that 'Edward Airving' would be 'the very man were he alive and in his right mind'.[1] Smith was clear, however, that Greenwood was the man. Greenwood's words are, 'the designer of the paper was to be editor against his will'. But 'he doubted his capacity and looked for preference to a life less journalistic and more literary.'

One part of Smith's work was to write to a number of people who were to lend their aid to the paper, explaining its scope and its 'platform' in politics. 'It was understood that we were to support the Liberal Government under Lord Palmerston; at the same time we were to be faithful to our purpose of independent criticism.' Greenwood, writing in the vigorous 'Looker-On' notes he contributed to *Blackwood* after his editorship of the *Pall Mall Gazette* came to an end, acknowledges that the paper started under 'more favourable circumstances than we were sensible of; journalism was at a turning point'. His own long spell of journalism had begun 'at a time of emergence from small credit and a poor wage, to pay that was a good enough return for the commodity supplied, and to as much consideration in the world as modest worth should look for whenever it cares about the world at all. I do not know what intellectual or artistic employment could be called flourishing in the dull years from the thirties to the fifties. I know of a London morning paper, which, even to the end of that period, filled its pages with reviews and other high critical matter at 10*s*. per yard-long column!' He said that years after *Pendennis* came out he knew 'a very perfect Bludyer'. He recalled that, even in the days when Coleridge and Hazlitt 'ennobled' the practice of journalism, 'writing for a newspaper was thought more respectable than to edit it. Lord Blachford, at the age of twenty-nine, was repeatedly pressed by the proprietor of *The Times* to undertake its editor-

[1] Edward Irving, 1792–1834. He had given lessons to Jane Welsh as a girl, had introduced her to Carlyle and would have married her. If he had, Mrs. Carlyle was to say, 'the tongues would never have been heard'. An early book of his was *An Argument for Judgment to Come*. For a time the Dr. A. J. Scott mentioned above was Irving's assistant. See Carlyle's biography of Irving.

ship. This he declined to do; but on being urged to write for the paper he almost thinks that he will try his hand. "This unattached way of things seems to me very feasible. No-one will know." This was in 1840 when the newspaper press had already made considerable progress in gentility, and a yet more pronounced advance to the authority of the Fourth Estate of the Realm. Bohemianism was its reproach, and the poverty which, in denying the means of cultivating the graces and refinements of life, perfects in some hurt minds the affectation of despising them.'

'But at the advent of the *Pall Mall Gazette* a better order of things—mainly signalised by the victorious advent of the *Saturday Review* (1855), and, by the attraction of many fresh bright strong and scholarly minds to journalism as a power—was coming in.' The intention of the *Pall Mall Gazette* was 'to bring into daily journalism (but with more legerity and less of the doctorial) the full measure of thought and culture which was then found only in the reviews. The newspaper press moved on to a higher place and to great prosperity'. The article concludes by recording the fact that 'one of the reforms achieved by the new journalism of sixty years since was the complete supersession of the formal artificial and hackneyed style by a style more idiomatic and familiar, unpedantic, flexible, good English of common life, never without humour, which men of education use in their talk and in their letters'. But to-day the reader of some of the best editorial writing in the *Pall Mall Gazette* will find not a few turns of expression which have become, in their turn, outworn! Some of mine, an octogenarian's, have probably become outworn also.

Sydney Smith said that in order to appreciate the value of the *Edinburgh Review*, 'the state of England at the period when it began'—he said England not Britain!—'should be held in remembrance'. When the *Pall Mall Gazette* came out in 1865 it entered a world in which there were men and women—in their nineties, it is true—who had been born before the Declaration of Independence. Two years were to pass before slavery came to an end in the United States, and two more before serfdom was formally abolished in Russia. In the American Civil War, *The Times* had sided with the Southern States, and *Punch* had pictured the President with hoofs. In 1865 Abraham Lincoln was assassinated and Palmerston and Cobden died. It was a year before the Atlantic cable was successfully laid, and five years before the overthrow of Napoleon III. Japan was ruled by a Shogun—and by samurai wearing two swords—a Shogun whose heir, Prince Tokugawa, was to come to my house in Tokyo; he made an admirable President of the House of Peers.[1] Spain was fighting Chile, and the Franco-German War was five years ahead.

For twenty more years boys of twelve were to work in the mines, and, for many more, half-timers between ten and eleven were to serve half a day in the mills before they went sleepily to school. Sailors had to wait nine years for a scene in the House of Commons which gave ships the Plimsoll line. The police system as we know it was only coming into being. Dissenter undergraduates were still hindered at the universities, and Newnham and Girton were years off. There were no postcards, typewriters, or telephones. Electric light was to come, anaesthetics were a new thing, and antiseptic surgery was of the future.

Dickens had five years to live, Huxley thirty-one. The word 'agnostic' was not invented. School boards were not to be set up until five years later—and it was then left to the boards' discretion whether education in their areas should be compulsory or not. Men had whiskers or side-whiskers or Dundrearies, the women crinolines, and the boys long hair.

The new books were Tennyson's *Maud*, Burton's *Mecca*, and Carlyle's final volume of *Frederick the Great*. *The Origin of Species*, *Adam Bede*, and *Idylls of the King* were six years old. Herbert Spencer's *Education* had been out no more than two years, and John Stuart Mill's *Liberty* but six. *Das Kapital* was two years forward (in German) and Mill's *Subjection of Women* four.

[1] *The Foundations of Japan*, J. W. Robertson Scott (Murray).

The *Standard* was seven years old, the *Daily Telegraph* ten, and the *Daily News* fifteen.[1] As for the fashion of journalism, only thirty years earlier *The Times* had called the *Chronicle* 'that squirt of filthy water', the *Standard* had spoken of a 'blubber-headed contemporary' and the *Chronicle* of 'that slob of corruption, the *Post*'. In 1865 Joseph Chamberlain was one of the rank and file in the Birmingham Liberal Association, formed in that year, and smoked a clay pipe in the street.

[1] The *Morning Chronicle* had been started in 1769, the *Morning Post* in 1772, and *The Times* in 1788 (as the *Daily Universal Register* in 1785).

A CONCEPTION OF JOURNALISM

From the first I conceived journalism as something larger than the getting and the publication of news. I found in it a means of working out and applying a philosophy of life, a chance to help things forward on the road I thought right, a quest taxing to the point of exhaustion every energy of heart and brain but having in it what I hold to be the true secret of happiness —constant striving towards ends which, even if they recede upon approach, yet reveal themselves, in receding, as truly worthy of pursuit.

To some men journalism is an occupation into which they have drifted for want of a better, a second-rate calling that evokes no sense of pride. To others, again, it is a trade or, at best, a business of which the success is to be measured by the number of advertisement columns, by circulation certificates, and by balance sheets. They have their rewards—and their disappointments. A few men take to journalism because they cannot do otherwise, because it draws them with an attraction too potent to be resisted, and because, with open eyes and discounting the drawbacks, they feel they will find, in the daily interpretation of events and in a self-constituted wardenship of the public interest, the only sphere of activity in which such powers as they possess can be satisfactorily employed. These may be called journalists by predestination. The test of their vocation comes when, later in life, they look back upon their efforts, failures and achievements, their mistakes, successes and shortcomings, and ask themselves whether they would have preferred to change places with any of the monarchs or statesmen, financiers or diplomatists, scientists or artists with whom their work has brought them into contact. If they can then honestly say 'no', and aver that they would not wish to be other than they have been, could they begin again, they may fairly claim to be journalists by right of temperament and predilection.

This test I have applied to myself, and can truly say that there is no other work I would rather have done during the past thirty years nor any other branch of public service in which I should have preferred to be engaged. While under modern conditions the making of newspapers must necessarily be a business, the making of that which newspapers exist to print is at once an art and a ministry.—*Through Thirty Years*, Wickham Steed (Heinemann, 1924).

CHAPTER XIV

The Early Numbers

'A PRINCELY PROPRIETORSHIP' — A VIEW OF JOURNALISTIC INDEPENDENCE — A WORD WITH THE QUEEN — SALE, 613 COPIES — MRS. SMITH AND HER JEWELS

THE *Pall Mall Gazette* came out two years after the death of the author of its prototype in *Pendennis*. Of its commercial head it is not too much to say that he was one of the most business-like, most honourable, and most courageous members of the immense family of his name.[1] 'A publisher of strong nerve', a fellow publisher describes George Smith. 'One of the most admirable personalities of nineteenth century publishing' is Siegfried Sassoon's phrase in his *George Meredith*. Smith could speak his mind, but one reads of his 'kind, wise face'. 'Christian to the backbone', said an agnostic, Leslie Stephen, 'he had some of the qualities which one desires in a friend, the staunchest, most straightforward and heartiest of men, pugnacious enough to be a good hater, but the best of backers to those he really loved.'

We all have books with the imprint of his firm, Smith, Elder & Co. It was enterprising, self-respecting, and thriving. The new paper was to enjoy what Sir Henry Lucy called 'a princely proprietorship', a phrase reflecting possibly what G. A. Sala had said about his relations with the *Daily Telegraph*: he enjoyed 'the treatment of a prince and the salary of an ambassador'. Smith was forty-one, Greenwood thirty-five.

The first number of the *Pall Mall Gazette, an Evening Newspaper and Review*—for half of Greenwood's *Evening Review* survived as a sub-title—appeared on Tuesday, February 7, 1865.[2] It was a large folio (13½ in. by a little more than 10 in.) of

[1] Fifty years ago there were more people called Smith in the *Dictionary of National Biography* than persons of any other name.

[2] Most of the tri-weekly evening papers which had done service since the days of Queen Anne were extinct or languishing when the first evening daily appeared, eighty-six years after the establishment of the first morning daily. This evening paper was the *Star* (1788), with rivals in the *Courier* and *Evening*

THE

PALL MALL GAZETTE

An Evening Newspaper and Review.

No. 1.—Vol. I. *TUESDAY, FEBRUARY 7, 1865.* *Price Twopence.*

THE QUEEN'S SECLUSION.

A LITTLE paragraph appeared in the newspapers lately, to revive a hope which was to have been fulfilled to-day, and has not. "We "are informed that Her MAJESTY the QUEEN will open Parliament "in person next session:" this was the little paragraph—printed, too, in that authoritative large type which carries conviction straight into the minds of most newspaper readers. But somehow the herald who brought such good tidings from Court was little credited. The trumpet sounded—that we all heard; but no confirming echo answered it—not even in those hollow places in our own hearts where dwells the hope of what we much desire. The most timid inquirer hesitated to believe; and he whose faith in editorial announcements had hitherto been complete, found himself disturbed by a strangely courageous scepticism. Was the announcement authorized at all by any one? Had we not been told of journalists and politicians who endeavoured to achieve what they wished by declaring it already certain? These questions were asked by many people. The answer to the first one is that the QUEEN never at any moment intended to open Parliament this session—(here is our own authoritative large type to prove it)—and to the other, that if the trick was played, it was a trick which only a very few philosophers can muster morality enough to condemn. There may be some politicians of the fermentative platform kind who secretly rejoice that (if tried) it did not succeed, but they are not philosophers.

It is when we consider what these gentlemen *are* that we most regret the QUEEN'S long absence from what is called public life. If it were not for them, and if Her MAJESTY'S retirement were not brought home to us strongly *now*, when a Parliament is about to end and agitation to begin, we should say nothing about it. There are, indeed, other reasons for regret but none that we can think of which justifies the remonstrant tone in which some journalists have lately discussed the subject. What *would* justify such a tone is a state of things which does not exist. The Sovereign of England is not an autocrat, sold to cares and committed to responsibilities which must necessarily be neglected in the indulgence of personal sorrow. Her Ministers are able and honest; and, what is more—what is conclusive, in fact—the QUEEN is known never to neglect the real duties of her sovereignty. Their faithful performance goes on, and has always gone on; and while that is so, our concern that her grief also continues should cease with the sympathy of a loyal and home-loving people. Of such sympathy there cannot be too much. Taking it for a moment out of the region of mere human kindness where it were better left, we may go so far as to say there are sound political reasons why it should be encouraged; unless, indeed, the country has had enough of the great blessing which the QUEEN'S reign is said to have brought upon it ever since her rule began. We have all been lying under a mistake for twenty years if the nation has not been purified by an example of homely affection and of household faith in that place where example is so potent for good or evil—the palace. Some observers are of opinion, indeed, that a certain reaction against this beneficent influence has set in: be that as it may, we cannot think the reaction likely to be forwarded by the sincere and lasting sorrow of a wife for the loss of her husband; or by our respect for it.

There are some other considerations which have been almost as much forgotten as these. There is the fact that a monarch is still a human being; and that a people has no right to ask him to smile when his heart is ill at ease, or violate the most natural, most pious, most imperative instincts of his human nature in order to make a pageant. Again, our affection for the QUEEN, our deepest reverence for her, has grown out of the knowledge that she is not only a queen, but a good and most womanly woman: and yet how many people have considered that the very qualities they reverence in the woman have embittered the grief of the queen? We all understand what is meant by the "sacredness" of sorrow, and know that to turn our eyes upon one whose heart is deeply smitten, is to add to the pain a new and intolerable distress. This is so if you are happily unknown to all but a dozen people, whose gaze you easily can and do escape. But if you are a queen, then you cannot escape; your grief, which should be secret to be endurable, is known to all the world—talked of by all the world—gazed upon wherever you turn. And the more womanly you are, the more you are conscious of an observation which is scarcely the less painful for being sympathetic. Therefore we say Her MAJESTY'S seclusion is exactly what might have been expected of her position and her virtues; and that inasmuch as we respect them we must respect their natural consequences, nor forget that her retirement is the most natural one of all.

But this is not saying we wish the seclusion to continue. What we do say is, that with the fullest sense of what is due to Her MAJESTY, with the strongest inclination to take no part in the discussion of this subject, we cannot resist the suggestions of the ceremony of to-day. In brief, we cannot help speculating, not upon the regret or the disappointment of the nation at large on seeing another fair occasion for the QUEEN'S re-appearance amongst us pass by, but upon the satisfaction it may give that small, determined coterie of Americanized politicians who are so particularly active just now, and whom we shall behold still more active before another Parliament can be assembled. Who can doubt that they *do* find satisfaction in the QUEEN'S absence, once more, from the most important and significant of all State ceremonials? To be sure, they are not likely to acknowledge such sentiments. There are many bold speakers amongst them, and a carnival of declamation is fast approaching; but we do not suppose any demagogue so rash as to suggest the question yet awhile, that as the country gets on very well with a monarch in retirement (the Board of Trade returns will sufficiently prove it), why not abolish the monarchy altogether? We do not expect *him* to point out so soon that people may become so accustomed to the absence of a Sovereign from public business as to make them ready converts to Americanism and the democratic idea. But it is just because he is not likely to speak that we feel bound to speak for him—now, while the people are *not* quite accustomed to the QUEEN'S seclusion, and earnestly desire her back again. Perhaps the event of to-day was not the most fitting occasion for her return to public life; perhaps we may hope that when the new Parliament is called together, Her MAJESTY will come once more face to face with her people. If so, we shall all rejoice—all but those who are speculating hopefully now upon the probability that her seclusion may be confirmed by habit, and, who are perfectly prepared to turn it into a political argument.

Private letters from St. Petersburg and Moscow say that the example of the Moscow assembly, which has adopted by a very large majority an address in favour of a constitution, will be followed by the nobles of the other provinces of the empire. The proceedings at the Moscow assembly were published without being submitted to the consorship, and the printer of the journal in which they appeared is being prosecuted criminally.

The *Standard* published a letter yesterday from St. Petersburg, in which the writer, apparently an official, sets before the English public, with great complacency, the reasons current among Russian functionaries of all classes for discountenancing the courageous endeavours of the nobility to obtain the establishment of a representative assembly. Such an assembly would, of course, be a terror to the members of the public service, whose acts it could criticise, if it could not legally control them. This is just the good—perhaps the only good—that the Reichsrath has done in Austria. "But," say the functionaries and the democrats of the baser kind, "if a legislative body were to be formed by election "in the present day, only members of the aristocracy would be chosen, "for it is well known that they alone are capable of discussing political "questions. The merchants are careless about such matters, and the "peasants are steeped in the greatest ignorance." The functionaries, then, from fear of exposure, and the democrats from mere envy, would postpone the formation of political assemblies indefinitely, or what comes to the same thing, until the spread of education throughout the empire should raise the other classes to the level of the nobles! These views, in default of more plausible ones, have been adopted by the Russian Government, and we find them expressed with great earnestness in a paragraph which bears the following curious heading:—"The Moscow Nobility demanding a Constitution!"

How perverse on the part of the Russian nobility! So in ancient times the discontented Hebrews, in the sinfulness of their hearts, called out for a King! But the Hebrews *had* their King; whereas the Russian landed proprietors, with an autocrat, supported by a mass of bribe-taking officials on one side, and with hordes of newly-liberated serfs on the other, have no chance whatever of getting a constitution. A few of the leaders may have the privilege accorded to them of going to the East of Russia in their own carriages, and remaining there until further notice. The others will have to be silent; or they may have the same measure meted out to them which they were so glad to see meted out last year and the year before to the Poles.

The first number of the *Pall Mall Gazette*. An expostulation with the Queen and a letter from St. Petersburg.

eight pages, price twopence. As Mr. Stanley Morison says, 'it was deliberately set in the "old style" tradition of the early and not the late eighteenth century, which had not been seen in newspapers for sixty years', and was printed on a creamy paper, 'used only for books in Canning's days', Greenwood notes.

The aim of the *Pall Mall*—I must now shorten its title to what its staff and most of the public called it—was 'to give each afternoon, along with a careful epitome of the morning's news' from the morning papers (which, a quarter of a century later, I was myself to do for it)—'two or three such articles on political and social questions as had hitherto been rarely offered except in the *Saturday Review* and the *Spectator*'. And 'our news reports will be written in plain English'. 'By far the greater part of the paper', said the prospectus, 'will be made up of original articles upon many things which engage the thoughts or employ the energies or amuse the leisure of mankind. Public affairs, literature, the arts, and all the influences which strengthen or dissipate society will be discussed by men whose independence and authority are unquestionable, and who are accustomed to regard the public expression of opinion as a serious thing.'

But we by no means intend to make the Paper pedantic or solemn. Humour is too powerful, as well as pleasant, to be left out of the design; which will lose none of the advantages of occasionally trifling. If a thing can be said better in verse than in prose, it will be said in verse. Epigram, but not in spite—burlesque but not vulgarity—will be readily admitted into its columns; and since a joke is often as illustrative as argument, good jokes will be welcome too.

In an account of how the *Pall Mall* began, contributed by Greenwood to the 10,000th number (April 14, 1897), long after the paper had passed out of his control, he explains its political standpoint and notions of independence.

Look to the prospectus and it will be seen that the word 'politics'

Gazette (1792) and the *Sun* (1792). All of these lived well into the next century alongside the old *St. James's Chronicle* (1761–1866) and had among their contemporaries the *Globe* (1803).—*A Newspaper History* ('*The Times*').

The *Evening Standard* began in 1827 and the *Echo* in 1865. The *Evening News* and the *Star* date from 1881 and 1888.

does not occur in it, let alone the word 'party'. This was by no means because political affairs were excluded from the original plan of the paper, which indeed gave to their discussion the foremost place, the first page and the most inviting type. The omission is explained by a resolve (perhaps too prudishly observed) to hoist no political ticket, and by an opinion which every year's experience has confirmed: namely, that journalism cannot be true to its duty—which is to the public—and true to party obligation. Independence might have been explained of course. It is usual to do so, but whether sincere or otherwise, that is a pretension which even thirty years ago I read as common form. Therefore the readers of the new evening journal were left to discover that its politics would be from day to day whatever the public credit and the public advantage seemed to determine; without the least reference to Ins and Outs.

'Some things that we intended from the first were left unmentioned.' One was that,

at no price should the publisher accept scandalous advertisements that were commonly found at that time of day in journals the most respectable. Quacks made fortunes, money-lenders made victims, practitioners in actual crime furthered their trade through newspaper advertisements at (in some cases) special rates of payment! But all quacks are not rogues, and some money-lenders deal fairly enough, so that to distinguish among them is difficult: therefore the rule was made to exclude the advertisements of them all.

May I mention that, as a loyal son of the *Pall Mall*, I went even better when I started the *Countryman*. On our advertisement rates card we specified thirteen kinds of advertising we should not accept, and stuck to the rule![1]

'With a full commissariat of such good resolutions', Greenwood goes on, 'we set forth to produce our No. 1, and there it is, distinctly sampling a new "line" in daily journalism, but imperfect and disappointing as all first numbers seem fated to be. To travel over the widest difference between dream and reality,

[1] Yet, in a few years' time, in nine successive issues we printed—those were the days of unlimited paper—an average of 200 pages of advertisements per issue at good prices.—*Faith and Works in Fleet Street* (Hodder & Stoughton).

start a newspaper.' He once called it 'an ungrown, unshaped, ungroomed thing'.

The 'leader', by the editor, was a sober intimation to the Queen that her subjects were becoming impatient at her continued retirement since the death of the Prince Consort four years before.[1] Among the articles was a diverting 'Letter from Sir Pitt Crawley on Entering Parliament', by Sir Reginald Palgrave, Clerk to the House of Commons. Sir Arthur Helps—his 'gentle wisdom of words', Greenwood once said, 'had brought him into great consideration'—contributed one of his 'Friends in Council' (two and a half columns). A signed 'Letter on the American Question' was by Anthony Trollope, 'he who with the aspect of a wild boar, and with not infrequent resemblance to the manners of the same', Greenwood afterwards noted, 'wrote those charming drawing-room novels on gentlemen and ladies, clergymen and clergymen's wives'. Trollope was 'extraordinarily ambitious to figure as a politician, but a politician he was not born to be: he was born to write *Barchester Towers*'. On the American War, Trollope says in his autobiography, 'my feelings were very keen', on the Northern side.

There was also in a newspaper which was to have on its staff, under Stead's editorship, the first woman journalist to be given the work, hours, and pay of a man, and was to champion the women's cause in every sphere, a skit of the time called 'Ladies at Law' by John Ormsby, a *Saturday Review* humorist and student of Cervantes. The style of the *Anti-Jacobin* was followed even to the extent of reproducing two of its headlines, 'Lies' and 'Misrepresentations'.

[1] A few months later there was a paragraph in the *Pall Mall* on the private landing of Her Majesty at Woolwich. This was copied into *The Times* under an account of the landing of the Prince of Wales and headed 'A Contrast'. General Grey sent 'an explanation to *The Times*' but Delane wrote to Lord Granville that it would be consulting the Queen's dignity to omit it. Lord Granville sent the letter to General Grey who wrote in appreciative agreement with Delane, after consulting Her Majesty, and nothing appeared. On another occasion, the Queen had *The Times* informed that she disapproved of the tax on matches.

The *Pall Mall*'s famous 'Occasional Notes', which became such a distinguishing mark of the paper—they were known in the office in my time as 'Occ. Notes'—occupied one column only the first day. 'Then a novelty', they were 'by various hands, as always'. Stead describes them as being, at the beginning—they soon got livelier—'long and cumbrous, and sometimes only a leading article cut into two'. Which reminds one of Greenwood's remark to a later contributor, Mrs. Drummond, on leader-writing: 'You understand writing occasional notes? Well, if you are entrusted with a leader, just string together six of these notes of average length on one subject, and there is your article.' Greenwood said that

> nothing served the popularity of the paper better than its Notes, of which two to four columns a day were printed after a while. They were no less attractive to writers than to readers, every variety of matter being admitted, from a joke of Lever's to a touch of science from Jermyn Street. 'Jacob Omnium' wrote little else. The work exactly suited his piquant, pungent humour. He was unrivalled, and he took such pains that after sending in two or three finished bits, ten or twelve lines long, he would come down to the office and spend half an hour in reducing them (in proof) to eight or ten. Lord Strangford,[1] a priceless contributor of laughing criticism and Eastern knowledge, wrote many notes; but a man who did much, and all best, in a style that has been hacked and hacked until it sickens us, was Mr. Maurice Drummond,[2] a true 'original' in mind and character. The *Pall Mall* owed a great deal to Maurice Drummond who, however, was not among its first year's contributors.

Besides the 'Occ. Notes' there were sound reviews and 'middles' of quality.

The printer was Richard Lambert, who served until 1889, when he was succeeded by the efficient and somewhat irascible Thomas Hunt, who, at times, when overburdened with 'copy' would, as I remember, rush downstairs to us with a handful and desperate expostulations. He was clever in making blocks—it was the early days of newspaper illustration—with bent brass rules and plaster of Paris. The paper was 'printed and published

[1] 1826–69. Linguist and diplomatist. See page 152. [2] See p. 162.

by F. K. Sharpe for the proprietors at 14 Salisbury Street, Strand'.

Greenwood speaks of 'beautifully orange-coloured posters—themselves surpassing everything of the kind theretofore seen—making bold advertisement all over the town. There are orange-coloured posters now; but to liken their originals to them is to compare Mr. Liberty in his own muslins to Mr. Colman in his own mustard.'

The proprietor was not at all pleased with the first number. The paper had, he said, 'anything but a brilliant' start. 'We had printed, under strict conditions of time', a sample number, but, in spite of the rehearsal, the first number appeared 'three hours too late and in a very imperfect condition. The reception was of the most chilly quality. Of the first number—as to which there was naturally some curiosity—exactly 3,897 copies were sold.'

Nor did the first number satisfy George Smith's partner, H. S. King. He wrote to say that its support of the Liberal Government placed him in a somewhat false position, for he had always belonged to the opposite party. His wife was a Miss Hamilton, a niece of the Duke of Abercorn and of Lord Aberdeen, both of the Conservative party. King hoped, for his partner's sake, that the paper would be a complete success, but he must relinquish any interest he had in it.

This incident, Smith says, 'promised to help me out of one difficulty. Mr. Greenwood had intimated to me that he expected to have a proprietorial interest of some sort in the paper, but I had had to tell him that it was not possible to propose anything of the kind to King. When, however, King wrote to me in the terms mentioned I thought I could do something to meet Mr. Greenwood's wish and wrote him the following letter——' Alas, this communication has not survived. When the editorship came to an end, and there were difficulties between editor and proprietor, Greenwood made a statement on their business relations which the letter would probably have cleared up.

During the first few days Sir James Kay-Shuttleworth called on Smith one day to tell him that in starting an evening paper he had 'taken leave of his peace of mind for the rest of his life'. Sir Charles Jackson implored him to have courage and give up at once. 'It will soon be forgotten', he said soothingly, 'but if you go on you will land yourself in very serious loss.' A fellow publisher, Longman, inquired sympathetically if he had ever sold 500 copies. 'Yes,' replied Smith, 'we have.' The only encouragement the proprietor of the paper had, he declared, was at home. 'I would rather pawn my jewels', his wife said, 'than see the paper discontinued.'

The *Courier* at threepence and the *Globe* at fivepence had but a microscopic circulation. The *Pall Mall*, as Smith contended, was the forerunner of the cheap evening press. From twopence the *Pall Mall* came down to a penny. 'We had to create the appetite for a good evening paper. I used to be told that a newspaper was all very well for the morning, but nobody wanted any high class reading after dinner. I venture to think we deserved success. We always gave good matter, the very best we could get. The idea of the paper was new, with its note of independence and courage. Our articles were excellent in a literary sense, and a certain wholesome atmosphere of independence about them was unusual up to that period. The men who wrote the articles were of high character and of independent position as well as of special knowledge. The quality of the writing soon came to be recognised.' There was to come a stage in the paper's history at which Smith believed that it 'had a greater influence on public opinion than any other paper save *The Times*'.

In the second number the editor gave himself enough room for his leading article, for it was two columns and a turn. The pessimism, in the 'Occ. Notes', about the Suez Canal is amusing in the light of Greenwood's future relations with the enterprise.

The announcement that communication has been opened between the Red Sea and the Mediterranean by means of the Suez Canal takes us rather by surprise.

A steamer towing a barge barely accomplished the distance between the two seas in twenty-four hours. How can such means of communication compete with the existing railway—goods and passenger can be transported from Suez to Alexandria in a quarter of the time, and at a much lower rate? The steamers of the P & O and Messageries Impériales Companies more than suffice at the present for the goods which will bear steam freight between India and Europe. Twenty times their collective tonnage would scarcely defray the expenses of maintaining the Canal.

What is the result in the Canal of the tideless Mediterranean mingling its waters with the ebb and flow in the Red Sea?

Then there is the security of the harbour in the Mediterranean extremity of the Canal to be enquired into, and the facility of reaching it in stormy winter months.

The general impression of sufficiently informed men so far is decidedly unfavourable. These considerations practical men, we feel persuaded, will carefully consider.

Lord Beveridge, in his *India Called Them*, speaks of his mother going through the Canal three years after it was opened, and the fee paid by the steamer being £785.

Stead, quoting Captain Shandon's phrase, 'The field preacher has his journal, the radical freethinker his journal: why should the Gentlemen of England be unrepresented in the Press?' pointed out four coincidences. The first was that the *Pall Mall* was, 'in turn'—under Greenwood, John Morley, and himself—'the organ of all three, Gentlemen, Radical Free Thinkers, and Field Preachers'. The second was that, when the first number came out, there was a sharp comment on the newcomer in the *Morning Star*, on which John Morley, who was to succeed to the editorship of the *Pall Mall*, was serving his journalistic apprenticeship. The comment, Stead thinks, 'might have been written by Morley, so entirely do the sentiments and even the phraseology accord with his:

Journalism has also received an accession in the *Pall Mall*, an evening paper professing to be conducted by scholars and gentlemen *par excellence*. We are ready to concede that its articles are generally written with polish and vigour, sometimes with eloquence, but they are unhappily too much pervaded by that sneering snobbism, of which the *Saturday Review* is the recognised type. However this tone of twopenny blood and culture, as it has been aptly called, may conciliate the prejudices of a class, it is not the way to permanent success. The moral dignity of a high purpose outweighs all the polished sneers and patronising superciliousness of your *soi-disant* gentlemen and scholars.

The third coincidence was that, when the *Morning Star* stopped publication, a member of its staff became the first editor of the *Northern Echo*, and a contributor of his and his successor was Stead, who was to be the successor of Morley on the *Pall Mall*. Finally, a compositor who shared in the setting of the first number of the *Pall Mall* had set up the type of some of the books of Ruskin, a conspicuous disciple of whom was E. T. Cook, 'a man', wrote the Brantwood sage, 'who knows more about my works than I do myself'. Cook not only edited (with Wedderburn) the thirty-nine volumes of Ruskin's works, but became, after Stead, editor of the *Pall Mall*. I might add a fifth coincidence that, although Greenwood and Stead were so unlike one another, they had both an interest in what Stead called 'spooks', and were both particularly fond of children.[1]

George Saintsbury speaks of 'the elevation' of the *Pall Mall*. In *The Tradition Established*, the second volume of 'The History of *The Times*', it is stated that the *Pall Mall* appealed to 'those who disliked the vulgarity, as they considered it, of the *Daily Telegraph* and the stiffness of the *Standard*'. They had in the new paper 'a journal conducted with great political and literary ability and written throughout in a light, easy-going modern style'. G. W. E. Russell quotes a rhyme, 'Agreeable Rattle':

> This news from abroad is alarming;
> You've seen the *Pall Mall* of today?
> Oh! Ilma di Murska was charming
> Tonight in the Flauto, they say.
> Not the ghost of a chance for the Tories,
> In spite of Adullam and Lowe:
> By the bye, have you heard the queer stories
> Of Overend, Gurney and Co.?[2]

[1] See pages 335 and 193, 407.

[2] The banking firm the failure of which had such disastrous repercussions. *Sands of Time* (Hutchinson).

'Even in the nineties', the author of *Moberly Bell and his Times*[1] says, 'it was an unwritten law that no concession should be allowed to human emotions; men were supposed to be absorbed in politics, law and foreign affairs, money, stocks and shares. Women, if they were considered at all, were taken to have the sombre interests of their menfolk.' 'Look back', says Mr. Hamilton Fyfe in his *Press Parade*,[2] 'at a morning journal of fifty years ago. The leaders fill a page. Reports of political speeches run to four, five, even six columns. There are two or three pages of Parliament. I remember *The Times* printing day by day, for years, despatches about the *Ausgleich* between Austria and Hungary.'

Abuse of the *Pall Mall* by Edmund Yates—'Edmund Yates with two or three chins', says E. V. Lucas—was of the type that makes it easy to understand how, before long, that *flâneur*, first of the *Morning Star*, and then of the *World*,[3] was turned out of the Garrick Club and afterwards landed himself in jail for criminal libel.

> If rumour may be credited [Yates wrote] the paper was established for the acquisition of increased social status, and a seat in Parliament for the distinguished proprietor. Of course the editor is a scholar and a gentleman, a man of blood and culture, and so no doubt in such an undertaking is the printer. No, sir, blood and culture and twopenny gentility is all very well, but they will have to come down to the honest British liner, who tells the public about the young person of prepossessing exterior, etc.[4]

[1] Richards. [2] Watts.

[3] The *World* was started, on a small sum, by Yates in partnership with Grenville Murray 'one of the most brilliant and most unscrupulous journalists of the Victorian era', and was soon a highly profitable property. Yates was a telling after-dinner speaker and is described as running Chauncey Depew close.

[4] THACKERAY, GEORGE SMITH, AND SCREENS. Yates had previously made an attack on *Cornhill* (in the *New York Times*, May 26, 1860) in which his disposition is fully illustrated. 'The success of the *Cornhill* magazine is already on the wane; went up like a rocket and beginning to come down like a stick; its first number sold nearly 100,000, its second reached 70,000, and now 4,000 is about the mark. There have been already four tremendously heavy dinner parties given by Smith. Thackeray is great fun, and comes out with the greatest geniality, speaking of G. H. Lewes as "The Bede." Smith is a very good

The fact is, as his daughter assures me, that George Smith had at no time any inclination towards the House of Commons.

man of business, but totally unread; his business has been to sell books, not to read them, and he knows little else. Thackeray remarked, "This is a splendid dinner, such as Cave, the bookseller at St. John's Gate, gave to his principal writers when Dr. Johnson's coat was so shabby that he ate his meal behind the screen." Then calling out to his host, Thackeray said "Mr. Smith, I hope you've not got Johnson there behind the screen?" "Eh!" said the astonished bibliopole, "Behind the screen? Johnson? God bless my soul, my dear Mr. Thackeray, there's no person of the name of Johnson here, nor anyone behind the screen. What on earth do you mean?" ' Yates also mentioned that the paper, 'Little Scholars', in the current *Cornhill* was by Thackeray's eldest daughter—'her first attempt at literary composition but touched up by the parental hand'. Thackeray's scathing and categorical reply to Yates I turned up in *Cornhill*. It is headed, 'On Screens in Dining Rooms'. According to my information, Smith took the matter lightly. In the manuscript of Trollope's *Autobiography* a cancelled passage throws some light on Yates's story. A page and a half, vigorously crossed and scrabbled through, reads: 'I do not know whether I did not put an end to these dinners by an indiscretion of my own. It was, I think, at the first of them that Thackeray, sitting opposite to his host, asked whether Dr. Johnson was getting his dinner behind the screen. The old story is too well known to require any further telling here. Our munificent publisher being engaged with his neighbour did not hear the question, and Thackeray, naturally anxious for his little joke, repeated it. Whereupon Mr. Smith, who was still very eager with the friend at his elbow, replied across the table that he did not think there was anybody of the name of Johnson in the room. There was not much fun it it, but, what there was, consisted in Thackeray's vain attempts to have his allusion recognized. On the next morning I unfortunately told the story to a friend—but I told it also in the presence of a man to whom nothing could be told quite safely. He was, though I did not know it then, a literary gutter-scraper—one who picked up odds and ends of scandal from chance sources, and turning them with a spice of malice into false records, made his money of them among such newspapers as would pay him. This story, altogether be-devilled and twisted from the truth—crammed with bitterness, both against Thackeray and Smith, loaded with poison—was sent to an American newspaper. That alone would not have mattered much because American newspapers are not much read in this country. But the *Saturday*—which everybody reads, or at least everybody then read—got hold by chance of the American paper, and, *more suo*, tore everybody concerned to pieces. Why were such dinners given? Why were such stories told? Was it creditable to anybody that the conversation of a private table in London should be made gossip to satisfy the evil cravings of New York readers? This article afflicted Thackeray much. It annoyed Mr. Smith greatly. I taxed the gutter-scraper with his offence, and he owned his sin, praying to be forgiven. I confessed my fault to the others;—for it was a fault to have told anything in the presence of such a man. I was pardoned, but there were no more *Cornhill* dinners.'

With regard to Greenwood, the former printer's reader certainly did not accord with Yates's conception of 'a man of blood'. As to Smith's character, it is illustrative of his scrupulousness that he would not have any Smith & Elder books reviewed in the *Pall Mall*. 'The one exception to this rule of honour', says Leonard Huxley, 'was when, as a matter of loyalty, Sir Theodore Martin's *Life of the Prince Consort* was noticed', and Sir Theodore, who we have seen was a friend of Smith's, 'was not at all pleased by the independence of the review'. Yates had also some doggerel about 'George Smithins', 'Shadowy Elder, who never yet was seen, and Margaret Denzil of the *Cornhill Magazine*'.

If the paper had a circulation manager he must have been a poor stick, for within six weeks of the start the sale had dropped to 613 copies. The advertising manager, if there was one, must have been no better, for in March, the month following that in which the paper had appeared, the receipts averaged £3. 4*s*. 10*d*. a day, and from this amount commission had to be deducted. The ups and downs in the proprietor's mind are seen in the following extract from his diary:

March 6. I am beginning to fear the *P.M.G.* cannot succeed.
March 22. Very low about *P.M.G.* which does not look like success.
March 23. Out of spirits about *P.M.G.*
April 17. Paper looking up a little and I am in better spirits.
May 11. Two extracts from *P.M.G.* in *Times*; this gives me some hope.
August 5. *P.M.G.* published 6 months; sale 1,400 to 1,500. Hopeful of success before this time next year.
October 7. *P.M.G.* published 8 months; sale over 2,000 and increasing regularly. Very hopeful—almost confident—of success.

One day in December, when the paper had reached the age of ten months, and there was 'an accidental influx of advertisements', 'a small profit' was recorded.

It was when the *Pall Mall* was a little more than a year old that John Morley—one day to edit it—wrote in a review that

Swinburne's *Poems and Ballads* was 'full of mad and miserable indecency'. There were passages in the 'unmanly book which bring before the mind the image of one who has got maudlin drunk on lewd ideas and lascivious thoughts'. A 'libidinous laureate' had 'a mind aflame with the feverish carnality of a schoolboy'.[1]

A member of the staff from the beginning was James Hannay (1827–73) of the *Edinburgh Courant*, who had written for the *Illustrated Times* and *Cornhill*.[2] Few of us have read his *Singleton Fontenoy* and *Eustace Conyers*, but they have been called 'the two best nautical novels since Marryat'. Escott[3] writes of him that he stood by Greenwood for years—as 'the English Pierre Loti' who 'had not a little of the French writer's grace and skill in reproducing the colour and scenery which as a sailor he had observed'. Moreover, 'he combined with a style at once graceful and terse, wide historical as well as literary scholarship, and a fresh, breezy humour which gave all his work a distinction of its own'. James Hannay's son, David, who succeeded him on the *Pall Mall*, was also to be on the *St. James's Gazette*. Mr. Eric Parker has spoken to me of the pungency of David's writing and of his passion for short words—'I remember him telling me once that he was always pleased, when his proof came down, if he could find a whole line made of words of one syllable.' Greenwood said to Escott that 'Hannay's articles were those of whose immediate effect on the public he seldom failed to find some definite proof', but it is not quite clear whether he is speaking of father or son. In that excellent book, *Memory Looks Forward*,[4] Mr. Parker tells a story which David Hannay related to him of his father. Hannay senior was sitting with friends in a tavern when a stranger introduced himself with the excuse that he had gathered from the conversation of the company that they were literary gentlemen, and that he was a descendant of Addison. Hannay surveyed him

[1] The book was withdrawn from circulation, but was reissued by another publisher.

[2] His father was David Hannay, a man of letters of 1794–1864.

[3] *Masters of Journalism* (Unwin).

[4] Seeley.

and spoke: 'Sir, since the only descendant of Addison was a daughter, who died before the age of puberty in a lunatic asylum, my respect for facts compels me to address you as a bloody liar.'

An early member of the office staff was J. Hamilton Fyfe, father of Mr. Hamilton Fyfe, the well-known journalist and author, who kindly tells me that Fyfe senior was born at J. M. Barrie's Kirriemuir ('Thrums') and was a weaver there before he became a journalist, that he worked in Edinburgh, and ultimately became a reporter on *The Times*.[1] Hamilton Fyfe of the *Pall Mall*, who is described to me as 'bearded and bookish', combined his work there with assistant editing at the *Saturday Review*, and wrote *Triumphs of Invention and Discovery*. The post he occupied on the *Pall Mall* seems to have been that of assistant editor. He left 'somewhere about 1870'. F. W. Joynes was chief sub-editor from the start till 1880.

In the second year of the paper Professor Tyndall sent in a report of Carlyle's moving inaugural address as rector of Edinburgh university, and in 1867 Carlyle wrote correcting, as 'altogether erroneous, misfounded, superfluous and even absurd', something that Ruskin had written about the people of Chelsea.

[1] 'So when I joined the staff, I was the third generation to serve it.' *My Seven Selves*, Hamilton Fyfe (Allen & Unwin).

CHAPTER XV

Some Famous Contributors

LESLIE AND FITZJAMES STEPHEN — MATTHEW ARNOLD — TROLLOPE — LAURENCE OLIPHANT — MEREDITH — RUSKIN — THE DRUMMONDS — THE 'MIDDLE' — 'WITH PRAYERS AND TEARS'

No editor adventuring with a newspaper has had a more distinguished band of faithful contributors than Greenwood.

With the second number [he writes] Fitzjames Stephen began the long fast-following series of articles which were a delight to him to write and to us no small credit to print. No journalist that I have known took so much pleasure in his work or brought more conscience to it or more eagerness and endeavour. Leading articles were the main of his contributions and he also wrote in what we call the literary columns of the paper.

Leslie Stephen was in the second number, and G. H. Lewes. [Lewes is said to have had £300 for 'general assistance' during the first year.] Philosophers say that Lewes was no philosopher, and the more philosophers they are the more they say so. He is no longer here to suffer under what he felt as scholastic ostracism and described as scholastic ignorance, and if he were here he would not be consoled by what I am going to say, which is that, as a writer for such journals as the *Leader* or our *Pall Mall*, he could not be easily matched, so versatile was he, so lucid, so sparkling and adept. Lewes wrote dramatic criticism that lasts and is quoted still, and in the *Pall Mall* he offered the first thoroughly appreciative and adequate welcome to Darwin's *Origin of Species* that appeared in print; as Darwin always remembered.

Before the end of the month to these writers were added Mr. Richard Holt Hutton and Mr. Meredith Townsend, also of the *Spectator*, Charles Lever, John Kaye[1] and Mr. John Addington Symonds, Mr. Dallas[2] and Mr. Higgins, better known and well-

[1] Author of military history and geography and of 'Essays of an Optimist' in *Cornhill*.

[2] E. S. Dallas, 1828–79 of *The Times* and *Saturday Review*. 'Few men wrote more careful, graceful English.'—*Dictionary of National Biography*.

known to the world as 'Jacob Omnium'. The pages of the paper were further graced and strengthened by contributions by George Eliot, Miss Thackeray, Theodore Martin and Mr. C. D. Yonge.[1] Trollope contributed some admirable hunting sketches and some imitations of Captain Sterling's political thunder (once so telling in *The Times*).[2] Mr. George Goschen[3] and Mr. Thomas Hughes[4] came into our leader pages early in the first year, Matthew Arnold began to write before the end of it, and, sooner or later in the same year John Tyndall, Lord Houghton, and Robert Giffen,[5] who was for a long time our best of City Editors.

Just before the *Pall Mall* appeared 'Jacob Omnium' had quarrelled with *The Times*, had a lively correspondence with the proprietor, and had reprinted it in a pamphlet in an edition of four copies. One was sent to Walter and another to George Smith. Higgins threw himself into the *Pall Mall* work with great earnestness, coming to the office every morning. 'He could write', in Smith's opinion, 'the best Occasional Notes that have ever appeared in a newspaper.' A note of his dwelt pointedly on the extraordinary number of memorials to Prince Albert in England. They supplied, he gravely urged, a new justification for country jaunts. The tourist, instead of confining himself to cathedrals and objects of interest of that kind, was now beckoned in every direction. A curious thing is that this particular note brought a message to Smith through Sir Arthur Helps, saying how pleased Her Majesty was with it, a surprising incident for which only Mr. Laurence Housman is likely to be able to account.

Once a wine merchant sent a hamper to the *Pall Mall*, hoping no doubt to get a puff. Smith happened to be in the office and

[1] Charles Duke Yonge, philologist and author.

[2] Edward Sterling, the Thunderer of *The Times*.—*Harriet Martineau*. See also account of Sterling and portrait in ' "The Thunderer" in the Making' in *The History of 'The Times.'*

[3] G. J. Goschen, afterwards Viscount Goschen, who became Chancellor of the Exchequer when Lord Randolph Churchill 'forgot Goschen'. There is no reference in A. D. Elliott's *Life of Lord Goschen* to this association with the *Pall Mall.*

[4] Of *Tom Brown's Schooldays.*

[5] Afterwards Sir Robert Giffen, the economist.

told the messenger to take it back. Higgins thought copy might as well be got out of the incident. 'The editors and contributors of the *Pall Mall*, possessing the finest cellar in London', he wrote, 'were not accustomed to drink wines of this class, but, in order to do justice to the contents of the hamper, their effect had been tried on printers' devils. Sample 1 was administered to the first printer's devil with the result that he immediately fell asleep. Sample 2 was of a more stimulating quality, for the second printer's devil, after he had drunk two glasses, insisted on having his wages raised. Sample 3 was tried on the smallest printer's devil. After a single glass he offered to fight the biggest compositor. Sample 4 was tried on the remaining printer's devil and its effects were so startling that we must positively decline to describe them.'

Higgins, when suffering from a rheumatic attack, was directed by his doctor to put soda in his bath, and discovered that the grocer was charging twice the ordinary rate. This led him to compare the prices he paid for his household supplies in general with the prices charged by the Civil Service Stores and to give the respective figures in the *Pall Mall*—as I have said, the advertising manager does not seem to have been alert. The result was greatly to advertise the Stores, then in a little corner house in St. Alban's Place.

As to Higgins's great height, the tall Thackeray had a story, which he may have invented, that, when he once went with him to a fair and wished to see the giant, the man at the door of the tent refused their money with the remark that they never charged the profession. It was true that, in order to save Higgins from knocking his hat at the *Pall Mall* office in Salisbury Street, the proprietor had a special archway cut over the staircase. Higgins was a man of fortune and lived in a fine house in Eaton Square 'at which he entertained his friends nobly'. He died from a chill caught when driving home after having bathed with his son in the river near Petersham. Mrs. Higgins was a relative of the Tichborne family and her husband wrote an article in the *Pall Mall* about the famous case. It was regarded as contempt of court, and cost the paper a hundred guineas. A leading article by Higgins ridiculed Charles Villiers, father of the House of Commons. Later Higgins described to Smith how he had met him at Lady Molesworth's. 'He asked me to walk across the square and smoke a cigar with him. He talked of nothing but the article without knowing it was mine. It has gone in deep.' A few evenings later Smith sat opposite Villiers at dinner. 'He said to my neighbour but obviously, I thought, for my information, "I got hold of old Higgins the other day and persuaded him to walk part way home with me and I *did* go at him about his article. It was such fun to see him writhe." ' Thus is history written.

At one time Smith saw much of a brilliant man of varied experiences, Laurence Oliphant,[1] a contributor to both *Cornhill* and the *Pall Mall*. 'The charm exerted by his face and voice, and especially by the frankness and beauty of his eyes—the most sincere eyes that ever looked out of a human head—amounted to nothing less than fascination.' When Smith had his office in Pall Mall he used to see him call every morning on the Prince of Wales, for whom he absorbed the news of the day from the various journals and then 'translated it into the terms of vivid conversation'. This duty discharged, Oliphant came to Smith. He was often useful to the *Pall Mall* in other ways than as a writer. 'He knew everybody and could name the right man to write on particular topics.' His sixpenny weekly, the *Owl*, an aristocrat among journals, 'fluttered through a brief but brilliant existence'. It was printed on superfine paper and was published during the season only. It was believed to have access to 'special sources of information in very high quarters. No engagement prevented Oliphant from taking his sweet-faced, distinguished-looking mother for a morning walk in the Park.' After his dealings with the American prophet, Harris, Smith encountered him during a short visit to England. 'He was as genial and friendly as ever, but his face was haggard and scribbled over with the hieroglyphics of worry.'

[1] Traveller, correspondent of *The Times*, official, M.P., author of *Altiora Peto*, *Piccadilly*, and *Episodes in a Life of Adventure*.

The proprietor of the *Pall Mall* enjoyed a close friendship with Lord Strangford, who wrote a good deal for the paper. Said to have been the original of Coningsby, he was 'curiously wanting in outward personal attractions but had grace of manner and charm of talk, and could clothe his knowledge—he had seen much of the world and knew everybody—in the most fascinating shape'. His literary style was severe and in reviewing in the *Pall Mall* a book by a Miss Beaufort he expressed his disapproval plainly and forcibly. 'The lady wrote a piteous letter to the editor, who handed it to Lord Strangford. He was rather touched by it and said, with a kind of rash courage, that he would call on Miss Beaufort. He did so, and she became in due course Lady Strangford.' Lord Strangford had a particular acquaintance with the Danubian principalities, and, during his association with the paper, the *Daily Telegraph* was afflicted with a correspondent in the Balkans for whose work he had a special scorn. 'The fun he extracted from him was the joy of the town.'

Friendship's Garland by Matthew Arnold appeared from 1866 to 1870. 'For anything better of its kind we must go to Voltaire', writes Herbert Paul in his *Life*; 'plenty of salt in his wit and not much pepper. Sala, one of Arnold's favourite butts, regarded his tormentor with friendly and respectful admiration.' It was in one of Arnold's articles that the phrase occurs, 'The magnificent roaring of the young lions of the *Daily Telegraph*.' Smith described *Friendship's Garland*—someone has spoken of its 'deadly banter'—as 'a curious production made up of gay and witty gossip about everybody, with pen pictures drawn in slightly satiric ink of well-known people'.[1] Of Frederic Harrison, for example, Arnold wrote that 'he always looked as if his coat had come home from the tailor the day before and as if the rest of his dress had just been taken out of a bandbox'. When Smith pointed out that 'though this description was perfectly accurate it was hardly worthy of his pen', Arnold replied, 'Good heavens, you don't mean to say he is like that. I have

[1] Herbert Paul speaks of it in his biography as 'the most amusing book he ever wrote'.

never seen him.'[1] It turned out that Arnold, with the most disconcerting success, had deduced Harrison's appearance from his style. 'Curiously, Arnold had no sense of music. And yet an ear for cadence and harmony is a necessary part of a poet's equipment. One of his children was an exceedingly clever musician. Arnold could hardly be called a handsome man, but he was a man of fine and impressive appearance. He was over six feet high, very upright, with a striking well-set head, crowned with abundant hair in which, to the last, no grey was visible. He liked, and, with that naïve and charming vanity of his, confessed that he liked, to be thought younger than he was. He was delighted to the point of absurdity by a lady telling Mrs. Arnold that she had seen "her and her son" at a certain church. Mr. Watts in the National Portrait Gallery portrait gives far too rugged a look to Arnold's face.'

'But of course', as Greenwood says, 'the paper was not "made" in the first year, nor in the second; and some writers who came in the third, the fourth and the fifth are to be thanked as much as any.'

The elder Herman Merivale,[2] as belonging to the earlier of these—a writer of admirable leading articles, and wiser than half the men who sit in Cabinet Councils; and Sir Henry Bulwer,[3] and Mr. John Morley, and Mr. Meredith and Mr. Huxley, and Sir George Grove, and Reade and Winwood Reade,[4] and Laurence Oliphant, and Sir George Chesney, and Sir Frederick Pollock,[5] and (among foreigners)

[1] As this is neither in the *Pall Mall Gazette* nor in the book it may be that Smith prevented it getting into type. Perhaps it was cut down to this (*P.M.G.*, April 22, 1867): 'Sir, I tell you confidentially that I saw the other day with my own eyes that powerful young publicist, Mr. Frederic Harrison, in full evening costume, furbishing up a guillotine.'

[2] 1806–74. 'As a boy', says the *Dictionary of National Biography*, 'of extraordinary precocity.' Professor of political economy at Oxford, assistant under-secretary for the Colonies, and called by the first Lord Lytton 'one of the most extraordinary men I ever met', 'of no less calibre than Macaulay' and of 'great promptitude of judgement'. Wrote a great deal in the *Edinburgh Review* and regularly in the *Pall Mall*.

[3] Colonial Governor.

[4] Charles Reade, author of *It is Never Too Late to Mend*, and Winwood Reade, author of *The Martyrdom of Man*.

[5] Author of *Legal Cases done into English*.

Barthélemy St. Hilaire—they and a score of such; and when they were reckoned, either injustice would be done of omitting the names of other most competent and serviceable writers, or else there would be an additional list no more intelligible to the public than if all made up of Mr. Joneses and Mr. Browns. So no more, except to say that the loss of Fitzjames Stephen when he went to India in 1867 as legislative member of the Council, was followed by the accession of Sir Henry Maine, who was a frequent contributor to the paper till the Radical flag was hoisted upon it in 1880.

This is a moderate reference to Maine, who 'used to write two or three leaders a week at special rates of pay'. He was once described by his editor as one of two men he had known who wrote as well from the first as they ever wrote afterwards. It is curious that in the *Life and Speeches of Sir Henry Maine*, which has an eighty-two page memoir, there is no mention either of the *Pall Mall* or of Greenwood. *Cornhill* and the *St. James's Gazette* are referred to once.

I asked Mr. Bernard Shaw whether as a young man he contributed to the *Pall Mall.* He wrote to me: 'When I finished my first novel—this was in 1879—and offered it to Macmillan's, John Morley was reading for them; and he was sufficiently struck with it to give me a recommendation. H. M. Hyndman did the same; but nothing came of it; I was too young and raw to be possible.' Shaw's historiographer, Mr. F. E. Lowenstein, was good enough to inform me that Shaw 'submitted a paper on "Open Air Meetings", on which he was certainly an authority, but it was declined'. Hesketh Pearson, in his life of Shaw, asserts that he was 'turned down as a book-reviewer because the editor, to whom Hyndman had recommended Shaw as "another Heine", was horrified by the indifference to the death of his wife displayed by a character in one of Shaw's novels'. It will be remembered in what a courageous way Shaw expressed himself when he suffered the heavy loss of his own kind and able wife. Years after his rebuff by Greenwood he reviewed for the *Pall Mall* under Stead.

I may add, higgledy-piggledy, a few more names of contributors—some writers got to work in later years: Palgrave of *The Golden Treasury*, Coventry Patmore (his biographer speaks of his regarding the paper as 'the only fit one for a gentleman'), Alice Meynell (of whom we have biographies by Esther and Viola), Drummond Wolff of the Fourth Party, Spencer Walpole (author of the six-volume *History of England* from Waterloo to four years before the foundation of the *Pall Mall*), Frederic Harrison (the Positivist), Ruskin, Sidney (later Sir Sidney) Colvin (who speaks of Greenwood's 'fighting editorship'[1]), and H. D. Traill (author of the six-volume *Social England*[2]), with whom, when he was editor of the *Observer*, I served for a few Saturday nights. After a week's work at the *Pall Mall* I soon found it too much of a strain. In 1868 Meredith said he was writing 'almost every week', and *Beauchamp's Career* was given two columns by Traill.

Ruskin contributed many letters in 1865, and wrote in a footnote to *Sesame and Lilies*: 'I am heartily glad to see such a paper as the *Pall Mall* established, for the power of the press in the hands of highly educated men, in independent positions, and of honest purpose, may indeed become all that it has been hitherto vaunted to be.' In 1871, however, he found the paper 'a mere party paper like the rest, but', he added, 'it writes well, and does more good than mischief on the whole'.

Many of the most important odes in Coventry Patmore's *Unknown Eros* first appeared, over the initials C.P., in the *Pall Mall*. In 1876 'The Toys' got some attention. Greenwood was one of the few of Patmore's friends who were allowed to see the prose work, *Sponsa Dei*, before it was destroyed on his advice, in support of that already given by Gerard Hopkins. The poet's relations with Greenwood are described in Derek Patmore's *Life and Times of Coventry Patmore*.

To the work of Leslie and Fitzjames Stephen in the *Pall Mall* some special attention may well be paid. It was Leslie to whom

[1] See also *The Colvins and their Friends*, E. V. Lucas (Methuen).

[2] A 'Record of the Progress of the People in Religion, Laws, Learning, Arts, Industry, Commerce, Literature, Manners, etc. to 1885'.

Greenwood referred when he spoke of 'the sensation of the editor when he broke open an envelope and caught a glimpse of his neat, small handwriting'. Among his contributions were letters from Cambridge signed 'A Don'. In 1869 Stephen said that though he contributed to the *Pall Mall* he disapproved of its 'whole politics'. He writes to George Smith about some articles: 'I signed my name expressly because I want my friends to understand that I utterly disagree with my brother. Of course if I had any personal quarrel with my brother I should not write to the papers about it; but on certain political matters I not only disapprove of his views but should be glad that my disapproval should be known to the few people who care about it one way or another.' Stephen was the original of Meredith's 'Vernon Whitford', and when Greenwood wrote an obituary notice of him he quoted a phrase of Meredith's 'Phoebus Apollo turned fasting friar'.

Fitzjames Stephen was one of the most vigorous intellects of his time; to Thackeray's daughter Anne, when she wrote to him, he was 'Dearest Fitzy'. We have a vivid portrayal of this remarkable man, whose career as a judge came to a tragic end in mental failure—in a photograph in *Paradise in Piccadilly*[1] there is a wild look in the eyes—in the *Life* by his brother,[2] and from various chapters it is possible to realize his outstanding service to the paper. He had been an early writer of 'middles' in the *Saturday Review*, and had begun to contribute to *Cornhill* in 1860. As a 'regular' he ceased in 1864, but told George Smith that when the *Pall Mall* got started he would be glad to write upon 'matters of a more serious kind'. The 'middle' 'he considered to be the speciality of himself and his friend Sandars'.[3]

> The 'middle', originally an article upon some not strictly political topic, [writes Leslie] had grown in their hands into a kind of lay sermon. For such literature the British public has shown a considerable avidity ever since the days of Addison. In spite of occasional

[1] By Harry Furniss (John Lane).

[2] *Life of Sir James Fitzjames Stephen*, Leslie Stephen (Murray).

[3] T. C. Sandars (1825–94), well known for his *Justinian*.

disavowals, it really loves a sermon, and is glad to hear preachers who are not bound by the proprieties of the religious pulpit. At this period the most popular of the lay preachers was probably Sir Arthur Helps, who provided the kind of material—genuine thought set forth with real literary skill and combined with much popular sentiment—which served to convince his readers that they were intelligent people. The '*Saturday Reveiw*-ers' in their quality of 'cynics', could not go so far in the direction of the popular taste; and their bent was rather to expose than to endorse some of the commonplaces which are dear to the intelligent reader.

I notice that articles for the centre of the paper in the *Spectator* still bear on the galley proofs the catchline 'Middle'.

With a fellow contributor to the *Pall Mall*, Frederic Harrison, Fitzjames 'fought in a chivalrous spirit; on one occasion a controversy between them upon the theory of strikes ends by an acceptance of each other's conclusions'. A sharp encounter was with 'Historicus' of *The Times*, Sir William Vernon Harcourt, once a *Saturday Review*-er and, in the House of Commons, the doughty Chancellor of the Exchequer who declared that 'we are all Socialists now'. George Smith kept a record of Fitzjames's remarkable tale of work for the *Pall Mall*:

Dates	*Articles*	*Occasional Notes*	*Correspondence*
1865	143	103	8
1866	147	36	22
1867	194	27	9
1868	226	29	11
1869	142	5	—
1870	14	—	—
1872	112	3	2
1873	96	1	7
1874	39	2	8
1875	6	—	5
1878	1	—	—

'Making allowances for Sundays, it will be seen that in 1868 Fitzjames wrote two-thirds of the leaders, nearly half the leaders in 1867, and not much less than half in the three other years.' As for the 'Letters to the Editor', it is surely the mark of a good editor that he has plenty of them. I remember that the first night I spent in a morning newspaper office I was handed a 'Whitaker' and told to 'write some Letters'. Fitzjames was 'a tremendous worker, rising very early in the morning, and occupying every spare moment of his time'. One of his leading articles, Smith states, was written in the train between Paddington and Maidenhead.

Leslie Stephen is led by his brother's exertions to consider the problem, What constitutes the identity of a newspaper; what is meant by the editorial 'We'?—on the use of which, it will be recalled, G. S. Venables of the *Saturday Review* expressed himself clearly.

The inexperienced person (Leslie writes) is inclined to explain it as a mere grammatical phrase which covers in turn a whole series of contributors. But any writer in a paper, however free a course may be conceded to him, finds as a fact that the 'we' means something very real and potent. As soon as he puts on the mantle, he finds that an indefinable change has come over his whole method of thinking and expressing himself. He is no longer an individual but the mouthpiece of an oracle. He catches some infection of style, and feels that although he may believe what he says, it is not the independent outcome of his own private idiosyncrasy.

Now Fitzjames's articles are remarkable for immunity from this characteristic.

When I read them at the time, and I have had the same experience in looking over them again, I recognised his words just as plainly as if I had heard his voice. A signature would to me and to all in the secret have been a superfluity. And, although the general public had not the same means of knowledge, it was equally able to perceive that a large part of the *Pall Mall* represented the individual convictions of a definite human being, who had, moreover, very strong convictions and who wrote with the single aim of expressing them as clearly and vigorously as he could.

Leslie explains that his brother's general plan was to write before breakfast, but that he used to call at the *Pall Mall* office on his way to his chambers. There he chatted with Greenwood, and sometimes sat down and wrote an article straight away.

On circuit he kept up a steady supply of matter. I find him remarking, on one occasion, that he had written five or six leaders for the *Pall Mall* for the week, besides two *Saturday Review* articles. Everyone who has had experience of journalism knows that the time spent in actual writing is a very inadequate measure of the mental wear and tear due to production. An article may be turned out in an hour or two; but the work takes off the cream of the day, and involves much incidental thought and worry. Fitzjames seemed perfectly insensible to the labour; articles came from him as easily as ordinary talk; the fountain seemed to be always full, and had only to be turned on to the desired end. The chief fault which I should be disposed to find with these articles is doubtless a consequence of this fluency. He has not taken time to make them short.

One morning—it was the day of the funeral of Palmerston—Fitzjames proposed to write the leader on that statesman.

He went for the purpose into a room divided by a thin partition from that in which Mr. Greenwood sat. Mr. Greenwood unintentionally became aware, in consequence, that the article was composed literally with prayer and with tears. No one who turns to it will be surprised at the statement. He begins by saying that we are paying honour to a man for a patriotic high spirit which enabled him to take a conspicuous part in building up the great fabric of the British Empire. But he was also—as all who were taking part in the ceremony believed in their hearts—a 'man of the world' and 'a man of pleasure'. Do we, then, disbelieve in our own creed, or are we engaged in a solemn mockery? Palmerston had not obeyed the conditions under which alone, as every preacher will tell us, heaven can be hoped for. Patriotism, good nature, and so forth are, as we are told, mere 'filthy rags' of no avail in the sight of heaven. If this belief be genuine, the service must be a mockery. But he fully believes that it is not genuine. The preachers are inconsistent, but it is an honourable inconsistency.

Leslie ventures the opinion that 'few leading articles have been written under such conditions or in such a spirit'. Most of his brother's articles are written in a strain of solid and generally calm common sense; and some, no doubt, must have been of the kind compared by his father to singing without inflated lungs—mere pieces of routine taskwork. Yet there was one doctrine which he expounds in many connections, and which had a very deep root in his character. What is the true relation between the Church and the world; or between the monastic and ascetic view of life represented by Newman and the view of the lawyer or man of business?

One of his ablest pieces of work in the *Pall Mall* was a review of a pamphlet by the Archbishop of York upon 'The Limits of Philosophical Inquiry'. He could not always carry his editor with him. When a Lord Chancellor, Lord Westbury—the judge who 'dismissed Hell with costs'—came to grief, Fitzjames Stephen could not persuade Greenwood to take the view that the accusation had been exaggerated for party purposes. But upon Westbury's resignation 'he obtained the insertion of a very cordial eulogy upon the ex-Chancellor as law reformer'.[1]

When Greenwood's indomitable helper took a post in India he did not cease to give his aid.

He had written twenty articles for the *Pall Mall* between the days

[1] The following (from the *Pall Mall* of Mar. 3, 1868) is a fair example of Fitzjames's style—in the journalism of our own time the number of Biblical allusions has been reduced: 'One of the most grievous and constant puzzles of King David was the prosperity of the wicked and the scornful. Like the Psalmist, the Liberal leader may well protest that verily he has cleansed his heart in vain and washed his hands in innocency; all day long he has been plagued by Whig Lords and chastened every morning by Radical manufacturers; as blamelessly as any curate he has written about *Ecce Homo*; and he has never made a speech, even in the smallest country town, without calling out with David, How foolish am I, and how ignorant! For all this, what does he see? The scorner who shot out the lip and shook the head at him across the table of the House of Commons last session has now more than heart could wish; his eyes, speaking in an Oriental manner, stand out with fatness, he speaketh loftily, and pride compasseth him about as a chain. That the writer of frivolous stories about *Vivian Grey* and *Coningsby* should grasp the sceptre before the writer of beautiful and serious things about *Ecce Homo*—the man who is epigrammatic, flashy, arrogant, before the man who never perpetrated an epigram in his life, is always fervid, and would as soon die as admit that he had a shade more brain than his footman—the Radical corrupted into a Tory before the Tory purified and elevated into a Radical—is not this enough to make an honest man rend his mantle and shave his head and sit down among the ashes inconsolable?'

of leaving England and of landing at Bombay. 'If I were in solitary confinement', he says, 'I should have to scratch newspaper articles on the wall with a nail. My appetite, natural or acquired, has become insatiable.' When he had entered upon his duties at Calcutta he felt that there were objections to this indulgence, and he succeeded in weaning himself after a time. For the first three or four months he still yielded to the temptation of turning out a few articles on the sly; but he telegraphs home to stop the appearance of some that had been written, and breaks off another in the middle.

On his return home in 1872 he 'found that the time might be adequately filled by a return to his beloved journalism. He proposes, at starting, to write an article a day till he gets to Suez'. The day after his arrival he called at the *Pall Mall* office. 'He had written an article on the way from Paris which duly appeared in next day's paper.'

Fitzjames Stephen assailed John Stuart Mill in a series of contributions which he collected and published with his name as *Liberty, Equality, Fraternity*. 'I confess that I wondered a little at the time', writes his brother, 'that the editor of a newspaper should be willing to fill his columns with so elaborate a discourse upon first principles.' Greenwood himself said that 'no such work was ever seen in a daily or weekly paper'. A few articles in 1874–5 were Fitzjames's last contributions to the paper.

It was through the *Pall Mall* that Froude, in respect of his *History of England*, addressed his famous challenge to Freeman that the Deputy Keeper of the Public Records should check its accuracy. 'The Deputy Keeper of the Public Records shall compare 100, 200, 300 pages, wherever he pleases, with the MSS. at the British Museum, and shall report the result to the *Saturday Review*.' The challenge was not accepted by Freeman, in what Paul calls a 'disingenuous barrage of insinuation', signed 'Mr. Froude's *Saturday Review*-er'.[1]

[1] 'I lay no claim to be free from mistakes. I have worked in all through nine hundred volumes of letters, notes and other papers, private and official, in five languages and in difficult handwritings. I am not rash enough to say I have never misread or overlooked. I profess only to have dealt with my materials honestly to the best of my ability.'—Froude in Herbert Paul's *Life* (Pitman).

In 1865 Ruskin engaged in 'a long controversy on work and wages', and later he wrote 'a Letter from Utopia'. Among the things which Sidney Colvin contributed between 1869 and 1872 was an article on the Albert Memorial, in which he spoke of it as creditable to engineer and mechanician.

A neighbour of the Smiths in Hampstead was Maurice Drummond, Receiver to the Metropolitan Police, a post onerous only as regards responsibility, leaving him 'plenty of leisure'. Before he became Receiver he was a clerk in the Treasury, 'an appointment he is supposed to have received as compensation from the Government for the murder of his kinsman, Edward Drummond, who was mistaken by the murderer for Sir Robert Peel'. He had been private secretary to Lord John Russell and Sir George Cornewall Lewis. Lady St. Helier, who speaks of her 'life-long friendship' with Greenwood, says Drummond was 'a curious, interesting, wild-looking person, very able and very original'. He wrote 'Occ. Notes' 'almost daily', and it was said that if he did not invent the feature he brought it to perfection. His wife, the eldest daughter of Lord Ribblesdale, was also a contributor. Her knowledge of languages is described as being of 'the utmost service' to the paper. Basil Champneys, her son-in-law, says,[1] 'She was from the first incapable of careless or slipshod writing; I can recollect with what warmth Greenwood spoke of this and her other accomplishments, as also the very high value he put on her husband's contributions.' She writes: 'Mr. Greenwood told me that he would never look at any chance MS. which bore signs of having been through a copying machine. The more modern typewriter, is, on the other hand, I am told, in great favour with most readers for the press; and no wonder.' She also tells the following story of her association with the *Pall Mall*:

A large parcel of new novels had been sent me to be reviewed, as I supposed. Two or three days after, a boy was sent from the office with a note asking that the books might be returned to the editor,

[1] *The Honourable Adelaide Drummond, Retrospect and Memoirs*, Basil Champneys (Smith & Elder).

as they had been addressed to me by mistake. Having made up the parcel again, I took it into the hall, where I found a very small boy sitting on a long chest, very much at his ease. He sat with his little hands on his knees, looking at me with a benevolent expression. Having received the parcel in a condescending manner, he rose and said, 'Don't be downhearted about this; they're sure to send you some more very soon.'

A review of hers of a book by Walter, afterwards Sir Walter, Besant, so pleased the author that he sent Greenwood a copy of *Ready-Money Mortiboy* to give her.

Mrs. Drummond was an early Home Ruler and supporter of votes for women. Her eldest daughter, Adelaide, also wrote for the *Pall Mall*. Walter Sichel[1] mentions that Mrs. Drummond was one of the very first heroines of an elopement to Gretna Green:

> Her incensed stepfather, then Prime Minister, posted after in a chaise but the young people were married before he could overtake them. In a long life she was by turns High Church, Low Church, Agnostic, Salvationist, until finally she found peace in Rome. Mr. Drummond, on the other hand, was a staunch Protestant, much vexed by these 'vagaries'. His articles in the *Pall Mall*, splendidly edited by Mr. Greenwood, were sometimes worthy of de Quincey, and the public took him quite literally when he wrote a thrilling account of how he had committed a murder.

In order to take us back into the period, here are the titles of three leading articles in the first year of the *Pall Mall*: 'Mr. Stuart Mill's "Alleged Atheism"'—he is, Greenwood says, 'one of the greatest writers and most influential thinkers in Europe'—'Dissenters' Chapels', and 'The Sausage Meat of Journalism'. In 1867 there are such topics as 'Advertising Quacks', 'The Philistine Priesthood', 'The Pauper Roll', 'The International Working Man', 'The Finance of the Abyssinian Expedition'. 'Occ. Notes' concern themselves with, among other matters, voters who 'see no objection to taking a pound', shoddy publishing, the

[1] *Sands of Time* (Hutchinson).

Overend-Gurney case—'Is there no code of honour in commerce?' it is asked—and the escape of 250 horses of the First Life Guards. The *Pall Mall* accused bishops of 'impotent caution' and 'misplaced decency'. On the marriage of Princess Helena to Prince Christian of Schleswig-Holstein, the comment was: 'H.S.H. must be rather astonished at the pinnacle on which his betrothal to Princess Helena has put him. In their own country Serene Highnesses mostly travel about in second-class carriages and smoke cheap cigars. Here they put in motion generals, admirals, troops and paragraphs.'

Alas, Greenwood writes, 'anonymity was an inflexible rule for journalists then, and the public was slow to descry our galaxy of shining ones through the universal veil'.

The new evening journal was not to achieve an immediate success. The winter thorn remained with us in May, the June rose perished and there was no rise (that a man should joke about such things!), indeed, if memory serves, it was on a lovely summer day, all nature beaming, that our circulation figured at little more than half a thousand and our advertisements receipts totalled only four and six. To within a week or two this is a faithful account of a very miserable time when to stop or go on became a question daily renewed, but without any question of fighting sturdily and spending handsomely as long as we did go on. When things were at their worst there was an interesting suspensive stage in these hesitations to go on, of which I say nothing except that it was an immense relief to one who never for a moment doubted that success lay ahead. And from the beginning of that suspensive stage the new evening paper began to move star-ward. Not much, but yet a little more and a little more as autumn went and winter came again, and then we had a piece of luck in a rousing sensation.

But for this we must wait a page or two.

As Anthony Trollope was to acknowledge, after buying his experience with a publication of his own, 'literary men will hardly get a magazine afloat'. 'If the *Pall Mall* had been run entirely on *Saturday* lines', Escott writes, 'it would have come to grief.' It was not. 'Greenwood did not forget the secrets of popular success he had learned from Vizetelly.' Leslie Stephen found it 'keeping its ground; nay more, it advances'. Sir William Hardman, editor of the *Morning Post*, notes that 'my favourite' paper lays itself out for 'curious, interesting and early scraps of information. The other day they picked up a book, recently published in Paris, consisting of notices of the various literary and scientific societies of the world.' He is taken by an article on the possibility of the Pope coming to live in England or Ireland—he would 'sink at once into the position of a president of the Wesleyan Conference; one can hardly fancy the benediction being given out of a window in Grosvenor Square'.

As for Greenwood's admission, like Smith's, that there was a time when the sale of the paper was somewhere about six hundred, I remember that when I came to the office there was a tradition that, early in the paper's history, a message might come down to the machinists through the speaking-tube, 'Run off another quire!' Which reminds one of Sidney Dark's story of later years. The *Standard*, under Arthur Pearson's ownership, found its circulation getting smaller and smaller; 'the subscribers died off and it found no new ones'. 'Damn this east wind', Pearson said to Dark as they turned from Shoe Lane into Fleet Street; 'six more readers gone.' Greenwood once spoke of how, when the circulation of the *Pall Mall* was to be counted in hundreds, his friend W. B. Rands (also known as Matthew Browne and Henry Holbeach)[1] upbraided him for having got him to come on the staff. Smith had a story of himself making 'three or four visits a day' to the office and of thus becoming an object of interest to the maidservants at lodging-houses near by. At a time when things were taking a turn for the better with the paper he heard one girl say to another, 'He looks a good deal more lively today.'

[1] Author of *Liliput Levee*, 1868, which contains the amusing poem about the children who 'turned the tables on the old folks'.

CHAPTER XVI

'The Amateur Casual' and the Fenians

'OUGHT TO ENTITLE HIM TO THE V.C.' — JAMES GREENWOOD — PROPRIETOR AS REPORTER — A MORNING PAPER EXPERIMENT

'TALKING with Mr. Smith and Mr. Lewes one afternoon of the prospects of the paper', writes Greenwood, 'I happened to say that my sensation was that of a captive balloon, ready to soar and restive against the rope that held it down. Could we but cut the rope? At this Lewes opened his remarkably wide mouth and said with a loud guffaw, "And whose business is it to find the knife?" A fair taunt and a deserved, it went *through*. Pain is always a mental stimulus with me; and that evening I set about looking for the knife (for the seventy-seventh time) in confidence that this time it would be found. And so it was. It came wrapped in the recollection of some dreadful reports of investigation into certain infirmaries, which reports excited no public attention whatever, being printed in a medical journal. This recollection suggested a night in a casual ward of a London workhouse as a sort of knife that might accomplish several beneficent bits of business at one stroke.'[1]

It was a very ordinary piece of enterprise to the present-day news-editor. Greenwood made the proposal to his brother James, a fellow contributor to the *Welcome Guest*, who is described as a rough diamond. James was not keen on the job, but ultimately agreed to do it for £30 or £40 down, and more if it turned out well. 'A friend of his, a young stockbroker named Bittlestone, expressed his willingness to take part in the adventure', one finds Stead writing years afterwards in the *Review of Reviews*.

[1] J. A. Spender, who may have known Greenwood, speaks of the sale of the *Pall Mall* at this time as 4,000, a figure which, if accurate, was not so bad as circulations went then.

JAMES GREENWOOD, 'The Amateur Casual'
From The Seven Curses of London, *by James Greenwood, published by Stanley Rivers & Co.*

They happened to select Lambeth workhouse.[1] The casual wards would only accommodate sixty-one casuals. Any applicants over this number were placed in an open shed. Here a herd of homeless wretches passed the night as best they could.

James Greenwood and his companion got themselves up in the style of the regular dosser, and one bitterly cold January night Frederick Greenwood drove them to within easy walking distance of the casual ward. As he drove away, he saw his brother and Mr. Bittlestone sitting on the stones shivering, without any great-coats, waiting until the attendant answered the bell.

Next morning he was there with the carriage, supplied with sandwiches and wine. After a time he saw two miserable-looking objects walking down the street. 'I never saw', said Frederick Greenwood, talking about it afterwards, 'so great a change wrought in a single night in the appearance of any human beings. When they went in they were well disguised, but any close observer would have perceived that they were got up for the occasion. After spending sixteen hours in the cold, squalor and obscene brutality of the casual ward, they seemed absolutely to have become confirmed tramps and vagabonds.' When they got into the carriage they gave way to some natural exclamations of disgust. After a while they calmed down, but they were still smarting under the recollection of the horrors through which they had passed, and it was not until they had gone home, had a bath, and were comfortably warmed and fed, that they could be induced to talk quietly about their experience.

James Greenwood wrote the story, assisted by the observations of Bittlestone. The editor 'retouched it by the light of what he had heard of the visit, and always with intent to avoid suspicion of exaggeration'. 'All that might have been written was not written', Greenwood said afterwards; it 'could not be described in public print in that insufficiently advanced period of the century. But what was suppressed could be otherwise made known; and so altogether, here was a good stroke for poor-house Reform, and a knife was applied to the tethering rope.'

To the modern reporter, who would take such an assignment in the course of his week's work, all this may look a strange

[1] Mrs. Robinson thought it was St. Pancras workhouse.

pother. But Sir William Hardman, the editor of the *Morning Post*, actually writes of 'an act of bravery, at, it is to be hoped, a very handsome fee, which ought to entitle him to the V.C. or rather to some unique order of merit which should stand quite alone. I would rather brave a Crimean campaign or an Indian Mutiny than undertake such a deed of daring.' Which shows the gap which existed at that time between what might be called 'high life' and 'the poor'.

J. P. Symon has a story that a famous actress, on being asked if she knew that one of the *Pall Mall* men had passed a night in a workhouse, replied sympathetically, 'Really—do they pay them as badly as all that?' It is an anecdote to be set beside the remark of the fine lady, du Maurier's neighbour at a party, who showed some interest in the *Punch* dinners. 'Ah, I see', she said, 'you do your little sketches and then they give you your dinner in return.'

The articles ran through three issues. Strange though it may seem, in the light of present journalistic practice, the first instalment of 'The Amateur Casual' was not given any prominence, and was not even made the subject of an 'Occ. Note'. On the completion of the series Greenwood did have something to say editorially. 'Part of the picture', he wrote, 'was too disgusting to be drawn.' The articles—the authorship, Trollope declares, was attributed to him and also to Lord Houghton—undoubtedly made 'a great sensation' at a time when such writing, common form in Fleet Street a few years ahead, was unfamiliar pabulum in the daily press, and few readers of daily papers had any real knowledge of the lower strata of the population. *The Times* paid the *Pall Mall* the remarkable compliment of reprinting the articles in full, and the *Saturday Review* testified to the 'magnificent heroism to which they bore testimony'. But the *Spectator* sagaciously remarked that, 'after all, the "Amateur Casual" had only spent one night under conditions to which hundreds of his countrymen were condemned any day of their lives'.

'The Amateur Casual' was issued as a pamphlet, and in later years, Stead, who, during his editorship was to produce so many

Pall Mall 'Extras', remembered the results secured by his own 'Maiden Tribute' and his book *In Darkest England and the Way Out*—which he prepared for General Booth some years after the publication of the ship-owner-sociologist Booth's *Life and Conditions of the People in London*—said that from 'the storm of indignation' over 'that one night in a casual ward may be traced the beginning of the reform of our Poor Law'.

'It was thought at the time', wrote Greenwood towards the end of his life, that 'the publication of the articles had an immense effect at once on the sale of the paper; but that was not the case. Yet it had a very good effect, if not enough for joy, enough for satisfaction. A considerable number of subscribers was added immediately to the list, and from that day the paper rose steadily to a high position of favour and authority.' In plain figures, 1,500 copies extra were sold on the three days the articles appeared and there was a permanently increased circulation of 1,200.

A few words may be added about Frederick Greenwood's brother, James, who lived to become a 'character'. There are references to him in J. Hall Richardson's *From City to Fleet Street.*[1]

I knew Jimmy as the author of articles on London life signed by 'One of the Crowd'. He wrote apparently with difficulty, laboriously on quarto sheets, in a hand which had never become cursive. His style and manner were his own. He had invented a jargon for the talk of the Cockney which never was heard in real life, but passed muster as the vernacular of the Londoner. The Greenwood costermongers and cockneys spoke a dialect of their own, and lived in a land of their own. If they were ever true to life, then Chevalier and all the other impersonators of the coster were poor artists.

I rather fancy that Jimmy was the author of the phrase which has been attached to a more distinguished colleague: In a common lodging-house this man wrote of a tramp, 'In this fraternity of misery, he called me mate!'

I found him to be a short squarish, good-humoured man, dressed in a long black frock-coat, and black tie—the cut of a slum missionary.

[1] Stanley Paul.

James was the initiator of the *Daily Telegraph*'s Children's Country Outings Fund. Mr. W. McG. Eagar, C.B.E., director of the National Institute for the Blind, who is writing a history of the Boys' Club Movement, sends me a note in which he says: 'James is important to me because of his vigorous and adventurous gospel for boys in the 1860's and his romantic low life articles which depicted the boys of London at that date. He also, I think, invented the phrase "working boy" which, for a long time, denoted recognition of the problem of employed

Signature of 'The Amateur Casual'.

adolescence. Books he produced suggest that he must have spent part of his early life in Africa or some savage lands, but I have not found any biographical note on him. Apparently he wrote a story of a fight between a man and dog in the Potteries which was found to be bogus.' The report is in the *Daily Telegraph* of July 6, 1874. The fight was between a bulldog and an undersized man called Brumary. There was a correspondence in *The Times*, the letters of July and August being the most important. To questions in the House of Commons the Home Secretary first reported that the account was substantially true and then that the chief constable of Hanley had been unable to get confirmation. Greenwood stuck to the accuracy of his account.

A book by Greenwood I have looked through is called *The Seven Curses of London* (*Neglected Children, Thieves, Professional Beggars, Fallen Women, Drunkenness, Gamblers, Waste of Charity*). It is poorish stuff, and was probably written when he was hard up, not an uncommon condition, I understand. A relative helped him occasionally. Another volume is called *Behind a Bus*. He died in 1929 at ninety-seven. Richardson speaks of him 'flickering out in police court newspapers'. James and Frederick do not seem to have been on cordial terms in early life or later. Frederick, I have heard, did not forgive him for deserting the *Pall Mall* for a paper which he regarded as a rag. (Even in my time at the *Pall Mall*, when the *Daily Telegraph*, which has had such vigorous management, was in what might be called the Arnold and Sala period, we sniffed at it, in the superior atmosphere of Northumberland Street, as 'the landlady's paper'.)

A relative of James, speaking to me of the two brothers said: 'Their dispositions were different. Frederick was high-principled. James's principles were not one of his strong points. To be tied to an editorial chair would never have suited him. But he knew his public, and his articles signed "One of the Crowd" were looked for. At the Cheshire Cheese and other Fleet Street taverns, where journalists gathered, he was sure of a welcome from the company. Hearty laughter would greet his ready humour and repartee. He could sing a good song of the patriotic order, "'Twas in Trafalgar Bay", "Tom Bowling" and "The Powder Monkey". Only men of some eminence in their calling were caricatured in *Vanity Fair* and he was one of "Spy's" subjects. At the height of his popularity his earnings were high. In his home life he had the devoted affection of his wife and family. He was 5 ft. 6 ins. and heavily built, and had glistening curly black hair.'

Now for a very different character, Anthony Trollope. He wrote for the *Pall Mall* not only the hunting notes which pleased his editor, but he tells us in his autobiography, 'a set of clerical sketches which brought down on my head the wrath of a great Dean'. He also did some literary criticism. It was 'not to my taste', he says, but he adds virtuously, 'in conformity with strict conscientious scruples, I read what I took in hand, and said what I believed true, always giving time altogether incommensurate with the pecuniary result'. It is evidence of the close attention which George Smith devoted to the paper he was financing—for a considerable period he was at the office daily—that Trollope should assert—no one else has made the statement and it is not implied in anything Greenwood has written[1]—that 'in the early days of the paper the proprietor acted as chief editor'.

> In that capacity [Trollope states] he suggested to me that I should, during an entire season, attend the May meetings in Exeter Hall[2] and give a graphic and, if possible, an amusing description of the proceedings. I did attend one, and wrote a paper called, 'A Zulu in Search of a Religion'. But when the meeting was over I went to the spirited proprietor and begged him to impose upon me some task more equal to my strength. Not even on behalf of the *Pall Mall*, which was very dear to me, could I go through a second May meeting, much less endure a season.

Which from the creator of so many fictional clerics is rather odd.

Trollope, who stresses Smith's 'untiring energy and general ability', thinks 'the strongest staffs of the paper were Jacob Omnium', 'the most forcible writer', and Fitzjames Stephen, 'the most conscientious and industrious'. The novelist also particularly mentions Lord Houghton, Lord Strangford, and Hannay, 'but I have met at a *Pall Mall* dinner a crowd of guests which would have filled the House of Commons more respectably than I have seen it filled even on important occasions'. He adds that he found himself 'unfit for work on a newspaper'. He 'had not taken to it early enough', he was 'fidgety' and he wanted to write on his own subjects and when he pleased.[3]

[1] See page 181.

[2] Exeter Hall was on the site of Lyons's Hotel in the Strand. The May meetings held there were the annual gatherings of religious and philanthropic organizations. People would come up from the provinces to attend a selection of them.

[3] Nevertheless he accepted a proposal from Virtue, the printer, to undertake, at £1,000 a year, the editorship of a magazine. The stipulations he made were that he should be free to put in and keep out whatever he pleased, should pay what he liked, and retain the job for two years. He would not agree to the proposal to call the periodical *Anthony Trollope's* and settled on *St. Paul's*. Although his writers included Dicey, Percy Fitzgerald, Layard, Allingham, Leslie Stephen, Mrs. Lynn Linton, Lever, Austin Dobson, R.A. Proctor, Lewes, George MacDonald, W. R. Greg, Mrs. Oliphant, Sir Charles Trevelyan, and Dutton Cook, the periodical failed to sell more than 10,000. The 'enterprise had been set on foot on a system too expensive to be made lucrative short of a

Some anecdotes may be related illustrative of Smith's keenness to make a success of the paper. Sidney Lee says that 'for the first two years' he 'kept with his own hand the "contributions ledger" and the "register of contributions" and devoted many hours at home to posting up these books and writing out and despatching the contributors' cheques'.

One day, in the paper's first year, as he was leaving the office he noticed the 'telegraph' spelling out 'President Lincoln', and then the word 'Assassinated'. 'I rushed back into the editor's room with the news, and asked who was to write the leading article. We discussed several names, but the man who seemed most suitable and at the same time available was Fitzjames Stephen. I jumped into a cab and raced to his chambers, found he was at court and drove there. He was on his legs addressing the judge. I scribbled my news on a scrap of paper and added "You must write the leading article". Stephen finished his address with praiseworthy brevity; I went with him into one of the waiting rooms and finally bore the leading article back to the office.' The paper was getting out with its first edition at a more leisurely hour than in my time.

One year Smith bestirred himself over the Oxford and Cambridge boat race. 'We trained two or three pigeons. I told our reporters they might lavish money in trying to keep the telegraph wire in their hands, and I confided my aspirations to Mr. Woodgate, our boating contributor and also the coach of

very large circulation'. His wisdom is: 'Literary merit will hardly set a magazine afloat, though when afloat it will sustain it or the hubbub, flurry and the excitement created by unbiquitous sesquipedalian advertisement; merit and time together may be effective, but they must be backed by economy and patience.' He says nothing about editorial aptitude and skill. His view is that 'publishers themselves have been the best editors of magazines when they have been able to give time and intelligence to the work. Nothing has been done better than *Blackwood*. *Cornhill*, too, after Thackeray left it, and before Leslie Stephen took it, seemed to be in quite efficient hands, the hands of the proprietor. The proprietor, at any rate, knows what he wants and can afford, and is not so frequently likely to fall into that worst of literary quicksands, publishing matter not for the sake of readers but for that of the writer. Such editors as Thackeray and myself will always be liable to commit such faults.'

the Oxford boat. Woodgate was somewhat of a sporting character and rode a used-up thoroughbred screw. He galloped off as soon as he saw how the race was going to end, and I happened to be in Northumberland Street when he came clattering down to the *Pall Mall* office. Knowing what I did about the mare's forelegs, I felt somewhat anxious till he pulled up at the door of the *Pall Mall*. We were first in the street with the news, but the *Evening Standard* came out within five minutes. This puzzled me. I used frequently to go up to the compositors' room and exchange a few words with the men, many of whom had been drafted from the printing office of Smith, Elder & Co. I said one day, "I don't wish to invite anybody to betray confidence, but I would give a £5 note to know how the *Standard* got out with the result of the boat race as soon as we did". The money was soon claimed. The *Standard* people had printed a number of copies announcing that Oxford had won and another lot announcing Cambridge as the victor, and on the arrival of the news, had been ready to pour the right one into the streets.'

On another occasion Smith betook himself to the reporters' gallery of the House of Commons when Gladstone was to unfold Government policy on an important subject. 'I listened while, with many a convolution, he reached the decision of the Cabinet. I had heard enough, and jumped into a cab and drove with speed to the office. I ran up to the compositors' room and asked for men who could set from dictation. I walked from one to the other dictating the speech. The words were so intelligently taken that not many had to be set right in proof, and in a few minutes the boys were crying the news. After so many years I cannot help smiling as I recall the simple vanity with which I walked home.'

Another reporting effort was when the Queen opened St. Thomas's Hospital. Smith thought he would rather like to go. He duly attended, and 'hurried back to the office and dictated an account in true reporter's English, a rather high-falutin' account of the scene, plunging into all the terms of millinery with most audacious courage. I read the report side by side with that of the *Morning Post*, and with the partiality of a parent preferred my own, but I had to endure some ridicule in the family circle over my description of one of the dresses.'

In the early days of the paper Smith had tried, for a month, the experiment of issuing an edition of eight pages as a 'morning review'. When, with one effort and another, the *Pall Mall* began to grow in circulation and influence, an ambition developed in 1870 to make it a morning as well as an evening paper. In advance, the price of the existing paper was reduced to a penny, on the assumption that this would give a much larger constituency of readers and make a broader foundation for the coming morning journal. This change did raise the circulation, and six months afterwards the morning paper was announced. It was to be, in Sir Henry Lucy's words, 'less bulky than *The Times*'—a tremendous and portentous production in those days—and to 'excel' it not only in compactness and convenience but in 'journalistic and literary excellence'. Smith was at the office from nine in the morning until six at night, and still contrived to give time to his other business. He said he watched the experiment 'very vigilantly'. But after four months of the struggle he decided that 'the prospects of success did not justify further trial'. The experiment had the effect, however, of increasing the circulation of the evening paper.

Unfortunately no figures of the financial returns of the *Pall Mall* have survived. The paper was not very old when it showed, Smith states, 'a margin of profit', and, after the morning paper experiment, it is recorded that 'the profits now began to be considerable'. But as one looks at the moderate volume of advertisements, it is difficult to believe that the word 'considerable' would be applied by a modern newspaper to the yield on the total expenditure from the start. Smith's phrase is 'The paper went on in my hands with varying success.' On the *Pall Mall*'s birthday Smith and Greenwood and the literary staff used to dine together, and there were several 'large entertainments at Greenwich and elsewhere' for the contributors. The publication of the thousandth number on April 29, 1868, was celebrated with a dinner at the Garrick.

Smith's most exciting experience was when Colonel Henderson, the chief of the Metropolitan Police, came to warn him that there was a Fenian plot to blow up the offices of *The Times* and the *Pall Mall*. 'You will easily understand', said Henderson, 'that anyone may come in and ask to see the editor and, when shown into a waiting room, leave a packet the contents of which would blow up the place.' It was arranged that fourteen detectives should be told off to watch the premises and that there should be two more on the roof. When Henderson was leaving, Mrs. Smith happened to pass him, and later asked her husband who he was. 'I told my first and last domestic fib and murmured "an author".' But this was not the end of the matter. On reaching home his daughter Dolly, in giving him a hug, felt the revolver that, as a result of the police chief's news, he had put in his pocket, and she had to be taken into his confidence.

No Fenian explosion occurred at the office, but a man in the basement, already under police suspicion, was one day found to have tampered with the machinery, with the result that many of the men might have been killed or maimed. There was an outburst of rage among them, and when the proprietor, hearing the tumult, hurried down, he found the man 'about to be lynched'. Smith said everything should be done to punish him if proved guilty, but he would not have him ill-used on the premises. In the result enough evidence was not forthcoming to sustain a criminal charge.

During the scare, Delane of *The Times* walked to and from his chambers with two detectives before him and another two behind him. Smith declined a similar escort, but carried, as well as his five-chambered revolver, a life-preserver with the cord wound round his wrist. He said that he acquired a reputation for cool nerves when, owing to a piece of machinery collapsing on an upper floor, there was a loud bang, and everybody in the editorial room, where he happened to be, jumped, and he did not do so. This was, he explained, because he was sitting with his legs extended to a second chair, and his lap 'full of proofs he was correcting'. So, at that time, he took some share in the editorial work.

Reverting to the Fenians, Greenwood shared police protection with his proprietor. For weeks he was 'seen into his cab at night, and out of it in the morning, by plain clothes constables stationed at each end of the street'. 'And one night at the corner of the street, and on another night near Queen's Gate. . . .' But there he breaks off. During Stead's editorship also—in 'The Maiden Tribute' time—the *Pall Mall* was glad to have policemen at its doors.

CHAPTER XVII

The Housing, the Editing, and the Libel Actions

GREENWOOD'S APPEARANCE — 'CRAZY AND OFFENSIVE CONTRIBUTORS' — AN EMISSARY FROM BISMARCK — MARX AND ENGELS — THE FRIENDSHIP OF GEORGE MEREDITH — A 'SCOOP'

IN the last few chapters we have been concerned with what the *Pall Mall* contained, with the impression it made, and with the men who wrote it. Not much has been said about Greenwood after he became editor, and nothing about the physical conditions in which his work and the work of his staff was done.

First, about the editorial, printing, and publishing office, Greenwood, in the long article he wrote towards the end of his life in the ten-thousandth number, when the paper was no longer in his hands, has himself given a memorable picture of it.

> We began modestly but efficiently with a printing office on the then naked foreshore of the Thames where the descent was made to its melancholy flats from Salisbury Street, and with editorial and publishing offices in a dwelling house in Salisbury Street itself. It has a castaway, precarious look, the printing office, as if, washed up from Wapping or thereabouts by one tide, it would probably be carried on by the next; but it was well appointed and perfectly comfortable except on the rare occasions when excessive rain or spring floods compelled the printers to go in and out on each other's backs. It was a narrow, gloomy brooding little street, in which the roar of the Strand was lost; and its No. 14 was so near the river (on the right hand side going down) that if any printer had really been in danger of drowning a life line might have been thrown from the editor's window.
>
> But what made the street dull also made it quiet, which was compensation heaped up and running over. We published in the front parlour. My office was on the first floor—three rooms approached by a dark, narrow stair, and one of those rooms a cell

scarce seven feet wide. The narrowness of that room was no obstruction to the deliverance of some of the best bits of journalism ever committed to print.

Salisbury Street, which is no more, ran parallel with Northumberland Street, between Adam Street and Carting Lane. It was demolished in 1896, and Shell-Mex House stands on part of the site. The *Pall Mall* was on the west side of the street, near the Strand, about forty yards from the river and low-lying. This was from the start, in 1865, until early 1867,[1] when the paper moved to 2 Northumberland Street. There it stayed until, long after Greenwood's time, it was sold to the first Lord Astor.

Northumberland Street is the narrow way opening from the Trafalgar Square end of the Strand, to which Grand Buildings, formerly the Grand Hotel, shows its back. The hotel is on the site of Northumberland House, built in 1605. As that edifice was not pulled down until 1874, when Northumberland Avenue was made, Northumberland Street in the early post-Salisbury Street days of the *Pall Mall* must have been, as Aaron Watson says,[2] a 'mean-looking thoroughfare, more like a passage than a street'. It was, however, convenient to the West End and to official London. The archivist of the City of Westminster has been kind enough to examine for me the rate-books of the time. The Northumberland Street offices had been two separate houses, one quite small. The premises had been occupied before Queen Victoria came to the throne by Turner Skinner and William Gilpin, army clothiers, but they had left in 1865.

I do not remember seeing anything of a warehouse and yard when I was at the *Pall Mall*. The office consisted of what looked rather like two houses made into one. The machines were in the basement, the compositors on the top floor, and the by no means elaborate publishing was done on the first floor. The editorial rooms, also facing the street, were still 'three rooms approached

[1] George Smith is also shown as a ratepayer for a warehouse, part of a wharf, a counting-house, and part of the ground floor of 78 Adelphi Vaults, the rateable value of which was £100. These premises were given up when the paper moved to No. 2 Northumberland Street, where the rateable value was £368.

[2] *A Newspaper Man's Memories* (Hutchinson).

by a dark narrow stair'. They were on the left of a dark passage and began with the largest, the editor's room. Then came a rather narrow apartment where, in my day, the editor's secretary sat, and books that the editor's room could not accommodate were shelved. There was a sliding panel for speaking to the small next room where two colleagues and I, the sub-editors, worked at, I think, an old dining-room table. This room communicated, by another panel, with the third room, which was that of the city editor—during my service a canny Scot, Mackay, who owned the *Chatham Observer*. Every room on the floor was shabby-looking. On the right of the narrow passage there was a store-room, also a place where one could wash, and a small room in which I once interviewed Oscar Wilde.

Aaron Watson says that Richard Savage got into one of his worst scrapes in Northumberland Street (originally Hartshorn Lane), and about the middle of the last century 'the very building in which the *Pall Mall* was published' was 'the scene of a sensational occurrence' referred to by Thackeray[1]—again the Thackeray connexion.

> The brave Dumas, the intrepid Ainsworth, the terrible Eugène Sue, the cold-shudder-inspiring *Woman in White*, the astonishing author of the *Mysteries of the Court of London* never invented anything more tremendous. It might have happened to you and me. We want to borrow a little money. We are directed to an agent. We propose a pecuniary transaction at a short date. He goes into the next room, as we fancy to get the bank-notes, and returns with 'two very pretty, delicate little ivory-handled pistols', and blows a portion of our heads off.

'The thing actually occurred as Thackeray describes', Watson states.[2]

[1] *Roundabout Papers* ('On two Papers I intended to write').

[2] A well-known authority on Old London, Mr. William Kent, writes to me: 'I cannot trace any connexion between Hartshorn Lane and Richard Savage. I looked up a life of Savage in the British Museum. It was certainly the first written, and it actually appeared years before his death. This mentions the fracas in which he was involved as taking place in Robinson's Coffee House near Charing Cross, and this of course would be quite close to Hartshorn

As we have seen, Smith did all he could for the paper, and was a most helpful and stimulating proprietor, but Leslie Stephen is right when he calls the *Pall Mall* 'the incarnation of Greenwood'. The editor was a personality. There is plenty of testimony to his vigour and ability, and power of holding a staff, and to his sincerity and his influence. It may be added that there are frequent references to his impressive personal appearance, which is borne out by his portraits. 'Still in the prime of life, the freshness of youth just mellowing with middle-aged maturity', is Escott's phrase.[1] Sichel speaks of his 'sanguine colour, both in countenance and intellect; he looked like some alert robin in the act of flight'.[2] In the *Vanity Fair* cartoon his beard is red. And it is the same in the original of our frontispiece portrait. I have seen it stated somewhere that Sir Archibald Geikie, the geologist, looked 'a sort of blend of Benjamin Jowett and Frederick Greenwood'.

Sichel makes the point that Greenwood was '*par excellence* a man of letters', which, as we have seen, he had hoped to be. 'Originative, penetrating, a censor of language in all its branches, he strove to classicize journalism and not to journalize literature.' Escott, who knew Greenwood, pays his tribute to 'a practical newspaper man of wide experience, shrewd insight and first rate judgement', who 'might have taken pure letters rather than journalism for his career. Notwithstanding a certain subacidity, due chiefly to his surroundings, his mind was traversed by a gentler vein than had an opportunity to declare itself in the drive and clash of newspaper editing.' In a book called *The London Daily Press*, H. W. Massingham, the editor of the *Daily Chronicle* and the *Nation*, a highly competent judge, speaks of Greenwood as 'an uncommon man, one of the few writers who, while they

Lane, but there is no reference to it. It appears that his subsequent biographer, Makower, has followed this book. Hatton's *New View of London* (1708) says that Hartshorn Lane was "on the south-east side of the Strand near Northumberland House". South-*east* is rather an odd indication. Perhaps it was intended to show that it was on the east side of the house referred to.'

[1] *Masters of Journalism* (Unwin).

[2] *Sands of Time* (Hutchinson).

may be called self-educated, have developed a style which for elegance and flexible quality would be hard to match outside the classical models of written English'.

An editor 'in his intellectual and imaginative prime', writes Escott, he 'really inspired as well as directed the clever pens whom he had invited to help him. The sport made by Matthew Arnold between Arminius and Adolescens Leo (*Friendship's Offering*) owed as much to Greenwood's suggestions as to Arnold's originality.' Greenwood is described by one of his staff as 'a man whom it was a pleasure to serve; he had a cheery confidence in his contributors and a belief in the goodness of their work'. Comyns Carr, who preceded Sidney Colvin as art critic of the *Pall Mall*, and wrote, among other things, articles on the reform of the Royal Academy—when were attempts not being made to reform it?—which were the subject of an unsuccessful motion in the House of Commons, says, in *Some Eminent Victorians*, that among all the editors he served he 'should signalize Greenwood as being by far the most inspiring to his contributors'. Not that to be numbered among his contributors 'always implied a peaceful career; he was an autocratic commander whose powerful personality loved to assert itself in every department of his paper, and he and I had sharp encounters with regard to that particular area of art criticism over which I thought I was entitled to exercise independent control'. George Meredith spoke to Carr of what he called Greenwood's 'Jovian editorial stroke'.

On the relations of editor and contributors, Greenwood said at the end of his career that he had 'always tried to help, with at least a little patience, even crazy and offensive contributors'. If he found something in a man, he did not let him go, even if he were not doing himself justice. 'It is part of an editor's duty', he declared, 'to take pains to discover good writers, and he can do much in the nursing of a suitable man.' Escott[1] notes that Greenwood

kept a keen lookout for rising talent in clubs, in the Inns of Court

[1] *Masters of Journalism* (Unwin).

and even in University common rooms. Literary experience or skill he did not ask for, but only practical knowledge and a habit of clear, fresh thinking about subjects which some special interest had caused them to make their own. He did not indeed command these to write a leading article; he invited them to submit their ideas, as they might in a letter to a discriminating friend. If it had good stuff in it, it might be elaborated. In this way Professor Lewis Campbell's brother, Robert, a Chancery barrister, first made his appearance, and afterwards often repeated it in leader type.

To quote further from Escott:

Greenwood arranged his daily bill of fare with an eye to making his journal the political or literary mouthpiece and leader of the cultured class. His own style may have been influenced by the study of Swift, but really grew from his topical mind and his habit of vigilantly looking for, and tenaciously storing with a view to future use, whatever struck him as specially good and wise in well bred and intellectual company. Even so late as the middle of the nineteenth century, newspaper writers had not shaken themselves free of a tendency to a stilted heaviness of phrase, a diction formal, artificial and hackneyed. Some of the best known and even effective *Times* contributors such as S.G.O. (Lord Sidney Godolphin Osborne) made no effort to rise above it. No one did more than Greenwood to substitute for it a style idiomatic, familiar, in short the natural good English, spiced with humour, that, in their letters and conversation, always remained in fashion with clever and educated men. Thus, for the first time, the reproach of 'newspaper English' was in a fair way of becoming obsolete.

But Greenwood 'represented only one among several literary forces visibly affecting for good the journalistic style of the period'. The names Escott mentions are Froude, Newman, and Jowett, Laurence Oliphant, Kinglake, Warburton, George Eliot, and Borrow. 'Following Douglas Cook, Meredith Townsend and R. H. Hutton, Greenwood's editorial methods and opportunities co-operated to make the *Pall Mall* more than it had ever been the literary mirror of the talk and mind of the average intelligent and educated Briton.' I see that in 1868 Greenwood was a guest at Alexander Macmillan's 'All Fools' Day' dinner with John Morley, Browning, Arnold, Tom Hughes, Huxley, Sidgwick, and Sir Arthur Helps.

Greenwood's aim has been described as being 'to make the Press more readable and therefore more powerful'. In time, 'he had his pick of regular correspondents all over the world'. P. W. Smythe, before and after he became Lord Strangford, was one who 'helped him to give the *Pall Mall* something of a European position'. Among his useful writers were the *Kölnische Zeitung*'s London representative, Max Schlesinger, and Camille Barrère, a refugee who was afterwards to be a French ambassador. A little book about Great Britain by one Thieblin appeared first in the *Pall Mall*. So also did what Greenwood called 'a little series of papers written by a young Boer about Boer affairs, which, being printed in his own quaint imperfect English to prove them genuine, were for that reason suspected of fabrication'.

> Greenwood's editorial course [I am once more quoting Escott] formed one long protest against the growing tendency to confuse the functions of the news collector and leader-writer. He would have nothing to do with and never printed what he called long screeds of speculation. Because they were telegraphed, contended Greenwood, these screeds took in the public. Far from conveying new facts, they were apt to be evolved from the sender's agility in jumping to a conclusion, and coloured by the fancy, the prejudice, it might even be the interests of himself or more probably of others. Greenwood's insight and precaution gradually won for the *Pall Mall* a reputation that stung even Bismarck with a desire to nettle it. More than once the Chancellor sent emissaries from Berlin to Northumberland Street.

Years after, in *Blackwood*, Greenwood himself described the arrival of one of them in the early days of the paper.

> I had a visit from a certain Dr. P., the Berlin official. He introduced himself as coming direct from the German Chancellor with a proposal which von Bismarck took a personal interest in. He often read the *Pall Mall* and was greatly pleased with, much desired, and sincerely respected, the variety of qualities which he habitually found there. On that account the Chancellor desired to be of use to

the *Pall Mall*, as he might be by supplying the paper occasionally with really good information of foreign affairs. If that would be agreeable to me, Dr. P. would be the means of dispatching the said news from time to time. Further, to enable me to see that this was a genuine offer, von Bismarck had entrusted to Dr. P. a few lines of his own hand to say as much. Document then produced, shown to me, and returned to Dr. P's pocket book.

With the best face at my command, I asked whether it was proposed to send news alone, or to send letters of observations and comment; to which the reply was that both news and comment were intended. What I then said I do not remember, but my meaning was to point out as inoffensively as possible that the *Pall Mall* being a small paper, the value of his kindness would be much enhanced if nothing but concrete news was sent, or such information, as could be conveyed in a single paragraph of affirmation, explanation, correction or denial. We seemed to understand each other at once; and though Dr. P. said very politely that no doubt this could be arranged, I never heard another word of the business he came about after he left the room.

It is one of the many surprising things in the history of the *Pall Mall* that Engels, the Communist, was a contributor, and was introduced by Marx! It was during the Franco-German War, and Engels' work was a series of 'Notes', signed 'Z', with which, according to *The Tradition Established*, the second volume of *The History of 'The Times'*, Greenwood was 'pleased'. Moreover, Hyndman, to be one day head of the Social Democratic Federation, whom Mr. Bernard Shaw has caustically described, was of the staff. Much of Hyndman's work was anonymous, but some of it may be identified by the signature 'H.' Independent of his journalistic writings in London, there was his service as war correspondent with Garibaldi. Hyndman had a high opinion of Greenwood, and his praise may well be added to the encomiums already recorded.[1] He was 'keen, incisive, humorous and original, the best and most generous of editors, a good editor in every sense; I never knew a contributor complain of his editing'. He 'collected around him a remarkable set of men, because they had,

[1] *The Record of an Adventurous Life*, H. M. Hyndman (Macmillan).

2 Woodside
Surbiton
Surrey

March 29th

Dear Sir,

I enclose continuation of the 'Gamekeeper'. In a leader to day 'Submission & Admission' I see you have clearly demonstrated that the difference between the two Governments is of a substantial character & not one of form only. The attempt which you explained to me in conversation the other day to substitute the San Stephano Treaty, for the Treaty of Paris, is just the very point.

I have written to Messrs Smith & Elder informing them that the ~~[illegible]~~ series will b

A Letter from Richard Jefferies to Greenwood.

concluded in 24 articles: as No II. was of extra length this is really equal to 25, & with the 3 on 'Poaching' to 28.

May I say something without giving offence — I do not feel quite easy in making use of your experience & advice & friendly assistance generally, without some acknowledgment. I have no idea what Messrs Smith & Elder will offer but I should be very glad indeed if I could induce you to take a little pecuniary share in the payment for republication. Of course I know very well that the money itself would not be of the slightest consequence to you, but that is not it: I feel that the articles would never have been written had it not been for your kindly encouragement, & in addition they have had the benefit of your literary knowledge in the elimination of unnecessary phrases & various other ways. To make use, as you have so freely allowed me to do, of your assistance without even a nominal return is contrary to my ideas of right, & if you would only accept some small part of only ten or fifteen per cent of the sum they give, I should not feel so ungrateful. I most sincerely trust you will not take offence at what seems to me a natural & proper suggestion: please look at it in the spirit which dictates it. I remain

propose to put my name to the book — unless you think it desirable — I think it would be better to remain anonymous which will enable me to write with more freedom for the P.M.G. in the future, than if the authorship was known to every one.

I remain, Faithfully yours

F. Greenwood Esq   Richard Jefferies

and believed they had, something to say which they were anxious the public should hear. Goldwin Smith called the *Pall Mall* "an atheistical Tory organ", but it allowed free expression to out-and-out democratic opinion ably expressed'.

Greenwood was a townsman, but, as we shall see later on in his letters to his daughters, he spent a good deal of time in the country and delighted in it. He was an early admirer of Richard Jefferies and rejoiced in having pioneered in publishing his work. He writes: 'One or two of those beautiful books of Jefferies first came out of the *Pall Mall*, all to receive an exasperatingly small amount of attention, a not inconsiderable amount in itself, but so much less than their manifest worth and charm deserved as to be painfully disappointing to Jefferies' editor.' Among some letters from Greenwood to George Bentley, the publisher,[1]

[1] The firm published some of the work of Disraeli and Dickens and had

which I bought in London, is the following (see pages 192–3) dated September 23, 1878: 'Permit me to introduce to you Mr. Richard Jefferies: the author of a series of papers which, after proving very successful as published in the *Pall Mall* has been rapidly bought in book-form: I mean, *The Gamekeeper at Home*. Mr. Jefferies has in MS. a novel of Country Life: this he wishes to offer to your attention, and though I have not read the story, I am strongly inclined to think it of the kind that deserves an hour's consideration at any rate.' The letter from Jefferies to Greenwood on pages 186–9 has not been published before.

'Literature owes much to Greenwood for honest criticisms and the encouragement of his subordinates thereto', George Meredith told Clement Shorter. Nowhere are the literary and journalistic standing of the *Pall Mall*, its varying fortunes, and the feelings of Greenwood's friends towards him reflected more faithfully than by the stalwart of Box Hill in the following extracts from his vivacious correspondence picked from different pages of the *Letters of George Meredith*, collected and edited by his son,[1] which, 'with pleasure', the trustees kindly give me leave to reproduce and arrange chronologically:

Jan. 27, 1870. I'm afraid the *Pall Mall* can't be doing well, though when I sent to Greenwood he insisted on the cheerfulness of its condition. All speak with regret of it and of what they hear of it. The tone—eh? of the leaders doesn't seem to me so good, though it's above the newspaper type. You see they have dealt with Bradlaugh. I spoke to Greenwood about him, insisting that he was a man of power, and was not to be sneered down.

Jan. 1, 1873. My dear Greenwood [all his letters begin so]. Open your heart a minute to receive a greeting of the New Year from me. May you fight as victoriously—bravely you always will—this year as last! Fitzjames Stephen's articles are fine out-hitting and have judicial good sense. They are prose of Carlyle's doctrines, valuable, profitable, but to me, though I take their smashing force, just not conclusive enough to make me anxious to hear the rejoinder. It is of

been in relationship with Colburn, the firm which had published Evelyn and Pepys.

[1] Constable.

great importance that what he says should be said. His side of the case has hitherto been woefully dumb—unable to supply an athlete. So bold and able a writer will set a balance. Only guard against a certain sombrely prognosticating tone that he has. Some one assured me that George Smith had yielded his part in the *Pall Mall* to Spottiswoode; not true, I hope?[1] All states of life have their privileges, and mine is to be behind the scenes of many illustrious and ringing names, and to laugh. I would run on, but you are a busy man. If we can't meet, I will invite myself to you for the evening. From your loving, George Meredith.

March 12, 1874. I should like to review *Spain and the Spaniards* of Azamur Batuk; and also *Yu-Pe-Ya's Lute* by Mrs. Webster, if I see stuff in it. Will you leave them out for me? I want work. My poor *Beauchamp* is not thought good for the market by George Smith, who is (as he always is) very kind about it.

Dec. 31, 1874. Though you are rapidly becoming insubstantial to me as well as elusive, I believe in you still, and will wish New Year's happiness to an Editor so deep in his retirement as to be but the animating spirit of a newspaper. Sometimes I see you glowing through the bars of the *Pall Mall*, roguish as Holbein's Harry 8th Jester at Hampton Court, or awful as Eblis with the fire at his heart. Some day I shall call for a talk of five minutes. Meantime I salute you with all my heart.

March 9, 1876. Don't laugh at my simplicity: I'm treating you as if you really meant to come. And who knows? Faith has been rewarded and unfaith astounded before now. I've a great appetite for you.

Nov. 11, 1878. I go strongly with you in your work. Your affectionate George Meredith.

Dec. 31, 1878. I wish you health and strength for the New Year. You do the work of a good soldier; I see your watchfulness perpetually, besides the big strokes and thwacks; and for no man have I so warm a desire to see him sustained to keep to his task, as for you.

Queen Victoria in 1878 found the *Pall Mall* 'very strong in the right sense'.

The editor of the *Pall Mall*, like one of his successors, Stead,

[1] I have been unable to obtain, from any quarter, confirmation of this rumour.

Sepr. 23. 187[illegible]

PALL MALL GAZETTE
NORTHUMBERLAND STREET,
STRAND.

Dear Mr. Bentley

Permit me to introduce to you Mr Richard Jefferies: the author of a series of papers wh. after proving very successful were published - - - - -

Facsimile of part of Greenwood's letter to Bentley.

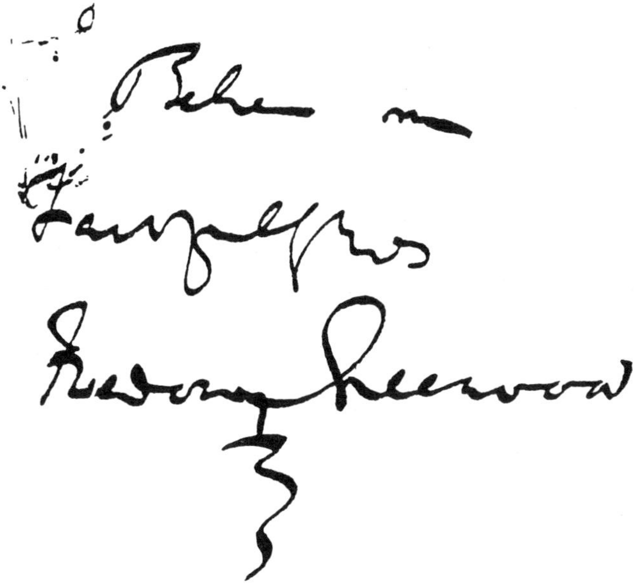

had, as has been stated, a particular feeling for children—Stead would take his own children out donkey-riding in the early morning on Wimbledon Common before starting for the office about eight o'clock. Greenwood, suspecting the genuineness of many advertisements in the Press for babies to nurse, had inquiries made, with the assistance of 'a courageous, good-hearted woman', whose name he did not disclose—one thinks of Stead's own 'Maiden Tribute' investigation with Mrs. Jarrett. She obtained a 'bundle of letters from advertisers', and a woman who had been one of the advertisers was arrested and eventually hanged. Severe though Fitzjames Stephen, Greenwood's right hand for so long, might seem to be, he was also a friend of young people. In 1872 he wrote an article in the *Pall Mall* on 'The Rights of Children', and W. H. G. Armytage has published in *The Times Literary Supplement* letters from him to A. J. Mundella offering to put aside work in order to draft a Children's Bill. This he promptly did.

What is an editor's worst trouble? Many persons who know nothing of journalistic technique suppose, no doubt, that it is having to write against time. Greenwood once admitted that though pressure may be 'too great for a favourable and satisfactory deliverance' it may 'be strong enough to produce warm and spirited work. An apt and ready mind constantly employed in beating over certain departments of political study is usually prepared for whatever may happen within its own range of observation and expectancy. This is the answer to the reproach of writing at an hour's notice on the most important political events. No political event is unrelated to past and present. But the hour's notice—the hour's notice is very desirable. It gives the writer ease, it smoothes his way; it may even be accounted necessary for his own good and the good of his work.'[1]

But, Greenwood says, 'the sharpest pang the editor's mind can know, a mental pain that smites the Herr Pretender to Critical Acumen through midriff to backbone', comes from his discovery that 'some good thing which all the world applauds and buys was by him declined with thanks. After that the worst pain is when a fine piece of work which he knows to be fine and sends forth with anticipation of another procession of Cimabue, goes almost disregarded. That it slowly but surely makes its way is satisfaction served up much too cold.' But, he says philosophically, 'in one shape or another, such disappointments are common enough'. He took pleasure on one occasion in what he

[1] A man who had a wide acquaintance with journalists, T. H. S. Escott, had evidently Greenwood's article before him when he wrote in his *Masters of Journalism* (Unwin): 'Work done under hot pressure ought not, nor as a fact is likely, to be less thoughtful than that produced at leisure, for the properly endowed and equipped journalist has beforehand for weeks, months, perhaps years, meditated on what he commits to paper in a few minutes. He thus finds, in the very severity of the conditions under which he puts his paragraphs together, an inspiring, a methodising and a concentrating force at once stimulating and quickening him.' Escott, Arthur Waugh writes in *A Hundred Years of Publishing*, was 'an energetic and competent journalist, with a wide knowledge of the world, and a fluent, rather old-fashioned literary style, which tended to become, under stress of exercise, both flowery and monotonous'. Towards the end of his life his work was affected by a breakdown in health.

regarded as 'a remarkably good stroke of what is called "journalistic enterprise"'.

> After Waterloo [he writes] there had been no such tremendous event of its kind as the Battle of Sedan and Napoleon's surrender. Many newspaper correspondents, furiously emulous, witnessed the conflict; but ours was the man, who by theretofore unthought of tactics, got home the news first; crossing the Channel by special boat and writing his account of the battle and the surrender in a special train from Dover to London. And practically he was first by two days! Arriving late on Saturday afternoon, Mr. Holt White got in a brief but telling report for the late edition. In Monday's *Pall Mall Gazette* the whole history appeared; and no other report was published in England till the next day. Mr. Holt White brought from that desperate field—which he crossed on his way home in the dark of evening while the battle was fretting to an end—a very remarkable trophy. He was on Sedan heights with the Prussian King's staff while the battle was going on, and was present when the wretched Napoleon's messenger approached with a letter of surrender. In token of his office he carried a table napkin at the end of a stick. Holt White begged the rag of the King, and brought it home in his pocket. What is that piece of linen worth to the reigning German Emperor?

'I know what it is', Greenwood added, 'to have a "handful" of a war correspondent and yet a remarkably clever man.' The *Pall Mall* was enlarged to twelve pages with this 'exclusive'. The conductors of a journal which had been, in its own words, mainly devoted to public affairs, literature, and the arts, and aimed at offering 'sound thought, knowledge and style', had it borne in upon them that even a select public expected from a daily paper not only ideas but news.

We shall find Greenwood telling George Craik that he left the news side of the *Pall Mall* to the sub-editors, and seldom looked at it until after the last edition. Account was certainly not taken of the competition of his evening paper rivals, which showed greater keenness as collectors of news. Greenwood was not the only editor who was to suffer for this limitation of editorial interest. Lord Pethick-Lawrence, writing in his autobiography, *Fate has been Kind*,[1] of his connexion with the *Echo* (started in the same year as the *Pall Mall*), is candid. In noting that the *Echo* lost him a good deal of money, he says, 'If I had had more experience of journalism I should have devoted myself first and foremost to news and circulation; I ought to have scoured Fleet Street for the best news editor and the best circulation manager. But my interest was centred on the political side.'

In the ten-thousandth number, from which I have been quoting Greenwood, H. D. Traill also had some reminiscences. He says the production of the paper 'might be described as leisurely, and assuredly that word would quite accurately qualify the manner in which its contents were prepared'. Comparing newspaper office conditions then and now, he writes:

> No merry police court case lightly and facetiously handled. Fun was more decorous. Quaint Americanisms and knowing slang of the race course did not adorn the paper. Articles and reviews were more discursive, more essayish, less 'actual'.
>
> As to books for review, there was no weekly wagon-load of new volumes shot into the office. The books were usually considered 'worth a column' or at any rate got it. The difference applied to the treatment of thought as well as of 'actualities'. If two of the ablest contributors, Sir Fitzjames Stephen and Sir Henry Maine, were still living and doing the same masterly work, no evening paper would have any use for it. They would have to expand it over ten pages of a 'high-class monthly review'.
>
> To-day the evening paper has ceased to be an evening paper in everything but name. It is a midday newspaper with afternoon and evening editions. The hastily swallowed breakfast of the editor and his staff conduce little to a genial and happy frame of mind. It is a 'heavy change' from the days when work began at ten.

When I was one of the sub-editors of the *Pall Mall* I arrived, if I remember rightly, two hours before that, and even earlier at times, having rushed through and blue-pencilled the most arresting things in the morning papers, as I travelled up by the London, Chatham and Dover from Loughborough Junction to

[1] Hutchinson.

Ludgate Hill, and thence by bus to Northumberland Street. The editor and his assistant gave themselves a little later hours.

Mr. Joseph Thorpe's report, in his *Happy Days*, is that the *Pall Mall* in Greenwood's time 'gave us news in a quiet, dignified fashion and provided us with interesting articles, reviews and criticisms; readers were given credit for average intelligence'. A veteran Gallery man, Sir Alexander Mackintosh, wrote to me shortly before his death that 'Greenwood's paper was unlike any other'.

A special appeal to the public interest beyond 'The Amateur Casual' and the score over Sedan was the exposure of a quack doctor who, after a five days' hearing in court, received a farthing damages. But Smith had costs to pay, and was the recipient from medical men and others of a silver vase and salver. Some sympathizers sent him farthings.

Another lively action, which is mentioned in the article by Smith in a *Cornhill* article under the title of 'Lawful Pleasures', was that brought by Hepworth Dixon, the author of *New America* and *Spiritual Wives*. An 'Occ. Note' writer had suggested that he was 'best known as a writer of indecent literature'. The finding was again damages, one farthing.

When a vexed correspondent of the paper expressed his feelings about a passage in W. S. Gilbert's *Wicked World*, the dramatist brought an action, during the hearing of which Buckstone and Bancroft, if not Gilbert, entertained the court. In this instance the verdict was in favour of the *Pall Mall*.

Although, by the accidental substitution of the name of one banking firm for another, Baron Grant (born Gottheimer) was undoubtedly slandered, that financial gentleman was not bold enough to bring an action.

General George Henry de Strabolgie Deville Plantagenet Harrison was more confident. To him Smith had to pay £50 and costs, in spite of the fact that the plaintiff had asserted in court that he was the heir-general of Henry VI, and the rightful Duke of Lancaster.

By Dion Boucicault the proprietor of the *Pall Mall* was taken not to a civil court but to Bow Street. An assurance that 'no prejudice to private character' was intended was enough, however, to end the proceedings.

How many people dip into Miss Braddon nowadays? Time was when she was a best-seller. Light on her abundant production was thrown in an incident in which the *Pall Mall* was concerned in its second year. An account of it was given by Mr. Montagu Summers in *The Times Literary Supplement* four or five years ago. A novel called *Circe*, bearing the name of Babington White, came out in a magazine of Miss Braddon's called *Belgravia*, a stray copy or two of which I remember looking into with wonder as a child. The *Pall Mall* said the tale had been pillaged from Octave Feuillet and suggested that the author was a popular lady novelist. A letter in the *Pall Mall* purporting to be from Miss Braddon spoke of 'a thunderbolt' and offered to refund to subscribers to her magazine the price of the numbers containing the novel. This letter, Miss Braddon wrote to say, was a forgery, and she offered £100 for the detection of the ill-doer. Next the *Pall Mall* printed an advertisement in a Dutch paper of *Circe* as by Miss Braddon. The editor naturally invited 'Babington White' to come forward, for he continued to contribute to *Belgravia*. He did not put in an appearance, and twenty years or more later some of 'Babington White's' books were included in a list of Miss Braddon's works published by Maxwell. Mr. Summers concluded his article by mentioning that Miss Braddon had other pseudonyms than 'Babington White', and that pen-names were also on books by Louisa M. Alcott, another popular writer of the period. But neither the *Dictionary of American Biography* nor two Lives support the second assertion.

CHAPTER XVIII

Who got us the Suez Canal Shares?

DISRAELI AND THE ROTHSCHILDS — GREENWOOD AT THE FOREIGN OFFICE — THE STORY OF THE PURCHASE OF THE SHARES — HOW THE NEWS WAS PUBLISHED — SOME PLAIN SPEAKING

The great engine never sleeps. Her officers walk into statesmen's cabinets. They give news to Downing Street.—*The History of Pendennis.*

No incident at the *Pall Mall* during Greenwood's editorship was comparable in importance with the part he played in the paper's tenth year (1875) in relation to the British Government's purchase of the Khedive's Suez Canal shares. For this he was held in respect by those who knew the facts, he must be valued in the history of journalism, and the nation is substantially indebted to him. His action was no doubt in the mind of George Meredith when, he wrote, thirty years later, 'Greenwood is not only a great journalist; he has a statesman's head'.

In the thirties Goethe had expressed a wish to see England 'in possession of a Canal through the isthmus of Suez'. In 1854 de Lesseps, in a letter to Cobden, could not believe that it was possible for England, with more than half the commerce of the East, to oppose his project. But the British Government, Palmerston said, would 'use all its influence to delay the realisation of a project which is but a bubble to ensnare unwary investors'. The Canal 'is physically impracticable and would be far too costly to earn any return', this 'foul and stagnant ditch' was 'one of the greatest frauds of modern times', de Lesseps was 'either a lunatic or a swindler'. Disraeli had thought the Canal 'most futile—totally impossible to carry out'. But it had been supported by the great editor of *The Times*, Delane.

When the project was set about, 90,699,000 francs were subscribed in France but only 42,500 francs in the rest of Europe (including Great Britain) and America. The balance was supplied by the Khedive.

With the opening of the Canal in 1869, when the *Pall Mall* was four years old—'in the name of His Highness the Viceroy and by the Grace of God', said de Lesseps at the ceremony, 'I command the Mediterranean to enter Lake Timsah'—the sea route to India was shortened by 4,888 miles. There was now a hundred-mile channel from Port Said on the Mediterranean to Suez on the Red Sea. Lord Clarendon, the Foreign Secretary, sent a generous letter and the Indian Government wrote that the enterprise had been carried out by Frenchmen 'in the interests of the universe'. In the summer of 1870 de Lesseps received the freedom of London, and *The Times* said he had come to a country which had done nothing to bring about the Canal but 'since its opening, has sent through it more ships than all the rest of the world. Great Britain will furnish the dividends the shareholders will receive. May they be the compensation for our error.' Yet for two years the General Post Office sent its letters overland. Waghorn of the Overland Route, it may be mentioned, died destitute.

The British proportion of the traffic which was soon passing through the Canal was three-quarters. But Great Britain had no control over the management of the waterway. And de Lesseps, like the spendthrift Khedive—Ismail, Wilfred Scawen Blunt declared, cost Egypt £400,000,000—was continually in financial difficulties. British shipping had trouble over raised tolls. There even came a time when de Lesseps threatened to close the Canal. And an Eastern Question was developing.

The strange thing is that Great Britain had had a chance, perhaps more than one chance of acquiring the ownership of the Canal, the value of which came to be understood by the Admiralty, the India Office, and the Board of Trade; but nothing had been done. Mr. R. C. K. Ensor, in his *England, 1870 to 1914*,[1] notes that 'in December 1870, when Lord Granville was Foreign Secretary, and France in the throes of her war

[1] Oxford University Press.

with Prussia', the Khedive, who owned seven-sixteenths of the shares, 'not merely offered to sell this interest to Great Britain, but suggested (apparently with de Lesseps' concurrence) that she should buy up the whole of what was then a non-paying concern'.

When, in 1874, Disraeli entered upon his second Prime Ministership, he tried, through his friends the Rothschilds, to make up for missed opportunities. The problem before him was not an easy one. An attempt to buy the shares in the open market could hardly be considered a prudent proceeding. Someone who, in 1872, suggested open purchase, allowed for an addition of £3,000,000 to the price! And France, which had got rid of the incubus of her indemnity to Germany, might encourage action by a French syndicate. The British Government was 'faced with the necessity of finding some large holder not accessible to the influences swaying the French, and disposed to sell at a reasonable price'.

The impecunious and unscrupulous Ismail was plainly the 'large holder'. But, as Baron Rothschild told a Government Committee, it had been a tradition of his house 'to avoid business relations with profligate and ill-governed States', and the firm had 'no influential representation' in Egypt. So in 1875, Disraeli had to be content with telling Ismail that the British Government 'relied on his friendship and his continued ownership of a large share interest in the Canal as a guarantee for the security of communications'.

The Khedive was politely described by *The Times* as 'a man credited with a good understanding, a liberal temper and a remarkable spirit of enterprise', and, more accurately, by Aaron Watson, who had had a good look at him, as 'a fat, florid, comfortable gentleman in a frock coat and a fez, commonplace almost to the limit of commonplaceness', with 'the cheerfulness of a person who has never denied himself anything and is troubled neither about the past nor the future'. Moberly Bell of *The Times*, who during his long residence in Egypt knew Ismail well, explains how he maintained his oppression 'by doubling

England in the Far East
(? Frederick Greenwood)

With the excuse of being quite without instruction from official guidance. Public opinion has never been more confused or uncertain than upon those affairs that most concern the public safety. Now when the central point of curiosity is Pekin, it is as it was when all ears were attentive to rumours from Constantinople. Every third day, public opinion swings up or down, to this side or that side, according to the latest news: & it is not even necessary that the news should be of essential importance to make the change.

Specimen of Greenwood's 'copy' from an article showing his interest not only in the Near East but the Far East.

the tribute to the Porte and incessantly "backsheeshing" the Sultan'.[1] But when, in October 1875, Turkey went bankrupt, the Khedive saw Egypt going the same way. His country's loan of 1873 fell from 70 to 54 without buyers. With heavy payment due on December 1, he had plans before him for loans at 15 and 18 per cent.!

At this juncture, on Sunday, November 14, 1875, Greenwood, who was interested in the future of Egypt and in Near East politics generally,[2] happened to be dining with his friend Henry Oppenheim, who directed the Austin Friars branch of Messrs. Oppenheim of Cairo and Paris. He was 'the cheeriest and kindest of Mayfair hosts', and Greenwood was frequently his guest. As one of the proprietors, with Henry Labouchere, of the *Daily News*—*Truth* was not started until 1877—he was politically an opponent of Disraeli. He is described to me by his daughter, Mrs. Campbell, as 'a very retiring man who never bothered about kudos, and worked only to serve his country'. The story, as it has been often related, is that he told Greenwood of the plans which were being made to transfer the Khedive's Suez Canal shares, 'within a few hours', into French hands, and expressed his regret that the British Government was not acquiring them. Whereupon Greenwood said he did not think a British move out of the question. He would himself, with Oppenheim's agreement, make the situation known in the right quarter.

Next morning, Monday, November 15, Greenwood, who in the *Pall Mall* was giving the Government 'strong but independent support', called on Lord Derby and urged the importance of securing the shares.

As readers who care to look up the correspondence in *The Times*[3] will see, efforts have been made to belittle the service Greenwood rendered, or to secure the reputation of having had

[1] *Life and Letters of C. F. Moberly Bell* (Richards). In 1914 the then Khedive became Sultan of Egypt. The Kingdom was proclaimed in 1922 and Egypt has been an independent State from 1936.

[2] See page 230.

[3] Dec. 27, 28, and 29, 1906, Jan. 13, 18, 26, 30, and Feb. 10, 1907.

a share in it, or to give the whole credit to Disraeli. In order that the facts may appear, it is worth the trouble to bring together some of the narratives. The task is by no means tedious.

G. E. Buckle,[1] in the fifth volume of the Monypenny and Buckle *Life of Benjamin Disraeli, Earl of Beaconsfield*,[2] says the 'startling suggestion was not at first welcomed by the cautious Derby', but 'the Prime Minister was sanguine of the immense benefit which would result'. Mr. Ensor, in the valuable work already quoted, says 'the decision to purchase was entirely Disraeli's, and that he carried it in the Cabinet against strong opposition'.

There is no question about that, and no one would wish to diminish the amount of credit due to Disraeli's imagination and vigour. But let us get it clear beyond doubt that Greenwood was the man who raised the alert, the revealer of the situation which would develop 'within a few hours', the initiator of the plan of immediate purchase.

H. M. Hyndman, later the stockbroker-head of the Social Democratic Federation and at that time on Greenwood's staff, gives a vivid account of his chief's action:

> I saw the whole of that Suez Canal business very close indeed and remember it all as if it were yesterday. The Khedive was pressing for sale in Paris. Greenwood heard of this and the idea occurred to him that the best possible buyer would be the British Government. In the *Pall Mall* office he asked me what I thought of it. I said it seemed to me a splendid idea. Greenwood then called in Traill[3] from another room. He was quite as confident of the merit of the scheme as I was. Then and there Greenwood went off in a cab to Lord Derby.
>
> What is not so well known, and Greenwood never referred to it afterwards, is that Lord Beaconsfield, according to him, was, or pretended to be, at first unfavourable to the project.
>
> Another point is that he [Greenwood] made not a shilling by the business himself, in the way of purchasing shares on the market; neither did the two men to whom he mentioned the matter. Green-

[1] Editor of *The Times*, 1884–1912.

[2] Murray.

[3] H. D. Traill, author of *A Social History of England*.

wood died a poor man. Traill was certainly not rich, and the writer is permanently short of cash.[1]

A colleague of mine years ago at the *Daily Chronicle*, Mr. James Milne, says, in his *Window in Fleet Street*,[2] that A. J. Wilson, well known for his ability and probity as a financial editor, and in 1875 on the staff of the *Pall Mall*, also 'knew for three critical days'—presumably from Monday morning, November 15. Mr. Milne, a friend of Wilson's, tells me that his memory is clear on the matter: 'Wilson left no doubt in my mind that the idea of buying the shares originated with Greenwood.' Wilson's daughter, Miss Laura Wilson, concludes a letter before me with, 'Dizzy grabbed all the credit'.

A Conservative journalist, the late R. D. Blumenfeld, formerly editor of the *Daily Express*, a neighbour of mine in Essex in the nineteen-thirties, who would be unlikely to belittle Disraeli, says 'the historians did not give Greenwood all the credit he deserved, the Disraeli cult being too strong for the romantic tendencies of the recorders'.[3] T. E. Kebbel, an admirer of Disraeli, in his article about him in the *Dictionary of National Biography*, gives the credit to Greenwood; 'there is no doubt about it'. Justin McCarthy in his *History of Our Own Times*, is also definite: 'Greenwood was the man to whom the idea first occurred.' J. L. Garvin spoke of Greenwood's 'unique stroke of genius'. Sir Ian Malcolm, a British representative on the Suez Canal Board, in his *National Review* article which is at the Treasury in a revised and re-revised form, agrees with these authorities.

Greenwood himself has two accounts of the transaction; the thirty-four lines of definite statement in his biography of Beaconsfield in the *Encyclopaedia Britannica* and a fuller statement in a spirited and characteristic address of great interest which he made at the dinner given to him by a distinguished company in April, 1905, towards the end of his career.[4] The

[1] *The Record of an Adventurous Life*, H. M. Hyndman (Macmillan).

[2] Murray.

[3] *All in a Lifetime*, R. D. Blumenfeld (Benn).

[4] *See* Chapter XXXVIII, 'The Great Occasion'.

speech is not orderly, but every sentence is relevant, readable and characteristic of the speaker. So it is well worth reproducing from *The Times* third-person report. After saying that 'the transaction had benefited the peasantry of Egypt, who, as a consequence of the purchase, enjoyed more freedom, liberty and personal comfort than they had enjoyed for 5,000 years', he went on:

> It was not very easy to accomplish, for Lord Derby did not like it and Sir Stafford Northcote, the Chancellor of the Exchequer, did not like it. After his first interview with Lord Derby, he had a visit from the Under Secretary for Foreign Affairs, Mr. Robert Bourke, afterwards Lord Connemara, who shook his head vigorously and gave him to understand that the Prime Minister himself was rather doubtful of the venture.
>
> He [Greenwood] had heard that possibly within a few hours the Khedive's Canal shares, which amounted to nearly half of the shares, would pass into French hands. He also happened to know that just before that opportunity arose, Lord Derby had been persuaded by the mercantile community of this country to obtain a reduction of the Canal dues. The British merchant was paying the dividends and the French public was receiving them. The correspondence had never been published, but he had seen it.
>
> At his first interview with Lord Derby not a syllable of the political effect of the purchase of the Canal shares was uttered. He dealt solely with the commercial side, and asked Lord Derby to consider what were the chances of ever getting the dues lowered if the whole of the property, instead of about half, passed into the hands of the French. He thought that view rather impressed him.
>
> But the Khedive's shares were his private property. There was, therefore, no authority whatever to interfere with his selling them at any time for any price he chose. To the question, 'How are you going to get them?' he had no answer to give except, 'Look at the alternative if you do not purchase'.
>
> Then Parliament was sitting. If it was asked for four millions, to use Lord Derby's own phrase, 'the gaff would be blown'. Mr. Morley [in the chair at the dinner to Greenwood] would want to know why. These questions were put to him like, not a five-barred, but a six-barred gate. However, he stuck to it that somehow or other the

shares were to be competed for by the British Government, and Lord Derby then showed what a very capable, prompt, ready, quick mind he possessed.

Going back to how he heard of the impending sale of the shares and to the arrangement of his talk with Lord Derby, Greenwood said:

He first heard of the opportunity one Sunday from a gentleman with whom he was dining. He went home immediately and wrote to Lord Derby at his house in St. James's Square, saying that he had heard what seemed to him news of very great importance, that he felt pretty sure Lord Derby was not ignorant of it, but at the same time it seemed of so much importance that he would take the liberty and the chance, of being permitted to see him the next morning at the Foreign Office. In his ignorance, he even named the time, 10.30. When he got to the Foreign Office he found the Foreign Secretary there. He had probably never been at the office in his life at that hour.

Lord Derby most kindly and graciously said, 'I know you do sometimes get very good information, but you are wrong this time' (about the imminence of the shares passing into French hands). He replied that he thought not. Lord Derby then said, 'I will give you my reasons. We had despatches only the day before yesterday from Colonel Stanton (our Consul in Egypt) who says not a word about it. Now it is impossible that a transaction like this, in a place like Cairo, could go on undetected under the nose of Colonel Stanton'. He replied that he was afraid, however, that that was the situation. Lord Derby then said, 'You have put me in a very awkward situation. Either you are right or you are wrong. There is only one way, and that is by directly interrogating the Khedive, 'Is it true or not that you are now engaged in negotiations for the sale of your shares?' Now we all know that he is very hard up, and if you are wrong what we shall do is to put the sale of the Canal shares into his head. In the next place we shall present ourselves as having some claim, which at present I do not see exists, to interfere with the sale. At any rate, the question will be opened in this way, and we do not want the shares. They are better where they are. Well, what shall I do? Shall I ask the question?'

It was not that Lord Derby was seeking his counsel, but he was putting upon him the fullest responsibility. He was testing perhaps his confidence in the information he had supplied. Lord Derby went to a table just behind him, wrote out a telegram, brought it back and read it out. 'This is to Stanton. "Go to the Khedive immediately and ask him whether it is true that he is negotiating for the sale of the Suez Canal shares, Yes or No. And do not come away without getting an answer." Now shall I send that?' Then he said 'Well, suppose we think of it.' Greenwood said, 'Yes'. On that his lordship said, 'Very well, if you will come to me tomorrow afternoon I will tell you what the result is.'

He [Greenwood] went back to Lord Derby. 'You are quite right', he said, and then, very characteristically, 'Master Stanton shall hear of this'. Master Stanton did hear of it. He was quietly removed from his post, to some consulship on the Black Sea.[1]

The end of it was that communication was then made with the Prime Minister and all these questions were seriously discussed.

Lord Derby most handsomely told him [Greenwood] that he thought he had a right to know how things went on. 'Come in when you please and I will tell you how it is going on.' He did not avail himself of that offer because he knew it was all right after the second day, and things went through quite easily.

The Paris correspondent of *The Times* had a story that when the news was conveyed to the French Foreign Minister he was relaxing himself in a game of billiards, and that when he heard the news he broke his cue across his knee and uttered threats of the most alarming description. He always doubted the story because he was informed that the French really did not make any objection at all.[2]

[1] Greenwood later accepted a correction from Stanton's son that his father 'for purely private reasons and on the score of health, asked for a change', and accepted in 1876 the position of chargé d'affaires in Bavaria.

[2] THE TRUTH ABOUT DE BLOWITZ. The correspondent was de Blowitz. He had been assistant in the Paris office of *The Times* from 1871 and was Paris correspondent from Feb. 1, 1875. On the Continent I have heard his claim to the 'de' questioned. There is a Life of him published by Arnold. The third volume of the *History of 'The Times'* is cutting: 'His inexhaustible fluency enabled him to write dogmatically on all subjects, all men, all countries and all events, including some events that never happened. Lacking convictions of his own, he felt the temptation to study his audience and their wishes. He never wasted discretion on news that could be obtained without it. He regarded Bismarck and himself as by far the most important people in Europe.' To which it may be added that the French Minister who broke a billiard cue across his knee must have been a muscular fellow.

Lord Rowton was sent down by Mr. Disraeli a day or two after to Baron Rothschild, who was rather staggered at the idea of finding 4 millions in the next few days and without any security. The whole transaction occupied eight or ten days, not a whisper got out and nobody heard a word of it, and there came a certain Friday when the air of England was filled with hats. All through England there was an acclaiming of this great achievement which would redound for ever to the honour of Disraeli.

On the previous Thursday Lord Derby sent for him and said, 'We shall have this out in the newspapers tomorrow but we think you have the right to make the first publication of it.' Those were endearing traits in a Minister. He did not avail himself of the offer, and the next day *The Times* and other papers published the news which was received with a great roar of approbation.

He was fully content with that. The following Sunday he had a message from Lord Derby asking him to call. He did so, and Lord Derby said, 'Well, we have done the job. I think it will do. And now what can we do for you?' That was handsome too. At that time the Government was in a very bad way, and the Suez Canal transaction set them up very much. He was young [at 46!] and had his moments of flightiness. He did an irreverent thing. He laughed a little and said he did not want anything but the satisfaction of having done something of service to the country and the administration.

Greenwood's statement was certainly 'good copy'. It was also circumstantial and specific. *The Times* said in reference to it that the country had had the story of the shares '*from the lips of one qualified beyond all living men to tell it*', and that 'it will remain for ever memorable as a turning point in the Imperial policy of Great Britain'. As for Greenwood's phrase, 'The air of England was filled with hats', a leading article in the *Spectator* gives an impression of the Prime Minister's triumph and the advantage gained by the Government: 'The slowly sinking reputation of the Government has been suddenly revived by one of those dramatic and yet statesmanlike *coups* in which the author of *Alroy* delights. An act of far-sighted courage, its entire history, its suddenness, its complete success, its audacity—for the news will fall like a thunderbolt in Paris and Constantinople—' and so on. And Hutton and Townsend proceed to reprove Gladstone for opposing the transaction. Another Liberal, Herbert Paul, in his *History of Modern England*[1] writes much in the same tone:

> Never in his long life had Mr. Disraeli been so popular before. The Ministerial Press was naturally and properly jubilant over this beneficent legerdemain. Mr. Disraeli had appealed to national pride, and got the response he desired. The Opposition picked all the holes they could. The shares did not give a right of voting on the Board of the Company proportionate to their number and value. The interest paid to the Rothschilds, who advanced the money, was too high, and they were fortunate in being Mr. Disraeli's friends.

Mr. Goschen, afterwards a sapient Chancellor, thought the purchase bad business commercially.

What struck one of the future editors of the *Pall Mall*, E. T. Cook, many years afterwards, was that 'the shares were not secured by shrieking captions in Greenwood's paper, but quietly and behind the scenes. If the editor adopt the noisier way, with incidental disadvantage to the public interests, when another and quieter would, or might have, attained the same end, he must expect to find his motives questioned.'[2] Quixotically, as most journalists would say, Greenwood, as he explained in his speech, chose not to be the first to publish the news of the purchase.

I turned with curiosity to *The Times* of November 26, 1875, in order to see the way in which the intelligence was actually given. The first time I looked through the file for November I did not find the statement. On a closer scrutiny I discovered it tucked away in 'Money Market and City Intelligence', a feature without a single cross heading. Between an account of a provincial bank in difficulties and a bit of commercial news there is this paragraph:

> The following telegram was handed to us today by the Bank of Egypt. The announcement is most important for this country and

[1] Macmillan, 5 vols.
[2] *Life of Sir Edward Cook*, J. Saxon Mills (Constable).

for Egypt. The political importance of the step cannot be overrated: 'Egyptian Government sold to English Government Suez Canal shares for four million pounds sterling. Ministry is authorised to draw this amount on Rothschild at sight.'

The transaction was, however, the subject of the first leading article. (Those were the days when the array of leading articles occupied almost the whole of a page.) The 'somewhat startling announcement', it was said, 'had no place in the conjectures of the time'. The next day another first leading article again expressed satisfaction and further discussed the subject. On November 28 there was a column and a bit from de Blowitz, but, strangely enough, there had been no Letters to the Editor. It was not lack of space. The Wainwright murder trial was having a solid page of small type daily.

I have turned over a large and entertaining correspondence which accumulated at the Foreign Office and the Treasury on the transportation of the shares to England. As delivered to Stanton in Cairo, they were, he reported, in 'seven large cases' occupying '100 cubic feet'. He had 'four chests, lined with zinc, a deal case and hoops and wire' made for them. These, with the registers in which he was instructed to make, with 'extra clerical assistance', a list of shares, cost the sum of £21. 15*s.* 0*d.* Getting them on board H.M.S. *Malabar*, which was to take them to England, ran up a bill for £35. 5*s.* 9*d.* The expenses of the messenger from Portsmouth to the Bank of England, which agreed to keep open 'after the usual business hours', were, with £7. 4*s.* 0*d.* 'passenger's excess luggage', £14. 12*s.* 5*d.* The naval captain applied—on the ground, he said, that the shares represented £4,000,000!—for a preposterous gratuity for himself. No, wrote Mr. W. H. Smith, the First Lord of the Admiralty, indignantly, to the extent of several sheets. The businesslike head of the famous bookstall firm pointed out that the shares were not 'treasure'. If they had been lost they could have been replaced. Had not the Lords Commissioners of Her Majesty's Treasury intimated that, for this reason, they 'were not prepared to insure the shares on their voyage'? Besides 'the whole time of the captain' belonged to the Government. But, somehow or other, he managed to get a nice little douceur of £500.

This was not the only incident. For a time a high financial authority at the Treasury was not sure that there ought not to be a special Act of Parliament to enable the British Government to hold the shares, as if, someone minuted, it was not already holding millions of property of all kinds.

It may be mentioned that the Treasury, in discharging the Government's indebtedness to Messrs. Rothschild, followed a precedent, by adopting 'the method of payment of the Alabama claims'.

The next thing of interest about the shares came a generation later, on December 26, 1906. Lucien Wolf[1]—animadversions on whom will be found on p. 214—had a portentous article in *The Times* headed 'The Story of the Khedive's Shares'. Because it extended to no fewer than five and a quarter columns, and in the future may be taken as wholly gospel, it is worth while, and certainly interesting, to read it and the correspondence which followed. Writers got elbow room in those days. There were in the same issue seven columns on 'The Legal Poor of London', not to speak of two and three-quarters on 'The Situation in Jamaica', and two on 'The Elephant in East Africa'.

Wolf's article, Greenwood wrote to *The Times*, was 'a complete inversion of the facts, a statement which, if it could not be corrected by absolute proof would bring me under suspicion of taking credit to myself under audaciously false pretences'. Wolf's report of what passed at the Oppenheim dinner table 'turned the whole story upside down'.

The following day there is a letter from Oppenheim. 'Without referring to Mr. Wolf's general statements, with many of which I am not in accord', he writes, 'it is due to my friend, Mr. Greenwood, that I should state that *the idea, as well as the*

[1] Died Aug. 23, 1930, aged 73. There is a portrait of him in his *Essays in Jewish History* and a cartoon by Spy in *Vanity Fair*. See also reference to Wolf, *National Review*, Sept. 1914, but the Wolff Press Agency had two 'fs'.

initiative which led to the purchase of the shares, came from him and not from me. All credit is due to him. The information I was able to give would have been of no use but for Mr. Greenwood's clearsightedness, promptitude, ability and knowledge of affairs. I myself never entertained the possibility of the British Government buying the shares.'

Wolf's reply was lame, but he does take note of the fact that 'Mr. Oppenheim concurs with me in regarding Mr. Greenwood's prompt and skilful representation to Lord Derby as the essence of the matter'. The next day Wolf rambles on about some misunderstanding of his own with Oppenheim. After the Christmas holidays Greenwood feels it to be imperative to return to Wolf with a letter of a column and three-quarters. He says 'only two persons now or at any time'—query, Hyndman and Traill?—'could speak to the truth, and both repudiate Mr. Wolf's misrepresentation'. Wolf, he said politely, 'in his general history of the relations of Disraeli, Rothschild and Granville with the Suez Canal is greatly in need of good authority'. And he adds with precision, '*When the Khedive's shares were actually passing into the hands of the French, neither of them (Rothschild nor Derby) was aware of the transaction*'.

On February 10 Greenwood once more returns to the subject. 'It is one thing', he says forcefully, 'to be ignorantly wronged, another to be insistently belied. The lighter injury may usually be remedied, while as to the other it is never so easily dealt with, and the business of repelling it is humiliation itself.' With regard to the Rothschild of that time, he goes on to say,

> In good faith beyond all question he disputed my claim, insisted that the purchase of the shares was an affair that lay between his father and Lord Beaconsfield. Since then, however, there has been time and occasion for thinking the matter over at New Court, and therefore I begged Lord Rothschild in my last letter to this journal to say whether and why he still believes that the credit I take to myself belongs to his house. Or if any part, what part, and what there is to show for it. That appeal to Lord Rothschild had not been answered.

To take my appeal in silence is not as it should be. And so I must go further into particulars, produce my bits of evidence, and show that Lord Beaconsfield, who had so much glory from the purchase of the shares, and Baron Rothschild, who, so far as I know, never pretended to any, were wholly and entirely out of it when I called upon the late Lord Derby on November 16, 1875. But for that 'accident', as it is described in a recent history, the shares would never have been gained, but even within a few hours would have been irretrievably lost.

After the death of Greenwood and Wolf, *The Times*, in the course of its obituary of Greenwood, wrote, regarding the controversy, '*Mr. Greenwood's "one small claim to distinction", as he called it, remained untouched*'. But, with the following letter which I have received from Mr. Hamilton Fyfe, the judicious reader may well consider the matter closed. Mr. Fyfe (whose father, as has been noted, was Greenwood's assistant editor) knew Wolf: 'I knew him when I was secretary to Buckle at *The Times*. He used to send in letters and occasional articles. I wouldn't believe a word he said or wrote about anything without proof. I may be doing him an injustice, but that is the impression of him which remains in my memory. I should not hesitate for a moment between taking Greenwood's word and his.' Later, Mr. Fyfe was good enough to draw my attention to *A Rebel in Fleet Street*,[1] an autobiography of Comyns Beaumont, a man with a wide experience of London journalism. In this there are several pages of plain speaking about Wolf.

Here it is as well, perhaps, to correct statements in Sir Henry Lucy's *Sixty Years in the Wilderness*[2] and Escott's *Story of British Diplomacy*,[3] which may one day mislead somebody. Lucy has this inversion of the fact, 'Oppenheim suggested to Greenwood that he should call on Lord Derby', while Escott (who commends his narrative by saying that he was in the habit of seeing several persons in high authority at the Foreign Office and knew three Foreign Secretaries), is so far wrong as to state that Greenwood suggested the purchase to Oppenheim!

[1] Hutchinson. [2] Murray. [3] Unwin.

Buckle, who wrote the 1920 volume of the life of Disraeli, begun by Monypenny,[1] mentions as a possibility that Disraeli may have 'got wind of the Khedive's negotiations from another quarter', independently of Greenwood's communication to Lord Derby. I have found nothing whatever pointing to this. Buckle's reference to Disraeli's social relations with the Rothschilds is as follows:

> Baron de Rothschild, to whose good offices Disraeli had already had recourse in connexion with the Canal, was, like Disraeli himself and at Disraeli's request, on the look-out for an opportunity; and he may well have got news from Paris or Cairo of what was in progress. It was Disraeli's frequent habit when in town on official business, out of the season, to offer himself to the Baron and Baroness for dinner, especially on Sunday evenings. At their house, he told Lady Bradford, in a letter dated Nov. 20—during the very week whose events we are describing—'there is ever something to learn and somebody distinguished to meet'. There was also a tradition in the Foreign Office that the information reached the Government from more sources than one—a memorandum respecting the negotiations of the Khedive with a French group is understood to have reached the Foreign Office from Sir Stafford Northcote [afterwards Lord Iddesleigh] at the Treasury on the day on which Greenwood called.

'This may explain', the ex-editor of *The Times* goes on, in a curiously balanced sentence, 'the strange omission of Greenwood's name in the private correspondence of leading Ministers during the negotiations,[2] unless indeed we are to attribute the omission to that dislike and contempt of newspapers and editors which has often underlain the outward flattery and deference exhibited by statesmen, but which could hardly be felt by one who, like Disraeli, had boasted in Parliament that he was himself "a gentleman of the press and have no other escutcheon".'

[1] *Life of Benjamin Disraeli, Earl of Beaconsfield,* Monypenny and Buckle. 5 vols. (Murray).

[2] I am indebted to the Record Office for an examination of the Foreign Office papers of the time—the three volumes for 1875 are now in the 'open period'—but they do not contain any correspondence between Lord Derby and Greenwood, or between Greenwood and Disraeli.

(The reference is to his connexion with John Murray's paper, *The Press*, which ran for six months in 1826.)

Buckle also gives the picturesque tale of Montagu Corry, Lord Rowton, Disraeli's secretary:

Disraeli had arranged with him that he should be in attendance just outside the Cabinet room (on Nov. 17) and when his chief put out his head and said 'Yes' he should take immediate action. On this signal being given, he went off to New Court and told Rothschild that the Prime Minister wanted £4,000,000 'tomorrow'. Rothschild, Corry was wont to declare, picked up a muscatel grape, ate it, threw out the skin, and said deliberately, 'What is your security?' 'The British Government.' 'You shall have it.'

The recorder evidently accepts the details of the story with some hesitation, but Sir Sidney Low, who was Greenwood's assistant editor on the *St. James's Gazette*, writes: 'I believe it to be true, for I heard it from Greenwood himself. Corry called at the *Pall Mall* office on his way back from the City, after seeing Rothschild.' As to New Court's commission,

I find [Northcote wrote to Disraeli on Nov. 24] Smith and Welby a good deal startled by the largeness, 2½ per cent. When it is considered that two million were provided by the firm for the Khedive on Dec. 1, another million on Dec. 16, and the last million on Jan. 5, the commission will seem moderate for so vast and prompt an accommodation. The withdrawal of four millions for a considerable period from the resources even of so commanding a firm as that of the Rothschilds necessarily entailed a large derangement of the routine of its business; and they had obviously to protect themselves against fluctuation in the value of money, and against the conceivable, though remote, risk that Parliament would refuse to validate the purchase. It was a transaction entirely without precedent, as Rothschild pointed out to Corry in a conversation at the time of the debates in Parliament.[1]

It is stated that, 'on the question of providing the funds, Baron de Rothschild, taught by his experience of Egyptian intrigue',

[1] *Life of Benjamin Disraeli, Earl of Beaconsfield*, Monypenny and Buckle (Murray).

sent for Oppenheim, Greenwood's host, and 'secured his valuable aid in carrying the operation safely through'.

What the Rothschilds actually did was to place a million at the disposal of the Egyptian Government on the handing over of the shares in November, and to provide the remaining 3 millions in December and January.

In one of the documents 'The First Lord and the Chancellor of the Exchequer state that Messrs. Rothschild undertake'—in one paper the wording is 'Baron Rothschild'—'the heavy liability on the pledge of H.M. Government that they will submit the engagement for the sanction of Parliament and endeavour to obtain the necessary power to repay the advance and pay Messrs. Rothschild's commission as soon as may be practicable after the meeting of Parliament.'

On the question whether the Government should not have applied to the Bank of England rather than to the Rothschilds, Corry reports the Baron as declaring that 'the Bank could not have found the required sum without grave disturbance of the money market. It is upon the entire absence of such disturbance, under his operations, that he, from the public point of view rests his vindication of the commission charged, and is content that the matter should be judged by the results.'

The British public, Mr. Ensor records, welcomed the purchase 'as securing the route to India, but in itself it contributed little to this; its principal direct fruit was merely to assist in obtaining reasonable tolls for the merchant shipping which used the Canal (then nearly four-fifths British). It did, however, give England a new concern and standing in Egypt, which she began almost at once to develop; and this led on to her eventually taking control of the country'.[1] But there was also the cash gain to the Exchequer.

[1] Although there was 'a little soreness' in France over the transaction, there would have been, but for the sale to Great Britain, 'a serious financial *krach* in Paris'. De Lesseps was wise enough to put aside his disappointment and congratulate his shareholders on the British acquisition as 'a fortunate occurrence for the commercial success of the Canal'. And in 1880 the Credit Foncier bought up the Khedive's lien of 15 per cent. on the net profits of the Canal. As the

In his *Life of Joseph Chamberlain,*[1] J. L. Garvin states that when, a few days after the Unionist Government took office, Great Britain entered upon the full possession of the Suez Canal shares free of further cost—twenty years after the purchase, 'Chamberlain drew up a memorandum for the Cabinet summarising the fabulous results'.

They were indeed remarkable. The precise sum paid, without commission, was £3,976,584. 2*s.* 6*d.* for 176,602 shares. (It was discovered that there were not 177,642 as had been supposed.) Commission and other expenses came to £100,016. 7*s.* 7*d.* The total cost, therefore, was £4,076,600. 10*s.* 1*d.* The receipts by our Chancellors of the Exchequer count up as follows:

	£	*s.*	*d.*
Interest received on Purchase money 1876–7 to 1894–5[2]	3,635,188	9	9
Total Dividends and Interest received 1894–5 to 1948–9	63,511,010	16	7
Total received 1876–7 to 1948–9 . . .	67,146,199	6	4

Or £63,069,598. 16*s.* 3*d.* net! The precise figures have not, I think, been published before in any book.

sum paid was 22,000,000 francs and by 1905 they were worth 192,000,000 francs, France had as good a bargain as Great Britain over its purchase.

[1] Macmillan, 1932–4.

[2] The Khedive agreed to pay interest, at 5 per cent., until 1894 'when the dividends—the coupons had been pledged—would again be payable by the Canal Company'.

CHAPTER XIX

Dizzy, Lady Bradford, and the Faery

EXULTING MESSAGES TO THE QUEEN — THE CHARACTER OF DISRAELI — 'THE FAME HE COVETED' — THE JUDGEMENT OF HISTORY — THE SHARES AND THE CANAL TO-DAY — SHOULD JOURNALISTS ACCEPT HONOURS?

INTERESTING though one finds the politico-commercial facts disclosed in the previous chapter, and the view of human nature they provide, there is an even more entertaining part of the story to be read in the correspondence between Disraeli and the Queen. Buckle, in the fifth volume of the estimable Monypenny and Buckle work,[1] prints letters between the Prime Minister and his sovereign which occupy in all, in small type, two and a half pages. In a first letter to the Queen, which he marks 'Confidential', Disraeli says:

> I was so decided and absolute with Lord Derby that he ultimately adopted my views. The Khedive now says that it is absolutely[2] necessary that he should have between three or four millions by the 30th of this month. Scarcely breathing time, but the thing must be done!
>
> Mr. Disraeli perceives that, in his hurry, he has not expressed himself according to etiquette. Your Majesty will be graciously pleased to pardon him! There is no time to re-write. The messenger for Balmoral is waiting.

Her Majesty telegraphs 'Approval', and Disraeli tells her that 'Your Majesty's approbation greatly strengthens me'. On November 24 the Premier's exulting message is, 'It is just settled; you have it, Madam', which reminds one of Lord Ellenborough's telegram from India, *Peccavi* (I have Scinde):

> The French Government has been outgeneralled. Four million

[1] *Life of Benjamin Disraeli, Earl of Beaconsfield*, Monypenny and Buckle (Murray).

[2] It has been noted that Disraeli was fond of the word 'absolute'.

sterling! and almost immediately. There was only one firm that could do it (Rothschilds). They behaved admirably; advanced the money at a low rate, and the entire interest of the Khedive is now yours, Madam. Yesterday the Cabinet sat four hours or more on this, and Mr. Disraeli had not one moment's rest today; therefore the despatch must be pardoned, as his head is rather weak. He will tell the whole wondrous tale tomorrow.

It was Lady Bradford's turn on November 25.[1] Disraeli wrote with 'a great State secret, the most important of this year, and *not one of the least events of our generation*':

After a fortnight of the most unceasing labor (*sic*) and anxiety, I (for, between ourselves, and ourselves only, I may be egotistical in this matter) I have purchased for England the Khedive of Egypt's interest in the Suez Canal. We have had all the gamblers, capitalists, financiers, classed, organised and platooned in bands of plunderers, arrayed against us and secret emissaries in every corner, and have baffled them all, and have never been suspected. The day before yesterday Lesseps, whose company has the remaining shares, backed by the French Government, whose agent he was, made a great offer. Had it succeeded, the whole of the Suez Canal would have belonged to France, and they might have shut it up. We have given the Khedive 4 millions sterling for his interest, and run the chance of Parliament supporting us. We could not call them together for the matter, for that would have blown everything to the skies, or to Hades. The Faery [his usual word for the Queen] is in ecstacies about 'this great and important event' and wants to 'know all about it when Mr. D. comes down today'. I have rarely been thro' a week like this last—and am today in a state of prostration—coma. Sorry I have to go down to Windsor—still more sorry not to have had a line today, which would have soothed your affectionate D.

A letter from the Queen on the same date ran: 'This is indeed a great and important event. The Queen will be curious to hear all about it from Mr. Disraeli tomorrow.' In reference to this visit, Disraeli writes to Lady Bradford:

Nothing could be more successful—I might say triumphant. The

[1] *Letters of Disraeli to Lady Bradford and Lady Chesterfield*, edited by the Marquis of Zetland (Benn).

Faery was most excited—'what she liked most was, it was a blow to Bismarck', referring, I apprehend, to his insistent declarations that England had ceased to be a political power. This remark she frequently made. She received me almost with caresses, absolutely said she never saw me looking so well and all sorts of things. She showed me a couple of telegrams she had received from the Prince of Wales, and she wishes me to write to him about Suez and all that 'because he likes you'. *The Times* is evidently staggered. I believe the whole country will be with me.

On November 30 Disraeli returns to the subject in a further letter to his close friend: 'The Faery was in the tenth Heaven, having received a letter of felicitations from the King of the Belges on "*the greatest event of modern politics*", etc.'

In thanking Her Majesty on November 27 the Prime Minister says: 'There was only one opinion in the City yesterday, and the accounts, from all the great centres of Your Majesty's kingdom, this morning re-echo the same feeling. He believes it may, now, be looked on as a great, perhaps unparalleled success. But Your Majesty predicted this when no one had given an opinion, and when many great judges looked demure.'[1]

On New Year's Eve the Queen sends the Prime Minister two hundred words from a letter 'from her daughter the Crown Princess' in Berlin 'which she thinks will gratify him'. 'I must congratulate you on the newest deed of your Government', writes the future Empress Frederick. 'It sent a thrill of pleasure and pride, almost of exultation, through me; a delightful thing to see the *right thing* done at the *right moment*. Everybody is pleased here. Even the great man (Bismarck) expressed himself to Fritz in this sense.' And 'Willy' (who was to die in exile at Doorn) writes to his mother from Cassel: 'Dear Mama, I must write you a line because I know you will be so delighted. How jolly!' The Crown Princess concludes: 'This will rank in history among the many great, good and useful things done in your reign, and that makes me so proud and happy.'

[1] *Life of Benjamin Disraeli, Earl of Beaconsfield*, Monypenny and Buckle (Murray).

In his reply to the Queen's 'most gracious letter and gratifying and very interesting extract', the Premier concludes: 'It must be an additional solace to Your Majesty that it was greatly owing to the sympathy and support which Mr. Disraeli received from Your Majesty, and to the clear-sightedness of which Your Majesty evinced in the affair from the outset', &c.

But, at the end of all this, journalists and the interested general reader will ask the question to which the ex-editor of *The Times* addressed himself, Why is none of the credit given by any of the characters to Greenwood?

In the two volumes of Disraeli's correspondence with Lady Bradford and Lady Chesterfield, from which, as well as the Monypenny and Buckle Life, I have been permitted to quote so freely, the statement about the editor of the *Pall Mall* is, we know, untrue—that he had 'the privilege of being the first to announce to the public that it (the purchase of the shares) had taken place'. His name does not occur at all in Froude's or Mr. Harold Gorst's life of Beaconsfield. Walter Sichel's *Disraeli* speaks of the Prime Minister's ideas that 'prompted the stroke of the shares', and Wilfred Meynell's two-volume *Disraeli*[1] refers to his 'great commercial and political *coup*', but Greenwood might as well have never existed. Neither does Greenwood's name appear in Dasent's two-volume *John Delane* (editor of *The Times*, 1841–77),[2] nor, except in a single footnote, in *Delane of The Times* by E. T. Cook, one of Greenwood's successors in the editorship of the *Pall Mall*. And it is odd that, though the *Dictionary of National Biography*, in its article on Greenwood, has the clear statement on the shares transaction to which reference has been made,[3] Sir Sidney Lee, the editor, in his eighteen and a half pages on Disraeli—under Lord Beaconsfield there is the reference 'see Disraeli'—makes no mention whatever of the subject. Nor, in the two-volume life of the Duke of Devonshire, is there in his account of the shares transaction a word about Greenwood. One could wish that Buckle—the

[1] Greenwood is mentioned in a list of thirteen magazine writers.

[2] Murray.

[3] See page 205.

valuable Monypenny–Buckle Life has been said to record 'all that is known and all that is probable'—had left things clearer than he did, for, as a former editor of *The Times*, he must have felt that something was due to the memory of a man who was to him 'a journalist of high distinction'. Before 1919, when the last two volumes of the biography of Disraeli were sent to press, there were at the Foreign Office, and probably in *The Times* office, or in retirement, men who knew well what actually happened. Greenwood lived until December 1907, Oppenheim until May 1912, and Buckle himself until March 13, 1935.

My own inquiries at the Foreign Office, as I have noted, yielded nothing concerning events more than seventy years back. In Lord Beaconsfield's papers at Hughenden, which Mr. C. L. Wayper is examining, there is not in the Suez Canal section, he kindly tells me, anything about Greenwood. I naturally asked for permission to look into the archives of *The Times*. Alas, the bomb which hit Printing House Square during the war 'destroyed, among other valuable things, the Greenwood file', the much regretted Barrington-Ward kindly wrote. He was so good, however, as to send me three cuttings from *The Times* which had survived. One is an article, 'Suez Canal Shares/A Great British Achievement/50 Years After', and the leader in the same issue 'The Suez Canal', which appeared in *The Times* of November 25, 1925. A cross-heading in the article is 'A Journalist's *Coup*', but the writer says, 'Mr. Greenwood's information is believed to have confirmed an official despatch received at the Foreign Office at the same time'. I am in a position to say that neither in the Foreign Office nor Treasury archives is there any record of such a document. In *The Times* leader the statement is historically correct, '*It was by a happy accident that Lord Derby learnt from Mr. Frederick Greenwood*, the distinguished editor of the *Pall Mall Gazette*, that the embarrassed Khedive was negotiating for the transfer of his holding'. It is little wonder that article and leader brought from Mr. Lowther Bridges a letter saying what was in other people's minds: 'Full credit must be given to Mr. Disraeli for not having turned down the suggestion made to him, but Mr. Greenwood merited some signal mark of public approbation for his great public service.'

Mr. Attlee was good enough to inform me that at Downing Street there is no record of Disraeli having offered Greenwood any distinction.[1] He kindly added that 'it used to be the practice for Prime Ministers to take away many of their papers at the end of their tenure of office'. I addressed myself to two eminent historians of the period, Professor E. L. Woodward of Balliol, and Mr. R. C. K. Ensor of Corpus Christi, the latter of whom I have twice quoted. Professor Woodward had come across nothing, but sent me the interesting letter in the footnote.[2] Mr. Ensor, noting that, 'in Queen Victoria's reign, honours were far rarer than in this century', was good enough to give me an example: 'An uncle of mine was an admiral and held for a period of years the third highest command in the Navy—with complete credit, and on top of another very high special post. Not only was he not knighted, but he never received an "honour" of any kind (he died in office). Today he would automatically be a K.C.B., and probably have a string of other letters after his name.'

In the course of his Life of Disraeli, the careful and highly

[1] Disraeli in offering, as Gladstone had done before him, a baronetcy to Tennyson, had said that 'a Government should recognise intellect; it elevates and sustains the spirit of a nation'.

[2] 'I am always very much puzzled about this Suez Canal business. Mr. Gladstone's view was right—the control of the Canal depended ultimately on sea-power, not on the ownership of shares—and there is some reason also to suppose that the French Government really wanted to buy the shares—they knew we should suspect them if they bought them: and they didn't want to offend us because they were in our political debt owing to the line we had taken over the 1875 war scare. At the same time they wanted a rise in Egyptian bonds generally because some French banks were heavily involved in them and wished to get out, and the only hope of a rise in Egyptian credit was that the Khedive should have some cash in hand. I don't know whether this version is correct—it is referred to in an odd and interesting American book, L. H. Jenks's *Migration of British Capital to 1875*. If this story which sounds plausible is true, I wonder whether Disraeli knew about it—Rothschild would, of course, have known—and if D. did know about it, then all the talk of a brilliant *coup* was D. once more with his tongue in his cheek!'

informed Buckle deems it necessary to make a statement which students of the matter under consideration can hardly pass by. He writes, 'The fundamental fact about Disraeli was that he was a Jew'. 'No Englishman could approach Disraeli', Greenwood says in the encomiastic biography of Disraeli which he contributed to the *Encyclopaedia Britannica* after the ex-Premier's death, 'without some immediate consciousness that he was in the presence of a foreigner. He was thoroughly and unchangeably a Jew, but one remove by birth from southern Europe and the East.' To the close of his career in the House of Commons he was, as Greenwood reports Lord Malmesbury saying, 'prejudiced by a pronounced foreign air and aspect'. 'His mind, neither English nor European', says Greenwood, 'should accompany the traveller through all the turns and incidents of his career.' 'To the end of his days', writes Viscount Cecil, 'he was distrusted by many of his colleagues and friends.'

In the course of his *Encyclopaedia Britannica* biography, of eight pages or more,[1] Greenwood in his temperate account of the shares purchase, says 'it was a courageous thing to do, but it was not a Disraeli conception, nor did it originate in any Government department'. Greenwood makes no criticism whatever of Disraeli, but at the end of the memoir, in the two columns or so in which he discusses Disraeli's complex character, he has this sentence: 'It is said to his honour that he "never struck at a little man", and that was well; but it is explained as readily by pride and calculation as by magnanimity.' And elsewhere, when he is mentioning the common belief that Disraeli looked in the glass when, in *Coningsby*, he described Sidonia, he quotes the novelist: 'In his organisation there was a peculiar, perhaps a great deficiency: he was a man without affection. It would be hard to say

[1] Greenwood seems to have cherished until a late period the notion of writing a book on Beaconsfield. How serviceable it would have been we may judge from his appreciative but discriminating biography in the *Encyclopaedia Britannica*. I know that he at first refused to assign the copyright of this painstaking piece of work to *The Times* and only yielded after some correspondence with Moberly Bell, who explained the necessity for protecting the interests of the newspaper.

that he had no heart, for he was susceptible of deep emotions, but not for individuals.' 'Whether Disraeli's likings were strong or not I do not know; I doubt his feelings of friendship being warm', writes Sir William Fraser, and adds unequivocally, 'no rewards awaited those who had sacrificed everything in their support of him: no thought was given to them; they had served their turn.'[1]

Two generations have grown up since Disraeli passed away (1881). They scan with curiosity the portraits[2] of a rather strange, alien-looking, unconformable personality who, 'without a drop of British blood in his veins', was twice Prime Minister of Great Britain. They probably remember having once read about the rings worn above gloves in his younger days,[3] and notice, even towards the end of his life, a trained curl[4] on his forehead. They have met with astute, picturesque, flamboyant scraps of his speeches.[5] They have, no doubt, perused some letters he wrote to his friends which tell a little of the man; they may have conned one or two of his novels. What is the truth, these moderns may well ask, about a man of mark, station, and reputation, who, contending with varied antagonisms and, for many years, with the hindrance of heavy private debt, did some service to the cause of political enlightenment and gained the headship of a party which, in his time, was the party of aristocracy and the socially and financially well placed, and the full confidence, even affection of his sovereign?

The Canal shares transaction and what happened about it can hardly be regarded as having no relation to Disraeli the man. As those who are of another day than that of the Prime Minister-novelist spare what time they may to get at the rights of the matter, have we not to be prepared for some inquirers after

1 *Disraeli and his Day*, Sir William Fraser (Kegan Paul).

2 The full length in the Junior Carlton has been said to be the best.

3 Fraser.

4 So says Sir William Fraser. Horace Annesley Vachell in *Twilight Grey* (Cassell) writes that, at one time, it was pasted down. Viscount Cecil has the phrase 'perhaps naturally black hair'.

5 'Penetrating, flamboyant visionary' is Mr. Algernon Cecil's phrase.

truth asking bluntly, Was Disraeli entirely a gentleman? Did he or did he not (in Blake's phrase) 'bend to himself a joy'—take to himself the credit of a transaction which, in honour, he ought to have shared, in some measure, with another in a less powerful position? His narrative of events, in which he alone shone, was accepted by his Queen and most of his contemporaries. Can it be entirely accepted now? As Mr. Ensor said to me, 'Disraeli is entitled to great credit for carrying the purchase through, just as Mr. Balfour, in another sphere, merits credit for the way in which he translated the ideas of others into action in his Education Act'. But, unless evidence is forthcoming of Disraeli's acknowledgement of Greenwood's initiative, may it not be thought that the fame to which he is entitled in regard to the shares transaction is a little blurred?

It is not as if Disraeli did not know Greenwood. He saw him shortly after the purchase of the shares. He saw him later on, at various times. He had, as Sir William Robertson Nicoll notes, many opportunities of seeing him. And he read what he wrote. He is reported to have said indeed, on one occasion, that whenever he read Greenwood, he felt himself in the grasp or grip of a statesman. He knew that, in the Press, first and last, in his contentions with Gladstone and on many questions, no editor had given him, no editor was giving him support of a more telling, more discriminating quality—'strong but independent support' in Buckle's phrase.[1] It is pertinent to add that Disraeli had a considerable knowledge of the Press. He was in a position to appreciate to the full, at the time of the shares transaction, Greenwood's professional self-abnegation in refraining from publishing what would have been one of the most noteworthy 'exclusives' in journalism.[2]

[1] See Gladstone's view of the value to Disraeli of Greenwood's general support, page 236.

[2] I notice, as this page is written, the following in the *World's Press News* of July 3, 1947: 'REUTERS ON PARIS LEAKS. Sidney Mason, Reuter's chief news editor, said that it is Reuter's job to get the news, secrecy or no secrecy. "Any rules of secrecy which officials impose are merely an additional challenge to find out what is really happening." '

The problem is not only a problem of Disraeli's personality but of Greenwood's. The fact that Greenwood had not received from Disraeli the word or two of public acknowledgement which was his due did not lessen in the least the support he gave him. That support was continuous and vigorous, even vehement. It was so marked as to be the chief cause, as we shall see, of John Morley taking his place as editor of the *Pall Mall*, a professional jolt from which Greenwood only partially recovered. Greenwood sacrificed something for Disraeli.

Greenwood's leading article in the *St. James's Gazette* on his death contains this judgement: 'Lord Beaconsfield's ambition was as great as the patience with which he worked and waited for the fame he coveted. No man thought more of what is known as the verdict of posterity. He looked forward to a place in the world's esteem when he was gone.' Will posterity ask if here is the secret of why Beaconsfield could not bring himself to share any of the distinction gained by the purchase of the shares?

The student of history whose judgement is unwarped by party feeling will be sorry about it. 'If I were to endeavour to sum up the ultimate feeling with which he inspired me', said Sir William Fraser, 'it would be one of pity.' There will always be different views as to the extent of the claims of Beaconsfield to honourable remembrance.[1] He was a man of genius. He worked assiduously. His life was a struggle. He was racially at a disadvantage. He suffered undeserved contumely. It would be pleasant to find, in his relation with Greenwood, a finer spirit than the records seem to show he exhibited to a man to whom he and, beyond question, the nation of which he was Prime Minister, were substantially indebted. I hope that some public statement of his in appreciation of Greenwood's service may yet come to light.

Buckle writing, with some authority, in view of his journalistic experience, has a phrase I have quoted about what he calls 'that

[1] Some members of the Liberal Ministry felt so strongly about him that they walked out of the House of Commons when the vote was to be taken on the motion to erect a statue.

dislike and contempt for newspapers and editors which has often underlain the outward flattery and deference exhibited by statesmen'. Every journalist who has occupied a position of any influence on the Press has been amused by instances of ill-becoming behaviour on the part of men in the public eye, of at one time seeking the favour of editors, and, on other occasions, trying to escape blame for slips of the tongue or to place the responsibility on the papers for inconvenient developments of public opinion. It would have been a shining incident in the relations of public men and the Press—which are more intimate than most newspaper readers suppose—had Disraeli, in some letter to a colleague or a friend, or on a public occasion, acknowledged in one editor a conspicuous act of intelligent, ready, and disinterested patriotism. Greenwood felt no rancour. Ten years after Disraeli's death he wrote an article on the Eastern Question headed 'Disraeli Vindicated'.[1]

I have met with a story that the Rothschilds gave Greenwood 'a few shares'! Absurd though this is, it is well to scotch it. Hyndman, who was closely associated with Greenwood, vaunted himself on being a man of the world, and as a stockbroker knew something of the ways of the City, says, positively, as we have seen, that Greenwood got nothing and was content to get nothing. Although Lord Crewe told me that there was 'no chance of any of the present generation of Rothschilds knowing anything of so small a matter' as the Suez Canal transaction, I applied to New Court and had a courteous reply from Mr. W. Bulkely-Johnson, who after 'a search', wrote: 'I am sorry to say that it has been without result. I was myself surprised to find that there are practically no documents in our archives referring to the transaction in any shape or form. You will remember that this was not an issue, but a straight loan to the Government, and therefore it is quite probable that the Firm had no knowledge of the antecedent discussions or of any distribution of shares there

[1] With regard to my criticism of Disraeli, I may note that, in the hope that any further facts available might be evoked, much of the present chapter and the preceding one appeared in the *Quarterly Review* of July 1949.

may have been to individuals. The transaction was, I believe, a very quick and simple one, and there is no evidence that the Firm ever handled any of the shares.'

As we have seen, the shares were in Cairo and went thence to the British Treasury.

It may be just as well to mention, however, in case anyone unacquainted with the history of the Suez Canal business may one day be curious, or even be led into baseless speculation, that Greenwood, as I have said, had always been interested in Egypt, and was well informed about conditions there, and that I found in the probate of his will that, among his investments, were £5,680 worth of Egyptian Preference Stock and Unified Bonds.

It is an argument against a system of public honours that it is impossible to distribute them with perfect fairness. Merit may be rewarded; equal merit will be overlooked or neglected. If Disraeli, both as a commoner and peer Prime Minister, neglected Greenwood, in words or by means of some distinction from his Sovereign, how did it come about that the two Conservative Prime Ministers who succeeded him failed to repair his omission? Between the retirement of Beaconsfield and the death of Greenwood there were two Conservative Governments, Lord Salisbury's and Mr. Balfour's.

As Lord Robert Cecil, Lord Salisbury had been a fellow contributor with Greenwood to the *Saturday Review*. As Foreign Secretary three times over, he knew the value of the service the editor of the *Pall Mall* had rendered to British standing in the Near East. He was aware that the shares *coup* had brought substantial backing to Disraeli's Ministry at a critical time. He was acquainted with the aid which Greenwood—who was a visitor to Hatfield—gave to later Conservative Governments. It will be seen, however, in the letters which the ex-editor of the *Pall Mall* wrote to Blackwood that on several occasions Greenwood strongly disapproved of certain actions of Lord Salisbury—spoke even of 'mendacious ingenuities'.

There remains Mr. Balfour, who had made Alfred Harmsworth a Baronet one year and a Baron the next. How did it happen that, on the occasion of the remarkable tribute to Greenwood, paid to him at the great dinner in 1905, when so many persons of distinction were present,[1] this Conservative Prime Minister failed even to send a letter of felicitation? Leading Liberals, who were present in numbers at the gathering, had overlooked, in their recognition of Greenwood's personal integrity and patriotism, his steady animosity to Gladstone; Conservatives forgot all that Greenwood had done for their party and could only remember the occasional proddings which the *Pall Mall*, *St. James's*, and *Anti-Jacobin* had given them.

A well-known journalistic gossip, Sir Henry Lucy, states that, in later life, Greenwood's friends 'heard him speak with natural bitterness of his generous avowal' to Lord Derby at the time of the purchase 'being taken too literally'. One of the most interesting men in London, Mr. William Stone, of Albany, who became its chairman forty years ago, is the oldest member but one of the Garrick and the oldest member of the oldest Cambridge college, and, at ninety-one, had taken his turn round the Serpentine on the two October mornings in 1948 I saw him, gave me his recollections of Greenwood. He has the happiest memories of him. 'A charming man of character', he said, 'a pleasant companion, with all his friends a power. He was greatly respected and we all felt that he had not had his due for what he had done in promoting the acquirement of the shares. When I say "we" I speak, for example, of a circle at the Garrick which included such men as Sir Edward Clarke (Attorney-General), Sir Arthur Sullivan, Sir John Millais, Sir W. S. Gilbert, Harry Furniss, Linley Sambourne, George Grossmith, Sir Francis Burnand, W. L. Courtney, Edward Dicey (editor of the *Observer*), and H. D. Traill.' Mr. Stone, who is also a member of the Athenaeum, was for half a century a well-known rider in the Row, and had many friends and acquaintances in the society of the Disraeli period. He has an excellent memory and 'cannot recall any occasion on which he or anybody else read or heard of Disraeli, either publicly or privately, acknowledging the service that the editor

[1] See page 429.

of the *Pall Mall Gazette* had rendered'. He has an impression, however—'it was common talk at the Garrick and other Clubs', but he has no proof—that the Prime Minister did 'in the course of one of Greenwood's interviews with him', speak of a knighthood, but did not press it. 'It was the gossip that Greenwood, who was a proud man, went without the distinction by not then and there accepting,[1] and was afterwards chagrined at being without that which Henry Irving gained at a time when a knighthood for an actor was something new. It is not easy to exaggerate the kudos which Disraeli got from the shares transaction. It was the one topic of the time and gained the Government credit when it was in need of it. J. L. Toole had a joke at the Folly Theatre about the money straits of the Khedive and what could be done if he owed one money, "Sue-his Canal".'

But if I read Greenwood's character and temperament aright he, like George Smith, had no 'great regard for titles'.[2] Nice enough things to have, no doubt, and many of his friends and quite a number of contemporary newspaper men had them. He had indeed seen two newspaper proprietors advanced successively to knighthoods, baronetcies, and peerages. Towards the end of his life, when his *Pall Mall* had gone from him, and his *St. James's* and *Anti-Jacobin* were no more, and he probably felt—I have no record of his having written or said it—that he was merely an elderly, not too physically vigorous, forgotten freelance, and most of the friends of his strength and prominence were dead or away from him, approbation in the guise of distinction of some sort might have added something to his tranquillity of mind. But Greenwood would not have done as much as he did for J. M. Barrie if he had not had a relish for the droll side of life. Often enough he must have smiled at the small claim many men had to the dignities they had inherited or scrambled for. A ribbon he would have cared for less than for

[1] Is it not possible that the foundation for this gossip may have been Greenwood's account in his speech, reported at some length in *The Times* (see page 209) of how, in conversation with Lord Derby, he refused any reward for his services?

[2] Page 249.

simple public recognition, in an adequate phrase, by a spokesman of the State, of the service he had given.

The fountain of honour, which did not flow for Greenwood, or for George Smith, in appreciation of the *Dictionary of National Biography*, rewarded Henry Hucks Gibbs, who put down the money for the *St. James's* and had no doubt given other support to the Conservative party. It rewarded with a viscountcy John Morley, the second editor of the *Pall Mall*, and this and E. T. Cook's knighthood were presumed to be for support and counsel to the Liberal party. Or were Morley's valorous editorship of the *Fortnightly*, and those stirring books of his, and Cook's thirty-nine volumes of Ruskin, occupying nearly eight feet on our shelves, also considered? Stead, who put as plain a mark on our journalism as Greenwood, got nothing.[1] Can one readily imagine him accepting anything?

When one comes to think of it, is there not a case against rewarding journalists at all, until, at any rate, their retirement—

[1] HONOURS TO JOURNALISTS. Suez Canal shares bought Nov. 24, 1875. Administrations: *Disraeli*, Feb. 21, 1874. *Gladstone*, Apr. 28, 1880. *Salisbury*, June 24, 1885. *Gladstone*, Feb. 6, 1886. *Salisbury*, Aug. 3, 1886, *Gladstone*, Aug. 18, 1892. *Rosebery*, Mar. 3, 1894. *Salisbury*, July 2, 1895. *Balfour*, July 12, 1902. *Campbell Bannerman*, Dec. 5, 1905. *Asquith*, Apr. 8, 1908. May 29, 1915. Dinner to Greenwood, Apr. 8, 1905. Death of Greenwood, Dec. 14, 1909.

The following honours to journalism, up to the death of Greenwood in 1909, with the names of the Prime Ministers recommending them, are noted in *The History of 'The Times'*:

1880	Algernon Bathurst	Kt.	Beaconsfield
1887	,, ,,	Bt.	Salisbury
1895	,, ,,	Baron	,,
1885	William Hardman	Kt.	,,
1892	George Armstrong	Bt.	,,
,,	H. H. Gibbs	Baron	,,
,,	E. Levy Lawson	Bt.	Gladstone
1903	,, ,,	Baron	Balfour
1894	Wemyss Reid	Kt.	Rosebery
1895	W. H. Russell	Kt.	,,
,,	George Newnes	Bt.	,,
1903	Alfred Harmsworth	Kt.	Balfour
1905	,, ,,	Bt.	,,
,,	,, ,,	Baron	,,

if real journalists ever retire? How can they write at all times their full convictions if in their minds there lurk the chances of receiving or not receiving distinctions? Is not part of the price which the editor pays for his liberty to write with that freedom which is necessary to his calling, the knowledge that he may not figure in Honours lists? But if men and women who come to distinction in every other profession are honoured, may journalism be singled out, with complete justice, to be honourless? May honours conferred on journalists be regarded as honours to their profession? Are honours received by editors and proprietors in the same category? May a distinction be drawn between honours conferred on authors and on journalists? How about the journalists who are, not infrequently, authors as well? Can honours given to authors be said to have been always fairly distributed? The selections for O.M. have been happy, and have honoured the selectors. But outstanding men have not received it—in all probability have not wanted it. Men's achievements outlast titles. Do many people of this generation remember that Tennyson was a Baron? As far as freedom to accept honours is concerned, there is obviously a difference between honours conferred by the State and by universities. Stars and ribands are less frequently worn than in pre-Victorian days. But there are nowadays many more orders and distinctions, and Quakers accept hereditary titles. Has a system of honours been found to be, for a variety of considerations, a useful makeshift in a developing civilization?

CHAPTER XX

The Proprietor makes a Present of the Paper

THE VENDETTA AGAINST GLADSTONE — WHY GEORGE SMITH GAVE UP THE PAPER — THE 'PALL MALL' GOES LIBERAL — JOHN MORLEY AS EDITOR — GREENWOOD WRITES TO GLADSTONE

ON a noteworthy occasion in 1905,[1] John Morley, by that time Viscount Morley, said 'the *Pall Mall* started as a sort of pleasure yacht, but soon became an armed cruiser, with guns of heavy calibre and a captain on the bridge possessed of a gallantry and a martial quality that had never been surpassed in the history of English journalism'. To James Hannay, a Conservative, Greenwood once described the *Pall Mall*'s politics as 'philosophical Radical'. Hannay replied ironically, 'I see the Radical'. Hyndman refers to the feelings of his editor about Gladstone:

> Greenwood was quite an admirable editor, thoroughly impartial in views until he became an active political journalist and permitted his strong feeling against Gladstone to warp his judgement, a mistake from which I should have thought his admirable sense of humour would have saved him. He attributed to Gladstone all sorts of unscrupulous devices which were, in truth, no more than evidence of what Carlyle called his 'extraordinary faculty of convincing himself that he conscientiously believes whatsoever tends to his political advantage'.[2]

'Anti-Radical' on the Eastern Question, Greenwood withstood Gladstone with all his strength, and grew to detest everything he stood for. Indeed, Froude thought the editor of the *Pall Mall* 'must have Turkish securities'! Although now and then a critic of Toryism, the *Pall Mall* became an animating spirit in the Conservative party, its 'Abdiel', Leslie Stephen called it. Morley—and as Gladstone's biographer he had the facts—

[1] See 'The Great Occasion', p. 209.

[2] *The Record of an Adventurous Life*, H. M. Hyndman (Macmillan).

regarded the paper as the most vigorous and unrelenting of the G.O.M.'s critics. It was Gladstone's own view that 'no Minister in this country ever had a more able, a more zealous, or a more effective supporter than had Beaconsfield in Greenwood'; John Bright spoke of the 'raving lunacy of the *Pall Mall*'. There is no record, however, of Gladstone adopting, with regard to Greenwood's attitude, the course he took with another opponent. 'He considered the hostile attitude of the *Daily Telegraph* so important', I have noted reading somewhere, 'that he called at its office to see Lord Burnham and Sir Edwin Arnold'. It was Gladstone who in 1892 had made Levy Lawson a baronet.

George Smith was not an ardent Party man—his daughter tells me that she never remembers political questions being discussed at home—but he was a Liberal and had Liberal inclinations, and he did not feel comfortable over the lengths his editor went in belabouring Gladstone and exalting Disraeli. The paper 'had drifted into a Conservative organ' and had 'a good deal of matter with which I had no sympathy. The change in complexion was unintended but was visible enough.' In fact Sir Henry Maine, on his return from India, asked Smith if the *Pall Mall* had been sold to the Conservatives. Hyndman, who said he had good authority for the statement, declared that Smith 'could not stand Greenwood's attacks on Gladstone any longer'. Mrs. Reginald Smith, who once mentioned to me that she has 'lovely memories' of her father, thinks that he was 'somewhat disappointed by Greenwood and thought that he had been politically ungenerous'.

Robertson Nicoll, who used to see Greenwood frequently, and no doubt got his information from him, says that the *Pall Mall* 'was a paying property long before he left it', but, as I have indicated, I am in doubt whether the paper, taking one year with another, ever earned money to what Smith would consider a substantial amount. Publishers of books have, however, maintained publications which, while they did not earn a return of much account, or anything at all, brought some reputation to the firm, and there have always been well-to-do men, whether publishers or not, satisfied to maintain a publication of consequence, for a time at any rate, whether it paid or not. But the day comes when there are regrets about losing money, and interest in the enterprise flags. Saxon Mills, in his life of E. T. Cook,[1] a future editor of the paper, says, and he no doubt had information from the subject of his biography, who knew the journal's history well, that Smith, like some other proprietors of newspapers, 'found that most of the political influence and the personal fame fell to the editor and his staff, while he was left with the financial responsibility'. It is not difficult to understand then that, when Smith had been proprietor for a quarter of a century, lack of sympathy with the *Pall Mall*'s party attitude, combined with business interests in addition to those of a publisher—he had an extraordinary success with Apollinaris—and possibly less cordial personal relations with Greenwood, made it possible for him to consider giving the paper to his son-in-law.

At any rate he did so,[2] and, as Bentley the publisher noted in his diary, it was 'a triumph for Mr. Gladstone'. The son-in-law, Henry Yates Thompson, was a Liberal—had been a candidate for Parliament and secretary of a Liberal minister, Earl Spencer, Viceroy of Ireland—and a change in the Party temperament of the *Pall Mall* was imperative. Greenwood resigned, and on May Day, 1880, the following announcement appeared in the paper:

> Mr. Frederick Greenwood, who has had the editorial direction of the *Pall Mall Gazette* from the date of its first publication till now, will not be responsible for any political opinions in its pages after today.

The subject of the leader that day was 'Political Morality', but the only part of it which could be regarded as a reference to the news on another page was this:

> For transcendental abstractions of Political Morality we, in this

[1] *Sir Edward Cook* (Constable).

[2] It was possible even for so widely informed a man as my friend, the late E. V. Lucas, in that charming work of his, *The Colvins and their Friends*, to blunder so far as to say that the *Pall Mall* was *bought* by Smith as a gift to his son-in-law.

journal, have ever shown but scanty response. But for honesty, for consistency, for plain dealing, for good faith, we have always entertained respect, which we have striven, and we hope not unsuccessfully, to demonstrate by our own conduct. The acknowledgement of a universal and constant obligation to the practice of these virtues has always seemed to us a respectably sufficient political creed; and discovery that the transcendental moralists are so utterly careless of them consoles us for any appearance of undue brevity in our own profession of faith.

The story, in several books, that Smith gave Yates Thompson the paper 'as a wedding present' is not accurate, Mrs. Reginald Smith points out to me. The marriage took place in 1878; the paper did not pass into Yates Thompson's hands and Greenwood did not resign until two years later.

John Morley—'after the exercise of considerable persuasion', Wilson Harris says in his faithful *Life of J. A. Spender*[1]—succeeded him. A paragraph which appeared the day after the resignation paid Greenwood this tribute:

It is known to all our readers that the able and accomplished gentleman who has been from the commencement Editor of this journal no longer retains that position; and in bidding him farewell we feel bound to say how much the *Pall Mall Gazette* has owed to his untiring assiduity and unflinching independence. It is by the latter quality that this journal has been distinguished in the past and will be characterised in the future.

A letter from the retiring editor, which appeared in the *Standard* of May 3—the correspondence between retiring editors and their proprietors, and of retiring editors concerning their proprietors, has perennial interest—I owe to Mrs. Bentley, who found it in the diary of her father, George Bentley, and has been so kind as to transcribe it for me:

I beg your permission to explain how and why it is that I, who originated the *Pall Mall Gazette*, planned it, down to the little details of paper and type,[2] and have carried it on as its editor from the day

[1] Cassell.

[2] This definite statement as to his share in the launching of the *Pall Mall* under the proprietorship of George Smith should be noted.

of its first appearance in 1865 down to today have been forced to give up all connection with the paper.

About ten days ago (the elections were just over) Mr. Smith, the proprietor of the *Pall Mall*, informed me that he was about to assign the paper to his son-in-law, Mr. Thompson. I am aware of Mr. Thompson as an Advanced Liberal. Therefore, when I was invited to meet him, in order to talk over future arrangements, I had little doubt of the result. At this meeting Mr. Thompson expressed his anxiety that I should remain at my post, if he took over the paper. I told him I was quite willing to do so on the old conditions, and if the paper was to retain its old principles. Thereupon I was courteously informed that Mr. Thompson proposed that the paper should give 'a general support' to the New Administration. So, to bring matters to a test, I advanced three questions, and asked Mr. Thompson how I should be expected to deal with them if he became proprietor and I consented to continue my services as editor; 1. The enfranchisement of the Agricultural labourer; it must be advocated said Mr. Thompson. 2. Mr. Gladstone's Foreign Policy as lately proclaimed; it was to be supported. 3. The Disestablishment of the English Church; it must no longer be opposed if Mr. Thompson had anything to do with the *Pall Mall*.

It appeared to me unnecessary to enquire any further. I was invited to remain editor of the *Pall Mall* on condition of parting with my principles, of bidding good-bye to all the men who had done so much in helping me to raise the paper to its high and honourable place in journalism, and of setting about making the paper a turncoat to please Mr. Thompson and the new Government.

I declined to do anything of the sort; and so it is that, by a transaction, of the nature of which (though I have proprietary rights in the paper), I am not allowed to know anything at all, I cease to be editor of the *Pall Mall*.

Greenwood continues with a reference to 'the men who did me the honour to associate themselves with me; they go with me—all being men of conviction, angry and ashamed at what has been done. But we do not propose to allow our independent little paper to be extinguished. Its spirit resides in us, and will soon re-appear in a new shape and "with all the latest improvements".' And there is this further paragraph about the *Pall Mall:*

Hoping to redeem the paper from the threatened assignment, I personally offered a large sum of money for the copyright. It was refused. But it is fair to say that the copyright was valued at a much higher price a few months previously.[1]

On which Smith writes in the next day's *Standard*: 'It is not my intention to enter upon a newspaper controversy with Mr. Greenwood, and I will, therefore, only ask you to allow me to say that many of the statements in Mr. Greenwood's letter are inaccurate or based upon misapprehension.' And Yates Thompson, 'begs to be allowed emphatically to contradict a statement that the *Pall Mall* will henceforward be a Ministerial Journal'. On May 4 he writes further to say that 'in the account of the conversation between Mr. Greenwood, Mr. Smith, and myself, contained in Mr. Greenwood's letter printed in the *Standard* there are inaccuracies of fact, or in colour, as to my statements on that occasion. Assuredly, in respect of the disestablishment of the English Church, no opinion was expressed by me.'

George Meredith, when his friend resigned, wrote to him:

You are having thousands of letters and are deep in business. If I swell the list with my bit of sentiment, I can make it short because I am certain that you know me true to you. My first impression last Saturday evening was one of a personal catastrophe.

I have walked per annum about 450 miles for my *Pall Mall*. And I felt that it was a startling loss to the country. Yours was the one English paper that could boast of independent views and competent power of expression. On Sunday the Tramps[2] came down for a walk. We said Greenwood thumped, and hard: we loved him when

[1] The *World*, continuing its interest in Smith—Yates's lampooning of him in connexion with *Cornhill* will be remembered—asserted on May 5 that 'Mr. Greenwood offered £10,000 for the copyright' and that 'Mr. Smith's price was £20,000, with a considerable extra sum for plant, machinery, &c.' It was good enough to say that 'no one will deny the independent character which the paper has always maintained'.

[2] There were sixty men in this Sunday walking club, but the number who turned up was not large. Against the names of some of them is written 'Never came out'. The full list is in F. W. Maitland's *Life and Letters of Leslie Stephen*. Meredith writes: 'They are men of distinction in science or literature; tramping with them one has the world under review, as well as pretty scenery.'

we thought him right, we hated when we thought him wrong, but right or wrong, the first was honest, it was a giant's and it was English.

However, Monday brought the better news that you soon pilot and captain another vessel. The *Pall Mall* did not make you, but you the *P.M.* So it will be with the new venture, and I still believe that the country has enough of the right material in it to back your new conception of the signification of journalism.

On Yates Thompson, a man a good deal out of the common run, reasons of space compel me to hold over what there is to say until a later volume. One of his distinctions was that he formed the best private collection of illuminated manuscripts in the world—it was worth a quarter of a million—and made to the British Museum its greatest bequest. The time came when he who had made the Conservative *Pall Mall*'s politics Liberal, sold the paper to a Conservative!

This is a convenient place, in view of the long antagonism between Greenwood and Gladstone—see particularly the letters to *Blackwood's Magazine*, Chaps. XXV–XXIX—to insert in the narrative an unpublished letter of much interest which the retiring editor of the *Pall Mall* wrote to the Liberal leader. It is in the Gladstone archives in the British Museum and runs as follows:

Pall Mall Gazette, Northumberland Street, Strand,
April 29, 1880.

Sir,

When this evening I had the honour of being presented to you, there was a fortuity in it wh. impels me to write this letter. For many a year, you in your great sphere, I in my little one, have often contended vehemently in opposite ways for what each thought the good of the country. During that time it has been my good fortune to know many distinguished men of all parties, but to Mr. Gladstone I had never the honour of speaking. And now this evening, when you, returned to your splendid position of authority, desired that I should be made known to you, I was within forty-eight hours of retirement from my own small region of power. My paper (I originated it, & have carried it on uncontrolled through its fifteen years of existence) has since the elections been sold into the hands of a thorough-going party-man of advanced Liberal views, & is henceforth to be no erratic independent, but to be printed as a supporter of your government. If, Sir, you care about such matters at all, you will not in the natural order of things regret that. But when I remember that you have more than once gone out of your way to speak generously of certain good qualities wh. you found in the paper, & since in its fiercest opposition to your policies never a line appeared to cast a doubt on their profound sincerity & their exalted motive, I venture to hope that you will not be altogether pleased that (for a time at any rate) the *Pall Mall Gazette* is to be virtually extinguished. The men who wrote its politics with me all resign with me.[1]

You will I am sure understand the impulse that leads me to trouble you with this, & will pardon it. I am, Sir,

Your Obedient Servant
Frederick Greenwood.

It would have been pleasant to read the courteous acknowledgement which Gladstone no doubt sent to Greenwood.

[1] The words '& not being [of] your mind, Sir' are inserted after 'me' and then erased.

THE 'DICTIONARY OF NATIONAL BIOGRAPHY'

CHAPTER XXI

St. Paul's

THE MAKING OF THE 'DICTIONARY OF NATIONAL BIOGRAPHY' — CONDENSATION AND CORRECTION — THE EDITORS — GEORGE SMITH'S CHARACTER

GEORGE SMITH was to be engrossed by a publication which was to be read by more people—and to last longer—than the *Pall Mall*. The memoir by Sir Sidney Lee and his account of the *Dictionary of National Biography* tell the story of an immense and most laudable undertaking, 'the best record of a nation's past'—Dr. G. M. Trevelyan does not hesitate to say—'that any civilisation has produced, a monument of the business ability, the enlightened public spirit and the widespread historical scholarship of the Victorian age at its final culmination'. The work would have been on a still greater scale had it been possible to carry out its originator's first conception of a Dictionary, not of National, but of Universal Biography. With 'a great fortune', Smith had 'got his mind on making a munificent contribution to the literature of his country', which would 'surpass works of a similar character produced abroad with State aid or other subsidy'. Restricted, on the advice of Leslie Stephen, to a *Dictionary of National Biography from the Earliest Times*, the work was begun in 1882, two years after Smith had given the *Pall Mall* to his son-in-law. I am glad to be able to add some particulars of the enterprise to those which are in print.

In the fifties John Murray had spent hundreds of pounds on preparatory work for such a collection of biographies, *Biographia Britannica*, but when he realized 'the sweep and scale of it', had had to give up. Some of his materials he generously handed to the initiator of the *Dictionary*. Why did Smith undertake an enterprise marked by several failures?[1] 'For one thing', he said, and it was a speech typical of the man, 'these very failures tempted me. They appealed to what you may call the worst side of my nature! There would be some satisfaction in succeeding where many had failed. I resolved that this should be my gift to English letters. The idea floated in my brain for two or three days and then hardened into definite purpose.' He felt the expenditure in which he would be involved to be worth while, 'not so much for the accounts of the few great and rare men', but because 'the memories of an enormous number of useful and noble citizens' would be saved from perishing. His estimate was that he would lose £50,000 on the work. The sum proved to be at least £70,000 on an outlay of £150,000.

Of the editor, Leslie Stephen, who was to describe himself as 'a considerable autocrat', Smith said, 'He was a scholar, a student, a master of clear and exact English; I know no one indeed who wrote better English. He was an old and trusted friend, and there existed such perfect confidence between us that no scrap of formal agreement was required.' Sidney Lee was assistant editor and when the time came for him to become editor he also trusted Smith and said not a word about terms.

Stephen, who resigned the editorship of *Cornhill* to undertake the *Dictionary*, wrote no fewer than a thousand articles himself, equal to two and a quarter volumes; Lee produced as many as 1,870. It is stated that 'Stephen's great lives and Lee's minor lives, Lee's knowledge of the 16th and 17th centuries and Stephen's knowledge of the 18th and 19th' supplemented one another. Stephen was not first-rate with proofs; Lee was a determined verifier and corrector, had 'a passion for precision'. The total number of persons whose lives were recorded was 29,120, which

[1] The year before Waterloo the Society for the Diffusion of Useful Knowledge undertook a Dictionary of Universal Biography which was to be completed in thirty-two volumes, but the editor devoted seven to the letter A, and there it stuck.

is far in excess of the number in the national biographies of any country. The biographies were done by 663 writers. The article by Stephen on Addison was sent to each contributor as 'a model of terseness and balance'. The staff and its library were housed on the top floor of the house next to Smith, Elder & Co. Both editors received, in turn, testimonials from the contributors.

There was to be no fine writing in the *Dictionary*—as Canon Ainger said, 'No flowers by request'. 'Nouns were more valuable than adjectives', and 'the severest terseness and the severest accuracy' were called for. A member of the staff who had to do the work of verification 'almost lived at the British Museum'. 'The best authority' on the subject of the biography either wrote the article or saw a proof. Solicitors wrote threatening to take proceedings if certain persons did not have the opportunity of seeing biographies before publication, but no one was scared. Sir Theodore Martin's account of the Prince Consort, which Smith, Stephen, and *The Times* found too long, was seen by the Queen and was therefore not cut. Smith had just been reading the article when Sir Theodore came in. 'Smith', he said, 'I have been looking at the articles in the new volume. They are very good but some of them are too long, much too long. You really must guard against this.' That there were complaints of biographers leaving things out need hardly be said. The widow of an Indian officer 'paced the office with clasped hands and streaming eyes. "My dear husband", she sobbed, "slew with his own sword fourteen sepoys in one battle. All India rang with the deed, and there is not a word about it in his biography. Oh, Oh!"'

As for condensation, Smith said, 'Let anyone try to abridge a given article and he will find that the sentences are scarcely capable of compression'. The cost of corrections was 'at least ten times as great as in an ordinary book; no book involving the same amount of labour and anxiety has ever been published'. The editor had trouble over some contributors' delays, and worried over defects. 'I consoled him by saying, "If you suppose a book of this kind can be beyond criticism you are utterly mistaken. We can only do our best; we can and must be content with this even if it stops short of perfection."' But Stephen had once said himself that 'a book of which it is the essence that every page should bristle with facts and dates is certain to have errors by the thousand'. One of the difficulties was that, in a list of subjects ranging from Anglo-Saxon times, it was impossible for the editor to know all that was interesting in every man's career until the article about him was written. Hence it was never possible to specify to the writer the precise length it should be. Lists of names of celebrities whom it was proposed to include appeared from time to time in the *Athenaeum*. As to whether some of the biographies are at disproportionate length—'it is the second-rate people', Stephen said, 'who provide the really useful reading'—every reader will have his opinion. The following fifteen are among the longest articles: Shakespeare 49 pages, Wellington 34, Bacon 32, Cromwell 31, Elizabeth and Walpole 28, Marlborough 26, Scott 25, Edward I, Byron, and Charles II 24, Newton and Swift 23, Edward III and Sterne 22, Wycliffe 21. (Who have been our fifteen most remarkable men and women?) The *Dictionary* had one great advantage. At the printer's the same proof-reader read all the proofs from the first. As to the total cost of the work, Smith used to relate that when his children wanted to protest against any piece of extravagance they did not say, 'Remember us, papa', but 'Remember the *Dictionary*'. The original price of the work was 12*s*. 6*d*. the volume.

The first of the sixty-three volumes came out in 1885 and the last in 1900, a year before Smith's death. In 1892 Smith entertained the contributors at a congratulatory dinner, and in 1894 they entertained him. In 1897 he gave a dinner in relays to 'the whole body of the contributors and some distinguished strangers', including the Prince of Wales. This was the occasion on which, Sidney Lee told E. V. Lucas, the Heir Apparent asked him, 'And what is your special subject, Mr. Lee?' Lee said it was Shakespeare. 'Stick to it, Mr. Lee', said the Prince, 'stick to it. There's money in it.'[1] In 1900 the Lord Mayor banqueted Smith, his editors, and a large company of men of letters and public.

[1] *Reading, Writing and Remembering*, E. V. Lucas (Methuen).

The editions up to 1940 and the names of the men who have been in charge of the work are set out in a footnote.[1]

[1] In the autumn of 1889, four years after the publication of the first volume, Stephen had a serious breakdown. At the beginning of 1890 Sidney Lee became joint editor. From April 1891 Lee was sole editor until the *Dictionary* and its First Supplement were completed in 1901. He resumed control from Oct. 1910 to Dec. 1912, while editing the Second Supplement. But he retained throughout 1901–16 the general oversight. Lee set out his views on biography and biographical work in 'National Biography', Royal Institution, Jan. 31, 1896; 'Principles of Biography', Leslie Stephen lecture at Cambridge, 1911; and 'The Perspective of Biography', English Association, 1918. See also *D.N.B., 1922–30*.

As has been stated, the main work appeared in 63 quarterly volumes between 1885 and 1900 with a Supplement of three volumes (64–6) in 1901–2. The original design was to close the work at the close of the century, but it was extended to Jan. 22, 1901, in order to include Queen Victoria. A small volume of Errata was issued free to subscribers in 1904. The 66 vols. were reprinted with some corrections on thinner paper and reissued (1908–9) in 22 vols.

In 1917 the heirs of the founder of the *D.N.B.* presented the stocks and copyright to the Oxford University Press, who reprinted, in 1921–2, both the ordinary edition of 22 volumes and an edition on India paper in 11 double volumes. The work was reprinted again 1937–8, and a reprint of the ordinary paper edition only will be published this year.

In 1912 Smith, Elder & Co. published a 'Second Supplement', covering the years 1901–11; this was reprinted by the Oxford University Press in 1920 and became known as *The Twentieth-Century D.N.B.*, since (unlike the 3-volume supplement of 1900–1) it is a continuation of the main work. It has subsequently been reprinted. The Oxford University Press has since published Supplements covering the years 1912–21 and 1922–30. That for 1931–40 was published last year.

An Index and Epitome to the main work and the 1900–1 Supplement, in one alphabet, was published by Smith, Elder & Co. in 1903, and a second edition in 1906. An Index and Epitome to the so-called Second Supplement (1901–11) was published by Smith, Elder & Co. in 1913.

In 1920 the first *Concise D.N.B.* was published by the Oxford University Press. It consisted of the Epitome to the main work plus the Epitome of the Twentieth-Century 1901–11, and was in two alphabets. Later an Epitome covering the years 1912–21 was incorporated in the second alphabet, and in 1930 a further edition included the years 1922–30.

The editors of the work have been:

Vols. 1–21	Sir Leslie Stephen	1885–90
Vols. 22–6	Sir Leslie Stephen Sir Sidney Lee	1890–1
Vols. 27–63	Sir Sidney Lee	1891–1900
Vols. 64–6	Sir Sidney Lee	1900–1
1901–11	Sir Sidney Lee	1912

It will have been realized during the perusal of previous chapters that no publisher enjoyed greater respect and regard than George Smith. Men as dissimilar as Thackeray, Matthew Arnold, Browning, and Tom Hughes loved him; Millais, when he could no longer speak, wrote that he was 'the kindest man and the best gentleman I have ever had to deal with'. No publisher gave books of greater interest and worth to the world. None eclipsed in importance and financial courage the production of the *Dictionary of National Biography*. No publisher showed more imagination in journalistic enterprises, for, as we have seen, both *Cornhill* and the *Pall Mall* broke new ground. Smith's various activities—it used to be said, truly, that the nation owed the *Dictionary* to Apollinaris—enabled him to become a rich man; but all he made was got by honest exercise of his talents, and by hard work and with consideration for those who worked for him. He almost made us think that Johnson may have been right after all when he asserted that a man can seldom be employed more innocently than in making money.

Sir Sidney Lee says that 'it would not be accurate to describe Smith as a man of great imagination or one possessed of literary or artistic scholarship'. But surely he showed imagination, if not 'great imagination', again and again in various fields. Lee continues more accurately: 'His masculine mind and temper was coloured by an instinctive sympathy with the workings of the imagination in others; by a gift for distinguishing almost at a glance a good piece of literature or art from bad; by an innate respect for those who pursued intellectual and imaginative ideals rather than a mere worldly prosperity.' 'To the last of his life', writes Robertson Nicoll, 'he was full of energy, and enterprising, alert and far-seeing. His great success never spoilt him. He was never overawed by great names and smiled at vanity. He was the greatest publisher of the Victorian period.'[1]

1912–21	H. W. C. Davis	1919–28
	J. R. H. Weaver	1920–44
1922–30	J. R. H. Weaver	
1931–40	L. G. Wickham Legg	July 1944–

[1] For additional testimonies see page 133.

As for pictures of him, Mrs. Reginald Smith tells me that he was not photographed for many years before his death. She likes best the portrait by G. F. Watts, which precedes the memoir. It was painted in 1876, four years before her father gave up the proprietorship of the *Pall Mall*. The posthumous portrait by John Collier is in the National Portrait Gallery, and accords closely with the last photograph.[1]

Smith died in 1901 at the age of seventy-seven. He had received no honour from the State. The editors of his great *Dictionary*, Stephen and Lee, were knighted in 1902 and 1911. In 1875, however, Oxford had given him—*civem de civibus suis optime meriture Georgium Smith*, said the Public Orator—its honorary M.A. And Mrs. Reginald Smith writes to me: 'After my father's death my mother received a letter saying that it had been the intention of King Edward to offer my father a baronetcy in the next Honours List. It was nice of them to tell her this, but neither of my parents had great regard for titles—far more gratifying was it to have the memorial tablet in St. Paul's Cathedral and the undying regard of the literary world for the *D.N.B.*' The marble is inscribed, 'To the memory of George M. Smith to whom English literature owes the *Dictionary of National Biography* and whose warmth of heart endeared him to men of letters of his time this tablet is erected by friends who loved him'.

Mrs. George Smith who, on the death of her husband, carried out his wishes by defraying the cost of three additional volumes of the *Dictionary of National Biography*, passed away thirteen years later, in 1914, at the age of eighty-three. There were two sons, George Murray Smith, who was for nine years with Smith, Elder & Co. and died in 1919, and Alexander Murray Smith, who was active in the firm from 1890, but retired some time before his death in 1939. His wife was Emily Tennyson Bradley, a daughter of Dean Bradley and goddaughter of Lady Tennyson. Her sister was Margaret L. Woods, the novelist. Mrs. Alexander Murray Smith is known for, among other books, *A Popular Guide to Westminster Abbey*, which she wrote

[1] Facing page 82.

with another sister who became Lady Birchenough. She died in 1946. The eldest daughter married in 1878, as has been stated, Henry Yates Thompson. The second daughter, Ethel, remained with her father and mother until their deaths, and died in 1929. The youngest daughter married Reginald Smith, who had joined the firm in 1894, and from 1899 was sole active partner, and, finally, sole representative until his death in 1916.[1] (In May, 1917, the business of Smith, Elder & Co. was acquired from Mrs. Reginald Smith by John Murray.) George Smith's grandsons, the sons of Mrs. Reginald Smith's brother George, for some time chairman of the Midland Railway, died when young, two in the war of 1914–18 and one later. The great-grandsons who survive, George Anthony Murray Smith, George William Murray Smith, and Peregrine John Harry Murray Smith served in the last war.

[1] See page 97.

GREENWOOD'S LAST EDITORSHIPS

CHAPTER XXII

The 'St. James's Gazette'

BEFORE THE DAYS OF HEADLINES — TABOOS OF THE TIME — THE FINANCING OF THE PAPER — GLADSTONE AND BEACONSFIELD

WRITING to R. L. Stevenson in the early summer of 1880, George Meredith said: 'Gladstone's victory at the elections precipitated the fall of Greenwood, the foe of Gladstone. But the fall of very mighty heroes is to rise. Greenwood towers in his new paper: the poor *Pall Mall* drags on melancholily, as it were with bowels out, for Greenwood marched the whole of the *Pall Mall* staff away to his drumming, and Morley has to be abroad recruiting.' Another letter to 'Dearest Greenwood' said 'My heart to you! Warm wishes that you may always have scope for your powers.'[1]

With the first number of the *St. James's Gazette, an Evening Review and Record of News*, published on May 31, 1880—at last Greenwood got *Evening Review* in his title—there was issued eight pages of the size of the paper, headed, 'Introduction to the *St. James's Gazette*'.[2] Hear 'The Blowing of the Trumpet':

According to promise made one short month ago, we, who were then a discomfited little company of writers, with reek intolerable smoked out of our ancient quarters, are gathered together again, to fall to work in the old spirit and in very much the old accustomed ways. Thanks to the raisers of the reek, we had the benefit of twenty-eight days' contemplation of our past labours, and we fancy we see now as clearly as anybody certain defects in our old work, and where it is easy to do better and where better must be done whether with ease or not. Moreover, all sorts of new ideas have taken shape during this blest period of contemplation; and in fair time and in due course

[1] *Letters of George Meredith*. Collected and edited by his son (Constable).

[2] There had been earlier three papers with *St. James's* in their titles.

THE

ST. JAMES'S GAZETTE

An Evening Review and Record of News.

No. 1.—Vol. I. | MONDAY, MAY 31, 1880. | Price Twopence.

Notice.

Advertisements for the St. James's Gazette *should be sent to the Office before Half past Ten o'clock on the day of publication.*

Announcements of Births, Marriages, and Deaths are inserted in the St. James's Gazette *at a charge of Five Shillings. They may be sent through any Advertising Agency, Newsagent, or Librarian; or, properly authenticated, to the Office of the* St. James's Gazette.

The Subscription to the St. James's Gazette, *including postage to any part of the United Kingdom, is 10s. 3d. per quarter.*

BIRTH.

Robertson, the wife of R. B., Esq., Glasgow, at Montgreenan, Ayrshire, May 24—of a son.

ROYAL ITALIAN OPERA, COVENT GARDEN.
Mdme. Albani.
THIS EVENING, MAY 31st, Wagner's Opera, LOHENGRIN.

Elsa di Brabante	Mdme. Albani.
Ortruda	Mdlle. Pasqua.
Federico di Telramondo	Signor Cotogni.
Enrico l'Uccellatore	Signor Silvestri.
L'Araldo del Re	Signor Capponi.
Lohengrin	Signor Gayarre.

Conductor, Signor Vianesi.
TO-MORROW (Tuesday), June 1st, Gounod's Opera, ROMEO E GIULIETTA.
Mdme. Adelina Patti.
Signor Nicolini, Signor Cotogni, Signor Graziani.
Mdme. Adelina Patti.
THURSDAY NEXT, June 3rd. (Subscription Night in lieu of Saturday, July 24th), Rossini's Opera, IL BARBIERE DI SIVIGLIA.
Mdme. Adelina Patti.
Signor Nicolini, Signor Cotogni, Signor de Reszke.
FRIDAY, June 4th, Meyerbeer's Grand Opera, L'AFRICAINE.
Mdlle. Turolla. Mdlle. Valleria. M. Lassalle. Signor Carpi.
Début of Mdme. SEMBRICH.
An engagement has been concluded with Mdme. SEMBRICH, of the Imperial Opera of Dresden and she will make her first appearance in England on SATURDAY, June 5th, in Donizetti's Opera, LUCIA DI LAMMERMOOR.
Doors open at eight o'clock, the Opera commences at half-past.
The Box-office under the Portico of the Theatre is open from 10 till 5.
Orchestra Stalls, £1 1s.; Side Boxes on the First Tier, £3 3s.; Upper Boxes, £2 12s. 6d.; Pit Tickets, 7s.; Amphitheatre Stalls, 10s. 6d. and 5s.; Amphitheatre, 2s. 6d.

AGRICULTURAL HALL, Islington.

HORSE SHOW.—THIS DAY (Monday), May 31, 1s.

HORSE SHOW.—TUESDAY, June 1, 1s.

HORSE SHOW.—WEDNESDAY, June 2, 1s.

HORSE SHOW.—THURSDAY, June 3, 1s.

HORSE SHOW. — LAST DAY, FRIDAY, June 4. 1s.

HORSE SHOW. — Doors Open at Ten o'clock.

HORSE SHOW. — Parade of Prize Horses.

HORSE SHOW. — Hunters, Hacks, Harness Horses, and Ponies for Sale.

HORSE SHOW.—Register of Horses for Sale. Apply to Secretary.

HORSE SHOW.—Horses under Saddle and in Harness.

HORSE SHOW.—Leaping.

HORSE SHOW. — Leaping Competition.

HORSE SHOW.—Reserved Seats to View same.

HORSE SHOW.—Reserved Seats, 10s. and 5s.

HORSE SHOW.—Unreserved seats, 2s. 6d. and 1s.

HORSE SHOW.—Entrance, Islington-green.

HORSE SHOW.—Reserved Seat Entrance, Barford-street.
(By Order)
S. Sidney, Secretary and Manager,
Agricultural Hall Company (Limited).

HORSE SHOW.—CAUTION.—The only STABLE FITTINGS made by the ST. PANCRAS IRONWORK COMPANY are those on either side of the entrance to the exercising ring. All interested in the health and safety of Horses are invited to inspect them

[1]

GAIETY THEATRE, Strand. Sole Lessee and Manager, Mr. John Hollingshead.
TO-NIGHT at 8 o'clock, FROU-FROU, Mdlle. Sarah Bernhardt; MM. Dieudonné, Berton, Train, Chameroy, Faure; Mdmes. Jullien, Kalb, Strelly, Wegler, and Aamont.

FINAL EXHIBITION at BURLINGTON GALLERY, 191, PICCADILLY, of the works of ELIJAH WALTON, the whole of which are for sale at very moderate prices.
From 10 to 6. Admission, including catalogue, 1s.

BRAZILIAN FOUR AND-A-HALF PER CENT. LOANS of 1852, 1858, and 1860.—The DIVIDEND on these Loans, due on the 1st June next, will be paid by Messrs. N. M. Rothschild and Sons on that day, and on any subsequent Monday, Wednesday, or Friday, between the hours of 11 and 2.
Printed forms to be applied for, and the coupons left three days for examination.
New-court, St. Swithin's-lane.

RUSSIAN FIVE PER CENT. CONSOLIDATED BONDS OF 1873.—The DIVIDEND on these BONDS, due on the 1st June next, will be PAID by Messrs. N. M. Rothschild and Sons on that day, and on any subsequent Monday, Wednesday, or Friday, between the hours of 11 and 2.
Printed forms to be applied for, and the coupons left three days for examination.
New-court, St. Swithin's-lane.

EGYPTIAN STATE-DOMAIN MORTGAGE BONDS.—The DIVIDEND on these BONDS, due on the 1st June next, will be PAID by Messrs. N. M. Rothschild and Sons on that day, and on any subsequent Monday, Wednesday, or Friday, between the hours of 11 and 2.
Printed forms to be applied for, and the coupons left three days for examination.
New-court, St. Swithin's-lane.

THE STANDARD LIFE ASSURANCE COMPANY.—Established 1825.
ANNUAL REPORT, 1880.

Amount of Assurances accepted	£1,134,444
Ditto during the last five years	6,066,013
Total Assurances	19,044,745
Revenue	796,459
Invested Funds	5,514,732

DIVISION OF PROFITS, 1880.

THE PROFITS WHICH HAVE ARISEN SINCE 1875 will be divided among Policies in existence at the close of the current year, and assurances now effected will participate.
Since 1835 the Company has distributed THREE MILLIONS Sterling in Bonus additions to Policies.
London: 82, King William-street, E.C., and 3, Pall-mall East, S.W. Edinburgh: 3 and 5, George-street (Head Office). Dublin: 66, Upper Sackville-street. Manchester: 50, Spring-gardens. Liverpool: 10, Cook-street.

DR. BARNARDO'S HOMES FOR DESTITUTE CHILDREN.
Treasurer.
William Fowler, Esq., M.P., 33, Cornhill, E.C.
Bankers.
London and South-Western Bank, Bow Branch.
The ANNUAL MEETING of these institutions, in which there now are maintained upwards of 900 orphan, neglected, or destitute boys and girls, will (D.V.) be held in Exeter Hall on WEDNESDAY, 2nd June, 1880.
The chair will be taken at Six o'clock by
The Right Hon. the Earl CAIRNS,
Supported by the Right Hon. the Earl of Aberdeen, the Hon. Thos. Pelham, the Rev. Burnam Cassin, M.A., the Lord Kinnaird, Wm. Fowler, Esq., M.P., the Rev. Arthur Mursel, Samuel Gurney Sheppard, Esq., the Rev. Sinclair Patterson, M.D., the Ven. Archdeacon Grant, the Rev. H. E. Fox, the Hon. A. F. Kinnaird, the Rev. R. C. Billing, M.A., James E. Mathieson, Esq., and the Rev. William Tyler.
Seven hundred children from the Homes and Schools will form a choir, and sing a selection of pieces.
A few reserved and numbered seat tickets (price 5s. each) can be had up to the 31st inst. upon application to the HON. DIRECTOR, Office of the Institutions, 18, Stepney-causeway, E.

ADVOWSON.—To be SOLD, an Advowson, within a short distance of a good cathedral in one of the Home Counties. Population 500. Society good, and the church and vicarage in excellent condition. The net annual value is about £800. Age of present incumbent over 75. For particulars apply to Messrs. JOHNSONS, UPTON, BUDD, and ATKEY, Solicitors, 20, Austinfriars, London.

RESIDENCES for DISPOSAL, Unfurnished, Brook-street, Hans-place, Russell, Bedford, Brunswick, and Mecklenburgh-squares. Furnished summer residences at Bournemouth and St. Leonards, besides others.—Chapman and Coade, 9, Southampton-buildings, Chancery-lane, W.C.

LIEUTENANTS of MILITIA desirous of competing this year or next for Line Commissions can be RECEIVED by the Rev. WALTER BAKER, M.A., at Batcombe Rectory, Evercreech, Bath. They will be thoroughly prepared in all military subjects by Major R. V. Dickens (late 11th Foot), who, besides having passed the Staff College and held several Staff appointments, has for some time past been successfully engaged in coaching Lieutenants of Militia and also Sandhurst Cadets for their final examination in the same subjects. Other competent tutors assist in preparing for the qualifying examinations.

MR. STREETER, F.R.G.S.,
NEW BOND STREET, W.,
and
COLOMBO, CEYLON,
DIAMOND & PEARL MERCHANT

Mr. Streeter, having an Agent constantly in the East, is enabled to offer Buyers,
ALL KINDS OF PRECIOUS STONES AND GEMS,
AT WHOLESALE PRICES,
By which they save the usual intermediate Profit.

DIAMONDS.	PEARLS.
CATSEYES.	EMERALDS.
SAPPHIRES.	RUBIES., &c.

Estimates and Designs for Jewellery of all kinds.

GARDNER'S DINNER and TABLE GLASS SERVICES. Free, graceful, and original designs, of unequalled value. Dinner Services, from 21s. Table Glass Services of the best Crystal, for twelve persons, complete, 65s. Cash discount 15 per cent. Coloured Photographic Sheets and Illustrated Glass Catalogues post free.
453 and 454, West Strand, Charing Cross.

GARDNER'S CROWN WARE DINNER SERVICES, in appearance and wear equal to Porcelain; effective, useful, decorative. £3 13s. 6d. the set for twelve persons complete. Cash discount 15 per cent. Coloured lithographs post free.
453 and 454, West Strand, Charing-cross.

(By Her Majesty's Royal Letters Patent.)
METZLER'S AMERICAN ORGUINETTE. The American Orguinette is a musical instrument constructed somewhat on the principle of the American Organ, and adapted to be automatically worked by simple strips of perforated paper, each strip representing one or more tunes. There is no limit to either kind or quantity of music. It will play hymn tunes, popular airs, sets of quadrilles, polkas, waltzes, reels, and hornpipes, with a clearness, accuracy, and degree of execution which but few performers can equal. A mere child can play it.
Style A, with six pieces of music, price £1 10s.
Style E, with six pieces of music and attachment, price £3 10s.
Cabinet Style, with selection of music, price 10 guineas.

Any description of music from 9d. a tune.
METZLER'S MUSICAL INSTRUMENTS.
Cornets, Violins, Guitars, Zithers, Musical Boxes, playing "Pinafore," "Carmen," &c. Accordions Concertinas, Drums, Fifes, Clarionets, and all kinds of musical instruments, strings, fittings, &c.
Catalogues Post Free.
Metzler and Co., Great Marlborough-street, London, W.

TRAVELLING BAGS.—ASSER and SHERWIN.

WRITING CASES	Asser and Sherwin.
WEDDING PRESENTS	Asser and Sherwin.
BIRTHDAY PRESENTS	Asser and Sherwin.
LAWN TENNIS	Asser and Sherwin.
ARCHERY, CROQUET	Asser and Sherwin.

ASSER and SHERWIN, Manufacturers and Importers, 80 and 81, Strand, London.
The New Catalogue, 300 Illustrations, post free.

LAWN TENNIS. The Revised Laws for 1880, by the M.C.C. and A.E.L.T.C., sent on receipt of six stamps.
ASSER and SHERWIN, 80 and 81, Strand, London, W.C.

"AND TEETH LIKE ROWS OF PEARLS."
JEWSBURY and BROWN'S Exquisite Compound,
THE ORIENTAL TOOTH-PASTE.
The celebrated original and only genuine Oriental Tooth-Paste is signed "JEWSBURY and BROWN, Manchester. Established 50 years." See Trade Mark. PEARLY WHITE and SOUND TEETH, a healthy action of the gums, producing that firmness and rosy brightness of colour so essential to beauty, and fragrant breath, are all insured by the use of this most perfect Dentifrice. Pots, 1s. 6d.; double, 2s. 6d. All Perfumers and Chemists.

THE PUBLIC SERVICE NOTE PAPER. Similar in quality to that used in Her Majesty's Government Offices. Suitable for clubs and private use, per ream 6s. 8d. Five reams 32s. 6d.
T. PETTITT and CO.,
Manufacturing Stationers, Printers, and Publishers (to Her Majesty the Queen and H.R.H. the Prince of Wales).
22 and 23, Frith-street, and 50, Old Compton-street, Soho, London, W.
Established over Half a Century.

JOHN BRINSMEAD and SONS' PATENT SOSTENENTE PIANOS,
Exhibited at the Paris Exhibition of 1878, gained the highest honours.
The CROSS of the LEGION of HONOUR,
The GOLD MEDAL (L'ACADEMIE NATIONALE),
And also the SILVER MEDAL.
"There is but one class of gold medals for the Exhibition, and the decoration of the Cross of the Legion of Honour constitutes a superior recompense."
(Signed), A. Fetis, Official Reporter.

JOHN BRINSMEAD and SONS' PATENT SOSTENENTE PIANOFORTES were awarded
The CROSS of the LEGION of HONOUR, and also the GOLD MEDAL, Paris, 1878.
The GOLD MEDAL and DIPLOMA of HONOUR, South Africa, 1877.
The GRAND MEDAL of HONOUR and DIPLOMA of MERIT, Philadelphia, 1876.
The GRAND DIPLOMA of HONOUR, Paris, 1874.
The GOLD MEDAL, Paris, 1870.
The DIPLOMA of EXTRAORDINARY MERIT, Netherlands International Exhibition, 1869.
The MEDAL of HONOUR, Paris, 1867.
The PRIZE MEDAL, London, 1862, &c.

JOHN BRINSMEAD and SONS' PATENT SOSTENENTE PIANOS.
Patented 1862, 1868, 1871, 1875, and 1879, in

GREAT BRITAIN,	AUSTRIA,
PRUSSIA,	ITALY,
FRANCE,	BELGIUM,

And AMERICA.

JOHN BRINSMEAD and SONS' PATENT SOSTENENTE PIANOS,
With the Patent Perfect Check Repeater Action.
"Paris, November, 4, 1878.
"I have attentively examined the beautiful Pianos of Messrs. John Brinsmead and Sons that are exhibited at the Paris International Exhibition of 1878. I consider them to be exceptional in the ease with which gradations of sound can be produced, from the softest to the most powerful tones. These excellent Pianos merit the approbation of all artists, as the tone is full as well as sustained, and the touch is of perfect evenness throughout its entire range, answering to every requirement of the pianist.—Ch. Gounod."

JOHN BRINSMEAD AND SONS' PATENT SOSTENENTE GRANDS.
With the Patent Perfect Check Repeater Action.
"Paris, Sept. 8, 1878.
"We, the undersigned, certify that after having seen and most conscientiously examined the English Pianos at the Universal Exhibition of 1878, find that the palm belongs to the Grand Pianos of the house of Brinsmead.—Nicolas Rubinstein D. Magnus, Chevalier Antoine de Kontski (Court Pianist to the Emperor of Germany)."

JOHN BRINSMEAD and SONS' PATENT SOSTENENTE GRANDS.
With the Patent Perfect Check Repeater Action.
"Brighton.
"I have pleasure in expressing my opinion that the Paris Exhibition Model Grand Pianofortes of Messrs. John Brinsmead and Sons are unsurpassed. The tone is deliciously sweet, sustained, and extraordinarily powerful; the touch responds to the faintest and to the most trying strains on it, and the workmanship is simply perfect.—W. Kuhe."

JOHN BRINSMEAD and SONS' PATENT SOSTENENTE UPRIGHT IRON GRANDS.
"Beautifully light and elastic touch, and an instant repetition."—*Globe.*

JOHN BRINSMEAD and SONS' PATENT SOSTENENTE UPRIGHT IRON GRANDS.
With the Patent Perfect Check Repeater Action.
"The Legion of Honour has been bestowed on the founder of the firm of Messrs. Brinsmead and Sons, *apropos* of the late Paris Exhibition."—*Daily Telegraph.*

JOHN BRINSMEAD and SONS' PATENT SOSTENENTE CONCERT GRAND PIANOS.
With the Patent Perfect Check Repeater Action.
"This splendid instrument has the unusual compass of 7½ octaves, and has a greatly-increased length and weight of string between the bridges; while the Sostenente sounding board is so constructed as to respond to the vibration of the strings with extreme readiness."—*Graphic.*

18—20, WIGMORE STREET, London, W.
Illustrated Lists Post Free.

MANUFACTORY, The BRINSMEAD WORKS, Grafton-road, N.W.

First page of the *St. James's Gazette.*

(for a newspaper that is brought out in four weeks is necessarily a hurried and imperfect production) they will be used to make the *St. James's Gazette* something better, brighter, stronger of its kind than has yet been known. So at any rate we hope.

To 'cheery endeavour' the paper had 'every conceivable incitement; look where we may there is a friend':

The Gentle Reader, our gentle reader, can't get on without it; his friends can't get on without it; his club between 5 o'clock and 6 p.m. is a place of yawning without it; and we do not observe that the Radicals are grinning in all the bumptious blessedness of possession at every street corner.

The Newsvendor, this most significant man, speaks to us, under his breath, of all success. A witness of much mortality, a minister to many existences of lingering distresses, he is naturally inclined to gloom, looking upon all first appearances with a disposition to forbode. But, then, as he truly observes, this is no case of first appearance—nothing of the sort. It is a case of painful disappearance, he maintains, with suspicion of burking for the sake of clothes.

As for 'that other concern'—the *Pall Mall* was not named—it was 'a spark fallen into another system; and, as from a distance, we watch it circling and singing in harmony with the little *Echo* and such like orbs'—the *Echo* was not being directed, as yet, by Lord Pethick-Lawrence, but by the careful Passmore Edwards—'a tear may fall, a sigh may be breathed, but not another word'.

There is a young paper's judicious reference to the advertiser and then a complacent allusion to the 'character, consistency, knowledge, judgment, policy, pledges', which had marked the still unnamed *Pall Mall*. And so on, with an admission of 'earnest blunders and vigorous mistakes' in the past and of 'again and again going violently wrong when sure of going right'. There were, however, to the credit of the previous incarnation 'good guesses as to what would happen and what should be done which justify the past'. As for Downing Street, there had been 'discoveries of a dreadful state of ignorance on the part of divine genius and its satellites; miserable condensations of superheated oratorical steam in chilling drizzle, consequent upon contact with fact; a hasty recall of heroic instructions, stammering policies, pledges in pieces, principles revised for office use—altogether a very different outlook from that which was promised us by the United Winning Party'. Next came two and a quarter pages with the title, 'A Political Retrospect', and, after these, four and a half pages of first class advertising, largely books from the chief publishers—except Smith & Elder.

The paper itself was in the old *Pall Mall* format, on the stout buff, some called it creamy paper, sixteen pages for twopence. The office, to the end, was in Dorset Street, Whitefriars. The subject of the leader was 'The Future of Political Ignorance' and of the 'follower'—as the article which followed the leading article was termed—'Moderation in Politics'. The *Pall Mall* types used are what we called long primer, bourgeois, minion, and brevier. A feature was 'The Morning Paper' summaries occupying about two and a half columns. 'The Evening News' filled two pages, no item with more than a single headline! Then came two pages of Reuter's telegrams, with, for the special occasion, two short 'Own Correspondent' messages, one from Berlin and the other from Paris, and general news—again all with single headlines. The editorial 'Notes' ran to nearly three columns. In these, beyond home and foreign political topics, the subjects were unnecessary display in the building of Northumberland Avenue hotels, the Oberammergau Passion play, German bands—there were such things in those days—the National Gallery, and pawnbrokers. Two original features were 'Passages for Meditation' (bits from leading articles and speeches) and two inches or so of rather heavy humour, 'Political Weather Today'—'*England*: dull, cloudy; a theological breeze gathering', and so on. After a chatty 'middle', came a review, of nearly two pages, of Ward's 'English Poets'. Trade and Finance occupied a column. Next day there was also a 'Parliamentary Summary'.

For some time ahead it is rare for a news item to get two lines of heading. Even the proceedings against Stead and his associates in connexion with 'The Maiden Tribute' are in no way 'displayed'. The reports are merely: 'The Armstrong Abduction

Case. Proceedings at Bow Street' and when the time came, 'At the Old Bailey'.

One is struck by the number of leading and other articles and editorial notes on national finance. Mr. John A. Masterman informs me that many of the financial contributions, published from 1883 to 1888, were written by a friend of his, the late John Govan, a man in the office of a Glasgow insurance company. When Govan saw the proposals of Gladstone's Chancellor of the Exchequer, Childers, on the sinking fund for the national debt he marked their weakness and wrote trenchantly to the *St. James's*. He received a post card from Greenwood, 'Send more'. Govan, who repeatedly disputed with the *Economist*, was valued by Greenwood, who proposed a visit to London, saw him several times, and told him that the Governor of the Bank of England had called with congratulations on the value of his contributions. Govan dealt with the National Debt question not only in the *St. James's* but in the *Pall Mall*, to which he transferred himself when he fell out with Greenwood over some sub-editing of his work. In the course of time the newspapers of the country came round to Govan's views, and when Goschen became Chancellor they were adopted almost completely. It is to Govan's credit and Greenwood's influence that the nation was saved in seven years some £14,000,000—which may be added, perhaps, to the million a year from the Suez Canal shares!

Many of the *St. James's* 'middles' are markedly dated. 'The Tyranny of English Wives'—crude to present notions—runs through more than one issue. The headings of two letters of the period to the editor are 'The Over-Education of Girls' and 'How to be Freed from a Troublesome Wife without the Publicity of the Divorce Court'. (One thinks of Greenwood's own problems.) The taboos of the time are reflected in the fact that in a short article, in small type, an account of a woman visitor's—the paper said a lady visitor's—call on 'The Ex-Khedive's Harem', mention of the word eunuch is avoided, once by writing 'a species of giant', and then 'a great big fat personage'.

There is seldom any special news, and the writing, though

spirited, is not, as we should judge, lively. A good deal of facetious verse is printed, some of which is smart, but the attack is of the time. The paper is plainly for people of some leisure and, we should think to-day, rather old-fashioned. It was bought for its political personality, its 'Occ. Notes', 'middles', and reviews. Although edited in what our generation feels to be an out-of-date idiom, it had conviction, force, assiduity, and a certain distinction.

As has been said, Greenwood 'never became a Conservative in the party sense'. But an article 'The Revival of Political Jesuitry', with Mr. Gladstone obviously in the writer's mind, is one of the many indications of the paper's political tint. Other leader headlines one comes on in turning over the file are, 'Messrs. Gladstone and Wemmick', 'The Midlothian Failure', and 'The Perversion of Mr. Gladstone'. There are allusions to 'Mr. Gladstone's recent pranks', and 'the Gladstonian misrepresentations'. One title is 'The Birmingham Temper in Politics'; another 'Mr. Bright in the Dock'. Although professedly independent, the paper preached almost the full Tory faith. Fox Bourne, in his *English Newspapers*, states that it was 'often a too indignant and ungenerous critic of the administration'. Robertson Nicoll, who as he saw a good deal of Greenwood in his later days wrote on a basis of knowledge, doubts 'whether anyone enjoyed a closer friendship with Lord Beaconsfield'. Joseph Hatton, the novelist, said that it was 'an education in Liberalism, Conservatism, in current history and the polite arts to read the *Pall Mall* and *St. James's*'.

Company advertisements soon appeared in the young paper, but the circulation must have been small. The *St. James's* cannot have been profitable. As to the financing of it, the facts are as stated in the *Dictionary of National Biography*. Henry Hucks Gibbs, 'merchant and scholar', who was a member of the City firm of Anthony Gibbs & Sons, and had been a Governor of the Bank of England, founded it 'with other members of his family, in the Conservative interest'. He afterwards became member for the City and, later, Lord Aldenham, and died in 1896.

The following letters from Greenwood to George Bentley the publisher,[1] written between the spring and autumn of 1881, are from a batch which I had the opportunity of purchasing from a dealer in autographs. One is written at the Garrick—the editor of the *St. James's* was also a member of the Savile. They are preceded with 'most cordial' thanks for 'sympathy and friendship', and give us an accurate impression of the workings of Greenwood's mind, of the gap there was between him and, say, Morley, his successor at the *Pall Mall*, and of the politics of the time:

Jan. 24, 1881. It is difficult to get at any accurate estimate of the numerical values of the different classes of voters; but my own melancholy impression is that the middle classes, left alone, would be swamped by the electorate below. But I doubt, for my part, whether they are likely to be left without auxiliaries from the working man section.

Men like Morley *must* know that a people does not change its most rooted characteristics in six months: and scarce anything the Government has done, or left undone, or failed in on attempt (for it cannot boast of a single successful move, wise or unwise) but offends some good or bad characteristic of the English people. It is a vain supposition that the people like to give up anything it has won, or can be pleased at the retreat from Candahar. The Ministerialists may chatter of wisdom and humanity: all the world knows, and Englishmen know and feel, that it is weakness, helplessness, with some deadly folly and a good deal of mere funk.

And when was the ingrained English love of order, insistence on obedience to law, what we used to brag of as 'law-abidingness'—when was that sentiment washed out of the people? You do not believe it washed out at all, no more do I: and if it exists, what must the people think of the way in which Ireland has been managed?

Again: is this a people likely to thank a Government which, at a time of vast and imminent change in the affairs of the East, (which are the affairs of all Europe) reduces it to helplessness? I think not: the fact is that we are completely out of the game just now—com-

[1] Succeeded to the business in 1867. His father, Richard Bentley, died in 1871.

pletely. No, my dear Mr. Bentley: the country appears stupefied, perhaps is: but it has not become another people since 1879.

And what you read in the *Spectator* and in my poor little perishing *Pall Mall*[1] about the will of the people and its 'mandates' never withdrawn, is 'bounce' when it is not ignorance and thoughtlessness. The worst of it is, that the mischief that has been done within the last eight months, and is now in progress and cannot be arrested, is of the most signal and unparalleled kind. If a month hence the country were to wake from its stupor and strike out against its present rulers, it would be too late.

As to Candahar, which gives you so much concern, *we have not left yet*. We cannot leave yet. And before long it may be seen that not only are the best authorities in India against it—(Ripon himself doubtful, Lord Napier of Magdala, Sir Donald Stewart, Sir F. Roberts and others dead against it) but facts may tell in the same direction.

This is certainly writing 'in the Conservative interest'. A letter, dated April 1, expresses the belief that 'we shall get rid of our National Calamity [Gladstone] soon; whether we shall ever be able to undo the mischief of the last five years is quite another matter'. In another note Greenwood is deploring the lack of 'any vigour, any promptitude' in the Conservative leaders. It is easy to understand that he was not counted on as a sound party man.

After this politics we hear of a young novelist with a rich father: 'Some time since I read a novel in MS. written by the daughter of a gentleman of my acquaintance—Mr. Staniforth. Whether you would think it good enough for publication I do not know; but I do think it worth your attention. I read it all through myself (which says something for it, perhaps) and I have certainly seen many things of its kind fairly successful with fewer merits. I have promised to give the author an introduction to you, and she'll take it as a favour if you will have her MS. read. Her father is rich, and I do not at all suppose that she is looking for more than the advantage of publication, on whatever terms you think safe for yourself.'

1 In the old days Greenwood would speak of his 'little *Pall Mall*'.

CHAPTER XXIII

Relations with Contributors

W. E. HENLEY — COVENTRY PATMORE — THOMAS HARDY — 'THE SOURCE OF PLEASURE IN WRITING' — A WARNING TO RICHARD JEFFERIES

LESLIE Stephen thinks that the judicial position of his brother, Sir James Fitzjames Stephen, should 'have restrained him more completely' than it did from taking any part in party controversies, but at the start of the *St. James's*, 'personal and political sympathy induced him, as he put it, "to take Mr. Greenwood's shilling"'. He ceased to contribute when the paper was about three years old.

One of the *St. James's* men was H. D. Traill. There was also W. E. Henley, who writes to Colvin, 'The merry Greenwood[1] has sprung a guinea for a stall (to see Henry Irving in "The Two Roses") and expects an article of "good, quiet criticism".' At another time Henley speaks of having a rasping letter from Greenwood; 'I shall knuckle under', he says; 'I must keep the *Gazette*.' He writes that Greenwood 'and I are really very thick'. He did for him one of his three reviews of Meredith's *Egoist*.

The author of *The Angel in the House* was a constant contributor of prose. Among other things there were eight articles on 'How I Managed and Improved my Estate', a reprint of which I saw advertised the other day for thirty shillings. Religion, philosophy, politics, art, literature, architecture, landscape, jewels, and market prices were other subjects. In regard to one article, Greenwood wrote to 'My dear friend': 'I've a boy who made the round of your "Sussex Marshes" on the inspiration of your account of them, and now I shan't be content till I've seen that inn in which a monarch down on his

[1] 'In England, the "greenwood" coming up to the very walls of the towns, it was possible to be "merry in the good greenwood".' Ruskin, *Modern Painters*.

luck might find a fitting abode.' On a reference by Patmore to the dramatist, Marston, Greenwood remarks 'how much the earth has cooled since his time!' Greenwood was, for Patmore, 'for more than a quarter of a century the sole and heroic politician and journalist in our degraded land'. Greenwood once wrote that he had not had of late, 'much talk as good as yours at a certain hotel and a certain club'. Two of Patmore's later prose works were largely made out of *St. James's* articles. In 1884, 'stirred to patriotic indignation by Mr. Gladstone's attempt to dissociate reform of the franchise from re-distribution of seats', Patmore had written to Greenwood:

> I am by no means a rich man;[1] but I am willing to bind myself to contribute a thousand pounds towards raising a really practical opposition to the ministerial treason, and if necessary, 'meeting force by force'. If I could further assist by acting as a sort of secretary or intermediary, or in any other way with you, nothing would make me so happy as to leave my retirement and to live in London for the next few months and act wholly under your direction. You would not, I believe, find me afraid of labour, or of any inconvenience that might arise.[2]

Greenwood replied: 'One or two such patriots as you ought to save us from the fate of Sodom; and I verily believe there are others too. I shall see one or two good men this evening, and again on Thursday.'

A characteristic article of Patmore's among the 120 he wrote in the *St. James's*—F. L. Lucas calls him 'Mary Annish and mad-dog by turns'—was headed, 'How to Govern Lady-like Races'. (They were, it may be noted, the Celts—Irish, Welsh, and Scots!) In 1888, on the subject of the Navy's inadequacy there was a letter from him called 'The Revanche, Sedan or Waterloo?', and he had the satisfaction of hearing from Greenwood that he 'heard it gravely discussed at Hatfield'. The *St.*

[1] Patmore paid for the printing of *The Angel in the House* and gave it to Cassell's National Library. The sale, price 3*d.* and 6*d.*, reached a quarter of a million.

[2] This and the following letters are from Basil Champneys's *Memoirs and Correspondence of Coventry Patmore* (Bell).

James's was four years old when the editor wrote to him: 'Next year I want to bring out as many articles as I can from "eminent hands". Will you, then, take thought again to provide a little series or so that I may brag about? My aim is to get at least a dozen men of some sort of distinction (various of course) to keep the pot boiling pretty constantly with a spark of sacred fire.'

When Patmore told Greenwood how happy he felt in the work he was doing for him, he got the response: 'I think I know what the source of your pleasure is in writing for the *St. James's*. It is the consciousness, more or less acknowledged, that your work *tells*. This it certainly does; and it is my pride in the paper that no good article—no really good one—ever did or ever does appear in it, without full effect,—I mean, of course, where it was meant to have effect, and where the effect is of practical value. My praise (whatever it may be worth) is the praise of him who eats the pudding, and sees how it is relished. I do not remember any article of yours of which I did not hear afterwards in one way or another; and that is the gratification you give the editor, over and above the private and personal enjoyment of good work, and the satisfaction of working with good men. Then there is the blessed concordance of taste, of aims, and a common love of freedom, even like that of the wild ass when certain things and persons seek to put the halter on. This explains it to my mind: it is a pleasant explanation, any way.'

In an article on 'Courage in Politics' Greenwood made deletions 'not so much as editor as friend—there will be plenty of people to snarl at your paper', and had a few words on 'being blizzarded again to-day. "Blizzarded"—don't you think it would make a pretty winter oath or objurgation? "You be blizzarded!" "May I be blizzarded!" Tremendously emphatic, and yet a lady might use it.' In the summer of 1888 he says, 'I have not had a clear twenty-four hours' holiday (yes, one); and at the end of it I'm working, not like one man, but a man and a boy: not to go the length of two grown-ups exactly'. Several of his letters are signed 'Thine, F.G.' In one he speaks of talking over things 'at large and deep'. Referring to a book of Patmore's he says: 'Some of the matter is above me: I have to strive to it. With just flight enough to get to the gate, I stand there and look in at the lower heaven of your meaning without ability to enter and partake as liberally as you intend.' He asks him if he noticed that 'a first edition copy of your poems sold for £3 the other day'. He would have Patmore 'come out of your hermitage a little more'. A later book by the poet, Greenwood calls 'a bag of nuggets and polished stones; with here and there something which is I don't know what'. Patmore in his letters to his third wife twice speaks of going to luncheon or dinner 'with the Greenwoods'. Once he says 'Greenwood admired my coat very much'.

Champneys notes that 'occasionally the editor headed an article of Patmore's with a conciliatory note, as for instance in the case of one entitled, "Why Women are Dissatisfied", to which the following is prefixed: "What follows is a remarkable paper, which some of its readers will think very shocking and even outrageous; though in fact it proceeds from one of the kindliest as well as one of the firmest, keenest, and most subtle minds of the day".'

From time to time the contributor had to be kept in check, as the following letters bear witness:

Jan. 9. Your letter shows once more a very generous spirit. The truth is, that it *does* take a little time to get into the tactics of newspaper writing on controversial subjects, but 'it comes'. Here is your article on 'Inequality'. It is all perfectly true, with nothing in excess; and yet you don't know what offence it would give in its straightforward, cool assumption that everybody knows that you are right who knows anything of the matter. So they do. But the truth itself is hateful to thousands and tens of thousands. I do sincerely thank you for your forbearance.

A letter written at 11 p.m. says:

Jan. 27. And now to my pain and grief I must confess to you that I fear you may over-metaphysic our poor readers if you write such papers as these four, the 'Seer', and the two later ones. Believe me, there aren't two in ten who can appreciate your subtleties, or dive deep enough in your thought without floundering. Some of them can—a few—and to them your articles will be as 'nuts'. As for the rest—you know what a man feels he can't understand he thinks he has a right to be offended with. Pity a poor devil of an Editor who has to take such people into serious account. But that is my unavoidable fate. Of course the poet is wanted for such work as you have been doing for us lately; this is where he comes in as 'Seer'; a name for him however which in a general way I don't like at all.

Another time Greenwood explains, as other editors have had to do, that the 'humorous ironical is most dangerous to handle'. On the death of Patmore, Greenwood said in an article that he had for him 'a fast affection as well as a profound respect'.

Sir James Barrie tells in *The Greenwood Hat*,[1] which contains a speaking portrait of Greenwood, that he began contributing to the *St. James's* at the end of 1884. In two years 140 sketches were accepted—and 'far more than twice that number rejected'. *The Greenwood Hat* owes its title to the fact that Barrie, when he first came to London, bought a silk hat in order to impress Greenwood. 'I never wore it', he alleged, 'except when I made my periodic advances upon the *St. James's*.' At the dinner to Greenwood at the end of his career (Chapter XXXVIII) he said, 'I dare not say in public how much I love Mr. Greenwood. He invented me. I owe almost everything to him.' 'If I were writing a guide to London I would put three stars to the name of Greenwood.' 'There was a legend', he added, 'that Greenwood could not smoke a cigar without putting a pen-nib through it.'

There is an allegation that Greenwood's swift appreciation of Thomas Hardy was due to his catching sight of the title *Under the Greenwood Tree*. It may be as well founded as the story that his friendship with the editor of Maga (see Chapters XXV–XXIX) was due to one being *Green*wood and the other *Black*wood! Another tale is that Greenwood picked up the book at a second-hand bookseller's as he had picked up the *Anti-Jacobin*,

[1] Peter Davies.

and wrote a review of it which did Hardy service. A variation is that when Greenwood got *Under the Greenwood Tree* from the sixpenny box, he 'sought out the author and commissioned him to write a story for *Cornhill* and that that story was *Far from the Madding Crowd*, which made Hardy's reputation'.

Among the people to whom Greenwood was indebted for contributions were, in addition to Sir James Fitzjames Stephen (and his second son, J. K. Stephen, the witty author of *Lapsus Calami*, whose life closed prematurely), Sir Henry Maine—'that powerful minded man', in John Morley's words (he did leaders)—D. C. Lathbury (afterwards editor of the ably conducted *Pilot*), Grant Allen (who wrote pleasing scientific articles of a type for which many writers are now equipped, and shocked a large public with *The Woman Who Did*), Andrew Lang (*Letters to Dead Authors*), Anthony Hope Hawkins (who was to do *The Dolly Dialogues* for the *Westminster Gazette*), Mrs. Lynn Linton (of *The Girl of the Period*), Katharine Tynan (in regard to whose 'more than pretty piece of verse' the editor wrote 'I fancy I spied one of your lines running off upon two feet more than properly belong to it'), George Saintsbury, Edmund Gosse and Gilbert Parker, both afterwards knighted, Sir Frederick Pollock, Kenneth Grahame, James Hannay, J. Hamilton Fyfe, Adam Gielgud, and Richard Jefferies.

Some of Jefferies's best work appeared in the *St. James's*, and Mr. Arthur Rogers, the Newcastle-on-Tyne dealer in old books, draws my attention to the fact that this early, struggling 'nature' writer, to whom popularity came late, gave Greenwood the first and second edition and the illustrated edition of *The Gamekeeper at Home*. Mr. S. J. Looker, who tells me he has been 'collecting and studying Jefferies for forty years and has 'the most comprehensive collection' of his manuscripts, favours me with a copy of this admonitory undated letter from Greenwood:

On reading this, I feel obliged, as your anxious but possibly enough mistaken friend, to warn against the style you have adopted in these papers. I will take the liberty of saying that this so well-marked style, an entirely new-fangled one, was never before adopted (till you took it up) by any single writer who was not more or less of a literary impostor. It originated, I believe, in *Household Words*, or in *All the Year Round*. It has been used by Mr. Wilkie Collins in Mr. Wilkie Collins' worst days: and he was always a bad writer—a thoroughly and contemptibly bad writer, according to my standard at any rate, and now, just when the style has sickened even those who once found some sort of fascination in it, you abandon the straightforward, simple, and in all respects most appropriate English of your *Gamekeeper* to take up with this tricky flashy manner. You see by the bad language which I myself am using that I *detest* this style, wh. has no ancestry, and not a single respectable connection. Do please go back to your original manner.

Nothing can be more fit for the matter you put into it. These simple unpretending harmonies in the *Gamekeeper* compared with wh. all this is very poor and artificial indeed.

Forgive my warmth. I feel like a man who sees his son abandoning the society of a quiet nice-mannered lady for a painted person voluble in lace and ribbons not too finely kept nor handsomely come by.

The following letter from Jefferies to Greenwood was written at Woodside, Surbiton. There is a facsimile on pages 186–9:

I enclose continuation of the 'Gamekeeper'.

In a leader today 'Submission and Admission' I see you have clearly demonstrated that the difference between the two Governments is of a substantial character and not one of form only. The attempt, which you explained to me in conversation the other day, to substitute the San Stephano [*sic*] Treaty for the Treaty of Paris, is just the very point.

I have written to Messrs. Smith and Elder informing them that the series will be concluded in 24 articles: as No. 11 was of extra length this is really equal to 25, and the 3 on 'Poaching' to 28.

May I say something without giving offence—I do not feel quite easy in making use of your experience and advice and friendly assistance generally, without some acknowledgement. I have no idea what Messrs. Smith & Elder will offer but I should be very glad indeed if I could induce you to take a little pecuniary share in the payment for publication. Of course I know very well that the money itself would not be of the slightest consequence to you, but that is not it: I feel that the articles would never have been written had it not been for your kindly encouragement, and in addition they have had the benefit of your literary knowledge in the elimination of unnecessary phrases and various other ways. To make use, as you have so freely allowed me to do, of your assistance without even a nominal return is contrary to my ideas of right, and if you would only accept some small part, if only ten or fifteen per cent. of the sum they give, I should not feel so ungrateful. I most sincerely trust you will not take offence at what seems to me a natural and proper suggestion: please look at it in the spirit which dictates it.

I do not propose to put my name to the book—unless you think it desirable—I think it would be better to remain anonymous, which will enable me to write with more freedom for the *P.M.G.* in the future, than if the authorship was known to everyone.

Have you observed the telegrams in *The Times* about 'Atrocities' committed by the Turks in fighting the Greeks? Day after day the telegrams declare that dreadful deeds have been done, only there are 'no details'—'no fugitives, but the Consul can produce some from the interior if necessary'! This has a curious look, as if somebody was very anxious atrocities should take place.

Stephen Phillips, the poet and dramatist, whose fame so quickly faded,[1] writes to Greenwood in a letter which was once shown me by a friendly second-hand bookseller, Mr. Hayward of Hastings: 'I will stand or fall by it ("Paolo and Francesca"). I have learnt so much from your criticism (more indeed than from any one) that I should hope that you might continue possible that line of such sane and helpful criticism. I send you a first copy of the book, and I send it to no one with greater pleasure. Is it at all possible for us to meet? I should think it a very real privilege.' Years afterwards, writing in *Blackwood*, Greenwood was candid about the poet-playwright's work, 'If Phillips thinks that his house is for the most part well made, he ought not to be allowed to rest in that mistake'.

On the relations of Greenwood with his contributors,

[1] 'Phillips was the victim of laudation and of his inability to stand oats, as the grooms say.' *Reading, Writing and Remembering*, E. V. Lucas (Methuen).

Thackeray's granddaughter, Mrs. Hester Thackeray Fuller, recalls for me the feelings for him of a friend of hers, Mrs. Ella Fuller-Maitland, who had considerable success as a writer in the eighteen-nineties. He helped her with her first book, *The Day Book of Bethia Hardacre*. 'She always spoke of him as a sort of god of literature, and it was with trepidation that she showed him her MS. But he said "Go ahead".' Mrs. Fuller-Maitland ended by collaborating with Sir Frederick Pollock in *The Etchingham Letters*.

The many references in these pages to George Meredith's friendship with Greenwood make it of interest to note the appearance in the *St. James's* of December 12, 1885, of a letter from Lord Dufferin concerning his aunt, Caroline Norton. It will be remembered that Meredith inserted a notice in the later edition of *Diana of the Crossways*, accepting the denials of the story, revived in Sir William Gregory's autobiography, that Sidney Herbert had confided to her the secret of Peel's intention to repeal the Corn Laws and that she had given it to Delane. The ex-Viceroy of India (and ex-Ambassador in Paris) recapitulated the statements of Henry Reeve and Abraham Hayward, both associated with *The Times*, that the source of Delane's information was Lord Aberdeen, and added that he had had himself an assurance from Lord Aberdeen's son, Lord Stanmore, that there was nothing surreptitious about the transaction—Lord Aberdeen acted with Sir Robert Peel's knowledge and consent.[1]

Like other editors, Greenwood had his worries. Mr. Daniel Macmillan has been kind enough to let me see a letter of his to 'My dear Craik' of their firm, about one of Tennyson's pieces which 'we had acquired at considerable expense':

> I assure you I did not see the Ode in the *St. James's* till three editions of yesterday's paper had been issued. All the morning I was busy with the forepart of the paper and in fact the hinder parts are usually left altogether to my subs: these I look over in the evening to see that the work has been done properly, and it was in doing

[1] *Caroline Norton*, Alice Acland (Constable).

this that I came upon the Ode. It is not at all in my way to do the thing you complain of, and I am very sorry my News-Editor didn't show more conscience on this occasion. You will see that I have put a few lines into the paper today about the wrong-doing.

But an editor of an evening newspaper not looking at its news columns until the last edition has gone to press, whew!

CHAPTER XXIV

The 'Anti-Jacobin'

STEINKOPF — 'CORRUPT BARGAINS AT BERLIN' — A SIXPENNY WEEKLY REVIEW FOR TWOPENCE—THE SUCCESSION TO THE THRONE

THE audience to which the *St. James's* so ably appealed was limited, and the buff paper, since its second year a penny like the *Pall Mall*, felt the competition of two other penny Conservative evening papers, the *Globe* on pink paper and the *Evening Standard* on white. There was also, on the same kind of paper as the *St. James's*, the penny *Pall Mall* so soon to become Conservative also, and, later, there was the Liberal *Westminster Gazette* on green paper. 'Tay Pay' O'Connor's *Star*, in traditional format, came out in 1888.[1]

When I was on the *Pall Mall*, and afterwards the *Westminster*, we did not regard the *St. James's* as a rival. It had seldom any news of importance, and the *Dictionary of National Biography* says it could not 'attain the prosperity of the *Pall Mall*'. As I have said, I am doubtful about that 'prosperity'. H. W. Massingham, who, I know, had his own trials as an editor, says, 'Cultured the *St. James's* was from cover to cover —Greenwood was himself a severe stylist and contributed scholarly and pointed work which did not appeal to the general body of Conservative opinion—and too steadily subordinated news to opinion.'

The time came when, on the death of one of the proprietors, George Gibbs (Nov. 26, 1886), as recorded by the *D.N.B.*, 'the financial control passed to his cousin Henry, who was not equally in harmony with Greenwood's views'. So in 1888 Greenwood persuaded Edward Steinkopf to buy the paper. This was an odd choice for a proprietor by a man of Greenwood's stamp. 'Stonehead', whose acquaintance we made in

[1] His *Sun* followed in 1893.

Chapter XI, had little to recommend him but his money. A friend of mine, Mr. William Stone, to whom he offered the *St. James's* for £12,000, described him to me as 'a Pomeranian Jew from Glasgow, a very rich man who left a million and a half. He bought a house in Berkeley Square, pulled it down and built a palatial mansion on the site. He was one of three, or perhaps four men who each owned one share in the New River Company—its shares were ordinarily held in sixteenths or hundredths—and he paid £120,000 for it. He had a merry, witty daughter—now dead—who had, unfortunately, a crippled hand. She was being continually proposed to—one man did so, she told me, while they were eating ices. She rode in the Row on a poor mount, over which I remonstrated with Steinkopf, for he had a parsimonious side.' Another friend's recollection of the man is briefer, 'A vulgar, loud-speaking German'. Possibly Greenwood felt that if a man of George Smith's standing and temperament could get on with Steinkopf he might be able to do so. But he was not able. The new proprietor refused his editor the freedom to which he had been used, and Greenwood 'retired suddenly and in anger within a year'.

What Greenwood's feelings were may be seen in the following letter of August 15, 1888, to Mrs. Ritchie, Thackeray's daughter, kindly lent to me by Mrs. Hester Thackeray Fuller, Thackeray's granddaughter:

At this rate I shall break down under the kindness of my friends. All day long letters come in which make me feel ashamed, so full are they of commendation and sympathy; and now here is your treasure of a letter—a sufficient solace in itself for going through a considerable deal of fire and water. Only an hour ago, Stephen the Judge was here talking in so kind a way as to make one cry almost. So it goes on; and it all comes from the fact that I was suddenly and ingeniously placed in a position which, while it was intolerable at the time, would have been disgraceful if I had remained in it.

Perhaps you do not know that there have been rumours and *on dits* in print that there had been corrupt bargains at Berlin over the

St. James's; and lately I was told by a mutual friend that Mr. W. H. Smith[1] had heard the same things! Now the truth is that there have been traffickings of some sort at Berlin by Mr. Steinkopf; and in the transfer of the paper to him he tricked me so completely (tricked is my solicitor's word, not mine) that I could not doubt him capable of what in Germany is not thought disgraceful at all. But of course that sort of jobbery will not do here; no sort of connexion with it will do; no connexion with suspicion of it even; and therefore did I resolve to fly rather than accept what, on other accounts also, I had found out must be a dangerous and humiliating alliance. The last thing I heard from my German Jew himself was that he had only entered into this business to please me, that I had broken his heart by threatening to go, and that if I did go he would close the premises. And no doubt he was absolutely confident (that was his calculation) that nothing would induce me to break away from my little paper, of which I *did* feel proud. However, it had to be done, but you will know, and Mr. Ritchie will know; and all my friends will know, that it must have been no joke for me to do it.

Meanwhile, accept my poor thanks for your most generous letter, which is more to me, and much more, than all the offers of cash that come by every post.

The letter is signed 'Gratefully yours'.

With his resignation from the *St. James's* Greenwood's career as a daily paper editor came to an end. It was unlikely, however, that a man who had been in four editorial chairs, the *Queen's*, the *Cornhill's*, the *Pall Mall's*, and the *St. James's*, and had found his gifts and tastes to be in editing would not desire to be an editor again. An active and acceptable writer in the periodical press, from the time he left the *St. James's*—the *Saturday Review* was among the papers to which he contributed—he started, on January 31, 1891, a weekly paper with the not too fortunate title of *The Anti-Jacobin, a Review of Politics, Literature and Society*.[2] The price was twopence, but it

[1] Of the famous firm of newsagents and booksellers, who entered the House of Commons in 1868, and after serving in various offices, succeeded in 1886 to the Leadership and earned the soubriquet of 'Old Morality'.

[2] The policy of the original *Anti-Jacobin*, as Sir Charles Petrie has written

THE ANTI-JACOBIN.

EDITED BY

FREDERICK GREENWOOD.

SATURDAY, JANUARY 31, 1891.

TERMS OF SUBSCRIPTION (PAYABLE IN ADVANCE).

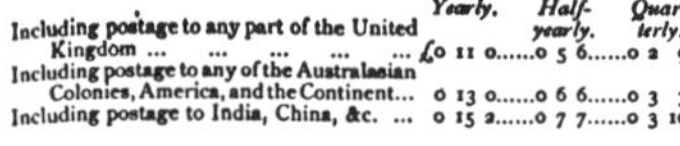

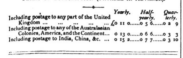

	Yearly.	*Half-yearly.*	*Quarterly.*
Including postage to any part of the United Kingdom	£0 11 0	0 5 6	0 2 9
Including postage to any of the Australasian Colonies, America, and the Continent...	0 13 0	0 6 6	0 3 3
Including postage to India, China, &c. ...	0 15 2	0 7 7	0 3 10

INTRODUCTORY.

FIRST numbers rarely satisfy. The first number of the original *Anti-Jacobin* was the least forcible and the least entertaining; and this sheet is issued in a spirit of apology for shortcomings which no experience and no endeavour seem capable of overcoming. Yet we may hope, and even promise, to bring our little paper much nearer to perfection before long.

The why and wherefore of its publication may be explained in a few words. The venture was decided on soon after that most timely and fortunate event, the Parnellite explosion, and for these reasons. The leaders of both parties had discovered a particular convenience in keeping the Home Rule question before the country as the first and greatest of all: the only one, indeed, that should be permitted to engage attention as long as it remained unsolved. If we would know why it took this importance in Mr. Gladstone's mind we should consider these facts. When that gentleman brought out his Home Rule scheme, he and his scheme were driven out of the field with a promptitude and vigour that amazed him. As one whose wits are scattered by a blow on the cheek, so was he; but in an instant his outraged feelings gathered in a set determination to force his will on an impious and ungrateful England. That he would do, with sufficient length of days and strength therewith; and nothing else, if anything else would hinder his desire. But what was a desire was also an obligation. He had put himself in bonds to men whom he had imprisoned either as criminals or as political offenders. It was all but impossible that he should come uppermost again without their aid, and that was to be retained at one price only: persistence in freeing Ireland from British rule. Without the necessity the incentive would have been enough—the necessity without the incentive. Who, then, but Mr. Gladstone should cry for Home Rule as a debt of righteousness and the only way of peace? So it was with this gentleman, in naming whom we name the whole Opposition leadership out of Ireland, where his masters live and move and regulate his being.

On the other hand, the Ministerial leaders were quite as much devoted to the Home Rule cry, ringing it out like a shout of "Fire!" and never ceasing. And no doubt there was danger; and yet if an instant means of suppressing it had been offered to the managers of the Ministeral party, is it certain that they would have been glad of the gift? Not at all: they would have been for cloaking it up and conveying it into darkness. Why? Because there can be no Liberal Unionism without a Union in danger. The tie dissolved by which Lord Hartington, Mr. Chamberlain, and the Liberals who follow them are bound to the Government, that semi-attached party would drift or be drawn away from Tory companionship, and what then? Without Liberal Unionist support, the Government would be in a minority; and where and what would be the place of its Liberal allies, if their mission suddenly ceased? Moved by such considerations as these, who can wonder that the Ministerial managers were almost as anxious to keep up the Home Rule hubbub as their opponents were?

It was seen long ago, however, that as soon as a General Election drew near, both parties would learn that the greater number of English voters have no hankering for Home Rule, no perception of any considerable Irish grievance, and very little interest in legislation that would do nothing for themselves. But, with the General Election a long way off, the Gladstonians had no temptation to advance Socialist projects, nor the Ministerialists to exhibit the ever-ready dish; and so the two parties went their several ways, the one more confident of success every day, and the other more apprehensive of defeat. Then came the Parnellite explosion, to change the whole aspect of affairs; and, looking to the probable consequences of that event, what struck us most was this: Already tired of Home Rule clamour, Englishmen had now before them the true character of the Irish conspiracy, and a faithful picture of what Ireland would become in the hands of the conspirators. Therefore it was less likely than ever that the Gladstonians would "go to the country" on the Home Rule cry alone, while the chances of an early dissolution of Parliament were much increased. In other words, the time had been brought nearer when the Gladstonian leaders would be compelled to declare for the New Radicalism, stoop to its prophets, adopt its doctrine, formulate its measures; the compulsion being all the greater, since with Home Rule they could do nothing.

And on our side? On our side, doubt. Before the ballot boxes close at the next General Election, the confused factions of to-day will begin to resolve themselves into two great parties, after the old fashion in England; but with stronger differences between them than any that have existed for generations. Whigs, Tories, and Radicals will still be heard of, no doubt: but the opposed parties will be—one Jacobin, the other Anti-Jacobin. How the first named party will be formed and led we know pretty well already. We also know how its opponent will be constituted. It will be formed of all the Conservatism, all the old true Liberalism, all the Radicalism that stands against the mad and tyrannical experimentalisings which Herbert Spencer and some other men denounce in their newly published "Plea for Liberty." But as to how this party will be led there is no assurance. If we had to judge from the recent legislation of a Cabinet the most powerful members of which are unofficial and irresponsible, we should be compelled to doubt whether there would be any leadership, for awhile, of the great party that will be thrown together against the New Radicalism. Their Free Education Bill, that grossly unjust and dangerous Irish Land Bill of theirs which Mr. Parnell rejoices in, these are but examples of a sort of statemanship from which the Jacobinism of the day has much more to hope than to fear. To be sure, those measures were introduced before "the Parnellite split" fully revealed what Parnellism means, and before Socialism appeared the necessary doctrine of salvation for English Radicalism. But we do not hear that such of them as lie before Parliament are to be recalled, and who knows yet whether the Policy of Dishing will not be steadily maintained, as if *that* could overcome the Irish conspiracy against England and the English conspiracy against property and freedom? Nobody knows. It is because of that doubt, as much as for any other reason that the *Anti-Jacobin* has been started; and perhaps enough has now been said by way of introducing it to the British public.

Editorial page of the first number of the *Anti-Jacobin*.

had to be raised to sixpence. Unlike the *Pall Mall* and *St. James's*, it was on dead white paper. Coventry Patmore, who had been a contributor to the *St. James's* to the end of Greenwood's connexion with it, is stated by Greenwood to have been 'the first person out of the house' to be told of the projected enterprise. He suggested as a title *Under the Greenwood Tree* and alternatively *The Twopenny Damn*! Who found the money for the paper I have not discovered. In view of Greenwood's friendship with the Baroness Burdett-Coutts I thought she might have been his backer, but no payment by her to him can be traced. Then I thought of Coventry Patmore, conflicting statements as to whose financial position have been made to me. His great-grandson, Derek Patmore, tells me 'he was always very secretive about his financial affairs, but he could have afforded it'. I have no proof, however, that he provided cash for his friend. The registered proprietor of the *Anti-Jacobin*, I find, was Greenwood himself.

Here are two letters which Greenwood wrote on his aims to the distinguished Edinburgh publisher, Blackwood, which are published for the first time.[1] The handwriting is a little shakier than it used to be and the paper is black-edged because of the death of one of Greenwood's children.

Jan. 7, 1891. As perhaps you have seen, I am about to bring out a new weekly journal, under the somewhat dangerous and ambitious title of the *Anti-Jacobin*. I mean to have a smaller sheet (i.e. fewer pages) than the other reviews, but at least as handsome as any in point of paper, print, etc. There is too much in most of the weekly reviews, and what there is is (generally) 'stodgy'. I mean to be quick, strong, brief, with more of the small sword than the sabre.

And another innovation: I do not propose to come out at *6d.* There are too many publications which men who want to know what is going on *must* buy, to make sixpence a welcome price any

in his *Four Georges*—strange that he should have adopted the same title as Thackeray—was to 'implicate the whole of the Opposition in the doctrines of its extremists, and in this it was remarkably successful'.

[1] See also next chapter.

longer. And there are lots of men, not poor, who don't believe they can afford 6*d*. for a weekly paper nowadays. So I mean to charge *twopence*: so that a smart, strongly written journal shall not be beyond any poor gentleman's pocket. If I can only approach my ideal you will soon see a first-rate sheet at a price that will content the richer classes, and be approved by others who are not rich.

Jan. 28. Thanks for letter of advice which I much value, and you shall see that I will try to work up to it. You may be disappointed in the first number—but I hope not much. There are more pages of it than I proposed to print, but that is rather forced on me by a number of advertisements which would not allow me to print 24 or 28 pages without giving too little matter, and yet oblige me to give more than I meant, and more than enough. However that will right itself.

I thoroughly agree with you about reviewing and shall strive to conform more in future to what is certainly the right way.

'Any poor gentleman's pocket.' In fact, still 'by gentlemen for gentlemen'!—which the father of the present Lord Salisbury was to parody on the appearance of the *Daily Mail*, 'by office boys for office boys'.

The first number gave its readers good value, for, in addition to the leading article, there are 'Working Men's Shackles', 'Proof Positive', 'The Age of Consent', 'The Colonial Temper', 'The Law of Conspiracy', 'What is an Anti-Jacobin', 'A Short Way with an Inventory', 'In the House', ' "Impressionist" ' Art' (by Coventry Patmore, the only contributor who signed his name), 'From Dr. Russell's Reminiscences'—a series on the experiences of Howard Russell, the war correspondent, which ran through several issues—'A Lost Leader', and 'The Playgoer', as well as editorial notes and a number of carefully written reviews. There is, as Greenwood had told Blackwood, a good show of advertisements.

In spite of the fact that the editor had previously launched two papers, he had to write that the leading article was 'issued in a spirit of apology for shortcomings which no experience and no endeavour seem capable of overcoming'; he promised to bring 'our little paper nearer to perfection before long'. In the following issues the editorial notes grew—in one number there were three and a half pages of them—and by November there were illustrations.

Greenwood had always an interest in the part played by the monarchy in a modern State. The leader in the first number of the *Pall Mall*, it may be remembered, had been a polite protest against Queen Victoria's years of seclusion after the death of the Prince Consort. Some time later Greenwood was to write the article, from which a quotation has been made, on the advantage of having a queen rather than a king on the throne. Now, in the *Anti-Jacobin*, he was saying: 'It is time to think of the comparatively few lives that stand between the Throne and the Duke of Fife, and whether it is well for the monarchy if the succession fell to the Duke of Fife's family. It would not be well that the succession would devolve on any child of the Duke's, an heirdom most untoward. It might be a very grave misfortune.'

What had moved him to write so strongly does not appear. The Duke, formerly Viscount Macduff and a Liberal M.P., had been advanced from his earldom on his marriage with George V's eldest sister, who brought the family into succession to the Throne; and although the contingency is now remote, the family is still in line. For one reason or another, the Duke was not in my recollection popular. It was said, for one thing, that he was tactless and inclined to rub people the wrong way. In his own countryside it was popularly believed that an ancestor had been a 'packman', and that the estates had been gained, in part, by a method of lending money to small proprietors and taking over their land when they failed to meet their obligations; and old wives had a story that in Duff House a Lady Duff had been heard calling 'Jamie Duff, Jamie Duff, come awa tae yer denner'! 'The worst thing I know about the Duke', an Aberdonian once said to me, 'is that he is blamed for having invented the Fife check and called it a tartan.'

The late Sir Alexander Macintosh, a well-informed Aberdonian journalist, who was so long in the Press Gallery of the

House of Commons, and passed his boyhood in Banff at the door of Duff House, wrote to me:

> Victorian gossip about the Earl when he became engaged to the Prince of Wales's daughter was that he belonged to the Marlborough House set, which was supposed to be a fast set. I cannot imagine what Greenwood had against him. The Duke's engagement to the Princess was believed to be a love-match, and the marriage turned out happily. There could not have been any trouble about finance. It was said locally that, on his succession to the peerage, the Earl took tight control over the great estates of the family. He was a good business man and became a partner in a banking firm. Duff Cooper has a strong resemblance in appearance to the Duke of Fife. His mother was a sister of the Duke.

An equally well-informed and responsible journalist in the county tells me that Greenwood's 'heirdom most untoward, a very grave misfortune' might have been based on the fact that he feared mental instability in the family. Greenwood was a frequenter of the Garrick Club of which the Duke of Fife was chairman.[1]

Greenwood, who, it is hardly necessary to say, was no sensationalist, also wrote, after the death of the Duke of Clarence, an article in the *Illustrated London News* in which he suggested with delicacy that if a marriage between Princess May and Prince George should come about it would be a happy occurrence.[2] The article was entitled 'Good for the Nation'. What the Duchess of Teck, a popular figure for her kindness, good humour, and frank ways, thought about this I do not know, but I do know that Greenwood was more than once a visitor to White Lodge and

[1] A correspondent in Edinburgh writes: 'There was some feeling that the Earl of Fife [raised to a Dukedom on his marriage with the Princess Royal] did not have a sufficiently exalted position in the peerage to justify a Royal alliance. Ideas on such matters were, of course, more exacting than they are today. The Duke is believed to have added considerably to the family fortunes through business activities in South Africa.'

[2] The betrothal to the Duke of Clarence took place in Dec. 1891, but he died in the following January. The betrothal to Prince George occurred in May 1893.

that she valued his friendship. It was noticed that on several public occasions he sat next the Duchess.

George Meredith continued to send his scraps of encouragement to Greenwood.[1] One note is dated 'Oct, first fog, 1896':

I read the *Anti-Jacobin*, liking all of it except the title. My domestic political views are on t'other side. But I share your feeling for the country, and am with you in your watchful outlook. Therefore I hail an extension of the Journal that has an air of prosperity—or at least of justified audacity. Much of the writing is excellent, in the tone of journalism which your supervision has always guaranteed. Often I wish to back an article or remonstrate. With my love to you.

Other letters from Box Hill are:

Dec 20, 1896. In old days of the *Pall Mall*, when you were under stress of battle, I used to send my New Year's word of hail on to you. You are out of the fray now, but still a ready fighter, and whether or not we are of a mind as to the means, we have an end in common. Your affectionate George Meredith.

Jan 3, 1898. When you were the constant evening star over Northumberland Street, I knew my mark. I am always forgetting Brittany Road, though not you at any season. Be sure of my lively good wishes now and ever. Your loving George Meredith.

And there is an epistle at the end of 1898 which concludes, 'How I wish to see you'. On another day 'Your loving George Meredith' writes, 'Here is a twitter of song for your *Anti-J.*, if you care to have it, just to show you my heart is warm'. Later, he explains in a note in which he is 'Ever Yours':

I thought it needless when I sent the verses to say that such tiny things were a gift, honoured by your acceptance. Do not, if you print me in future, pay me. We are not on the same side in politics, but at heart we are one. I never can help wishing well to an undertaking headed by you. Is the *Anti-J.* in a swim of success? This cheque insists on blowing a fine brass note, and I like it better than the money, although you pummel my poor lot of worthies and won't see things visible to me. But you do love England, where again we join.

[1] *Letters of George Meredith* (Constable).

The next spring he says, 'You are the prince of Editors, too good for you to have a party backing you. But take the title, and stand paperless.' Alas, by the end of the year the *Anti-Jacobin*'s advertisements had dwindled. The back page was wholly occupied by Beecham's Pills, and, to the experienced journalistic eye, patent-medicine advertising is never a healthy sign in a paper—as I write a leading advertising agent has just urged that it should be abolished. The issue of January 16, 1898, was the last. The *Anti-Jacobin* had lasted seven years.[1] When the struggle was over —someone said the weekly was 'too literary to live'—'Your loving Meredith' wrote: 'Your terse and pregnant few words of greeting told me so much, reminding me of the days when I was looking for the afternoon issue of the *Pall Mall*, sure of good writing. The words you sent were gold. If they had not been written from a sick bed, they would have inspirited me. I have to suppose that your enemy is gout.'

[1] Of the original *Anti-Jacobin or Weekly Examiner* (1797–8) there were thirty-six numbers. It was an eight-page paper, quarto, 9½ inches high, double column. All the headings were in italic caps. and the first article was leaded. It bore a 3½*d.* stamp (16 per cent. discount). The price was 6*d.* Advertisements were not admitted. The editor was William Gifford. The prospectus was written by Canning and most of the financial articles by Pitt. The office was at 169 Piccadilly, opposite Old Bond Street. Ingenious letters to the editor, reports of imaginary meetings and parodied speeches were a feature. Greenwood, in an article in the *Academy*, lxviii, 1905, speaks of the 'pungent, insidious, uproariously humorous' introductions to metrical pieces; 'the serio-comic has never been carried farther in our language' than in the notes to 'The Loves of the Triangles' purporting to be by a Mr. Higgins of St. Mary Axe. It is alleged that the publication 'came abruptly to an end at the insistence of Mr. Pitt, so alarmed became Mr. Wilberforce and others of the more moderate supporters of Ministers at the boldness of the language employed'.

FREDERICK GREENWOOD. Probably about 1892. He did use a quill

From a portrait kindly lent by Mr. J. H. Blackwood

THE BLACKWOOD LETTERS

CHAPTER XXV

Gladstone, Salisbury, and Chamberlain

THE 'PALL MALL' AND 'THE MAIDEN TRIBUTE' — GLADSTONE AND DISRAELI AS WAR MINISTERS! — LORD SALISBURY AND HIS COLLEAGUES — SHARP CRITICISM OF CHAMBERLAIN — LORD ROSEBERY AND 'A PLOT'

AFTER the collapse of the *Anti-Jacobin* some of Greenwood's most characteristic work is to be found in *Blackwood's Magazine*. Five articles—the first dates back to the *St. James's* period—include 'What has become of the Middle Classes?' (Aug. 1885) —a question still discussed—'Manners, Morals and Female Emancipation, being a Familiar Letter from a Woman of Quality' (Oct., 1892), and 'The Newspaper Press, Half a Century's Survey' (May, 1897). There followed Greenwood's series, 'The Looker-On', which was widely read, had a considerable influence, and continued from the January 1898 number until the issue of November 1899, when it came to an end in circumstances to be described.[1] Some years afterwards the connexion was revived and Greenwood wrote in February 1905 on 'The Marriage Bond' and in June 1905 about his old friend Coventry Patmore.

The veteran publisher, Mr. J. H. Blackwood, of the famous firm of Blackwood and Sons, kindly told me of a collection of 170 unpublished letters, with a telegram or two, which were received from Greenwood between 1888 and 1900. The letters had been presented to the Scottish National Library, the director of which, Mr. Marryat R. Dobie, was good enough to give me

[1] Mrs. Oliphant had previously used the title for occasional contributions. It was through Greenwood's introduction that Charles Whibley contributed to *Blackwood* the series which followed his, 'Musings Without Method'.

permission to have copies made. They are addressed to John Blackwood, with the exception of one or two to his nephew, George William Blackwood.[1]

In addition to this batch of correspondence, there are in the firm's possession unpublished letters of Greenwood's between 1901 and 1905. I was readily given leave to have copies made of these also.

'Ferreting out the story of a man's life from his correspondence', writes a biographer of Edward FitzGerald, 'is like reading a closely written manuscript by the light of a tallow candle.' The worth of the rich collection of Greenwood letters lies in the impression they give of his journalistic and literary character and his assiduity, from his editorship of the *St. James's* through the brief *Anti-Jacobin* term, to his time of free-lancing in his last years. They show his keen attention to home and foreign politics, the pains he took to keep himself informed and to express himself clearly, and the quality of his informants. The letters contribute something, therefore, to 'the story of a man's life'. They also contain scraps of gossip and touches of colour which students of the period will like to have.

To save space, I have cut out a great deal, but nothing, I am sure, of permanent utility. Frequently when I have been on the

[1] John Blackwood, 1818–79, grandson of the founder of the firm, William Blackwood, 1776–1834, was for thirty years editor of 'a magazine the continuity of which', he said, 'you will hardly match in periodic literature'. He noted that 'Dickens and Thackeray, when at the highest wave of their popularity, started, or were employed to start, periodicals, but they never touched *Blackwood*'. It was begun five years after Waterloo. While in John Blackwood's time all articles were anonymous, William Blackwood encouraged signatures. To write for him, Charles Whibley testified, was 'an office of friendship generously rewarded; the letters which he wrote at the end of every month to his collaborators were masterpieces'. His birthplace, like Thackeray's, was India. George William Blackwood, who succeeded him, was born in 1876, his brother, Mr. J. H. Blackwood, the present honoured head of the firm (now taking less and less share in its direction) two years later—they both saw the light in India—and his elder son Wing-Commander G. D. Blackwood, now in the firm, in 1909. That valuable three-volume contribution to the history of publishing, *Annals of a Publishing House: William Blackwood and his Sons*, comes down to 1898.

point of striking out, I have refrained because I felt that I might be taking away a fact or point that someone might be glad to come upon. I have also been loath to leave out every one of the bits about 'copy' and proofs—some I have deleted—for the relationship of an editor-turned-contributor with his editor makes its appeal. I have allowed somewhat irregular punctuation to stand, and the spelling is untouched. In his letters, if not in his manuscript for the press, Greenwood had a punctuation of his own. In reference to the copying of Thackeray's letters, one finds Hester Ritchie writing in *Letters of Anne Thackeray Ritchie*, 'It has seemed important to transcribe them exactly as they were written with their unexpected spelling, contracted words and peculiar punctuation'. But I have economized space by omitting addresses and subscriptions. The early letters are all headed *St. James's Gazette* or 19 Argyle Road, Kensington.

I have found the letters good reading as worth while comment on events of the time. In the first letter dated February 16, 1885,[1] the allusion is to 'The Maiden Tribute of Modern Babylon', a series of articles, startlingly outspoken for the time, written by W. T. Stead, the editor of the *Pall Mall*, with the object—in which he was successful—of raising the age of consent from thirteen. As a result of the publication of the articles, the *Pall Mall* lost most of its advertisements and many of its readers, and the editor, who had done his work with the knowledge and sympathy of Cardinal Manning, the City Chamberlain, and the Salvation Army, underwent a short term of imprisonment for a technical offence for which a Sunday paper had egged on the authorities to prosecute. 'The *Pall Mall* won't quite leave its filth, you see, or its hypocrisies. Both have done the paper a world of harm amongst decent folk, who will not take that sort of thing into their homes. This we find in the circulation of the *St. James's* wh. has gone up many thousand: our new subscribers, of course, being the best of theirs. It is pretty to see how the railway readers of the *P.M.G.* try to hide what they are reading: how queerly ashamed they look.'

[1] Greenwood was at the *St. James's* from 1880 to 1888.

In April, after one of his allusions to Gladstone as 'our National Calamity', he writes: 'Here is a story I can vouch for. Some time ago somebody was telling Mr. Gladstone of his great gifts, when he said, "Well, I doubt, after all, whether my capacity will ever be fairly tested till I become Minister of War!" And he is quite capable of plunging into a war (other things failing him) to show how much he can excel Mr. Pitt in that kind of business. Not that I believe he has the faintest idea of doing that now.' Which reminds one of what Sir William Fraser said, 'Had there been a European war, Disraeli would have felt that, in conducting it, he was in his true element'. And in our own day we have been indebted in war-time to military direction by a prime minister who, despite the strain, manifestly had uncommon satisfaction in the conduct of hostilities.

At the end of May, Greenwood hopes Blackwood will like his Middle Classes article, and admits that 'an Editor has sometimes very good reasons against printing an article that he *doesn't* dislike. So I am quite prepared for the return of my MS., & beg that you will send it back without a second thought if it does not quite suit you. Only let me have it pretty soon—it's all I ask.' The amenable ex-editor contributor adds that 'if you take it, it may be necessary to alter a line or two at the end'.

Up to now the letters have begun 'Dear Mr. Blackwood'; from now on Greenwood writes 'My dear Blackwood'.

An October letter refers to a book sent for review, at Blackwood's request, to a friend of his. Unfortunately,

> your friend has sent me a review so badly written that it is quite impossible to print it. I put it into type, but it is so confused, & in many places so thoroughly & hopelessly ungrammatical even, that I could not mend it without rewriting the whole thing from one end to the other. I tell you this to account for the non-appearance of the review: for I am most unwilling that you should suppose I neglected any man who came with your introduction.

Then we come to the Midlothian Campaign, and Greenwood, after making a bad shot as an election-results forecaster, writes:

It is a bad situation because of its immediate results abroad and in Ireland. Some conversation with Lord Salisbury and with Lord Carnarvon is enough (with what we can all see for ourselves) to convince me of that.

And—as you say—all these troubles and difficulties would have disappeared, if one man had disappeared three months ago. One single piece of incarnate mischief has done it all for us. Had he been out of the way, there would have been such a junction of Moderates, Conservatives and Liberals, to settle and overawe the Parnellites, as would have assured the foreign Governments that we had come to our senses again and could be dealt with accordingly.

I suppose Lord Rosebery is really looking to the succession, just as Chamberlain is.

About a year later, on November 15, 1886, 'Mr. J. M. Barrie asks me for an introduction'. 'I venture it with great willingness; for he is really a clever man at first hand—meaning that his cleverness is not of the second hand order; and I believe his work to be well worth your attention. At the same time, I know nothing of the book which, I understand, he proposes to offer to you, and judge by the work he has done for me.'

Later, Blackwood is told by Greenwood that he likes Laurence Oliphant 'extremely'. A letter of the summer of 1887 gets back to politics and Lord Salisbury:

Lord S., who is really in a bad Bill of Health, is so much occupied with foreign affairs, and so used up in transacting them that he has no time to look after his team and not much nerve in driving it. Nor has he anybody of importance in the Cabinet (except Goschen) to think for the Government, and work for it as a whole, and bear a share in its responsibilities. That he should be glad to get Hartington in we need not doubt. But, for my part, I don't at all think Hartington will join the Cabinet just now; while as for Salisbury, Goschen and [Lord Randolph] Churchill sitting in the same Cabinet, that's not credible.

The two correspondents introduce writers to one another and Blackwood sends 'most cordial and kindly invitations' north. In September 1891 Greenwood is writing from 5 John Street, Adelphi. The following year satisfaction is expressed that

Blackwood is 'content' with an article—'there is not a statement that you cannot stand by'—and there is this bit of news: 'Knowles (of the *Nineteenth Century*) gave me to understand that Gladstone offered him the "Outidanos" article [*Contemporary*, Oct., 1889]: wh. was not accepted on account of an unswerving determination not to print an anonymous article by anybody.'

The election of the summer of 1892 'can be fought on no ground so invincibly', Greenwood writes in June, as on foreign affairs. 'Of facts, circumstances, speculations, contingencies, I believe I have good knowledge; & I shall be glad if you will allow me to set them forth in the next number. I would undertake to provide an extremely strong, & close, & various argument in a very few number of pages,—say 8, & not a word of partisanship.' A letter from Blackwood next month is 'a great gratification'. Greenwood's article 'will be despatched by whatever post you appoint, & not by any later one. And I will write very plainly; & revise; so that proof will be needless.' Some small matter he has been 'told by Morley' is mentioned. A letter of July 3 speaks of 'a good deal of confusion & heart-burning among the Gladstonian leaders', and gossips freely about Lord Rosebery and 'a plot':

How far that *has* gone you may judge from what I am about to whisper—please keep it *quite to yourself* at present. When just before the elections some preliminary arrangements were made for forming a Gladstonian Cabinet, Rosebery refused to take any part in it. He declared that he would stand out altogether: had neglected private affairs to attend to; did not find himself in good health; & so forth. This rather bothered Mr. G. who would not take No, though Rosebery repeated it more than once. It is extremely likely that the matter was made up when Mr. G. was staying at Lord R's in Scotland. If so, I fancy a great deal more has been re-arranged. For why was it that Rosebery held off so resolutely & surprisingly?

The explanation is this, perhaps. The House of Commons captains (on Mr. G's side) are strongly of the opinion that it won't do to have Lord Rosebery as Prime Minister. They understand that in the master's place, master he would be; & seeing that he is a young man, vigorous, adroit, popular, enormously rich, & with more of real statesmanship in him than all the Harcourts & Morleys & the rest can show, the fear is that if he once mounts the box not one of them may hope to take the ribbons.

With these considerations in view, a plot was formed, more than two years ago to put Lord Spencer in as a figure-head Prime Minister should 'anything happen' to Mr. G: Spencer who of course would be as wax in the hands of the Commons men, & easily superseded on occasion. Now I should not be surprised if that plan was again brought up a couple of months ago—the time referred to above; that Mr. G. sanctioned it; POSSIBLY proposed to put Lord S. in *this* time, so that he (Mr. G.) should be able to devote the whole of his declining strength to his Home Rule Bill, with a sinecure place in the Cabinet, where yet he would do as he pleased, while escaping a multitude of worries, deputations, questionings. If Lord R. heard in any way of his colleagues' plans for keeping him out of the Premiership, his refusal to have anything to do with the new Govt. is explained. That refusal would naturally lead the way to explications, & probably to concessions: for Lord R is too popular & powerful a member of his party to be got rid of without subsequent sorrow: though that is not the opinion of some who like not the prospect of his domination in the party.

From these matters Greenwood gets on to a 'fear that haunts me, that Mr. Chamberlain will be still allowed to dictate the policies of a party nine-tenths of it Conservative, & still further to destroy all effective opposition to Radicalism in the future': 'I know him thoroughly. He is as "Red" today as ever he was in his life. He has never moulted a feather of his old Birmingham Radicalism, or ever whitewashed one; & he prides himself to excess on seeing the party that opposed him & scorned him going about in public in Highbury liveries. But perhaps you think I feel too hotly on that subject: & if so I can well believe you right, for on none did I ever feel more strongly in all my life.'

In August we are told that 'the *Standard* is in the right as to Lord Rosebery'. 'He consents "under considerable pressure, & with reluctance". And beautiful it is to see that the attempt to elbow Lord R. out has led to a demonstration of his popularity & power in the party of a very remarkable kind.'

At the end of August, from somewhere in Kent, Greenwood thinks that 'considering that this is the holiday season, when light writing & reading is preferred, & considering that there is always a stirring interest in "Society", & its tone, & so forth, you may like the enclosed paper: wh. is a short one. Written as if by a woman of the Great World, its style is imitated from the letters & conversation of one of the oddest, cleverest, & best known of Society's great ladies.' In a day or two he explains, in regard to his article, that the style he has 'tried to imitate (by way of giving dramatic individuality to the scrap) is that of Lady Dorothy Nevill'.

> But she is not older than other people, & she is very far indeed from being retired from society, as no doubt you know. Please don't mention the original of the Woman of Quality; for though, of course, there is no harm in a kindly application of her extremely odd & amusing talk, women (& men too) often take deep offence at little matters of the kind. I see one or two ways of communication between George Street, Edinburgh & Charles Street, Berkeley Square—where Lady D. lives—& I would not offend her for a great deal. On this account I hardly know how to draft the little paragraphs.

Here is a postscript about the shortcomings of the Foreign Office:

> When I published last year some papers about the Pamirs, with intent to explode the dangerous fallacy that military operations were impossible there, first I was privately assured by a high Indian functionary that I was totally misinformed—the country was altogether impracticable;—& then the Foreign Office people asked to be put in communication with the writer of my articles. Up to that hour they knew so little of the country as to be under the same delusion; & even then they showed every disposition to cling to it.

In the course of a long and rather portentous letter, which gives us more of Greenwood's political outlook, an article is proposed to Blackwood to show that

> a very great deal of what keeps all the world in uneasiness is at bottom the unfortunate law of things by wh. we can have no good without paying for it—the 'account' often coming in a most un-

> expected shape & surprising in amount. It is a matter of demonstration that whatever destruction of civilisation is threatened, proceeds in great part from the activities of civilisation itself: e.g. extraordinary facilities of communication, rapidity of transit & conveyance, erasure of 'barriers between nation & nation', & very much besides, of the same kind. Again: extension of civilisation, extension of demand, for comforts, appliances, & luxuries of civilised life. The frontiers of the competing states are extended beyond original natural boundaries into strange lands. The hopeful theory that advance of international commerce would destroy national hatreds, convince all mankind that it is a brotherhood with common interests, & therefore banish war, has turned out to be a total delusion. The competitions of commerce are more conducive to conflict than to brotherhood & peace.

The chief advantage this country has, he suggests, is 'a great command of alliances'.

The same month he mentions that he 'ought to be yachting now by rights' with Mackinnon of the British East Africa Company, which 'is in such low water'; and we learn that the tremendous article has not attracted Blackwood. 'I quite understand', Greenwood says, and adds: 'If you have a mind to see what sort of a fist I have for writing that does not come into the political & social essay category, there is a trifle called "Apology from Age to Youth" in type for *Macmillan* that may be read in a few minutes, when it comes out.' On January 4, 1893, he is sending a paper 'with a prayer that, if you don't like it, you will speed it back to me'. He describes it as 'giving voice in a dramatic form to feelings that must revolve in many an anxiously religious mind. Thousands & thousands of religious minds that pine under the ascendancy of science-bred unfaith; & my belief is that many of them cry out in their secret hearts as does my good Mr. Taylor of Baronsgate.' But 'Taylor of Baronsgate' comes back with 'a pleasant and courteous letter'. *Macmillan's* take it.

In his next letter Greenwood encloses a note from the French author of 'a very remarkable book—written from a foreign & entirely independent standpoint—on Gladstone; I wrote a longish notice of it for the *National Observer*': 'The question she asks, you see, is whether, in the excitements to come, a translation of it on her very easy terms (£10) would not be good business. It is certainly a most compact, most thorough, most pointed & condemnatory account of W.E.G's whole character & career.'

There is now a gap in the correspondence until a note of December 28, 1895: 'Up hats for that stout good article of Mrs. Oliphant's: so aboundingly courageous & so very much wanted. But I am in love with Mrs. Oliphant, you must know—as are many, many more.' Elderly readers will recall the indomitable and able novelist and literary worker, and shoulderer of other people's burdens, whose life (1828–97) is so touchingly unfolded in her autobiographic fragment and by Dr. Richard Garnett. Later on we shall have further evidence of the affection Greenwood had for her.

He is now living mostly at St. Leonards. In May 1896 he has a letter from Blackwood evidently suggesting, as Robertson Nicoll, among other publishers had done, an autobiography. The reply is:

> The purpose of your letter gratifies me much, & I am very sorry indeed that I cannot give to it a direct answer at once. Several suggestions of the same kind have been made to me: Macmillans, for one, made me a specific offer of so much for a couple of volumes some time ago. My difficulty does not lie there, however, for none of these offers leave me under any engagement: I took none of them. But nearly the whole mass of my papers & letters (a couple of hundred-weight or thereabout) are stowed away with my furniture in the 'Repository' of the Army & Navy Stores. In a few months I hope to have them at hand again: & then, if you are of the same mind, the matter can be reopened.

In August, Greenwood is asking Blackwood to 'look at this—A woman's conversation with her indwelling devil—a piece dramatical, domestical, psychological, in parts lyrical: & here & there, I hope, of the nature of the poetical'.[1] He says there is

[1] 'A Midnight Conversation' proved to be a seven-page poem (*Blackwood's*.

something in the new Maga 'I am specially attracted to, the contribution of your thoroughly sound A. Michie'.[1] In another note he mentions that he always reads Michie 'with respect and large agreement; he is one of the few who have understanding with knowledge'. As for the 'woman's conversation' he sends a few days later a motto from 'a hitherto unknown Bishop'—an imaginary one—and adds: 'This is not exactly a new line for me, but an old one, dropped thirty years ago, so that this piece will have the interest of surprise to most of my friends, if it have no other.'

The same month he is down on obstruction in the House of Commons, which is so reprehensible when carried on by political opponents, and is sententious on party principles: 'The unfair & blameable obstruction of the [Conservative] Opposition, has been much exaggerated. The whole history of the session shows that the destruction of the party system is mainly due to the general disintegration of party principles. There *are no* party principles: & without them there can be no party solidarity. (I have written a word or two to that effect in the *Contemporary*.)'

In October he evidently feels it to be judicious to send a note

September 1906) of which some readers must have had difficulty in making much. The first three lines are

Here lie we, baby, all alone
And you are mine and I am thine
But we are not our own.

The concluding lines are

For Prebendary Price was all
That you could call respectable;
'Twas said that none could be so nice
As Mr. Prebendary Price;
But Mrs. Price she still said No,
Her P. should not a-may—a-maying——

[1] Alexander Michie (pron. Mickie) is remembered as 'a short, rather rotund gentleman who struck one as having caught the appearance and mannerisms of the Chinese; recognised as the greatest authority on China and the Chinese of that time, second only to Morrison'. His *Englishman in China* was published by Blackwood. Morrison, who was long *The Times* correspondent in Peking, where I had once a profitable fortnight's stay with him, walked across China in a very simple way and wrote *An Australian in China.*

to Blackwood in reference to 'an article of mine [in *Cornhill*] on Disraeli, with some bits of reminiscence, written under a pressure of solicitation wh., for special reasons of a personal character, I could not well resist'. He adds 'Time & the fulfilment of events are doing so much for Disraeli, & are likely to do so much more, that it is almost too soon to take account of him as a political monitor. He will be seen to much more advantage in that role a few years hence, I believe: two, three.'

Though editors 'will suspect offices of friendship', he says he will do anything he can, in the way of reviewing, for those valuable three volumes, *Annals of a Publishing House: William Blackwood and his Sons*. The first two were by Mrs. Oliphant, the third by Mrs. Gerald Porter, granddaughter of the founder of the firm.

CHAPTER XXVI

Mrs. Oliphant, Thackeray, and de Quincey

IN DEFENCE OF DISRAELI — THE RUSSIAN ASCENDANCY — 'NO ACCURATE PICTURE OF THE GREAT THACK' — AUBREY BEARDSLEY

THE reminiscences were not the only book by Greenwood we have to go without. He writes on January 24, 1897, to Blackwood:

> My papers—most of them—are where they were: &, except for some planning & sketching, I'm no forrarder. Partly on that account (between ourselves) I have just declined an invitation of Lord Acton's to write the history of the Beaconsfield Administration (1874–80) for that many-volumed history of modern times wh. he has undertaken for the Cambridge Press. An extraordinary six years that, in many ways: in what came to growth from the past, & in what was sown for the future.
>
> I'll do the article you suggest on the Press—with pleasure; & set about it at once.

He adds a plea for a larger cheque:

> I wonder [whether] what I am about to say will offend you? It is that the difference of the page in Maga & the monthly reviews, & such publications as the *Cornhill*, makes a great difference to the writer in the ordinary pay of both. There is the greater pleasure of writing for Maga no doubt, but her pages swallow up so much more matter than theirs that the poor scribe cannot help noticing the difference with a sigh.

In acknowledging his next cheque he calls it 'quite satisfactory'. The new pay was, I learn, £21 or thirty shillings a page.

In about a week—the year is 1897—he suggests 'an article in defence of Dizzy, who is being very badly treated just now even by some spokesmen of the party, wh. he (who else?) set on its legs in the late years of his life.'

The way in wh. a little article of mine about him[1] was received convinces me of an immense popularity still; & I believe that a work in his defence would be much welcomed. I send you some of the heads of what I propose to write; by no means all, however. If you would like me to write this, & leave the Press article over, please favour with the one word 'Yes' by telegram.

A little book might be written out of my notes for this article—a book at any rate as large (or as small) as the Duke of Argyll's on the same subject, wh. Murray published last summer.

The article appeared. It is indicative of a less general custom of 'wiring'—the rate then was sixpence for the first twelve words and a halfpenny for each additional word[2]—that when Greenwood thinks of sending the conclusion of one of the articles direct to the printer—'I will write very plainly and correct MS'—he asks if a telegram might not be 'profitably spent'.

The Dizzy article, written with 'utmost economy of words', had a passage about 'Lord S's and D's real relations in the seventies, modified', and there were 'some softenings' at the instance of Blackwood. 'I could have been much spicier', Greenwood says, 'but not to the pleasure of Lord S.' Blackwood's satisfaction with the article 'gratified' Greenwood, who says, however, that it was 'too closely packed; even the last points in Dizzy's favour are insufficiently developed'.

In a previous letter Greenwood has mentioned chatting with Morley, his successor at the *Pall Mall*. Now he speaks of a later editor, Sir Douglas Straight. 'I should have thanked you for the offer of Tryon's Life. I shall suggest to the *Pall Mall* editor that he should do his best to get Lord C. Beresford to write. Lord C. regards him [Tryon][3] as a sea-deity, & I think will be glad to

[1] In *Cornhill*.

[2] Delivery was free within a mile of the office nearest the address or town area of a head post office where this exceeded one mile. Porterage was at sixpence per mile or part of a mile beyond this. If the address was more than three miles from the terminal office and a mounted messenger was employed, one shilling a mile was charged (except in Ireland where the rate was eightpence). If no horse messenger the charge was fourpence a mile or part of a mile over three miles.

[3] The Admiral who went down in H.M.S. *Victoria*, when, on a turning

say a strong word for a man for whom he has a boundless admiration; & will put his name to what he says.'

An article on how to meet 'the consequences of the Russian ascendancy, bad for the whole of Europe', is now proposed.

I doubt whether there is a single Govt. in Europe (except France) that would not gladly withstand an autocracy wh. already makes itself felt so portentously, if it could be done. Lord S. has done very well as far as we are allowed to see. But the Czar & his influence with the other Powers has put a dead check on the evacuation of the Turkish troops from Crete (itself a trouble for Lord S. both in his conscience & his management of affairs) & he can do nothing but sanction & join the coercion of Greece (wh. will embroil him at home) or go out of the Cabinet: wh. would be followed, I believe, by a great revenge. I could, I think, write a strongish article about, & roundabout, this, in no more than 9 or 10 pages. And for a change, it could be printed *anonymously*. But I do not urge it upon you.

He is surprised that *An Uncrowned King*, 'a very good book indeed, & especially good for its firm grasp upon life & its masculine use of the English language'—the author of which he had supposed to be 'a man of affairs'—had been written by a young woman.[1]

Concerning authors: 'I shall be only too glad to play go-between any good & promising writer & 45 George Street; & thank you for what you say about that. It has happened to me to come across some originals unknown: the last was the author of *Bethia Hardacre's Daybook*,[2] a charming farrago, wh. had a considerable success last year.'

Taught by his own experience, he is a manageable contributor.

April 16. Here is a remainder of article: revised: & with every

exercise on which, he insisted, she was rammed by H.M.S. *Camperdown.* I remember, on the *Westminster*, going in haste in a hansom to the Admiralty, to the constructor of the *Victoria*, Sir William White. A careless sub-editor had put an ordinary single line heading to the tape-machine announcement, and said nothing about it.

[1] Moira O'Neill, who contributed poetry to *Blackwood's Magazine.*

[2] Mrs. Fuller-Maitland.

word pretty clearly written: so that if holiday-making exigencies oppress, proof of this portion need not be sent.

April 19. If you would like this article shortened, there is a paragraph on pages 4 & 5 that can come out bodily: it begins 'there was a common superstition'.

Next month he writes that it is 'a great satisfaction to me when any bit of work of mine satisfies the giver of the job: in that I am like the good carpenter & cabinet-maker'. He is struck by an article in Maga, in wh. 'intellectual arrogance (at its worst & most detestable when it is academic) is trounced'. On the political situation he has references to Massingham and Chamberlain:

The editor of the *Daily Chronicle* is now hedging off: he never did encourage the Greeks to fight! I wonder what his idea of encouragement is.

The Boer affair is troubling me most. I can't at all believe that this Govt. proposes to force things to ultimatum-point there: it is in too ticklish a position everywhere out of England.

The likelihood that Chamberlain still remains rather too dramatically inclined to pose as first figure in any Govt. that he belongs to should not be neglected, I think. In some respects he is still what he ever was.

When Mrs. Oliphant died he wrote:

You were the nearest to Mrs. Oliphant of all whom I know, & I must say to somebody how profoundly grieved I am at the death of that dear woman & fine, clear, wholesome, vigorous mind. I did not see her often, or know her as well as many others did. But from the moment I set eyes on her & talked with her I was in love with her out & out. What beautiful eyes she had—all genius, & that so kindly. Add how savage it makes one to think of the fussiness of Fortune over a pack of women-writers who were & are Things of the Gutter compared with M.O.W.O. I hope you will write about her yourself in Maga. Do you know where a good photograph may be got?

Later he speaks of her 'good & constant fight for wholesomeness & commonsense in our social relations'. As to the proposed memorial he feels that the proposals should be made when the publication of 'the history of your House recalls attention to its fine & sweet-minded author & her merits'.

Whether then it would be best to set the memorial scheme afoot by means of a letter to the *Times* or by private appeal to old friends, I have some doubt; inclining, however, to the first-mentioned plan because the other seems to withdraw her claim to public gratitude. I shall be glad to co-operate in any way for anything in her honour. Your memorial notice of her in Maga was good & most fitting.

He thinks an article of his on Machiavelli in *Cosmopolis* 'you probably would not have cared about, though I think it puts M. right (as far as possible) for the first time. A clumsy, wild, & rather injurious attack by Frederic Harrison on this screed of mine obliges me (though F. H. is civil enough to me personally) to write a defensive explanation of my views where F. H.'s arraignment appeared.'

Therefore, & most truly to my regret, I am unable to put before you a proposal for the October number of Maga.[1] I could have sent you what I feel sure will turn out to be the right thing to say about the drift of continental affairs & the natural result of stifling Lord Beaconsfield's Eastern policy & providing no other. But my foreign politics you don't agree with; though, to my grief, I see the whole round of them justified by the present situation.

The reference to disagreement on foreign affairs and the way Greenwood's mind was moving about South Africa is the first indication of the break which was ultimately to come with *Blackwood*.

Meantime there are many matters on which the two men are at one. Greenwood revises his editor's 'drafts of the Oliphant letters', and says:

I sat up till one o'clock this morning reading the Book of the House of Blackwood: & most entertaining I found it: & many a time I stopped to think of the extraordinary change in things

[1] Maga, the familiar name for *Blackwood's Magazine*, is simply a shortening of the word 'magazine'.

between then & now. The old days & the old writers of Maga come out most forcibly; & of the Blackwoods, William the First, Robert, & John, are beautifully distinct figures. Alexander—there is art in the way in wh. he is made to move through the chapters like a shade. De Quincey, I suppose, was the last of your great original staff—though not of them at the first. My own first writing in the magazines was in some numbers of *Tait* when de Quincey wrote his Pope essays there. It was in 1851, I think: & the last of de Quincey's writing: & uncommonly good writing it was.

It is a pity Greenwood never put on paper all he could have written about Thackeray. But on November 26, 1897, he sent a letter of some importance to Blackwood:

I have been thinking of your suggestion that I should take Thackeray for a subject for your January Maga; & with every willingness to follow your wish, I'm in a difficulty.

All that has been written about him hitherto is in one vein of repetition. It is not wrong in itself, but wrong in its incompleteness; & though I do not say that completion would make a very different picture, or one that mortal man need be ashamed to own (we don't think much less of Goldsmith for his weaknesses) I hesitate about being the man to draw the true portrait. His daughter is one of my friends. I like her as most people do who know her, & therefore should be sorry to write anything wh. would seem to her unkind & even unjust. The truth is, all the same, that no accurate picture of the Great Thack exists.

Instead I propose a sort of article ['Looker-On' notes are in his mind] wh. seems to me altogether in the taste of the day: wh is for reading in brief spells, & especially of persons & things that impart a personal & table-talk interest. A roundabout: a macedoine of various matters treated in various moods. Enclosed is a list of some of the themes I should include—all being more or less 'topical'; & I should look out for what opportunity might arrive between now & the middle of December for a bit of reminiscence, memoir, or touch of anecdote. Perhaps this proposal will not strike you as seductive; but I am pretty confident of not sending you a disappointing paper. It would be better to print this proposed paper (if you like the idea) anonymously, perhaps: or under a pseudonym.

Here are some of the interesting suggestions for topics referred to:

The softening & otherwise lamentable influence of these insistent, these hot-foot reports of 'great British losses' in war: 'great losses' of a score or two of men. Bad, for one thing, that the men should be taught to think such grave losses grave, afflicting. The rapidity & eloquence of newspaper reporting far from advantageous here: what would such daily repetition be in case of a great & not at first a fortunate war?

The reasons why novels may be expected to continue as a large business product—feeding new appetites, & being turned out as the day's loaves are: & consumed & forgotten as the day's loaves are, without demand for anything in them that need be remembered after consumption.

Apropos of the 'Beth Book'—(Sarah Grand's[1] isn't it?) some remarks on the influence of such writing, & of the 'revelations' of women by women upon marriage. That is to say, how strongly they must persuade young men not to marry—young men having many cogent dissuasions from it already wh. did not exist a century ago. And how much would that consequence improve the position of women or conduce to 'purity'?

On a certain cant in criticism, both of pictures & books. The succession of 'booms', now of one painter, now of another: & of poets. The strange instability of taste where it seems there should be as much constancy as there is in the perception of the differing beauty of flowers & trees. And on artificial valuations—cash valuations, *eye* valuations—in art.

On a passage in Du Maurier's *Martian*, wh. betrays a serious belief that his long series of pictures of very tall & handsome women & men have had an actual physical effect on the new generation. (This to be treated lightly & chaffingly.) Not quite to be accepted; but there *is* the new crop of fine tall handsome boys & girls; &, compare the familiar theory that the physical beauty of the Greeks drew something from the perfection of Greek statuary so abundantly seen in public places. And then remember how many Ellen Terry chins & noses discovered themselves when that actress was so much the rage; & again, the Burne Jones type of faded, yearning face; &

[1] Author of a best seller, *The Heavenly Twins.*

now, lately, the appearance of a sort of young woman never seen before, every one of whom might have been models for Aubrey Beardsley, or have come out of the beautiful new 'posters' designed in Mr. Beardsley's manner.

Perhaps the appearance of Dizzy in a novel—where he placed so many other men.

Blackwood liked 'the sheaf', and the title of 'Looker-On' was adopted with subheadings for the subjects dealt with. Greenwood actually preferred 'Divagation' or 'Divagatory' instead of 'Looker-On', but 'Looker-On' it was, and surely Blackwood was judicious.

With liberty to ramble, & with accident & event constantly provocative [Greenwood said] such papers ought never to fail of being interesting; and it is certainly the sort of thing I *like* to write. You shall have the best I can supply. Your decision as to title quite contents me. You are right about it altogether. But I think the subheads will help.

In December an old editor commends the skill of the 'conductor of *Blackwood*'.

CHAPTER XXVII

John Morley, Two Poets, and Lord Wolseley

BURTON AND SPEKE — 'ZOLAESQUERIES' — 'MENDACIOUS INGENUITIES' — W. E. HENLEY — 'THREE GRAINS OF SPIRITUALITY FOR KIPLING'

ANOTHER indication of Greenwood's friendly relations with his supplanter at the *Pall Mall* is to be found in a long letter at the beginning of 1898:

> Morley told me that great preparations were being made in Ireland to celebrate 1798—& more in America. Boat-loads of American Irish coming over from the United States. Not a word of this had got into the press—much to Morley's surprise. Morley is not at all likely to be misinformed. Your contributor who is writing about a royal residence for Ireland might be told of what Morley told me (of course without mentioning names). Please do not use M's phrase of 'boatloads' of American Irish coming over. He (M.) might recognise it as his own: an equivalent word would be better.

Greenwood, in his next communication, is 'rather in a quandary about Disraeli'.

> Just before I wrote for Maga an article about Dizzy, Macmillan's asked me to write a new Life & Characteristics of that political hero: not as a volume in a series, but as a distinct book. Having some reasons against doing it, I excused myself. (And, unluckily, I had not long before declined a proposal from Macmillan's to write a memoir of Bismarck for a series they were commencing.) Not long afterwards, Lord Acton, as I think I mentioned to you, asked me to write, for the great Modern History he is preparing, the history of the Beaconsfield Cabinet of 1874–80. That also I declined. And now shan't I be put in an awkward position if so soon afterwards I take up the work I then put off? I am much afraid.

Here are some notes of things he has in mind for 'Looker-On'.

> The Jews: the apparently mysterious revival of hatred of them in

countries entirely dissimilar, at the same time, & almost universally. The cause of it? or causes? With an Explanation wh., I think, covers all cases.

Foreign Correspondents: a question as to whether we do not add to our unpopularity abroad by discussing in a critical way & from entirely British standpoint, the domestic affairs of foreign nations: affairs with wh. we have really nothing to do.

Ireland 1798: 1898.

The Theatre at present, & theatrical criticism.

Some portended extravagances of fashion in women's dress.

The probability that novels will become ordinary commodities, & be sold at the drapers, & with pounds of tea.

Attention called to a book of Meredith's, wh. I do not find that one reader of his books in ten has ever seen or made any account of: a wonderful book of imagination: *The Shaving of Shagpat*.

On some great & little tragedies in the newspapers. One of them about a little girl & her pinafore: another, the Soudanese Emir who, after suffering, with his men, days of thirst in a besieged African fort, sallied out to some wells hard by, was shot, & fell dead in the water he had longed for & had so desperately sought.

If Greenwood paid too little attention to the news side of his newspapers, he certainly had an eye for 'human interest stories'. The above list illustrates the range of topics on which he could write with facility and with something to say. In a letter in which he says ' "Looker-On" shall not go beyond 16 pages—even for an article of varied interest & colour 16 of your pages are enough'—he continues:

India, my dear Blackwood, offers a most grave prospect.

Finance is a matter I never allow myself to have an opinion about.

Your loyalty to the Govt I shall always keep in mind, & of course shall write nothing that would offend that loyalty.

Except that the *permanent* chiefs of the great political departments are generally its lords, & arrogant & narrow, though clever within the limits of their narrowness, I know nothing about them.

Many pages back in this book an appreciative reference was made by a printer to Greenwood's ways with a proof. One now finds this paragraph in a letter to Blackwood: 'Hating to make correction in proof, I had yet had to make more than usual, for wh. I am sorry: the plain truth is, however, that being unusually worried & pushed at the time, the MS. went off without final revision.' The care he took is illustrated by this extract: 'There will be a few pages more to make a better ending to the paper. But I send this off at once partly because you may think it better to *begin* the article with this portion; as it starts with a bit of imaginative writing more engaging to attention, perhaps, than the opening of the portion you have got.' On one occasion when he is late with the end of his notes, he says, 'it shall not only be written plainly and revised', but punctuated—his punctuation, as will have been seen, was sometimes irregular. He states that he always posts his copy himself. Once he apologizes, 'My MS went beyond calculation'. He is, as has been seen, always amenable. Of one batch of copy he says, 'If you think it too long, please instruct your people to cut it where they think the excision will matter least.'

A letter written in March is about Stephen Phillips and Oscar Wilde:

> I had it in mind to propose a screed founded on two poems: one contained in Mr. Phillips's volume (real poet, Phillips) the other *A Ballad of Reading Gaol.* They represent remarkably the greatest & gravest fault in modern English literature: profoundly immoral, debasing while affecting to elevate, & as corrupt ethically as possibility allows. It is everywhere almost in modern verse, & it is time to pray that it may be kept out of the pulpit.
>
> What do you say to the inclusion of Zola's new novel?
>
> There is always the chance of some taking new subject turning up, &, properly dealt with, up-to-datishness is a prudent thing.
>
> Do you think I could make believe that I had received a letter from a French rabbi saying that *he* can tell me what Moses bade the other Rabbi write, & then pour out a few hundred sonorous words of advice to the Continental Jews?

He had mentioned 'a letter from my Lord S. in wh. he sees everything that is natural, & yet most likely to be extremely mischievous, in the violent comment of our press in the Zola case'. A few days later Greenwood writes: 'I suppose there is something, a little, in the rumour that Lord S. was more shaken in that carriage accident at Hatfield than was acknowledged.'

If the half of Lord Salisbury's malady is not mortification, so much the less may we think of Lord Salisbury. Whether he can invent any redeeming policy now, we shall see. It does not seem probable; & if not, he 's a done man, after associating his name with some of the worst humiliations we have ever suffered. It is in *his* time that England's strength has reached its greatest, her wealth its fullest; while as for pluck & patriotism, there never was more in this island; & it is in *his time*, with all this, that England has fallen from her high place. It is absurd to talk of his extraordinary ability, wonderful authority, vast knowledge & experience: if we look to 'the proof of the pudding', all these fine qualities are as if they were not. Five or six—eight or nine years ago, perhaps, I wrote about him what some thought a too severe article in *Chambers's Cyclopaedia*. It can't be thought too severe now. [This was a curious slip of memory. The article in *Chambers's* was by F. H. Groome.]

There follows a paragraph with three stars in front of it: 'I had a letter this morning with a strong hint wh I should not notice if it came from a less knowing source: it is to the effect that *military* preparation has been quietly ordered & is going on: military, not naval. My informant can hardly be mistaken, I may add *can't*, in fact.'

This scrap about two explorers is interesting: 'As to Burton, I have always thought him a man of courage—a great brute though, in many ways. And the Speke affair, all through,—bad: unless my view of it was prejudiced by hearing of it from members of the Speke family long ago.' There is a reference to Kitchener in the Soudan:

He is a good man—looks it, talks it. And last year he very nearly got displaced from the chief command in the Soudan in favour of one of Wolseley's comrades at home!—a misfortune if he had been, for another good soldier would have gone unrevealed.

Wolseley was staying at Stratton Street while I was there last week, (the Baroness Burdett-Coutts' house) & over the evening cigar he let out to me a great deal about the actual state of army affairs. Some things that he said can be dealt with in Maga without impropriety.

It is certainly true that the feeling in favour of Spain increases: & the news of the destruction of the Manila fleet is sure to increase that feeling further: the little 'un so awfully over matched.

'I'm not much in love with George Moore's Zolaesqueries', Greenwood writes one Sunday regarding *Evelyn Innes*. As for Whibley—of whom E. V. Lucas said 'his *bête-noires* were so numerous that we might have been in Hayti: hardly a white to be seen'—'he will make a capital writer when, under your chastening eye (wh. has had its effect already, I fancy) the critic is still less concerned in turning out startling locutions'. Of a contribution by Sir Herbert Maxwell he says: 'Very interesting, with plenty of light & colour: you need not be told that here you have one of the best writers available for periodical literature: very versatile, always sound, & with a quick & lively touch.' Then comes 'a little misfortune':

An old enemy of mine, who looks in every three or four years at the change of the seasons, Gout, has just taken possession of my left foot. Experience makes me uncertain whether the plague will be dislodged in time enough to allow trotting about in the picture-galleries for Looker-On.

You know some-one, perhaps, in whom you have confidence. If not, I would suggest application to Claude Phillips, lately appointed curator of the Wallace collection. Or, as a good critic of the old school, Frederic Stephens, who writes in the *Athenaeum*. I have met Phillips, & know Stephens, &, if you liked, could address myself to either.

Within the week he is referring to

Dr. Creighton's amazing injunction to Mr. Kensit that Kensit could go & worship in another parish if he did not like the service in his own. Perhaps you saw that the *Times* had some strong remarks & in Convocation on the 12th the bishops fully admitted the prevalence of illegal practices: 'services of the kind', said the Bishop of Winchester, 'that brought about the Reformation three hundred years ago'. I am taking this subject into 'Looker-On', writing in a strong Protestant spirit, but of course carefully.

Later he quotes *The Times*, 'The air is thick with sacerdotalism'.

In a letter to Michie, Greenwood speaks of Lord Salisbury's

mendacious ingenuities which disfigure the whole of his career; too often have they been successful, but I think he may now spare himself the invention of them. They will not answer any more. I suppose that his speech to the bankers was another stroke of Italian ingenuity: an expedient to impress the French Govt—suggesting to it, without the risk of despatch-writing & more alarmingly, that the British prime minister had really got his back to the wall, at last.

In a post or two, however, he is writing about 'this humiliating flood of forced & false fine writing about Mr. Gladstone, extravagance palpably artificial: a commodity'.

Gossiping with Blackwood on the topics with which he thinks of dealing in 'Looker-On', he says, 'I shall be glad to get in a good word for Henley. (He has just come very well through a ticklish operation, & has now a good chance of being set up again—as no doubt you know.)' On his own gout he says 'I am able to get about after an experience corroborative of the saying that the worst provocative of gout is mental worry. From this last may you always be preserved: without it gout is of no consequence, nor anything else.' For some time he had been worried about his daughter Kate's health. 'Uncalculated developments', he writes in July, 'obliged my daughter to undergo an operation wh. had been thought too grave & hazardous to be attempted. For some days she has been in a very critical state, & is not yet out of the wood;—all of wh. has thrown me off work, wh. I never do very quickly.' Later, 'a hazardous surgical feat has been accomplished well, & the after-dangers are fast diminishing'.

Noting that 'regular partisan Conservatives may not have liked all that they read in the new Maga', he speaks on the basis of experience: 'There are far greater numbers who read with satisfaction, depend on it. And all experience shows clearly, I think, that undeviating support of a Govt. is fatal to the authority of whatever "organ of opinion" makes the mistake. And the Govt. itself ceases to be grateful for such support: takes it as a matter of ordinary course.'

He tells Blackwood of his 'imaginary "Midnight Conversation" between Bismarck & the Emperor William II, in wh. conversation Bismarck 'gave in his resignation & stated his reasons', and of an experience which every journalist could parallel.

> Next day, the news of Bismarck's resignation 'startled all Europe like a bomb-shell', as the phrase is. My article was written for the *Contemporary*; & as it did not appear, of course, till the end of the month, it was supposed to have been written after the event instead of before; & as Bismarck's reasons in my imaginary conversation were the *real* reasons (though not all) all the more did I feel robbed of my due as a prophet. How did I know then that they were the real reasons? Because Herbert Bismarck told me so a few weeks afterwards—adding that there were others, though these others were not the original ones.

He mentions that a story in 'Looker-On' about Crown Prince Frederick and the unification of Germany was 'told to me by Lord Lytton'. Ever mindful to keep his editor assured that he is giving him his best matter, he says:

> From its starting, I have been under an engagement (or understanding) to write for *Cosmopolis* occasionally. After we had arranged our 'Looker-On', *Cosmopolis* asked for an article on Bismarck. I offered them a better subject—(better, I mean, than a *set* article about B.), but nothing would do but a Bismarck article: probably as suiting the cosmopolitan & trilingual character of the review. So they have got it, but I do not think it will make you regret that you had not a set article yourself. There has been so much written about the Chancellor's career that I am sure Bismarck is better touched off in a few pages as in Maga.

He sends 'a page and a half (in print)' on 'The Marriage Market', a kind of subject which, as we have seen, always interested him.

In the autumn he is commending a book by G. W. Steevens on the Soudan war, 'Admirable! and oughtn't it to sell!' *The*

Times critic had written 'doltishly' about it. As for 'Looker-On', he has kept Crete out because 'I doubted whether you would quite agree with my very strong feeling that it would be better if we meddled between the Xtian & the Mahommedan ruffians in that island very much less.' He adds, 'I'm never in fear of want of matter'.

On Kipling he says that if he had 'three grains of spirituality in his temperament he would be the greatest genius of modern days'. Returning to Rosebery he writes:

I have always been a partisan of his, as against the House of Commons Radicals his enemies: knowing the ground & detail of the long intrigue against him. His continuation-of-foreign-policy principle alone ought to keep him in favour with all good Conservatives: for he has always maintained it—even in the Gladstonian days he did so firmly. What I say about the 'proscription' by the House of Commons Liberal leaders is strictly accurate: it would make a charming story if told in detail.

In thanking Blackwood for 'two gratifications: your cheque & your satisfaction with the commodity', he asks whether a good book could not be written on the West Indies by Steevens, and says:

I shall be proud to appear in the Thousandth Number of your great old magazine, & hope to suggest & accomplish an article not unworthy of it.

Before the end of the week I will go down to the Garrick & clap down your nephew's name. It will be better if Mr. Stone[1] seconds him—especially as your friend is much about the club: & I will get Barrie, for one, to put his name hard by. Barrie was of my introduction, as perhaps you have read in that lovely little book of his, *Margaret Ogilvy*. Your servant is the Editor who figures therein—I am glad to know of your nephew George's presence in London, & particularly that you find so much reason to be pleased with him as your 'prentice. Great must be that satisfaction to you. I will drop him a line anon, & we will meet & have a talk.

[1] Mr. William Stone, to whom I am indebted for memories of Greenwood, written at 93. See page 231.

The Duchess of Cleveland must be a very old lady now, I suppose:—very clever, & original.

'I am always glad', writes Greenwood in December, 'when I am thought to have earned my fee, & therefore read your first paragraph with a good deal of pleasure.' He adds: 'I *did* get a letter from Miss L. and—I didn't answer it. It is a horrid confession; but I have convinced myself that she is as troublesome as she is clever, & that it is the safer way to converse with her at a distance. All the same I am very sorry.' She was the author of a number of papers in Maga, and also wrote some books, which I do not think Blackwood's published.

CHAPTER XXVIII

New Light, through Cecil Rhodes and others, on the Boer War

'THE STEADY GLARE' OF GLADSTONE'S EYES — CONRAD AND MRS. OLIPHANT — LORD SALISBURY'S RELATIONS WITH JOSEPH CHAMBERLAIN — 'THE BLUNDER AND DISGRACE OF THE L.C.C.' — 'THE GRANNY WHICH IMPOSES SILENCE' — KRUGER AND MILNER

ON New Year's Day, 1899, Greenwood mentions that 'rheumatism came down on me, & made such a savage attack on my knee that I've not been well able to go across the room since; but, as little Tom Macaulay said, "The agony is abated"'. In the 'Looker-On' which he contributed to the imposing thousandth number of *Blackwood* [Feb. 1899]—460 large pages, making a volume more than an inch thick; it went into an eighth edition[1] —he said of Maga that it exhibited 'a steadier continuity of character than anything of the kind that can be named, a personality more individual, more constant and pronounced than is seen in any other periodical publication'. In his own contribution he is once more on the track of the bishops, who are 'chiefly to blame for the present troubles of the Church, the treacheries that infest it'; and is concerned with 'a second explosion in the ruins of the Liberal party'.

He has his accustomed slings and arrows for Gladstone—'everything in him, is 'subject to the ferments of a drop of essential unveracity'—but he sends a fine story told him by Boehm, the sculptor, about Gladstone's eyes.

[1] I looked with interest at the advertisements. They include the Brownings' Love Letters, Wheatley's ten-volume Pepys, G. O. Trevelyan's *American Revolution*, 'George Allen's New Books', mostly Ruskin, *Good Words* and the *St. James's Gazette*, which, it is stated, is 'in its literary department, without rival among the evening journals of the kingdom'. It 'gives with point, brevity and accuracy all the most important news' and financial news 'more fully than any evening paper'.

Boehm, who had made four or five busts of the Liberal leader, was at the dinner table with Gladstone, opposite whom was that redoubtable and fervent Grecian, Professor Blackie [with whom I remember once having an hour or two's talk]. At the wine and walnuts period Mr. Gladstone sang out, in illustration of the way in which, as he believed, Homer was chanted, not recited. This Professor Blackie could not endure to listen to. 'Mr. Gladstone', he cried, 'I don't believe a wurrd of it.' I looked towards Mr. Gladstone and marked how the outer lids of his eyes widened to the fullness of their steady glare. Something he said, too, nettled the choleric Blackie, who knuckling the table as he rose to speak, had only got as far in what he had to say as, 'Mr. Gladstone, if there is one thing——' when his tongue stumbled and he sank back into his chair in confusion. Again I looked to Mr. Gladstone and understood. The inner lids (here Boehm held two fingers of one hand upright and parted them) were opened. They had been opened on Blackie, and he had looked into the Pit. Go to the Zoo for it. Make your way to the place where the eagles, vultures, falcons and such like creatures blink on their perches. Select a bird. Stare at him with insult, and you will see the outer eyelids expand as Mr. Gladstone's did. The filmy vertical lids, through which he looks at the sun and opens to paralyse his prey, will part; and then you will see what Blackie saw and understand his feeling.

Greenwood adds that he told this story to a painter 'who stopped dead in the street to say in an awed voice hardly his own, "It 's true! I've seen it!" '

On February 4 he writes 'Lord Rosebery has asked me to his dinner on Monday: but as H.R.H. is to honour the board, political talk is very unlikely. Lord R. is sure to avoid that.'

The same month he returns thanks for 'your permission to write "beyont the twal" ' pages, and is gratified that what he has said about the Church is approved. 'All we *demand* (though not all we hope for) is faithful dealing with traitorous contumacy. What less should be expected?'

Nicoll[1] was no doubt right in thinking that the aim of the bishops

[1] The Rev. afterwards Sir William Robertson Nicoll, editor of the *British Weekly* and the *Bookman*, who practised agreeably what I once heard him

was procrastination, & their hope that the Protestant discontent would soon die down. But, as we all see, Lord Halifax & the Church Union have effectually disposed of that hope & expectation. Mutiny is the only true word for the demonstrationing & memorialising. All that the extreme Catholic party has been accused of it avows boastingly; all that it has been suspected of working for (consciously or in blind infatuation) is yet more to be suspected. And now we see whether the bishops were right or not in agreeing that the insurgents were only a few. It is a very grave state of things. But one thing we shall agree about, you & I;—that open mutiny definitely declared against law, & in violent opposition to sworn engagements (for every parson accepted the headship of the Crown at ordination) is no more to be permitted in the Church than in the army.

Writing on Maga, he says, 'The article you particularly mention is reserved for this evening's accompaniment to the evening's tobacco'.

Conrad's story will no doubt be a success—he seems to have caught the general favour. Yet, for my own particular taste he is so extremely wordy, so fixed to let nothing go till he has said it ten times over in as many different ways that I don't get on with him as well as I ought.

The Trevelyan review will be a bit of a surprise for others than the weak & vacillating politician but admirable writer, George T.[1]

Morley was never a politician—hadn't in him the makings of a statesman; & even as a writer is great more by style & industry than by judgement. His judgement is *exceptionally* good in no field: though he has all the graces & a great garner of reading.

This moment I got a letter from Lady Charles Beresford, who is, I fancy, rather anxious about her Charlie's excursion into China politics, & wants to talk with me about it. Afraid I shan't be able to say that I think he has been discreet.

A spring letter about a coming 'Looker-On' says, 'Mr Winterley proposes to write something about dining and about

preach to a man about to start a weekly, that an editor should always write some chatty feature as well as his leading article.

[1] Sir G. O. Trevelyan, the biographer of Macaulay, sometime Secretary for Ireland, and author, as a young man, of *Interludes in Verse and Prose*.

these continued proposals for a National Opera', Mr. Winterley being a character who had figured in one of Greenwood's sketches. As for his health, 'I've been sadly with small ills since I wrote last,—and now I have been, for a week, down with a bad throat-and-snivel cold—distressing & disgusting: entirely without the dignity that influenza has attained to, & am still unable to leave the house, except for such important affairs as dropping *Blackwood* copy into an adjacent pillar box'. He thinks April 'Looker-On' 'should have had some lighter matter'. 'There shall be a long screed from Mr. Winterley next time—about pictures & other things. And if you have no political article next month perhaps you will let me run to 16 pages, of wh. Mr. Winterley shall have half.' The letter goes on to criticize the Government. Mr. Ritchie 'should never have been allowed another chance of showing his want of judgement after his London County Council scheme': 'What ground the government have lost they will not recover with the Workmen's Dwellings Bill. The truth is, I suppose, that Lord S. being much occupied, & no longer greedy for work, & indisposed to step in between his Liberal Unionists on the one part & his Conservatives on the other, there is not the one-man grip over the administration wh. is as necessary for the right conduct of public affairs as of an Edinburgh magazine.' But he does not forget that 'I am to keep my notions of the Workmen's Dwellings Bill out of the magazine'.

He adds 'Lord Acton pursues me again to write the story of the Disraeli administration—(1874–80)—for his great history-book, but I hesitate'. He was interested in meeting the Irish leader, John Dillon, 'at a small dinner-party of men; not an immensely important personage but repaying observation'. For the next number he is 'in doubt as to whether, with my view of it', he should include some remarks on the Irish Local Government Bill. Eventually he 'wrote Pinero paragraphs & let Ireland go'.

Blackwood has sent him Mrs. Oliphant's autobiography and receives this response:

I go back again & again to the book after the slow & deep first reading. For all its careless & disorderly composition (wh, however, may really be part of its charm) it is one of the most fascinating & endearing bits of biography ever printed in English, to my mind; & you will learn from the sale of it, I believe, that that is a common impression. Spite of her failures as a novelist (2 in 5, I suppose) she had a very sympathetic public—drew out from countless readers a *friendly* feeling that was almost entirely denied to George Eliot; for example—a something that makes me say at this moment that I would rather have been Margaret Oliphant than Mary Ann Evans with ten times Mary Ann Evans's genius.

Greenwood sketches a paper that he thinks 'very much called for', 'a screed on the Tyranny of Sentiment: wh., in social & political affairs alike, is playing the deuce with us. This is the Granny wh. imposes silence on all the commonsense there is amongst us when old-age pension schemes & the like deceits carry away masses of light-headed people who think it a virtue to be blind to facts, probabilities, possibilities & impossibilities when they conflict with humane aspiration.'

He appends the question, 'Did you know that the English edition of Busch's *Bismarck* was a speculation of *The Times* people, though published by Macmillan?' The answer is, I understand, Yes; the book was published on commission.

Writing at the end of April, Greenwood reports that the Transvaal concerns the Government a great deal, and sends a notable admission by Cecil Rhodes during a talk with him.

I put to him this question: whether the demands now made upon the Boers would not, if conceded, sweep them *all* clean out of *all* share of Government in the Transvaal in a very few years; & whether the knowledge that that would be the certain & quick result did not account for their desperate resistance. He answered, with instant emphasis, that beyond a doubt the Boers would be 'absolutely annihilated—cleaned out altogether'—wh., he went on to say, was just what the country needed.

I daresay he is right, but we can't be surprised if knowledge that their complete suppression is meant *does* make them desperate. Like the rest of us, Boers are humans, & of the fighting sort.

Not that I think Kruger will fight if he can possibly help it. He is wise enough to give in as soon as the last moment for choice has come: the only question is whether he can persuade the ordinary 'old Boer' to do so, he being more stubborn than wise.

Greenwood is sorry that the price of Mrs. Oliphant's autobiography is high and for the reason for it.

Remembering that according to the 'Wills & Bequests' paragraphs in the papers (& great impertinences those paragraphs are) that Mrs Oliphant had left some thousands of pounds, I inferred that she had cleared off her debts & difficulties some time before she died. Of course I'll do all I can: have already sent every friend I have talked or written to to get this affecting book. Enclosed is part of a letter from Mrs. Fuller-Maitland (*Day-book of Bethia Hardacre*) wh speaks for many minds of sense & sensibility. This poor lady, Mrs. F. M., is a close invalid, wh. is why she often writes in pencil.

The letter to Greenwood from Mrs. Fuller-Maitland, from 131 Sloane Street, is as follows:

Did you ever read anything sadder than this book of Mrs Oliphant's? I feel really as if it has brought grief into the house to have read it. You no doubt knew her. I did not. To those who knew her it must be even more painful than it is to me. It is heart breaking. Do you think it should have been published? I don't know that I do, at least I don't now know that I do while still under the cloud of reading it. Of what curious stuff human nature is to hold with its whole strength to what may be gone for ever at any moment. The book has made me so sad that I feel as if some personal calamity had come to me! Which is very, very foolish, & I am wishing I could keep it from various people among my friends, whose children alive & dead are everything to them.

He has been at 'a little symposium' in which Chamberlain and Sir William Harcourt participated:

The long talk (to midnight) all of affairs. Chamberlain said that the latest Colonial office news of & from Kruger was *not* good, but the other way. In answer to something like an ultimatum (though not *precisely* that formidable thing I gathered) he had received a strong, disagreeable reply.

It will be found, I think, that Chamberlain has made the mistake of founding his ultimatum, in great part, on an assertion that the dynamite concession & its results violate the Convention: in wh he has the authority of the Crown Law-Officers. But we shall see that assertion strongly contested. I doubt whether C. himself is convinced of its soundness.

He is 'a little behind the scenes'.

Believe me I shall not only be most in the right of it, but most in harmony with the views of the more august members of the Cabinet, in taking a moderate line wh. shall at the same time give no encouragment to Mr Kruger. It is eminently a matter for fairness, firmness, prudence. A war that would make rebels of the Africander subjects of the Queen (not Transvaalers only) all over South Africa —that must be avoided; & can be, with solid gains to the Outlanders.

The foregoing letter was written on June 16. Later in the week he writes: 'The disturbing thing is that Chamberlain talks as if England had been placed under an unendurable snub by Kruger. The *fact* is that the Govt has been placed by him & his Milner in a very awkward situation—escape from wh. (in decent condition) depends on Mr Kruger.' Transvaal affairs worry Greenwood, for he is not of his editor's views, and Blackwood is an old man:

I have tried to be very discreet when I might have been sensational by letting out a little of the true inwardness of the business. All that is kept out—not to cross ministers (or the minister) in any but the gentlest way, & putting the thing more upon Milner where management went wrong. If you have any doubt now as to whether this is the right, correct. I have perfect confidence that the doubt will be removed by the end of the month.

War on the franchise point would be absolutely illegal—no *casus belli* supportable. (See a communication from Westlake[1] in this evening's *Pall Mall.*) Besides wh. it would be monstrously impolitic.

I *know* that, weeks before the Milner report came out, Jameson, Beit, & other men of that fraternity, knew of the franchise campaign, & were working together to push it on as 'the way of doing

[1] John Westlake, international jurist, 1828–1913.

the trick': these same people who were in the raid were then organising support for the 'franchise campaign'.

The subject is continued in a letter a fortnight later, and, as many people are even to-day in ignorance of the facts, and the war with the Boers is not forgotten in South Africa, it is worth giving a good deal of Greenwood, though there is not a letter that I do not cut considerably. The informed will see now and then where they can skip.

Chamberlain's course is marked out to commit his colleagues, of whose 'weakness' he complains, from step to step. The publication of Milner's report (certainly known to the Rhodes, Jamesons, Beits, here before it was received in Downing-street) was the first of those steps; his speech was another. What the next will be if any, is in his own breast. Meanwhile he says that he would have preferred a less pushing way of going to work if the weakness of his colleagues aforesaid did not oblige him to push *them*. Whether they like it or not doesn't matter, of course: they cannot publicly confess to being pushed, though they are.

My apprehension is that the Johannesburghers, or some moving spirits there, will be so set up by Chamberlain's speech (how 'clever' he was!) & by the recent cry of no compromise here, that they may reject what wisdom would call a fair & sufficient franchise concession.

Against that apprehension, however, there is one rather telling thing. The mine-owners are in great fear that, were war to break out, their mines would be destroyed. Their own belief is that that would be done before British troops could be brought up to protect the mines: the Boer Govt having instant command of the rails.

I remember—when Milner, Governor and High Commissioner, paid a visit to London—walking up and down the room in his chambers, and, as a close student of South Africa before he went out to South Africa, and as one ex-*Pall Mall* man to another, expostulating with him on the course things were taking. I said that if there were not a better understanding of the admittedly difficult Oom Paul and his Boers and a wiser approach to them, war was inevitable, with far-reaching consequences in the next half-century. But Milner, who with all his great abilities and desire to serve Great Britain, had something of the unyielding temperament of a German professor,[1] was no more able to get on with a man like Kruger than he had been able to do, when he was at the *Pall Mall*, with W. T. Stead. In another fortnight Greenwood is writing:

Things look black. The subjugation of the Dutch is preached as a patriotic duty by the provokers of the strife. It would be too monstrous to open such a war for the sake of the difference between Milner's proposals & these that the Transvaal Govt is passing into law. The truth is that the planner & worker of all this trouble is the curse of the Cabinet. Everything that his Milner was instructed to ask for (of course to bring on a crisis) at Bloemfontein, would not compensate for a tenth part of the mischief already done & impossible to undo.

You may not want all this said, & I do not propose to go beyond the meaning & spirit of last month's screed; though you see how deplorably Dutch & English are thrown into conflict all over South Africa by a singularly bad speculation in 'bluff' badly carried out.

Continuing on August 8 on the subject of South Africa he says: 'What I have said to you is true. Lord S. & Mr. Balfour's speeches are no contradiction of the fact that the Govt as a whole (with Lord S. himself) holds the prospect of war in something like horror, & is most unhappy at the present situation.' In the same letter he says, getting away from the threat of war, that 'for a domestic subject, a good one, I think' for the next 'Looker-On', would be,

after a slight review of the 'fashionable' season, the way in wh. nowadays the press is occupied with detailed reports of gay doings, fine spectacles, & *more particularly*, with rich & costly attire. Half the penny papers now are given to this sort of matter, wh. doesn't affect men, (unless to offend or annoy them) but must have no good effect on women—even the best of whom love to look smart—in making them longing & discontented. The cost of dress amongst fashionable women is something frightful. Similar competition,

[1] Born in Hesse-Darmstadt, son of Dr. Charles Milner and his wife, daughter of Major-General Ready. Was brought to England at four, but from twelve to fifteen was at school at Tübingen. His grandmother was Sophie von Rappard.

running down to the lower middle classes, would be bad indeed; & all this flare of publication has that tendency.

For a literary subject, I should propose that newest craze, the 'Celtic revival', wh. needs showing up a bit.

In one letter he speaks of seeing Michie 'on a tricicle' (*sic*).

CHAPTER XXIX

The Rift

'THEY LOST SIGHT OF THE QUEEN' — 'PRESS CLAMOUR FOR A FIGHT' — WHO ORIGINATED THE *Pall Mall*? — SUSPENSION OF 'LOOKER-ON' — LORD WOLSELEY'S TEARS AND MEMOIRS

GREENWOOD, who has been spending a day or two with George Meredith, had written several times scoffingly about the Dreyfus trial, reprehending in turn the military, the friends of Dreyfus, and the Paris Press. Now, he says that 'were this an English case in the English courts, there is hardly a newspaper publisher in London who would not be in gaol':

> I say *in gaol*, & not merely under heavy fine. For defamatory assertion & insinuation, the most constant, the most heaped, there has been nothing like it, ever; & besides that, the evidence is reported every day with the rankest dishonesty *as* reporting. Believe me, this is not only not well seen now, but is producing a strong reactionary feeling of disgust, wh. the erring newspapers say nothing about, of course. Meanwhile, & that is a matter of no small concern, this monstrously abusive criticism in the English press produces in France a degree & a kind of exasperation wh. in certain events might prove extremely troublesome.

'I've no interest & no concern with that filthy mass of lies & malignancy', he adds to his editor, 'except as it concerns our own country.' He hopes, therefore, that 'you will allow what I have written to stand'.

Greenwood, who has been visiting an excellent man, whom some of us remember, D. C. Lathbury, the future editor of the *Pilot*, returns on August 31 to the Transvaal:

> I am quite sure Lord Salisbury hasn't the least intention of going to war for any reason now known to the Govt; quite sure that there will be no such war unless some fool or deeply interested person throws a spark into the gunpowder so liberally spread abroad on all sides.

If Mr. Chamberlain published today despatches lately received, instead of keeping them dark, there would be a further change in the public mind tomorrow.

However, the main thing is that when Mr Chamberlain gives out that the Govt is ready to declare war on any point that now discontents him, he goes beyond his last; & his declaration to that effect has startled crowds of people who never believed that anything more than a game of bluff was meant, in wh. their silence was to assist. Here, the effect of that speech has been very strong: & you will find it reflected not only in this morning's *Daily News*, hitherto a strong supporter of Chamberlain in this matter,[1] but in *The Times*: wh. has been all for the war policy & will not give it up readily.

'All this, of course, is merely from F. G. to W. B., & not at all to suggest a line of writing for Maga. I've not the least wish to push my opinions, & only care that Maga shall stand safe out of error: her present situation in this matter.'

In September he is asking that a *Blackwood* shall be sent to Lord Rosebery. 'I find that he is deeply impressed with the mischief going on between France & England, & the consequent danger touched upon in the first section of my screed this month. And in all such affairs Lord R. is one of us—no Radical funker or anything of the kind.'

He is glad that in the 'Looker-On' 'we have made a success of the Transvaal', and has a reference to the Queen:

It *did* look as if we were at variance with the Govt. policy; all the ministerial papers going strongly & even violently the other way. But the mistake was theirs. They forgot that Colonial Secretaries cannot make war at will. Like Mr. C. himself, they lost sight of the Queen & her *certain* views & feelings in the matter (*she read that Highbury speech*) as well as the various facts & arguments wh. must determine Lord S., as Foreign Minister, to avoid a South African war by every possible means. I write, of course, before publication of that last despatch to Transvaal. No doubt it is stiff—probably minatory; for Chamberlain's face must be saved for one thing. But the Govt. policy, & the grounds of it, are not what

[1] Edited at this time by E. T. Cook, formerly editor of the *Pall Mall* and the *Westminster Gazette*.

Times, Telegraph, Post, Standard, Globe, Daily Mail so furiously imagined (& now drop) & of course not Mr Chamberlain's; but entirely accordant with what you permitted your Looker-On to say in that July number.

For the next Maga—'if you care for a "Looker-On" next month, but perhaps you don't, and of course I don't want to press you, having been an editor myself'—Greenwood has 'two or three non-political subjects'. But, in his next letter, he returns to the Transvaal:

You will see that the Cabinet despatch is in exact accordance with what I have written to you. A despatch making for peace in every line, wh is what the Council was called for. This is the *Government* policy, not Mr Chamberlain's, wh. it corrects & redeems from mischief.

Every condition named in the despatch has already been proposed from Pretoria, except what relates to the use of English in the Raad. The 'suzerainty' *is* dropped, according to this version of the despatch wh is not contradicted this morning. The 'sovereign international state' claim is a totally different thing, though the two are being confounded—sometimes innocently sometimes wilfully. The one (sovereign international state) would give up our right of veto on treaties with foreign powers, wh of course was never to be thought of. The 'suzerainty' objection on the Boer side is objection to the restoration of a vague general right of interference in Transvaal domestic government.

When, a day or two afterwards, he sends his 'Looker-On', he stresses the fact that the Government 'does not want the suzerainty claim insisted on in the Press; & one of its greatest embarrassments is the Press clamour for a fight. I know that this is true & right. And you must know that departmental secretaries have often got their Govts into bad trouble before now. That is the present case; & the Govt would be glad to be helped out of it.'

When the proofs come, 'two points of some importance are worked in', he says:

I have tried to carry out your wish as to Outlander rights—wh.

are thoroughly secured by the Convention itself: all but franchise, wh. in every 'foreign state' belongs strictly to internal government. It is impossible to exaggerate the badness of the suzerain claim, as (whether legal or not) a claim to be enforced. Don't fail to read Westlake's letter (Westlake very eminent international lawyer, you know) on that claim in today's *Times*. Sir E. Clarke's letter you did not miss, I hope.[1]

If what I have written at end about Outlanders' rights doesn't answer your question, you will cut it out.

It may be mentioned that George Meredith was one of the backers of Greenwood in the views he expressed about South Africa. The next letter says:

If you were satisfied with the Transvaal section of 'Looker-On' when you wrote you cannot be less so now after reading Lord Salisbury's little note & the Duke of Devonshire's speech. His Grace might have written the 'Looker-On' section himself.

Mr Chamberlain has made so frightful a mess of the whole business, to the sorrow & disgust of his colleagues. Yet I suppose that if the war begins, wh. Mr. C. intended all along, ministers generally will have to affect contentment with it. It is the way.

Believe them that tell you that this is a newspaper-made campaign, inspired from the Colonial Office & the City Rhodesians. (If Maga were talked of, openly, at dinner-tables where sit careful & considerable men of affairs, as *The Times* is, you would take to your bed with chagrin & never leave it again.)

I am afraid my paper gave you a great deal of trouble & worry; my only satisfaction on that score being that I had my share of the same; & in these days a publication like your magazine must not lag behind on great or exciting occasions.

In mid-October war has begun, and he has been for a day or two 'amongst people of various sorts worth dipping into'.

The main result of all is confirmation that nobody, literally nobody that I have seen, doubts what others know, that this war is grief & pain to every considerable member of the Govt, except 'Joe', who is himself suspected of apprehending that a war against Kruger is a much bigger thing, & more pregnant of sinister possi-

[1] See footnote, p. 323.

bilities, than he imagined when he started work upon it. At the same time, the war has been whipped into a hugeous, frothy popularity amongst the many who do not think for themselves, & [there is] no doubt about the effect of that immensely stupid Boer ultimatum as a work of art.

But, as you say, one of two great considerations is the opening of such an opportunity for push, squeeze, or worse, from the European Govts as they are not likely to get again for many years to come. And from a word dropped into my ear, I take it that this consideration partly accounts for the vastness of the expedition, & the enormous number of officers with it—a number wh., as a military 'expert' said, would suffice for an army a hundred thousand strong. The Cape is on the way to places that might be found in danger of disturbance before Xmas time.

Greenwood little suspected that Great Britain was in for a £200,000,000 war with the Boers—and £200,000,000 was £200,000,000 then—and no end of humiliations and complications. But the Maga position, as defined in one of his letters is that

we are in perfect agreement with the Govt. as a Govt., though this same Govt had at last to give way to 'Joe's' determination when he had so strong a wind of popularity behind him that his resignation could not be thought of calmly.

And also there was the Kruger ultimatum, wh. J. C. had manœuvred for, & wh. came in such terms as silenced all peace-making. And we are not only with the Govt. in feeling & reason, but with the facts & probabilities every one. Yet we must 'duck' a little, like the Govt itself, I suppose. That is to say, we must take the war as an enterprise to be worked through with the *utmost expedition*, on every account.

But (of course I am only giving you my mind) it will not do to speak a syllable in favour of the war as an act of policy, or to question what is the absolute fact,—that it was a contrivance of the Colonial Office.

For were we to do the first things we might find, & not *very* improbably shall find, that we had sanctioned a tremendous mistake running to calamity: suppose, for example, that the Russians walk into Herat when we have our 60,000 men entangled in South Africa?

'One thing is certain, it will be the most exasperated & exasperating war we have ever been engaged in', Greenwood prophesies, as I did myself, if I may say so, in two pamphlets, one published by the *Star* and the other by the *Manchester Guardian*. And, when the *Daily Chronicle* turned from criticism of Chamberlain to supporting him, I resigned from it and from daily-paper journalism for good. But to Greenwood's next 'Looker-On', and the problem of saying the right thing during the war:

It behoves us who write to go very carefully. The reckoning can & should wait of course. Yet when the time comes for it, what I hope is that the war, with all its benefit & glories, & with all the contraries of profit & glory, shall be well understood to be the Colonial Secretary's. Don't let it be the Govt's more than it must be, or the party's, or yours or mine. For it is quite impossible that *any* good can come of the war, in any shape or form—any good that could not have been attained without it. As to the amount of harm, in several shapes & forms, Heaven only knows. It cannot be little,—that is all that we know.

From now on it is plain that Greenwood has difficulty, with all his prudent letters, in carrying Blackwood with him. He is careful to prepare him for what he is going to say in 'Looker-On'. He is really very tactful. Writing on October 20 he says:

That, my dear Blackwood, is what I am about as the safest & best course. I am quite confident it is. Believe me, you will never regret it. The upshot of these negotiations, the conduct of them, has not been heartily approved by any Minister of importance—perfunctorily only; & remember that the whole thing will be judged by the consequences of the war, wh. have yet to unfold.

As to debate last night—Sir Edward Clarke's speech was smashing for Chamberlain.[1] I say that quite deliberately and thoughtfully, that no more *effective* speech than Clarke's has been heard for years. Wait awhile, till your next (December) number comes out, at any rate, before you give what cannot be recalled. Meanwhile, what I

[1] i.e. against Chamberlain. Clarke, the eminent counsel, who became Solicitor-General, took a strong stand against the war. It was he who, once alluding to leaders of the Conservative party, spoke of 'the great, wise and eminent'.

write goes not to the contrary of any opinion you may incline to, & has more novelty & originality than throwing up our hats with the rest would have.

He adds that Wolseley 'says with tears' that the army dispatched is too small. It was soon to be seen how true that was. It is clear that Greenwood is receiving troublesome letters from Edinburgh. In his next note he stresses the fact about the relations of Chamberlain and his colleagues. 'As for the diplomacy, as an absolute matter of fact it was a course wh. the Govt. itself keenly understands to have been unfortunate to say the least, & knows, too, that C.'s exposition of it lacks candour & even truth. No considerable Minister has defended it, except (in Lord Salisbury's case) in a half-ironical spirit, or perfunctorily, as in other cases.'

In my note to you I humbly suggested that it will be safer on the whole to reserve Maga's support to the Colonial Office procedure & its results till the war brings out its developments in the next week or two. God forbid that I should make impertinent suggestions, but you might, perhaps, have a separate article on the subject for the December number.

I hear that the Govt is already receiving representations & inquiries from Continental Govts.

'This bad man', he writes the next day, 'must send yet another page.' 'Included will be a word for that good deed of the Queen's in sending £400 to the father of the fisher-boy shot in our waters. To that I want to add, what I am sure you will approve, support to Sir Michael Beach's reported determination that all classes shall contribute to the cost of this very popular war.' On the last day of the month there is a reference to 'the intolerably murderous savagery of the natives employed by Wolseley—wh. Wolseley himself could not stand'. And the letter goes on:

No, my dear Blackwood. I can find no satisfaction of any sort in this deplorable war, except, of course, as it brings out once more the fine fighting qualities of our men.

I entirely agree with the two letters of Selous [the big game hunter] especially when he denies the 'inevitable' character of the war. It is a needless war, a contrived war, a war that no sooner begins than it takes an importance wh. its abettors had no idea of at the beginning of their labours, a war that can bring no honour, & one that if it ends a fortnight hence by the appearance of overwhelming odds, *must* have a long trail of untoward consequences.

'And now, having delivered my mind to you', he says, 'I need not add that I don't propose to offer you another word on the subject for Maga. There must be matters upon wh. we do not agree, of course; & this must be shelved as one of them, as I see by your last letter. But still I hope, as a matter of personal friendship & concern, that Maga will keep in view the abundant possibilities of misfortune, or even of disaster.' He proposed that 'Looker-On' should be dropped for the next number, and incidentally mentioned—and it is an instance of his varied sources of information—that he had 'a long letter from Cavagnari [in Afghanistan] just before he was murdered'.

It has been well worth while, I think, to give these extracts from the Boer War letters. Greenwood prided himself on writing on the basis of carefully sifted information, and he was favourably placed to get it, and was skilful in drawing it out. Also many people's impressions to-day of the parts played by Chamberlain, Rhodes, and his friends, including Milner, are inaccurate. I may perhaps mention that, in addition to the advantage of having made some study of South Africa before the war, I met several of the persons on both sides who were concerned in it, and, when it was over, I sat through the proceedings of the committee of investigation at Westminster, of which Chamberlain was a member and to which Rhodes and other South Africans gave evidence.

Then comes the end of Greenwood's gossip and comment in Maga. On December 3, 1899 he writes:

On clearing the deck today for a 'Looker-On' paper, & casting back & looking forward & all round about, it is borne in upon me that perhaps it would be better to suspend these contributions till the war is over. I don't believe that the war operations will be as tedious as many people think.[1] But in a few days we must have strong forces smashing away in several directions towards Pretoria, &, if our difficulties are confined to South Africa, we ought soon to see the end of the fighting part of them—according to present prospects. You are very likely of the same mind. I mean as to suspension for a month or so.

He remains, however, 'my dear Blackwood's', 'very sincerely'. 'I have a vague recollection', Mr. J. H. Blackwood, the present head of the firm, wrote to me, 'that Greenwood had become too Liberal in his ideas to suit my uncle, who was very much the Diehard Tory', and the old man was eighty-one. But no copies of the old gentleman's letters exist.

There is no other letter from Greenwood until February 10, 1900, when in it is 'dear Blackwood' and 'very truly yours': 'Have I your permission to reprint from your magazine the verses entitled "A Midnight Conversation" & to make similar use of the article about Disraeli?' Another letter from Greenwood was written a year later, when, on March 31, 1901, he says, still to 'Dear Blackwood' only: 'It would be ungrateful not to acknowledge the handsome way in wh. the writer of "Some Editors and Others" (Shand, I fancy)[2] speaks of me in the April Maga. By handsome I mean more than that word expresses, as I hope you will understand.' He refers to Shand's point that George Smith 'originated' the *Pall Mall*. 'The plan was mine; & George Smith was not even the first man to whom it was communicated or to take it up. I did not know George Smith then; & had half forgotten my scheme when one evening, while we were together, the thought of it recurred to me & I set it forth. Of course I don't deny that G. S. did a great deal in his own way to bring the thing to success, but he did not "originate" the *Pall Mall*.'

On October 28 he writes to 'Dear Mr. Blackwood': 'Your

[1] In this, of course, he was wrong, with a great many other people. I remember prophesying in a pamphlet a long war.

[2] Alexander Innes Shand, author of a life of Sir E. D. Hamley and *Mountain, Stream and Covert.*

card has just been sent on to me with some letters from the Club [Garrick] & I must acknowledge the courtesy. I hope the summer has given you a good holiday. My ill-luck has brought some weeks of illness.' On August 5 of the next year there is this note to 'Dear Blackwood': 'I should like to write an article (signed or unsigned) of wh. I enclose a pretty full sketch,—feeling that the sketch gives a rather feeble idea of what is intended.—Perhaps it would suit you. If it does, perhaps you would not mind writing a word in reply.' It is endorsed: 'Ansd. by Wire. Sorry space clean blocked for Sept. Would October be too late for subject?' Greenwood thinks that the subject will be 'too generally thrashed out'.

On February 23, 1903, a note comes from him to 'Dear Meldrum':[1] 'If your firm is inclined to make a proposal in the matter of wh. we spoke last week [the memoirs of Lord Wolseley] it might be as well to do so as soon as due consideration allows; not that I am aware of any new reason for haste.' The following letter to 'My dear Blackwood' is dated June 13:

> Lord W.'s memoirs are nearing completion—or rather the first two volumes—& the business arrangements stand just where they did when you sent your offer. Meanwhile, however, I find that Lord W.'s mind reverts strongly to his first idea—sale of the copyright out & out or fixed price. This I report to you accordingly, though of course I do not know if you incline to do business in that way. And you are not to understand that Lord W. has settled on that plan definitely. That I should not say.

Greenwood shows his willingness to be helpful by writing no fewer than four more letters on details. He even saw Constable's with a view to their giving the printing to Blackwood's newly equipped printing office. But Blackwood's did not after all publish the book. To a March 1 letter is added the sentence: 'You found that North Berwick really justifies its reputation, I hope'. For himself he is 'convinced rather painfully that Putney

[1] This is Davis Storrar Meldrum who helped Blackwood and then went to the firm's London branch as literary adviser. Blackwood's had published three books of his. Later, Mr. J. H. Blackwood kindly reminds me, he became art critic of the *Morning Post*.

is too damp to live in. Wherefore I am about to quit this region for a higher one' (Sydenham).

The old relations were almost re-established, though it is only 'dear Blackwood' and 'Very truly yours'. On September 15, writing from 6 Border Crescent, Sydenham, Greenwood makes another proposal to write again: 'Gosse is about to publish a memoir of Coventry Patmore. I knew Patmore very intimately for years, & believe I could write an interesting paper about him. Is it likely to suit you for Maga?' The suggestion is evidently adopted. In January of the next year he is writing, 'with all good wishes': 'By the next post I shall send you a short article wh. I hope will find favour. It is meant to be lively, dramatic, flagellant, & is aimed at the increasingly impudent degradation of The Marriage Bond by such novelists as Robert Hichens. Nobody named, however.' In acknowledging a cheque the following month he says: 'I hope London will be kind to you: its skies, I mean. And I shall be very glad indeed of an opportunity of seeing you again & of an interchange of gossip & idea thereupon.' Whether they met or not does not appear.

There is now a Balfour Government. In March Greenwood is writing: 'In home affairs the great mistake was the general assumption that Mr Chamberlain had the Prime Minister in his pocket. "A. B." has been all along his own man & in much the stronger position, as we now see.' The final letters are under the dates with which I have prefixed them:

April 13. To my great distress, I see now that two considerable upsets coming together make it more than difficult to write the Patmore article in anything like good time for your next issue. Believe it a real disappointment to myself, whatever it may be to you: & besides, it has been a point of pride with me never to fail in this way. You may now think the article better left undone, but I hope not. If it will do for the next number I'll take care (D.V.) you have the copy early.

May 20. It is a great gratification to me that you should like the Patmore article so well, & should interrupt your delightful holiday-making to tell me so.

You have lovely weather, summer days. I see that you are heartily enjoying them & I hope they will give you as much good as pleasure.

June 2. My thanks to you for a cheque sweetened by your approbation of what it pays for. I am very glad you like the article so well.

You had fine weather; hold fast by all the good you got.

Here, most people delighted with the Japs, & some more ready to believe than before that if we could only substitute their *bushido* for our Christianity, & so acquire the very different & much superior Japanese soul, we should do well to make any sacrifice with that view. Only at present nobody has any explicable idea of what *bushido* is.[1]

'The falling out of faithful friends, renewing is'—it is pleasant to find in this final letter of the long correspondence, Greenwood and Blackwood back on the old footing.

[1] Dr. Inazo Nitobe, of whom I saw a great deal during my residence in Japan, told us in his *Bushido* and was scoffed at by some old Japanese hands. But only last year my friend Professor A. L. Sadler, a sound authority on Japanese language and history, assured me that he was in the right.

THE MACMILLAN, BARRIE, AND MORLEY LETTERS

CHAPTER XXX

Greenwood's Books

The Lover's Lexicon — 'MUCH TOO BOUNCEABLE' — LADY DOROTHY NEVILL — MRS. LYNN LINTON — *Imagination and Dreams* — *The Moon Maiden* — J. M. BARRIE'S DOG — JOHN MORLEY AND 'THE MOST TOUCHING GOOSE'

MR. DANIEL MACMILLAN, who was good enough to have the firm's file searched for Greenwood letters, favoured me with the following, dated August 16, 1893, to 'My dear Craik', George Lillie Craik, a partner in Macmillan's and the husband of Dinah Mulock, author of *John Halifax Gentleman*, whom he married in 1864. Greenwood writes concerning the *Illustrated London News*:

I have got into a difficulty. They were to have begun, 'Lover's Dictionary'[1] end of July, my understanding. Royal marriages intervene. I get alarmed, knowing that you want the book out in November, as I do. I write to Shorter: he is desolated, and will start soon. Then he (who knew, of course, my engagements with your firm) sends me the enclosed with a lot of proofs. It now seems impossible to do anything worth while with the *Illus. News* in the few weeks of Sept. and Oct. It does not seem that more than eight numbers could be got out, perhaps only six: and that would be too small a portion to pay me, for one thing. What I propose to do, therefore, is to get Shorter to agree with me to drop the *Illus. News* publication (he knew of my engagements many weeks ago) and to plant a certain portion of the 'Dictionary' in the *Pall Mall* instead. [Then being edited by E. T. Cook.] They will be glad of it for the two very dull months before them (when London evening papers drop about half their circulation) and I shall get the pay anticipated

[1] *The Lover's Lexicon* (Macmillan.)

from *Illus. News* without deferring publication of the book. We shall lose the [*Illustrated London News*] illustrations, but you would rather be without them, I know, though I am of another mind. However, if the book has luck, you will be freer to have an illustrated edition to your own mind. It does lend itself to illustration beautifully I think. Of course the *Pall Mall* won't get more of the book than was meant for *Illus. News*.

A month or two later Greenwood is writing to George Macmillan:

Enclosed the last proofs of *Lover's Lexicon*. I suppose you will choose an appropriate sort of present-book binding. I've been dreaming of a rose coloured cloth—that wh is the imitation of morocco. Better still would be rose-pink sides and darker rose back. White soils too quickly—and too much. The morocco imitation seems to me very eligible. Perhaps to have the backs a darker shade than the clear pink sides would be too costly?—but it would look extremely well.

Do you propose to put a medallion on the sides? If so, here (I think) is a taking design: the figure of Dr Johnson, burly, bewigged, hat in hand, leading by other hand (as if by way of introduction) a Cupid with a big book under his arm. Cupid not to be too little: not a 'Love'.

Great print, of course, to make of it an attractive present-book.

Two further letters about binding will be of interest to every author who has been concerned about the appearance of the 'case' of his book:

I return the dummy copy—sadly. It is disappointing; looks—(I must tell you what I think) rather common—trivial: predisposing to disregard. The colour lends itself to streakiness, from the paste beneath perhaps. The material seems remarkably coarse and poor of quality. For my part, I should very greatly prefer a darker colour: as what is called cherry colour; or light maroon, like port wine seen through the glass. Any bright shade of claret rather than this. But this would be better if the baldness of the cover were carried off by a narrow band of ornament (or an ornamented band) at head and foot. And I *do beg of you* not to have the margins cut down even for the sake of the gilding. The margins are narrow enough without cutting (specially the top and side margins); and whatever dignity the page has as the printer designed is entirely cut away and destroyed by the binder. Please don't have the margins cut. Never mind the light gilt edges: they never go well with linen covers. *And* if the word 'Greenwood' on the back can be made smaller please have it made so. It looks much too bounceable as it stands.

I am very sorry indeed to make any objections, and wouldn't do so, depend on it, if I didn't feel them too much for silence. If you have a strong liking for the colour (which, however, will go streaky white) please relieve it by ornamental bands, and ask Mr. Brown for something less coarse. But I hope you will like a darker colour just as well and, above all, that you will indulge me so far as to leave the edges uncut. The margins will not stand the binder's irregular knife, and he spoils the dignity of the page completely. Time is getting on, too.

Two days afterwards there is this letter about the page and about author's blunders:

The binding of the American edition I like decidedly, and shall be glad if the home edition is bound exactly like it—Dr. Johnson and the Cupid being omitted. But whether the top margin will bear cutting, for gilding, I doubt: however, that you will decide upon. I daresay I can have a copy or two altogether uncut. Pardon the suggestion, but if we have the luck to reprint the American edition, it would be a wise instruction to printers to widen the top margin, so as to allow more for cutting that. There is plenty of bottom margin to go upon for the purpose you see.

The American page is good: the better of the two and all the more because the printer has not deprived the headlines and cross lines of their full points. [We have happily got away from this fashion.]

But there are some errors—author's blunders—in this edition (corrected in the English edition) which I shall be glad to set right if there is ever a chance. I believed you were going to print both edits. from Clark's type. You don't bring any of the American Edtn into England, I hope, on account of these errors, and some differences here and there.

Hope we shall be out soon now. The book is posted with this.

The Lover's Lexicon was a stout work of 322 pages, and was published in December 1893 after the collapse of the *Anti-Jacobin*. Its author described it in the title as 'a Handbook for Novelists, Playwrights, Philosophers and Minor Poets, but specially for the enamoured'. The little essays in it are arranged alphabetically. Under A there were Abhorrence, Absence, Acceptance, Addresses, Admiration, Admirer, Adoration, Advances, Adventure, Affection, Affiance, Affinity, Amour, Amourette, Assignation, Attachment, and Attentions. Other headings which catch the eye are Pride, Rake, Rapture, Responsibility, Sensibility, Temperament, Tendresse, Voice, Vows, Wedlock, and Wife. *The Times* found the book 'original and captivating', presenting 'in quite a new and unexpected light'—but not to us who have noticed his continuous interest in the relation of the sexes—'a brilliant publicist and political writer of rare force and insight, with a backbone almost too stiff for this invertebrate generation'. 'Subtle, wise, fascinating' were the *Spectator*'s adjectives. 'Not one of the least of this book's delights', said the *Athenaeum*, 'is its joyousness.' The New York *Nation* discovered 'tenderness, generosity, kindly humour, wisdom'. Greenwood is said, however, to have been disappointed with the book's reception and to have hoped to bring out a revised edition.

Mrs. W. K. Clifford, whose novel, *Mrs. Keith's Crime*, was once, I remember, a topic of conversation, was one of the friends who received a copy. She wrote:

> I am glad and proud to possess it. Please come soon and put my name in it. There is so much beautiful and witty writing in it. I think your definition of affection as the 'three per cents of love' one of the best bits. It ought to have a lasting career, for it is a book that all sorts and conditions will like.
>
> I hope your dear girls are well—mine are, and *horribly* tall, bless them.
>
> Did you see me (i.e. my short story) in the *P.M.G.*? I was rather stuck up at being in the same shelter with you.

The delightful Lady Dorothy Nevill's acknowledgement was: 'I am much interested in it as I have read most of it in the *Pall*

Mall. But you must put your name in it when you come to us. Come on Sunday.'

Mrs. Lynn Linton, who horrified her generation with her *Girl of the Period*, expressed herself as follows to 'My very dear Mr. Frederick Greenwood':

> Thank you a thousand times and one over for the prettily got-up book of exquisite grace and tenderness and humour which has embalmed those more scattered gems. It is lovely of you to give me this book—perhaps because you felt how I would be *sure* to appreciate all the loveliness of your work? I sipped it as a connoisseur sips his glass of '34 port—as he sniffs at the bouquet of a rare old bottle of Steinberger. I loved your *Lexicon* and thought what a big fellow you were to write both masculine politics and the tenderest and most graceful sentiment. So I thank you, my dear man, for your remembering me both because it was sweet of you to remember me at all and because I have in perpetuity a work I admire and love.
>
> I have been very ill, and have still to submit to regimen and restrictions. I am not allowed to see anyone, and, for all the glorious sunshine, I may not breathe the fresh air.

The wife of Sir George Lewis, the famous solicitor, writing in 'respectful admiration' of the book, found it 'delightful to have in a collected form your original and charming conceits'. That the invalided Mrs. Fuller-Maitland did her best to promote its success is seen from a letter which deals mainly with her dogs:

> I am sending you this photograph to show you how pretty my dogs are. They are such dear little creatures. I have had them now for nearly seven years, which is the length of their lives. The one on the table is a most romantic dog and full of sentiment. He will not sleep without a shoe or something of mine in his basket and his companion is just as affectionate in his own ways. 'Spaniels gentle or comforters' is the old name for such dogs.
>
> I am hourly expecting your book. I told Bumpus to send it as soon as he could capture it. I also began some time ago to ask Mudie for it.
>
> I don't think the depraved editors will print my produce. There seems to me to be something demoniacal about this. I will send to you whatever the *Westminster Gazette* prints of mine.

Next year Greenwood brought out *Imagination in Dreams*; and in 1903 *The Russian Empire and Czarism* by V. Berard, was issued 'with an introduction by F. Greenwood'. *Imagination and Dreams*,[1] which was to be followed by a book on somewhat similar lines by William Archer, is an expansion of articles in the *Contemporary* and the *New Review*. In addition to accounts of his own dreams, Greenwood mentions that, like Mr. Galton and M. Maury, he was accustomed to see faces 'in the dropping-off to sleep time and when I wake in the night'. They were 'never seen except when the eyelids are closed, and they have an apparent distance of five or six feet; they look as if traced with chalks on a dark ground'. The author explains that 'the dreams which have been chosen, exemplify the potentialities of the mind in sleep' and appeals to readers to report, care of Mr. John Lane, his publisher, or to the Garrick, dreams which are other than 'incoherent and inconsequential nonsense' and are 'psychologically informing'. His object is not to

> reinstate a superstitious interpretation of dreams or to encourage the practice of searching into them for omens. The sublime faculty of imagination has potentialities beyond any yet assigned to it. Its far greater force, intensity and creativeness in sleep are beyond doubt. If these large reserves of power seem capable of extending insight far beyond its present range, it would be absurd to close our eyes to the prospect in fear of falling into superstition. At divers times and places the supernatural has turned out to be the natural unascertained; and nobody can say that a great development of any mental gift, and especially of imaginative power, is beyond the laws of nature.

'The natural unascertained' appealed also to Stead, who was always referring to the subject in the *Review of Reviews*, and turned out one or two publications on what he called 'spooks'.

Now I may slip in some letters addressed to Greenwood's daughter Jessy from J. M. Barrie, in which we see him first gay and then grave. These letters are dated Strath View, Kirriemuir (1888), 5 Albany Street, Edinburgh (1889), 14 Old Quebec

[1] Lane.

Strath-view
Kirriemuir, N.B.
27. 12. 88.

Dear Miss Greenwood

I have not managed to get your fox terrier yet but hope to get a good one before long. I have been making enquiries and have been promised the first that can be warranted which comes along a good kennel. I had a dog from the same place myself once which was a success. The man tells me that ladies like dogs that are either very pretty or very ugly — which

One of several letters from Sir James Barrie to Jessy Greenwood.

seems profound. I am thinking it over.
If you hear of a [illegible] terrier [illegible] you happen [illegible] hear again of [illegible] [illegible]. You should [illegible] [illegible] promising small [illegible]. Please give your sister and the Professor my best regards and believe me

Yours very truly

J. M. Barrie

Street, Marble Arch, 15 Old Cavendish Street, Cavendish Square (1891 and 1892), and Kirriemuir and Anchor Cottage, Shere (1892). Here is the first one. It will be seen that it is all about getting Jessy a dog,

Three months later he writes from Edinburgh another doggy letter:

The lady of Dollar and her appeal for enlightenment about the dog were both genuine, and she was one of these perfect people who send an addressed envelope for reply. More humiliating to me was the result of a recent article in the same paper. A correspondent (English, I am proud to say) wrote a private letter to the editor, explaining that he and a friend had a small bet as to whether the article was humorous, and would the editor decide the matter.

In Edinburgh for a few days on my way back to London, I notice that the fox terriers all run from me, not knowing whom they are wanted for. The man next door has a good one, which he is training in the backyard. He little knows why I take such an interest in its education. I wonder if he will miss it much.

Two months after this he has still something about Jessy's dog:

I am glad to hear the dog is trying to do his duty. I see I must have made a dreadful blunder, and given you his name wrong. It is (or was) Dick, not Bob. Dick seems a good name in one way. You can say it with a sudden jerk that may pull him up sharply when he is on the warpath. I don't guarantee this.

I left the chain purposely in case you might find it useful. It may do for week days in the kingdom of Fife. I hope to see the dog before he goes north yet. Anything for an excuse, as the Parnellite said when he drank the Queen's health.

On January 21, 1889, there is a note about the closing down of the *Anti-Jacobin*; 'I am much taken up to hear that Mr. Greenwood is ill. Glad to hear the paper is given up, for he was working too hard. If you could let me know how he is, it would be very kind of you.'

It is in the spring of the previous year that we first hear of Barrie's sister Margaret. She is staying in Old Cavendish Street. He writes: 'She would like much to meet you. Could you lunch with us on Thursday at two o'clock? I wish you would.' But in May there is unhappy news from Kirriemuir: 'A terrible thing has happened to us. A telegram today announced that Mr. Winton, to whom my beloved sister was to be married in three weeks, has been flung from his horse and killed. I don't know whether my darling sister will live and my mother is old and cannot bear much.' The following paragraphs are from four black-bordered letters sent from May to July:

My sister is as well as can be expected. She is so entirely in God's hands that we can do little, but we do all we can. And you have done all you can, too. Her one solace is that he was so well prepared to face his God. There is no other comfort in such a trial. The letter you wrote her could only have come from a most tender and good heart, and I hope you will write to her very soon again.

My sister is not able to write to you yet but wants you to know how she is. I cannot pretend that grief has softened any yet, and she is still as broken in health. I meant to bring her to a village in Surrey this week but my mother is now down with bronchitis, brought on, I am sure, not by cold but by the sorrow at her heart. I suppose my sister's happiness always was infinitely more to her and to me than anything else in the world. We think and the doctor thinks that my mother is now a little better. With my sincere regards to all of you.

My mother is much better. Margaret is much as she was. I hope to get her south next week. She is willing to try to do anything. You who saw so little of her seem to have understood her as few have done. I can't tell you how much it is to me that your father's daughter is such a friend to her.

I have always been hoping to get out to see you again but my sister and I are alone now and I don't like leaving her. So she asks me to write in the meantime and tell you that she is a little better. I suppose she is in a sort of way, as she is able to go out walking with me. I was very sorry to miss you that day. I shall let you know when I am coming next time, and hope you will be in as I should like to see you. Margaret sends her love.

In May of the next year he sends a stall, made out in his name, 'to the Dress Rehearsal of the New Opera May 12 at 2·45 for 3 p.m.' from D'Oyly Carte.

In the chronicles of his time John Morley is not often found in a facetious humour, but on July 10, 1872, he writes to Greenwood's daughter Kate ('My dear Miss Greenwood, Always yours very sincerely'):

Your telegram has just reached us, and fallen on the lunch table like a bomb. We believed no telegram could possibly come to us, except in a tardy and orderly manner, through the post bag the day but one after. We see the delusion. My wife thought her son had been hit on the head with a cricket ball; I insisted that it was only her daughter who had been attacked by cholera. Then we turned cheerful, and wondered who had left her a fortune: or whether Longman & Co., wearied of an old woman, were going to offer the editorship of the *Edinburgh Review* to a young one: or whether . . . well, then we opened the envelope, and found nothing more tragical nor more comical, than that you are going really to have the most touching goose in Puttenham Parish for a kitchenmaid. After all, she is clean and honest and willing, and you might do worse. She shall be sent you forthwith, and ought to reach you shortly after this;—unless she goes to Kingston-on-Hull or Kingston Harbour, or Kingston in Radnorshire, by mistake. The ingenuity of the dull is unfathomable.

And that reminds me of the dullness of the ingenious. Why has your father cut me off from his friendship, and why do you not come down and try our air? 'Tis most salutary. I should be downright glad to hear good news of you. Can you really not come?

Our aspect at sight of a mid-day telegram has not been equalled since Crusoe saw Friday's foot-print on the shore.

Two years later, in July 1874, when Morley is acknowledging a letter of her father's, he speaks of a future visit by Kate and her sister.

The Portrait of GREENWOOD, towards the end of his life, in Sir James Barrie's book *The Greenwood Hat*
(published by Peter Davies)

A FATHER TO HIS DAUGHTERS

CHAPTER XXXI

Letters to Kate about his Friends and his Walks

AN EDITOR'S FOIBLE — BRINGING UP DAUGHTERS — DEPRESSION AND DESPONDENCY — PATTI — LORD CARNARVON — GREENWOOD ASSAILS BURNE-JONES

SCOTS speak pungently of a 'doo oot and a deil in', a dove out and a devil in, that is a person, amiable and 'clubbable' outside the house to his friends and acquaintances, who is, at home, in Carlyle's mother's never-fading phrase, 'gey ill to live wi'. A friend (and for some time a tenant) of mine, the late Harold Begbie, once wrote some verses, 'My wife could tell a tale of me'—jocular, of course, for he had a happy home life. My aim in this book is to give an impression not only of the character and quality of Greenwood's writing and editorial work, and of the way in which he was regarded by his fellow craftsmen and by statesmen and other people in public life; but, for a comprehension of Greenwood the man, some trustworthy particulars of his home life.

I have not found any portrait of Mrs. Greenwood or any letter she wrote, and hardly any allusion to her.[1] But happily there has come into my hands a large collection of letters—many more than can be used—from Greenwood to his elder daughter Kate, and several to his younger daughter Jessy. I have also a number of letters written by Kate and Jessy to one another, and a few letters from their brother Edgar. Kate, Jessy, and Edgar were the only grown-up members of Greenwood's family. The other three died young. These letters are full of domestic allusions,

[1] See page 444.

but they also give sharp impressions of Greenwood's rounds of visiting and dining out, and constant walking expeditions.

To read the letters in the order in which they were written has been almost or entirely impossible. It is curious that an editor, with a large and often important correspondence every day of his life, should have so frequently followed the reprehensible practice of neither dating his letters nor, commonly, setting down the addresses at which they were written. Nearly all the correspondence has been preserved in its envelopes, however, so I have secured a number of dates from the postmarks, when they are not blurred. I have had to use a magnifying glass constantly. Altogether the job has been rather exacting. When I came to the copying of the letters it was again frequently necessary to use the magnifying glass. The script of a man who was always writing—in the days before typewriters—is often, at its best, by no means clear. And Greenwood apparently used a quill—as I see it is stated his friend Coventry Patmore did—and often a quill which was not in perfect order. (Does the present generation know the origin of the word pen-knife?)[1] The fact that he uses long 's' has not mattered—on Kate's visiting cards the second 's' in 'Miss' is a long one—but some of the letters are in pencil. I have not grudged the time and eyesight given to the spelling out, for they have brought me, as they will bring readers, into closer contact with a kindly, sagacious, redoubtable man. It is a fortunate thing that Greenwood's letter-paper—the letter-paper of many people of the period, evidently—was always of stout quality.

The letters tell us just what we want to know about Greenwood, what he was like in the searching circumstances of his domestic life, without a wife to share the bringing up of daughters and a boy. He was plainly a man of tender heart. He could not have written more frequently or more affectionately to his family, could not have shown more continuous solicitude for their health. He tried to be a little disciplinary with Edgar, but he almost coddled his girls. In providing them with money

[1] See reference on page 378 to a daughter's quill-cutting.

for their constant holidays, in repeatedly urging them to spend freely, and in urging them to stay away longer than had been planned, he is generous, for he can never have been really well off. (Mr. William Stone, several of whose letters I have quoted, got the impression that Greenwood, in his club life, could not always do as much entertaining as he would like to do.) With his head full of his editorial work or his general writing, and with his many engagements, he not only writes constantly to his daughters but finds time to obtain anything of which the young women think they are in need. And he is always attending to the affairs of the house; he keeps an eye on the different flowers in the garden and on the pet birds, looks after tradesmen and servants, has a care even for 'the dustbin' and 'whitewashing'.

One marks his courtesy, even deference, to his daughters as they reached young womanhood, and the pains he takes in gradually transferring housekeeping and social responsibility to them and in introducing them to worth-while acquaintances. He discusses politics with Kate—I have a telegram he sent her announcing the death of the Emperor Frederick—and encourages Jessy with her novel writing, which did not come to much, and even provides the whole family with book reviewing, which, if one draft I have be a fair sample, was not of outstanding quality.[1] The health of the young women never seems to have been robust—they have always colds, and usually seem a bit sorry for themselves—yet they survived their devoted father. Whether, when they grew up, they looked after Greenwood well is not clear. They may not have been of the housekeeping kind. They suffered no doubt, like other young women of a time when entrance to public work, secretaryships, the Civil Service, and commercial offices was for men only.

Considering his life of unremitting work, Greenwood must

[1] On Oct. 3, 1885, 'the proprietors of the *St. James's Gazette* present their compliments to Miss Greenwood [Kate] and beg to enclose £2 for contributions during September'. I came on a poem of Kate's in *Country Life* the year after her father's death.

have been of sturdy build, but the dietary and hygienic notions of his period were unscientific. In reading Victorian and Edwardian biography and autobiography one laments the premature death of many men and women whom saner living might obviously have saved for the continuation of their good work. Greenwood had frequently gout or rheumatism, and probably the substantial 'hospitality' of the period, pressed on a good talker and well-informed and influential man, had some responsibility for the 'depression' and 'despondency' to which he refers at times. Happily he had a real liking for the open air, for walking and for scenery. He hardly writes a letter, whether in town or in the country, without references to the weather—considerations of space have usually required their elision—which are not conventional remarks but the notes of a man who was a gazer at the clouds and the sky. I am compelled to cut his holiday letters more heavily than his town correspondence, but his joy on moor, hill, and dale helps us to understand his appreciation and backing of Richard Jefferies.

I have not found in the hundreds of letters I have read one thing common, mean, or discreditable. I have suppressed nothing. There was certainly no point in leaving out piquant touches of character and temperament in acquaintances who have long passed away. After all, Greenwood was writing for his daughters' instruction and entertainment. But, while he missed nothing provocative of comment in the people he met, there are many signs of his having, for a large company of friends, acquaintances, and the casually encountered, a kind heart and an uncommonly understanding mind. One thing one notes in all his writing is his care for accuracy. When the methylated-spirit bottle in his bag was smashed and 'no harm was done, for the outrunning spirit did not more than saturate the paper', it is typical of him to add, 'To be sure there was plenty of it'.

I have given as much of the letters as I have done because I often felt that condensation would mar the effectiveness of the view they give us of a relationship between father and children which it is good to read about, apart altogether from the journalistic and literary chronicle with which this book is concerned. In recent years several books have been written showing up fathers. It is now the turn of a busy father to furnish some account of the hours he gave to his family.

I make extracts first from the letters to the elder daughter, Kate. It will be seen that at the time the early letters were written, Greenwood's father and mother were still alive. I include letter beginnings and endings only when they are not the usual 'My dear Kate' and 'Your affectionate Dad', and I omit unnecessary dates. Greenwood was editing the *Pall Mall* 1865–80, the *St. James's* 1880–8, and the *Anti-Jacobin* 1891–2. I give the years of the first two letters. They start off with small beer but are worth reading for the light they throw on Greenwood and his domestic environment. One notes how, as the girls grow older, the letters get more and more grown up.

1871. Will you be good enough to send up to P.O. Gothland [Yorkshire] my mother's address? [Presumably she was on a visit.] I am not sure of it. A sullen, determined deluge has begun.

1873. My dear Kitty. Except for the news of your cold—from wh. I trust you will take warning—your letter is very pleasant reading. From its whole tone, I gather that you are very comfortable, and so far satisfied with the change, at least. What is the name of the staring family? I am very glad indeed to know that you have one nice person to talk to, at any rate. It is very likely that those sulphur baths would do you good: have you courage enough to try one?

All goes as usual at home. The servants behave very well to me. I was away at Leatherhead Saturday, Sunday and till Monday night, and got good out of the expedition. I fancy I shall sleep somewhere out of town Friday night. Saturday the boy [Edgar] must come to me again.

The only news I have got is that the 'fern' has come out with a pretty but not large mauve flower, that the roses are coming out well against the house, and the rhododendrons showing bloom. And that the hostilities of those two cock birds have had a fatal termination. After another tremendous battle the young one died. The other has a damaged wing.

My father has had a very bad time of it, but seems now to be getting round again. This afternoon I am going to see him.

With this I send two cheques, so that the amount may be easier to the person cashing them. *Mind, no more* colds.

The next letter is to 'My dear little Kitty':

May 19. My father seems to be getting better, but slowly: he has been very ill.

I have to avoid hurry and hurried work as much as possible.

The boy was with me Saturday and yesterday: that cough sticks to him, but it seems better, and he looks pretty well. On Saturday he brought me one of three sweets.

On Saturday, I meant very much to go to Lady Waldegrave's, but was tired, and Mr. de Crespigny came in for a gossip, and that settled me in the little room for the evening. We had bagatelle before the parson came (he had asked me to dinner) and the boy won one game and his Dad another. He is getting more and more to be a very nice boy.

On Saturday Mrs. Stanley called, and purposed to come up with her dear Johnny to see the chestnuts, and take luncheon yesterday (Sunday) at our cottage.[1] But the day proved cold and threatening for rain, and they didn't appear, so that my nice little luncheon went for nothing. Today I get an apology; and this evening I dine with them.

Tomorrow I think of going to the Drummonds. Once a week I am regularly asked, and must not say no any longer. I don't intend to go for a trip next Saturday, because the following week I must go to Lady Portsmouth's[2] and the boy will miss coming home.

The cold weather keeps the garden out of countenance, but the wall-roses swarm with buds (and a good many nice blooms too) and the buds swarm with blight.

Your last letter seems to show that you are still very comfortable, and on the whole better for the trip. Three weeks have gone by since you started. I hope the Roman [*sic*] is not carrying on the tradi-

[1] Apparently at Burley.

[2] In a letter to him Lady Portsmouth once said that, although she had 'always a great conscience in worrying busy men', she was concerned about her 'distressed' butler 'who never meddles with a gun', being supposed to be the indirect cause of the death of a man at Chagford.

tional habits of conquest. Which of you is in love with him most? Jenny or Kate?

You got a registered letter from me, no doubt. Give me full warning, my dear, when more money seems wanted. You must make a few excursions when the weather is good for that purpose. It pleases me profoundly to hear that Jessy looks so well and bright. How does Jenny[1] look? My love, my dear and good little maid. The kitten grows pretty and funny.

The following note is from Chepstow, and, like some of the others, is addressed to 'My dearest Kitty':

From your letter I am a little afraid that my not coming home on Tuesday was a disappointment in spite of your cheerfulness and good nature. The fact is, I rather slipped back for a day or two, and wanted to recover lost ground—as I am doing. I fancy now I shall stay till Monday, wh. will make four weeks of it.

Of course I shall spend a week or so at home with you. For a little while I was afraid all was not quite well with you, and that therefore you did not write. Now that is off my mind.

I wish you could find out, either yourself or through Jess, what the boy would like for a present, and let me know. Jess would probably get it out of him easiest.

I often and often imagine how it is with you in our little study of an afternoon. The mornings are most difficult for you probably. I have broken my watch & greatly defaced my Thackeray ring.

'I very much admire', he says in another message from Chepstow, 'the names you have given to the kittens':

Gummidge, I foresee, will be the kitten in wh. I shall have most interest. I hope you don't mean that the other two can't be got out from the roof. And thanks for the boy's very characteristic observation: it is wonderfully funny; and I can well fancy how he spoke. It sets me going with a fresh impulse to see how cheerfully you write: and I hope that as your letter is so are you.

Today I am going for a three days' walk, with bits of river on the way, returning to Ross on Monday. I believe I know every road now for ten miles round. I send you two photographs.

My love to you all, and very very much of it.

[1] Query, one of the daughters who died. Or see pages 349 and 426.

'As soundly as ever I did at fourteen' is the way he reports he is sleeping, but 'for a couple of days I have been expecting to get a line from you, and this morning am rather disappointed'.

Nothing has gone wrong I hope: but that would be rather a reason for writing than otherwise. As for me, the whole holiday has done me so much good that I think I shall stay out a few days longer. But if you would prefer my coming home, or there is any reason to do so, of course you shall see me back at once. Tomorrow I hope will bring me a letter: if not I shall begin to feel anxious.

Patti, the Derbys, and Lady Granville are mentioned in the following note, the fifth in five days:

I was very much distressed to hear about your cold. My little girl is very unfortunate; happily she is stout of heart, and bears these troubles well. My hope, amounting to a kind of belief, is that you have got over the cold, and are all right again.

I dined with the Stanleys on Monday: they were very kind and nice. Did not dine with the D's [Derbys] on Tuesday—going to do so on Monday—with Francis D. [Drummond]. Have an invitation to the Countess of Granville's for tonight—grand Majesty's birthday evening—but shall not go. Went to the opera last night, Patti, 'Barber of Seville'—in my belief never to be surpassed.

Back in London in June, he writes:

What *shall* I send Jessy? I owe her a watch chain: that can come with the other article. I daresay she would like a ring, and I have a great mind to chance hitting off the right size. By all means the fête. Let it be a good one: I am very much pleased at the idea of it, and should like it to be carried out well. As to your expenses, I do not propose to make any estimate of them, or trouble my head with the details. I am sure you do not spend more than is necessary and becoming, and I only want to know from time to time when remittances are needed.

Why don't you ask Jenny how it is she doesn't get on with Jessy? It is one of the most mysterious things I ever heard of. Tell her you observe it, and that it distresses you, because you know there must be some reason for it, whether mistaken or otherwise.

Your American young man must have been a bore, but he is of those who teach us mankind. Was the lad going about alone?

A few days ago, I was caught by Mr. W. Saunders,[1] and was persuaded to go in and dine. It was not a pleasant evening. But he really did his very best to please me, and Mrs. Saunders appears to be a very thorough good sort of woman, natural and goodnatured. Nor is her daughter an ill girl, I think, but rather a good one.

And the other evening, while prowling about the garden, who should approach the bank but the parson, with his niece, Lady de Crespigny on his arm? She is a tall, fair, pretty girl: slender and rather elegant: *nez retroussé* kind of fair girl: not without possibilities of harmless sauciness, I should say.

The Stanleys have asked me to dinner on Saturday,—think I shall decline. I would sooner be at home with the boy, and I owe him a Saturday.

Solicitous as he often was that a holiday should be extended, he writes in an affectionate letter expressing satisfaction with his children: 'It will be better, I *quite* think, for you to stay longer. The misfortune of the weather ought to be repaired and another fortnight may make a great difference to you. Let me know how much money I should send you—taking care to have enough. The boy is better, certainly. Tomorrow I am going to take him and little Leonie [I don't know who she was] to the Crystal Palace.' Greenwood has had 'a very fatiguing week' with the Shah:

On Friday I was at the grand Guildhall Ball to the Shah: great crush, but I have seen more splendid spectacles. On Saturday there was a State performance at the Opera House: a fine sight. For Tuesday I have an invitation from the Countess of Granville (to have the honour of meeting the Shah) but levée dress is ordered, and I suppose my bourgeois swallow-tails would not be admitted: whether or no, I don't think I shall go. I had a similar invitation to the Duchess of Sutherland's: so that I have had offered to me a very fair share of these Persian festivities. I wish you could have been transported to one of them, and back the same night, in a flash.

Your account of yourself is profoundly grateful to me, and also

[1] The rather robustious founder of the Central News, a bit of a social reformer, who, as editor of the *Eastern Morning News* of Hull, set J. A. Spender going in journalism.

your account of Jessie. You don't know how much pride I have in the confidence that my children are all far above the littleness of little characters—and have good clear heads, and good wholesome minds. Every year this is to be a larger and more certain pleasure. Goodbye, my dear.

He expresses himself touchingly about his family: Kate is now a young woman and Jessy a schoolgirl.

As to Jess [he writes to Kate] I do not see how she can come with you because it would be necessary to pay for a term's schooling unless notice is given. What do you think about that? Jess would be happy enough if she knew she had only one more term to go through with. *You are to decide how it is to be*; nor do I care so much about the sacrifice of the money, especially as it will not be without compensation, by any means.

Don't worry about me. It is only in spells, when I get overtired, that I fall back. A few days of quiet, and I improve again. Do you let all that kind of care go, and take a comfortable lounge for a fortnight more. It will do you good, and that is doing me good.

After mentioning that the boy may have had 'a small attack of hooping [*sic*] cough', he speaks of the Prince of Wales's garden-party and other excitements:

Everybody is so civil to me that I ought to be contented and well: and you are getting better; and the boy is showing good stuff; and Jessie, according to your affectionate account is grown so good and nice—all these things ought to tell, and they do.

Last night I dined with the Stanleys, after one or two refusals: they were very nice to me: I don't think they are altogether in good running together. This afternoon I go to the Prince of Wales's garden party: the Queen is to be there, and 'civilians' are ordered to appear in evening coats and morning trousers; which has brought on me the expense of a new coat, for the other is far too white in the seams to show in a garden of an afternoon. It is a ridiculous prescription, isn't it?

The conservatory is in a blaze. But I had to quarrel with the gardener for slovenliness. You will be in time for the clematis, but not, I think, for the roses.

I am going to stop at Burley till February 9. The Stanleys asked to be invited: I should like them to come on Sunday when you return.

In August he is in Ross and has had 'a charming excursion—twenty miles out and twenty miles back by another road: both beautiful along the whole route. One night I slept at Raglan, two at Tintern. It is a long time since I enjoyed such walks and drives in such scenery.'

He mentions that 'Lord Carnarvon is going to send me some venison. What you will do with it I don't quite know. If Captain E. is at home, I should send him some—or all if it is a small joint, wh. it will not be probably.' In view of Greenwood's frequent visits to Highclere, I had hoped that some letters of his might have survived, but the present Lord Carnarvon tells me that nothing is to be found.

The next letter tells of Kate's induction into writing for the

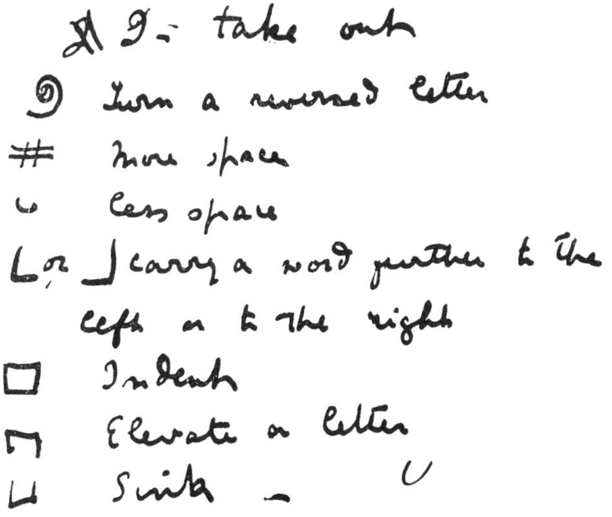
take out
turn a reversed letter
more space
less space
or carry a word further to the left or to the right
Indent
Elevate a letter
Sink —

Some printers' corrections written by Greenwood for Kate.

Pall Mall, and this time Greenwood is her 'ever affectionate Dad': 'Here is your first cheque, for your first earnings with the pen, on the first day of a new year [1874]. I could say a great deal about it, my dear, but I refrain.'

We jump to April in 1875. Hoping Kitty is none the worse for some trip, he writes to Jessy:

I had a really charming walk on Sunday. Spent the whole day, from 11 to 6, either on the ridge above Betchworth or in the meadows between Betchworth (through Bucklands) and Reigate.

Just as I came away from home this morning, there came a woman to say she thought she knew where Dolly [a dog] was (the bills were out yesterday). If Dolly *has* been found they will telegraph to you. Peg has been very distinctly not herself since you went away.

I have too much dining out: Sir H. Maine's last night, Baillie Cochrane's tonight: and I think I shall take the girls to the opera tomorrow. The Drummonds on Monday. I send you a letter from Mrs. D. My advice is, that you write and tell her you have promised to stop at Sandgate till Tuesday. [Mrs. Drummond used to send her brougham for Kate.]

In August he is largely domestic:

Before sending the enclosed cheque, please look to see at what dates the rent is due. It certainly does not seem time yet to pay another £45. I really forget now how much a week we were to pay.

You did quite right about the cretonne.

I am very very sorry about your sore throat. Of course you ought to be careful how you go out in hansom cabs, with a bad cold about you. When you first go, you must muffle up well.

As for me, the headache is gone, but I don't feel particularly bright: not unwell, you must know, but peevish and shaky rather.

You should just make a paragraph of that novel. If it is stupid, you can point out its stupidity. Now that you have had the trouble of reading the book you may as well earn half a guinea by saying what ought to be said about it.

If the boys make any more jam, mind you save me a taste.

He is in Wales. He finds the 'beautifully situated Llanidloes, amongst hills and river, about the filthiest place anywhere out of the main street that ever was seen. The people are poor, and foul: such swarms of dirty children that make you hot with anger at their parents and guardians. But there are dozens of chapels: godliness being a cheaper virtue than cleanliness.' He adds, 'Mind you have your cab-drives'.

Next year (1876), from Pickering in Yorkshire, he writes about 'poor Miss Shildrick': 'Your letter gave me a shock in spite of the certainty that she must soon die. Poor old woman. I am deeply and truly grieved. I believe she left the world almost as innocent as she came into it, and that is very much to think of.' He mentions that yesterday he 'had a long day on a high moor, and propose to spend today and tomorrow in the same way'.

From Thirsk he reports that Ripon has 'some exceeding pretty scenery of a gentle kind about it':

> The day before, a very pleasant three hours' stroll, but with no very good scenery—(all soft)—and the air more southern than northern.
>
> In all the outlying streets of this place, and at Kilverton beyond, the cottagers frequently grow fruit trees against the outer walls of their cottages—straight up from the footway, so that in passing you could knock down the fruit with a stick. And in four cases out of five these fruit-trees are apricots.
>
> Today the rain has been falling in a fine close torrent, and so I 'stick about'.
>
> Which is the boy's birthday?

The following year, in August, he is at Pickering again, and we get more indications of his delight in moor and sky:

> On Thursday morning, after the post comes in, I propose to go to Gothland, about ten miles on the edge of a broad moor, and commanding fine open views. This morning I was up there, blowing about under skies alternately inky-black and brightly blue, for three or four hours. Yesterday was spent at Grosmont, a little bit of Switzerland in miniature—crag and wood, and resplendent little patches of Alp, a roaring beck running down from dark moorland hills, the water bright-brown and foaming, like beer: the peat colours it, and it rolls through ironstone a good deal.

He reports on the air at Helmsley—'it invigorates, and stupefies'—and is 'off for a six miles stretch on a high hard road'. He has had 'three days on a fine moor, with good spacious views and splendid air; but at the little "public" had to take four meals of eggs and bacon in succession'. He adds 'no gout!'

He says sympathetically, 'I dread Miss G's coming on your account. I shall be able to get away a bit from what must be much suffering and melancholy, but for you it will not be so easy. There's where the matter touches me. But it must be done, I suppose, and indeed it would be brutal to say no.'

Hoping that his daughter's 'drives will go on, from time to time, satisfactorily', he writes from Gothland in September 1877:

> The rain has been of small hindrance, and the clouds only beautify the landscape. I had a splendid walk—from nine till one, steadily going on, and only stopping here and there to admire some new view or some fresh beautiful light on the rolling purple moors. The land all about is running with brown becks and watercourses: you are never long out of the sound of falling water: so that without rings on his fingers or bells on his toes, the saunterer has music wherever he goes. Before dinner I mean to have another hour's ramble (in this fine air you do not easily tire) and after dinner come the newspapers, and to bed at 9.30. Seven is my hour of rising, and I get a stroll before breakfast. It is very cold here. In the mornings I am glad to thrust my gloveless blue fingers into my pockets; and I write and read with a shawl over my knees. All very restful and quiet.

A year afterwards he is once again in Yorkshire and is realistic about life in 'Richmond—beautifully placed, very beautifully' but—

> dispiriting to the last degree. There are not twenty decent houses in it: and except one person in the garb of a clergyman, and one other who kept the stationery and fancy shop, I did not meet with a soul who looked of the middle class or above it. A great hotel in wh. I had luncheon was filthy; and I was waited upon by a foul old man with a black eye. It was quite irritating to breathe in so grey, dull. squalid a town so beautifully pitched.

At the doors of some six or seven of the fifty beer shops was a group of working people in their Sunday clothes: the women watchfully sober and the men all drunk: this was at midday.

In a letter reporting that 'Whitby is a miserable place', he says: 'I go daily in fear of an outbreak of gout. Being caught in a shower this morning, for instance, my left foot is burning; and so it has been off and on four or five times, careful as I am. My constant depression of spirits has the same origin, I hope.'

In August he sent 'memoranda of direction' by which the family is to join him, and enters into household problems:

I am very glad that you have got a pleasing paper for your room. I had rather you got the room done well and nicely once for all. Well painted, it will last for ten years as you use the room, and I want to see it look pretty: let it be painted in keeping with paper. Perhaps the enclosed scrap may give idea enough as to the shelves.

The servant Fanny is to be brought:

Be at the station a *good ½ hour* before train starts. While the boy and Fanny see the luggage into the van, you and Jess go to the train and take places; after getting tickets of course. Places soon fill up, and corners are in demand. The *left* side of train *going out* is the shadiest, I think. Don't mind drinking and eating on the way: my little boy might carry the provender.

On May 30 Greenwood sent his daughter four cuttings from the *Pall Mall* pasted down on copy paper of the fine quality he used. He heads the first—three quarters of a column—'F. G.'s Observations on Mr. B. Jones's Pictures'. An extract—about half of it—may be given of this entertaining notice as an indication not only of what a number of instructed people thought of Burne-Jones at that time, but of Greenwood's powers as an art critic. The five canvases are 'The Annunciation' and the story of Pygmalion, in its four successive stages.

We have on various occasions acknowledged that Mr. Jones is a painter of very remarkable gifts and capabilities; at the same time it seems to us that those gifts and capabilities might be yet more remarkable than they are without justifying the praises heaped upon him by the more excited of his admirers. Certainly these pictures do not justify rhapsodical encomium. They have only to be looked at soberly, only to be appraised as all such work should be, and they will be found very moderate examples of the painter's skill.

The Annunciation is unquestionably faulty in the highest degree. Look upon the angel, look upon the Virgin, and it will be seen that if one had come to declare and the other to hear that a child was to be born who would bring ruin on the human race, the expression and attitude of the two figures would be appropriate enough. Had an angel announced to Eve, on the expulsion from the Garden that her first boy would be a murderer, Mr. Jones might have painted the incident just as he has painted his picture. This is no picture of the Annunciation at all. It is not a picture of one who brings ineffable honour and glory to a lowly, innocent, unexpectant girl. Of course, if upon the theory which seems to underlie all the productions of this school, joy, rightly considered, is melancholy, and glory despair, the picture is all right.

Mr. Jones should be warned that a picture like this may damage his reputation, by suggesting the inquiry whether he does not doubt his own capacity for expressing any feeling but sadness supremely well; whether his woebegone style is entirely a matter of taste and preference.

This leads us further to observe upon the way in which this everlasting effect of weariness and woe is produced. Inspection will reveal that it is for the most part accomplished by means similar to those employed by women in the flesh for a like purpose. The eyes of Mr. Jones's angels and damsels take their expression not so much from what is in them as from the way in which they are painted round about.

Of the good points in this picture of the Annunciation the most excellent is the drapery on the Virgin's figure. Nothing in its way could be more natural or more graceful. Mr. Burne-Jones has been inspired to hang his messenger from Heaven about with heavy metallic or lava-like folds suggestive of no fabric known on earth below. The shallow tones of colour in which the picture is painted are also seen in the Pygmalion series. Here mistakes are to be found which no artist should commit, and imperfections which it would have been said no artist could possibly be guilty of.

We ask attention to the figure of Venus bringing a bit of blue sky with her into a room. Better, however, to pass all matter of this kind, and simply call attention to *the foot of Venus*. It will do the rhapsodist critic good if he will scan that bit of drawing, the great toe, the whole foot, with those hideous nails imbedded in the flesh, and every line bearing testimony to congenital bad form distorted by tight boots.

Greenwood followed up by writing a skit in the form of an anonymous letter to the editor in which, as 'Q.T.', he says:

> Just by way of pitting Nature against Art, you know—I am ready to back my pedal extremities for beauty, either or both of them against Mr. Burne Jones's Venus for any money not over £5,000 and not under £5. Or if that will not do, I'll back against her, in this respect, the first man that walks out of the Burlington Arcade after the clock strikes four any afternoon! I am to be heard of on application to the porter of the Marlborough Club, Pall Mall.

'Tremendous flutter in aesthetic circles' adds Greenwood on the slip for his daughter. 'Sidney Colvin, rising to the fly, replies by proposing that "Q.T." should ask the opinion which he proposed of the three first foreign artists of repute whom he may find in England on the merits of Mr. Burne-Jones's work in general this year, and of the picture of the Annunciation in particular.' In the *Saturday Review* 'Mr. Comyns Carr, director of the Grosvenor Gallery, and a quite too awfully fine-art person' has a two-feet long article on 'Art Criticism by Wager' in which the *Pall Mall*, mentioned eleven times or over, is vigorously belaboured. Greenwood also pastes on his sheets for Kate a letter in the *Pall Mall* in which Legros (Slade Professor of Fine Art, University College, London), W. B. Richmond (Slade Professor of Fine Art in the University of Oxford), and Sidney Colvin (Slade Professor of Fine Art in the University of Cambridge) unite in declaring that the roughly-handled work of Burne-Jones 'and most especially the Annunciation, are of the very highest order both of imaginative and technical power, and such as would have done honour to any school at any period of history'.

CHAPTER XXXII

More Notables and Family Cares

'THE ONLY ONE WHO HADN'T A TITLE' — THE FRESHMAN AT OXFORD —'THE WORST BLUNDER OF MY EDITORIAL CAREER' — 'STICK UP TO FATE ALL OF US' — PRINCE LEOPOLD AND PRINCESS CHRISTIAN

ONLY three of Greenwood's letters are written on *Pall Mall* paper—'*Pall Mall Gazette*, Northumberland Street, Strand', embossed in blue, which we were still using when I served in the office from 1888 to 1893. One of them says, 'I've been very unwell and very desponding for a good many days together. If I could lie by for a month or two I should go to [Sir Richard] Quain: otherwise I feel that it is useless.' He goes on to mention the parlour maid, the window box, and the bird Reuben who 'seemed very puffy this morning: I'm afraid there's no keeping these wilder birds long'.

When you go on the water—and it will be good to go just as often as you feel inclined—you ought to have all your wraps aboard. Buy any little thing, print or what not, that takes your fancy, or that Jessie [the name is usually spelt by the family, 'Jessy'] would like. (*How about* her *birthday* present? *Can you give me a hint*?)

I dined last night at Oppenheim's in very fine company, from ambassadors (German) downwards: I was the only man, of about 8, who hadn't a title, and only two of us were baronets. Tomorrow I dine at Putney with Mrs. Stanley.

Take care you stint yourselves in no way. The hotel bill was no bigger than that sort of document usually is. I send two *Budgets* [the weekly edition of the *Pall Mall*].

In June 1879 he wants Kate to 'stay on' somewhere, is concerned about a 'rheumatic touch' of hers—she is to 'see the best doctor in the town'—and, for himself, expresses a wish to live in the country for the rest of his life:

On Sunday a recollection of Lamb's love for the Hertfordshire lanes and of a wide stretch of really lovely quiet, reposeful country between Edgware (Middlesex) and Watford on one hand and St. Albans on the other, took me down to that district. I walked for five hours, and for six (counting a good three-mile walk after dinner, in the twilight) on Monday; and all the time amidst exquisite greenery —tree and meadow and gorse, now a little uphill, now a little down hill, without coming once upon a piece of brown earth or any sign or sight of ugliness.

I only wish I could live at rest in such a country for whatever time remains to me.

On Friday last, not wishing to disappoint Captain C, I accepted an invitation to dine in Eaton Terrace. I had a very stout woman who did her best to put me at my ease, bringing me out by asking me whether I took any interest in politics. Opposite was a parson who, as he ate and as he drank, and in every word that dropt from his lips, talked of sacraments, offices, services, vestments, in glib incessant drawl, and obviously with no notion whatever of his gross irreverence. 'I gang nae mair to your town.'

The Virginian [the parrot] has just burst into a blaze of jug-jugging in the dark of the dining room. He does that often now.

In the previous letter, an eight-pager, there was one page about the rhododendrons in the garden; in another note he speaks of the ferns, lilies, and carnations. He is disappointed at not having news from Kate—I have twice found him enclosing notepaper—and if she has not received money he sent her she is to telegraph. He proceeds about the people he is seeing:

I dined with Mrs. Stanley on Sunday: Lord and Lady Airlie, Sir Henry Thompson, Sir James Fitzjames Stephen, Mr. Froude, and Mr. Newton. Went to Cosmopolitan Club afterwards, where there were a dozen celebrities. Thursday I dine with Lord Reay.[1] Friday, I am sorry to say, I engaged myself to dine with Chamberlain M.P. at Richmond. Most probably I shall meet you at the station though, if you come home on that day.

[1] I remember a talk with this simple, useful public servant, the head of the clan Mackay, eleventh Baron Reay and first president of the British Academy. He was born in Holland, and was naturalized in England at thirty-eight. He was for a time an Indian Governor and Secretary for India.

All 'society' is in a rage with Carey for leaving the Prince Imperial[1] to shift for himself. I do not remember any more lively or more general feeling of indignation and disgust. It is not, perhaps, quite fair.

In an October letter there is an account of his boy's introduction to Oxford:

The journey would have been more pleasant if boy had not seemed so anxious, nervous and gloomy. It was more like going to prison than to the beginning of life in an easy and hopeful way. However, I think he is rather more at ease now. We have seen Dr. Percival, a pleasant man whom I rather took to. Tomorrow boy is to go to him again with other 'freshmen': he will then be handed over to the bursar; some pecuniary arrangements will have to be transacted; and on Saturday morning, probably (if not tomorrow) the boy will go before the Vice Chancellor for admission formally. We have got lodgings, recommended by Dr. Percival: they look upon a broad cheerful street, and are opposite the College gate. But they are mean rooms, and very poorly furnished; the rent about twice what it ought to be. However, he can shift next term if he does not go into residence. The lodgings are over a bookseller's shop; and Dr. Percival says the house is kept by very respectable people.

He notes that Edgar should 'become more self-reliant than unfortunately he is'.

With the following letter, we come to the starting of the *St. James's Gazette*. On May 28, 1880, he says:

I should say, Come back sooner, seeing how anxious you are to be at home just now, only it really hardly seems worth your while as matters stand. Saturday and Sunday and Monday I shall be at work (or worse) all the days, and should be little visible to you. By Tuesday, I hope devoutly things will be settling down.

I'm still haunted by a doubt whether we shall get our 3rd machine

[1] The son of Napoleon III. Slaughtered with his company by Zulus during the campaign against Cetewayo. 'The circumstances were not creditable to the officer in charge of the party.' Sir Evelyn Wood, one of the last officers to gain promotion by purchase, conducted the Empress Eugénie to Zululand to see the grave.

actually at work (and if we don't we shall not be able to make much more than ½ the supply of papers that seems demanded), but the people in charge say it shall be done. The most sanguine man of all is Vizetelly—who tells me he expects that we shall sell 20,000 copies of No. 1. I expect nothing of the kind, but V's judgment is generally good in such matters. Tomorrow we shall print a trial number.

I did not fail to observe how carefully and kindly you had gone over the house here to provide for my comfort and care, before you left London. I saw the print of your hand in a dozen places.

By August he is able to get away to Pickering for walks in his loved Yorkshire:

It has been all walking in mud, and for the most part in rain. Nevertheless on Tuesday I got a very good walk and came upon really fine scenery. Yesterday (rain for ¾ of the time) I had a yet longer walk and over much better ground. Here I came across a very fine bit of the striking order: and the scene, for five miles out of seven, was all very good. The roads are high roads in a double sense; and the hedges are for the most part delightfully low, so that as you walk you can see over a great stretch of country. That is the great charm. For an hour at a time yesterday I seemed to be on as high ground as anybody and to see over 20 miles of undulating land, prettily studded at intervals with timber. But all this 20 miles was by no means grand, or more than picturesque, to look at.

Yesterday's walk was diversified by an adventure wh. brought me to the verge of an attack of gout. This adventure was the chasing of three horses out of a great field of green barley: no easy business. The rain had gathered in the barley, and by the time I had got my horses out (you must know it was myself who had let them in) my boots were wetter than I knew perhaps. On I went for six or seven miles after that, and no sooner had got in than my left large toe began to burn and swell.

In 1880 Kate, Jessy, and Edgar have gone to Switzerland, and in sending them money he hopes 'you will do all you can to make your holiday agreeable. Don't mind a pound or so. You are all so good that I should be distressed if you missed any opportunities. My love to my other girl, and my boy.' There follow letters of credit for £50 with the injunction: 'Pray don't worry about the cost: I do assure you it worries me to think you give a moment's care about spending as much as you need to be quite comfortable. Say no more about it—think no more about it: but enjoy yourselves as much as you can.' There is a reference to the *St. James's*.

I've had no fresh troubles about the paper worth consideration. The worst of it is that fifty difficulties start up when I think of going for a rest: it really seems as if the whole machine here hangs upon my several fingers.

I dine at home almost every day (for some ten days now with one exception.)

My father, I hear, is very well indeed—my mother pretty well; and both as happy and contented as possible. I am going to see them soon.

He announces on August 11 that he has 'got rid of the worst fit of "depression" that I think I ever suffered from; never was more down in all my life without reason why very clear'. At home the pets are 'all right; but both seem downhearted'. 'Punch is dull, certainly I think: he misses the family, and the attentions of one member of it do not suffice for that large-hearted bird.' The travellers are not to 'worry about the bill; it's long since you had such a trip, and you deserve it ten times over'. [Next month, too, he is writing, 'Never mind the bills'.] 'If you wonder at the aspect of this letter, know that it is written by a sort of pen-pencil that F. Drummond has just given me.'[1]

At the end of the month he has been 'out of town most of the days getting afternoon walks and lounges—with goodish results'. He is concerned that he has forgotten Edgar's birthday. 'If you think him really ill send me a telegram.' 'On Saturday afternoon I went to George Gibbs'[2] place at Elstree, returning this morning: a nice place and very nice people: I hope you will

[1] The coming of the fountain pen. The year is 1880. See, for a remarkable series of types, three well-illustrated lectures delivered before the Society of Arts, Jan. 23 and 30 and Feb. 6, 1905, which Mr. F. C. Guildford courteously lent me.

[2] One of the proprietors of the *St. James's*.

be acquainted soon with the ladies,—homely, pleasant people, after your own heart, I think.'

In September we hear for the first time of the Baroness Burdett-Coutts, to whose friendship reference will be made later on. He dined with her at Holly Lodge, and 'came away with a whole essay in my head: a pretty page it would make in a journal all told'. The man the Baroness had married, much her junior, had been her secretary and took her name. A gossip of the time tells me that the ceremony was fixed for 'ten in the morning and that Sir James Lacaita was called out of bed at 8 a.m. to be best man'.

Greenwood continuing his letter, says: 'The animals are all right: though the Virginian's tail has been fretted to fiddle-strings. Punch is the dearest little creature. My foot is no sooner within doors than he calls to me with affectionate impatience, and he never fails to give me his little song when I go to him of an evening; and I do believe it is more tenderly sung than ever.'

Then he gets to Brussels and has his adventure:

> Yesterday, to the museum and came away in such condition that a glass of brandy at a confectioner's near by was eagerly swallowed. Five or six young ladies—(apparently a part of a ladies' school)—were in the museum, and seemed to enjoy it very much, lingering especially about the enclosed spaces containing pictures too horrible for public exhibition and the wh. are viewed (as probably you observed) through peep holes. I peeped into two; and it was the second that sent me off to the pastry cook's.

Writing from London he speaks of having good walks on three successive days and says: 'They sent me an invitation to Hughenden, on the day Lord Beaconsfield was buried, but I could not go; and am very sorry for it. Tonight I dine with Mr. Pender. It is what he calls his Academy dinner: at the festival of last year it was that I met Mr. Gladstone, you may remember.'

His news from home in May is: 'Birds properly attended to. Hedgehog lively, but does not seem to have made much impression upon the host [beetles] he was called in to disperse.' But he follows on with his views on Lord Salisbury:

On Monday a dinner at the Rabelais club (than wh. nothing could be less Rabelaisian.) This evening I dine with Sir Rutherford Alcock (I wish people would let me alone) and that is all for this week I hope.

Lord Salisbury is forcing himself into the leadership in the most resolute and unscrupulous way: if he goes to the top, there's an end to all hope of harmony in *that* party, and to all chance of their being helped against the Radicals (effectually) by Whigs and Liberals.

If Lord S. is appointed, as I don't doubt he will be, it will be because his friends knew he would make himself too disagreeable if they refused him. But it is a mistake, wh. his party will bitterly regret. It throws Lord Derby (his foe) more nearly into the opposite ranks, and Lord D. is the most popular man in the country, after Mr. G. and may even resolve Lord D. to take office with the Liberals, even while Mr. Gladstone lives.

He had been sending the *St. James's* and is 'concerned about a very grave error wh. Mr. F. Drummond let us in for'.

The oath, upon wh. that article about Bradlaugh was written, is *not* the oath in force now at all. It is the worst blunder we have ever made in the whole of 16 years of my editorial career. The form of oath was altered in 1868: *substantially* it is the same now; but the form has very much to do with the matter. I expect we shall hear more than enough about it. I begged D. to be careful of his facts; I had no memory of the change, nor had Mr. Traill. Pity!

At Seaford, which has 'a fine bright, clean, spring-water sort of air', he had 'some good cliff-downs to walk upon, and slept like a top'. Returning to London, he continues to dine out and to wish he hadn't:

I had an awful evening at ——. Nobody there but myself, a coarse greasy dinner (fault, the cook) and much gabble of talk, host and hostess speaking of different subjects at the same time, and I replying to both, that I went home with the bones of my skull jarring together. Yesterday I was out to dinner again—with Mr. Watts, to meet Mr. Woolner[1] and Colonel Moncrieff, both my friends, and

[1] G. F. Watts, the painter, to whom Ellen Terry was married as a girl, and Woolner the sculptor.

the evening was pleasant enough: but too long. This evening I go to the Lathbury's, on Lathbury's account, who wants to talk of the proposed new paper [the *Pilot*]. For tomorrow I was asked by Mrs. Stanley to meet Sir S. Northcote: but no: I've had enough of it for this week: and shall go into the country instead.

By the way, I went to see 'Othello' again on Monday: Irving a much better Moor than Booth: Booth's Iago not so good as Irving's.

He has twice urged that Jessy should see Sir Richard Quain. She and Kate are in the country as he is himself. He says, 'I get very knocked up from time to time: and either I have much more to do than I used to have, or I do not get through it with my old force and rapidity.' His chit-chat is

Mr. Grant Allen is a smallish, fair, feeble-looking man of about 35 or so—nearly beardless, if I remember right.

I had a letter from Wood[1] the other day, full of expressions of gratitude for a certain article I wrote in his favour.

I go downstairs of an evening to get a little bottle of wine. The hedgehog is reported very amicable and lively but not much of a match for the beetles.

Writing the same month he continues to be the attentive father: 'I can have no satisfaction in the world so great as the belief that you and Jessy and the boy are comfortable. I am exceedingly sorry about the little blaze on your cheek; but you may rely upon it it will gradually tone down. Jessie's freckles will soon disappear: I'm glad to hear of them: they are not bad signs at all. A couple of cheques I send. I'm as certain that I'm alive that you are a good little housewife, and I never want a word of explanation of any kind whatever. Stay on yet awhile.' He adds some town and country news:

I spend Saturday afternoon and yesterday in the country and am today quite bright and well indeed: wh. seems to show that no harm's done by all the worry and work.

The Oppenheims asked me to dinner on Sunday to meet Lord Hartington, (of course the Duchess of Manchester)[2] and various

[1] Sir Evelyn Wood.

[2] Whom Lord Hartington later married.

other great people; but I preferred the downs, and the gorse, and the cowslips: and my conscience approves the choice today.

Thompson's [election] defeat was very complete: a disgraceful beating.[1]

The Conservatives have reason already to regret that they made Lord Salisbury their leader. His pledges and promises, in the Tunis business, hamper them exceedingly: and he can't open his mouth (as I warned his party would be the case, you remember) without an instant cry of 'violent Toryism', 'opposition to the will of the people' and so forth.

He has been in the Welsh hills and has seen somewhere a dog that 'beats all the dogs I've ever seen (except Dolly) for native humanity'. But he has to get home 'very much on account of the paper, wh. for the last three weeks has been hideously pointless, spiritless, and dull'. Later, in a note to 'My very dear Kate' from Highclere Castle he says: 'This is to say Good Morning for me tomorrow (and for me it was a good day when you were born) and to convey the good wishes of your gratefully affectionate Father. I wish I were at home. Visits like this are usually poor, empty, and wasteful: and though I have found exceptions here, as well as elsewhere, this is not of them.'

But he finds the persistence of his daughter's cough 'most disappointing: I must go and talk to Quain about it; you ought to stop down at Hastings a little longer'. He is glad she walks 'as much as 4 miles a day, enough', says the Victorian, 'for any young woman at any time'. In a few days he is expressing 'a very great regret' that 'your outing seems to have done you no good'. He adds: 'I have to dine with the Gibbs tomorrow to discuss the affairs of the paper.'

In the autumn of 1882 he is writing from Derbyshire in country 'bald, bare and open and good to walk in'.

That you got downstairs is I hope a presage of better things. As to D. H., let him have some rope: a long absence, you know, and the worst would be any clouds between you and Jessie. It is possible

[1] Henry Yates Thompson, second proprietor of the *Pall Mall*. He had stood for Parliament.

that I may have crammed that little paper of trinkets into some drawer. Of course I do not for a single moment suspect the girls of knowing anything about it: it did not even occur to me.

Chapel-en-le-Frith I found a very beastly place, with an indescribable look of insolent slovenliness and dirt not unprosperous. So I plodded on Castleton way about four miles out and four miles in, and a beautiful walk it would have been but for a fog. I was solaced on the road by a luncheon of the best bread, the best cheese, the best butter I have ever tasted all together: and, (with a pint of beer in) I had to pay sixpence for it (6d.) There's a good high walk from here through Pilsley and that I shall go for tomorrow: I want to see that country and roam about in it for two or three days if possible.

He goes through 'bleak profitless-looking ranges of hill scarred with mine heaps and scorched with stone walls', but 'I had a walk in the direction of Edale wh. was very good'.

He thinks that Kate should certainly buy a servant 'a tea service' and hopes the girl 'will do well married', though 'the beginnings do not look very easy'. The business of getting a new servant (*temp.* 1882) 'will be very troublesome'. His New Year's Day (1883) greeting is:

My dear Kate, and Jessy, and Edgar, I have been blaming myself for not being at home this morning, and am all the more inclined to do so now that I get your little letter—though I half expected it. And a happy New Year to you, my dears, who are all my thoughts when I think for myself. And if it does not turn out quite so happy, as I'm a little afraid it may not for some reasons, I hope we shall be able to stick up to Fate like men, all of us. My everlasting love to you. Your affectionate and grateful Father.

He condoles with Kate and Jessy on the discomforts of getting to Guernsey, though they 'stood up against it in a manly way'. They are to be 'careful not to walk too much, and have a carriage often. As soon as you are lodged I had better send you a small case of wine: or can you get it good there? Probably you can.' But he is troubled by 'the boy's refusal to go with you; there has not been much conversation in Argyll Road since'. His news in May is that the oilcloth has come and he has dined again with the Baroness Burdett-Coutts. 'The enclosed will show Jessy that she has not forgotten her.' His intention is to 'go off on Saturday for a Sunday, and perhaps a Monday stroll'. '*Don't come home so soon*. Don't trouble about gas and water bills or anything of the sort. I'll see to that, with Edgar's assistance: he's good at it, if I'm careless.' He speaks of Oliver Wendell Holmes and also about a cab accident:

Had a pleasant dinner last night,—much pleased with Holmes—a delicate, fine, small, slender little figure; with a sweet face, genial, benignant, humorous. No swagger: homely and nice altogether.

Going home horse fell suddenly; body of cab, separating from the springs behind, came clean forward—like a hood—top of it falling in front and completely enclosing me. Horse's hind quarters just under my nose. Cabman pitched forward—unhurt: in a great state of funk (for me) calling for help. No getting out except through one of the side windows. Window accordingly smashed in—I covering my head and face to avoid flying fragments; when all the glass had been knocked out, I partly crawled, partly was hauled through—all safe. (*Moral*: ride in omnibuses or walk.) One hand slightly bruised and lacerated, and that's all. Felt not in the least fright, thank goodness, gave the cabman half a sovereign as a sort of thank offering, and got back, and slept none the worse. But it was a very ugly situation, to look back upon.

At the end of May a letter mentions being at Lord Carnarvon's again:

A nice small company, with Sir S. and Lady Northcote, Sir Matthew and Lady White Ridley, Lady What's-her-name who was Mrs. Lowe, Sir F. D. Acland, with Mrs. Howard (who was very nice to me, and seems a thorough good homely sort of woman for her rank) and her daughter, and of course Lady Winifred, (who is charming) and one of Lord Portsmouth's daughters. Afterwards I went to the Foreign Office reception (Lady Granville's) and there met, amongst others, Lady Portsmouth, who asked most kindly about you. Tomorrow I've a luncheon (Sir George Birdwood's[1]—

[1] The Anglo-Indian official who, in a letter to *The Times*, as the *D.N.B.* puts it, 'led popular sentiment to associate the primrose with the memory of Lord Beaconsfield'.

a downright nuisance this luncheoning) and this evening I must go to Lady Ridley's though I'm not much fit for it.

In June he is 'just off for Stevenage', but 'there's neither rest nor recreation in these visits to fine places and fine people. However, it will not last long'. He is 'rather bothered' at getting no letters from Kate. In August she, Jessy, and 'boy' are to join him in Yorkshire. 'Boy might bring me a couple of boxes of cigarettes.' At Reigate by himself he gets 'MSS and proofs etc. every morning and evening'. Back in Derbyshire he is glad of having 'a good thick pair of boots'. His eye troubles him,[1] and 'there have been floods of rain; the whole place steams at sunset with a reek like cotton-wool'. He is afraid Kate is 'dreadfully bothered: it is always the way with these plasterers and decorators—they get worse and worse'. November brings pencilled urgings to go to Bournemouth.

Today I send you two novels: either or both of wh. may be good for notice. And I intend soon to send you a small parcel of children's books, wh. you might take up at odd moments and intervals. These may help you: they will certainly give you some relief in the way of abstraction from the disagreeables about you. Of course you will keep a good fire in your room always and take every possible care of yourself.

I've a letter from Jessie, all agog again for going to Germany: has been assured by her German master that she can get into a clergyman's family for 30£ a year. It worries me very much to know what to say or do.

And here's my brother Alfred lost his wife (after confinement) leaving him with 12 children—three of whom are off his hands.

The next letter is mainly about a 'Mrs. C's exigence'. 'She has really no resources in herself and does not understand that anybody can wish to be alone or do anything more than gossip and saunter through the day.' His Sunday holiday was 'a very good one: splendid day for good walking'.

In March 1884 he is sympathizing with Kate over some 'larky children'. For himself in London he 'quite enjoyed walking

[1] See page 425.

about without a great coat: felt quite spry and young'. He is 'engaged in an endeavour to get Edgar to go to Mrs. James's At Home; but doubt my success'. Kate is to take 'great care not to go out, or only a little, and in the most favourable hours'. At home he has the comfort of 'the sober and well-endeavouring Ellen' and 'they seem to have cleared or to be clearing out the dustbin'.

I was to have gone to a Lord Mayor's dinner this evening, but, like many other entertainments, it has been put off in consequence of Prince Leopold's death. I have none but good memories and impressions of his demeanour and character. On Thursday I had luncheon at Wimpole Street with the Princess Christian, who wanted to see me about nothing in particular as usual.

He sends 'a batch of books wh. I believe you will find amusing; more magazines shall follow, and more books'. He adds, 'I think so much of quiet in the country that I forget its drawbacks.'

In August, 1886, he is back at Reeth, near Richmond. The road there,

a beautiful road, looked lovely in the light, rainy sunshine. But presently the clouds gathered and darkened, and while the dogcart spanked along at its best, down came as pretty a storm of wind, hail, and rain as you could wish for. There was nearly half an hour of this. But driving in that sort of weather is no distress to me.

Reeth village, on the side of a mound, with a good broad green, is surrounded but not hemmed in by good fall-back hills of very various line. Less than half a mile from the inn begins a stretch of rolling heath in full bloom. At the foot of the village, Swale-dale, softly picturesque. Ten minutes to the wild hills, ten minutes to the romantic dale. The road hard, the air fine and bright.

I am seriously thinking that you might do much worse than make up your minds to join me. The sitting room is big enough for us all, and I don't doubt there are bedrooms enough. The expense of travelling would be made up by the smaller amount of the weekly bills. Every place for fifty miles round London is very dear and *they* have to be travelled to also.

Under a 'high blue sky, masses of silver cloud with threatening undersides, the shadows moving fast over the hills', he has had 'a good breezy walk 2½ hours long'.

A later letter says:

This morning, at half-past ten, started to walk over the lofty ridge of hills that divides Swaledale from Wensleydale. Got over and down far enough to look into Wensleydale, and then back. Fine panoramic views, and your foot on heather almost whenever you chose to turn aside from the road. During the 3½ hours the wind very keen and F. G. very warm.

'Shootists' are banging or rather popping about here in great numbers and extraordinary *déshabillé*. It seems that to shoot well you must dress like a London costermonger as nearly as possible. I hate the sound of their guns, and don't doubt they would despise me for hating it.

Three days after his arrival at Reeth he wants his young people with him:

It does not at all interest me that you and Jessie and Edgar should have only a fortnight in the country. Now this is what I desire, and I hope there will be nothing against it. Come down on Friday morning. Get ready to do so. I mean to go over to Wensleydale on Monday morning. There is an inn at Aysgarth that will suit me very well, if I can get into it. I believe I can find nice accommodation for you in that neighbourhood for a week, and then we will come here for the rest of the time. My reason for this is that you cannot come here in one day: you would be too tired. You would get into Wensleydale at five o'clock: and it would not matter if you stayed for two or three days at Leyburn.

My only fear about *this* place is that you would find the accommodation rather rough. But there is a good double-bedded room, the sitting room is good enough, the room I occupy is quite satisfactory and Edgar will be all right. The people of the house do their best in everything, but I am not sure you would not find the living and service rather too 'homely'. However, I get on well enough, though a good deal spoiled by the perfect housekeeping at 19 Argyll Road. I am *particularly desirous* of you coming out no later than Friday. I have been counting on it. As for expense, I am sure you won't do better, probably not as well. And it is a really good change. Air and scene excellent.

Later he specifies requirements:

Arrangements have been made. You will find it well to bring some *warm clothing*, for it is cold sometimes. Also I advise the bringing of books, as many as you can. Please bring me the one-vol Shakespeare. I am afraid Edgar will not have a chance of bicycling, but lots of chances of photography. If he has a mind to spend a little money in enlarging his apparatus, tell him I beg him to do so. I found the second class very comfortable: take single tickets by all means, you will have to change at *York*. Please bring me a few sheets of copy paper, and if you have them, some of those correspondence cards. If you can find room for my frock coat and waistcoat, and for my hat-box with tall hat (the inside will carry small articles), good. I shouldn't bring *best* frocks to any extent if I were you, but the older ones that are good for pottering about. You must not be sure of linen sheets at Reeth: whether you would like to bring a couple is for you to consider. I recommend a *good* supply of chocolate: and a tin or two of game or other paste for sandwiches would be good.

When he gets back to town, and Kate is in Scotland, he mentions 'dining with Oppenheim'. Kate is staying with an old friend of Greenwood's called Kinnear, who is standing against Mr. Asquith. Her father says 'these clannish Fifeshire men will want to know "Who's Asquith"'?[1]

I am most heartily sorry about Goschen, and if Edinburgh is not ashamed of turning him out, so much the worse for Edinburgh. No doubt you marked the sudden scream of joy evoked at Hawarden, and 'wire' to 'dear old Edinburgh'. We are not so 'dear' to him in London, but I flatter myself we are much more worthy. All the metropolitan constituencies, as you have seen, have shown a splendid spirit of indifference to Mr. G's *cajoleries*: and I don't doubt but he has had some yearning thoughts about the baker's shop in Pudding Lane, where the Fire began wh. ended in Pye Corner. Not that I think Mr. G. will give up office without a more absolute compulsion than he would find in the present figures. There are more aces yet up that old gentleman's sleeve.[2]

[1] Asquith was successful and sat for East Fife for thirty-two years.

[2] F. G. is referring to Labouchere's saying: 'I do not object to Gladstone's always having the ace of trumps up his sleeve, but only to his pretence that God had put it there'.

Sir C. Dilke, I hear, is shockingly rejected: I almost begin to pity him a little, though against her (Lady D.) my heart is quite hardened, I'm afraid. However, he is out, and one or two more most objectionable creatures: Professor Rogers,[1] for example.

As to his health, 'I'm generally very well when there is a good scrimmage going on.'

What you tell me about yourself deeply distresses me. It is so unaccountable, so untouchable. I do hope the medicine and advice will help you.

You will be wise in keeping off those thorny questions of politics as much as you can: it doesn't do you good to discuss them. *I* don't doubt that you can take care of yourself, but it is better not to have to do it; and you need not tell me you are conscious of not being hardhearted and contemptuous of poor people, or the 'masses'. We *do* misunderstand each other, though, terribly.

Next day, however, he thanks Kate for her 'interesting and instructive letters', declares that she is 'a real politician', and shows her 'precisely how affairs have been going, and why'. He mentions that he is 'invited to the Marlborough House Garden Party to-day "to have the honour of meeting the Queen". But [the thought of] four or five hours in that garden, sticking about till 9 o'clock for dinner, and a cold ride home at night, has put my foot "back" enough to resolve me not to go. I confess, however, I am very sorry to give it up.'

[1] Thorold Rogers, the economist.

CHAPTER XXXIII

Royalties, Birds, and Hostesses

G. A. SALA — LABOUCHERE AND THE DILKE CASE — PRINCESS CHRISTIAN AGAIN — THE EMPEROR FREDERICK — 'FRIVOLOUS RELIGIOSITY'

GREENWOOD continues to meet well-known people at dinner, but their talk is not always so very interesting. 'I went out to dinner yesterday—a good company—Lord and Lady Salisbury, Lord and Lady Randolph, L. and L. Wemyss, L. and L. Pembroke, Goldwin Smith, Buckle, and your father:—yes, and Sir H. and Lady Maine. I've known nicer dinner-parties, but it was fairly nice. The conversation all political, but loose, and not a word of news or novelty in it.' The heat is 'terrible' this July and he has 'some lingering botheration' with his foot. 'It has kept me from going about, so that I am not so well informed at this moment of what is going on in the political world as I usually am. But I shall be able to go to dine to meet the Princess, this evening, and am pretty sure to see somebody there.'

A correspondent of his 'seems to have been delighted with the redoubtable G. A. Sala, and to have thought a great deal of Mrs. Sala'. 'Edgar', he records, 'is very nice to me now that he feels me under his care.' A letter of July 24 is nine pages long and affords the following extracts on a variety of topics:

I went to the grand party at the Colinderies [Colonies and India Exhibition]—really the nicest, most brilliant, the most splendid entertainment I have been at for some time. 'Everybody' there, from the Prince of Wales to Frederick Greenwood. Mrs. Drummond I took to somehow, with a little leap of feeling, as if she had at some time belonged to me. Still handsome and young-looking for her age, but *very* stout: on the verge of being thought unwieldy. Rosebery came up to me very cordially; even Harcourt gave me a cordial-sounding 'How are yer?' The supper-rooms were splendidly furnished with flowers, fruit, and goodies of the finest description. Electric light, carpet everywhere, garden illuminated—all really beautiful; and I did a dozen times wish you had been there.

The Dilke case has made a tremendous sensation. Yesterday (couldn't help it) I had a talk with Labouchere. This gentleman was in consultation with Sir C. D. over the evidence before it came out, and says the case was worse than it looked in court. Mr. L's own account of the dodges *he* recommended to get his friend out of the scrape were astoundingly impudent and cynical. He says Sir C. D. was very confident of success. I hear he is watched, in fear that he may kill himself.

Here's a piece of news I get in confidence. But can you believe it? Lord S. has offered the Viceroyalty of Ireland to Lord Carnarvon! What on earth it means is beyond my intelligence. Were it known, there would be shouts of laughter all over England—grins of delight all over Ireland.

Let me know in good time to send you money for your return, etc.:—good tips to servants.

I am very sorry and much disappointed that the change has not done more for you. Of course it is not an exciting place, Kinloch, but the absence of domestic solicitudes, and the good air, and the pleasant friends might have been expected to produce a better result than from your last letter I fear it has. In any case it will not be long before I see you again, and then we must see what is to be done next.

He concludes: 'My love to you, my dear, and to Jessy. You are both of you more and more to me, year by year: and it's the same whether you are at home or away:—that makes no difference.' 'Edgar will presently send you Mr. Stevenson's new book *Kidnapped*, wh. you will find good. The Virginian is flourishing and affectionate.' The same month he is at Silloth on the Solway Firth, much developed to-day since my Cumberland boyhood, when I was frequently taken there.

The hot sea bath *régime*, and the good air decided me to try it. The foot seems to be improved; a freer movement in the joints. The shallowness of the Solway probably accounts for the good air: at low water there are great stretches of sand between the coasts [of England and Scotland]. If I find a craft that goes out, I shall make the trip. One fine day enabled me to see the hills on the Scottish side and the Cumberland hills too. It is certainly a very strong air—strong enough to give me a headache and a terrible attack of 'nerves' for two days.

He hears of 'a lovely village', Wetheral, five or six miles from Carlisle, so happily placed on the Eden, where I remember being for the first time in a boat:

Really a very pretty place indeed and the whole country for a few miles round very picturesque. What strikes me most in this county is the complexions of the women: except at Lewes, I never saw so many fine, milk-complexions: half the women and girls would be thought remarkable for that, in London.

I am glad to hear that Edgar made the little trip over to Calais: *that* day was well spent.

He hopes Jessy is 'not worried over her story'. Coming south, he is, with Jessy, at Stratford-on-Avon. It has 'a sort of interest that nothing can surpass. The house was much larger than we expected to find it; Ann Hathaway's cottage really *looks* as if nothing had been changed in it or about it.' In the north again he is 'quite angry' with himself 'for having lingered at Lancaster when there was so much to see at Warwick.'

It is a clean place, too, and the scenery all about is rich and sweet, with beautiful grass-bordered roads. Though the air is a little too soft for pick-up purposes, I've quite made up my mind to bring you for a round of the neighbourhood, and then on to Keswick and Patterdale. I took Jessy to see Kenilworth on a beautiful road. If Edgar were here, he would go photographically wild, if anything could move him to delirium.

With regard to Edgar, this is the way Greenwood makes a proposal on the eve of Bank Holiday the next year: 'It is of no use suggesting, I suppose, that your brother should take you a bit of a jaunt somewhere.' In August, Kate is joining her father in the Lake district and he asks her to secure 'two second class Lake tour tickets, from Keswick'. Later he is at Kenilworth again and has been wandering about Stoneleigh 'and never was out of sight of good scenery for a minute'.

There is a letter in October in which he is sorry to have missed her when he left in the morning. But he will be 'at home (D.V.) at the hour of your birth: and shall see myself, once more, prowling about in a little back garden, listening to the first cries you ever uttered'. He is 'your grateful and affectionate Father'. In December she is away somewhere and he is solicitous about 'a distressingly cold journey down. You really couldn't have put enough wraps on, within or without your gown: and I do hope you will pile them on a little more for your return journey. I dearly hope to hear that you are better.' He offers to send books. Writing on December 14, 1887, he speaks of the future Emperor Frederick:

> You take so much interest in Mackenzie and the Crown Prince that I could not resist sending you that unhappy piece of news by telegram this afternoon. One of the young Mackenzies brought it to me: a young Mackenzie who *is* like his father—voice, and name and all. He says his father thinks the matter must be rather grave. His assistant at San Remo has been writing to him to say that the throat did *not* look as well as has been generally reported, and as the German doctors at San Remo thought. But on *this* information Mackenzie did not feel justified in acting. This is between ourselves at present.

Three days afterwards he writes that he has had 'a dreadful week of it, what with work and evenings out' and asks—Kate is at Bournemouth—'Is there anything amongst the pretty things in the shops you would like to buy?'

> The august people at Windsor say that the Crown Prince is better; that latest reports represent his case as much more hopeful. 'It's a muddle'; in wh. amongst small things, nothing is more remarkable than the anxiety of the Royal family to hush the matter up: to have as little said about it as possible. I am going to see the Princess Christian this afternoon, and expect prayer and remonstrance.

The Princess 'made it clearer than ever that they don't like a word said that tends to throw doubt on the Prince's recovery. "Had a crow to pluck with me", and so forth. However, I stood up a bit, and she was all through very gracious: had brought some violets for me, and promised me her photograph (a new one) etc., etc.' A letter from Bangor pictures a scene far away from Princesses:

At Conway there got into my carriage a ragged wretch—a young man and good looking, really a fine type of face—handcuffed to a constable. Dreadfully haggard he looked; and not knowing what he may have been guilty of, I liked him better than another young man whom I found in the carriage at Shrewsbury, and who, before we had gone ten miles felt bound, upon the inspiration of the Holy Spirit, as he said, to speak to me of his recent conversion to Jesus after a life of sin (he must have been about 20 years old) the shabby and disgusting details of wh. he informed me of, together with an account of his family and connexions. I was glad to get rid of him at Crewe.

Writing later of a three weeks' holiday with the family, he says he does not remember 'a more pleasant, more grateful outing. What makes it so is our common enjoyment. We all enjoyed it alike, and together: a real good holiday: and if that were possible, it leaves us closer together than ever before.' Later, he is by himself and asks, among other things, for 'a pen, adroitly cut by dear Jess, who must send me the exact address of Mrs. Mary Dodge: upon wh. I will indite letters to Mrs. M. D.'—evidently about Jessy's health. One place he has been at is 'a little too much like Shrimpington-on-Sea'. By this time he is away from the *St. James's* and writes about the Emperor Frederick, Bismarck, and the young Emperor:

I left at home an address book brought from the office. In it you will find the address of Dr. Geffcken—something Schulstrasse, Hamburg, I think. Please put the address on the enclosed envelope and post as soon as may be. My purpose is to warn him against any communications to the *St. James's Gazette* with regard to the Diary: for if he is concerned in that matter, and does write or tell anything to the *St. James's*, (thinking me still there) he will certainly be betrayed.[1]

I think it very likely that he is the real communicant of the

[1] For the German connexions of the later *St. James's* see page 270.

Diary. He is not a man of *very* good judgment in practical affairs, though he is a sound lawyer, and cool and telling in controversy. That he published without hint or permission I find it hard to believe; and he is in frequent communication with some members of the royal family *here*, as well as the Prussian royal family. So that if the Empress Frederick wished to give Bismarck blow for blow, you see how it could be managed without the Empress's own direct action.

I believe the consequences of this publication will extend very far. A 'wild' Bismarck (you know what I mean) already anxious to make things more secure, and to establish his own work more completely, works with a headstrong, selfwilled, military young cub like the present Emperor, becomes more dangerous than ever: and one result in all this is to deepen the dislike of England in Germany and wear away its disguises.

He adds, 'I'm sorry for Vizetelly [prosecuted for selling Zola] but he should do a more decent trade. What contemptible stuff the London newspapers write about these murders!' [Jack the Ripper.] While staying with the Carnarvons he says: 'From two sources I learn that a rumour has been put about that I have been taken ill. I am supposed to have suffered from "reaction" against so much work and worry. We may guess the authorship of those rumours.' He feels that when he was at Bournemouth he did not do 'nearly enough work'. But he mentions contributions to the *Saturday*, *Scots Observer*, and *Contemporary*. The following has interest:

I've heard once or twice since from Annie V. much as she seems to have written to you, but with (as I think) an extension of the hand for assistance wh. does not seem quite reasonable. However, I can understand that. I have told her that her father, while he is in the infirmary, is as well cared for as he would be out of gaol—the prison walls being the only but the unavoidable difference: and that when he comes out of the infirmary we will see what can be done to make him more comfortable. The truth is, Kate, that he does deserve his punishment; and if he were a younger man I should not pity him in the least. On the other hand, offences of that sort are worse in an old man than a young one.

Writing from home he says: 'The birds all right. The little Patches look bright and comfortable, though they do not seem to be yet done with domestic cares. Punch too, is in good order, and gives me a little song every evening. And the others are all right too, each in his way.' In 1891 he is on a coach trip in the Isle of Wight and would be all right if he had not on his mind the *Illustrated London News*, for which he had begun to write. 'Whether I shall be able to do anything much seems doubtful.' He wants Lady Jeune's address, and says—and it is of interest in view of the next chapter—he has been

> on the water in a brown paper boat that will drown some of the Patmores one of these days. They want me to stop till Monday or Tuesday, and I really think will be sorry when I go. But I shall be glad to be back:—not my own master ten minutes a day, and work, or anything conducive to work, quite out of the question. Impossible, however, for any people to be more hospitable in thought and intention and endeavour.

Going forward two years to 1896, he speaks of 'a pleasant quiet evening' with the J. M. Barries at their 'very pretty little house, appointments all in thorough good taste'. Mrs. Barrie—she was Mary Ansell, a clever actress—is 'a brightlooking, cheerful, pretty little woman, with no look of the actress about her, and nothing of it in her speech. He looked as well as I have ever seen him; both made much of me, and there were lots of kindly enquiries about you and Jessy.' A letter of April 26, 1898, the last of the dated series, is about a party at the Baroness's.

> Really very brilliant: over forty guests, at four round tables, with the Baroness at head of one, Coutts another and Lord Peel and Lord Wolseley heading others. Very pleasant altogether, and your father made as much of as he deserves, at least. This evening there is to be a theatre party: Wolseley and his daughter, and I don't know who beside. Thursday morning I shall be back, and glad to be back. For these pleasures and varieties I feel almost criminal when I think of you, wh. is at least ten times a day.

In a large batch of letters the dates of which it is not possible to fix, there is one with the confession that his declining a certain invitation 'was not wisely done or perhaps I should say I overrated the reasons for refusing'. In another he thinks of 'asking one or two men to come on Saturday afternoon to a sort of cold meat dinner'. Many notes continue to express anxiety as to the comfort of the lodgings which his daughters get at sea-side or other holiday resorts, and he keeps on trying to allay Kate's anxieties about the house and servants. She is to 'have a drive every day for an hour or two, to take every means of getting you into tolerable condition. If there's anything I can send to add to your comfort, name it; you must take care that your food is as nourishing as possible.' He promises to do his best with the birds. Alas, Dan had been 'very mopy' and had come to his end. 'Every morning I see that the cages are well cleaned, and that fresh water and food is abundant. Reuben is rather dumpy.'

Lady Salisbury's reception at the Foreign Office was 'really a splendid scene; light, flowers, music, grand staircases, flowing company, all stars and garters, diamonds and laces: the black coats quite distinguished by their fewness'. He is going to dine with the Duke of Manchester, and wants to know where he shall meet Jessy in order to take her to the Baroness's. In handling a certain lady visitor, Kate should 'invite her for such a period as will not exhaust worldly topics and lead on to the wretched chatter of'—skilful phrase—'frivolous religionism'. He writes from Reigate about wallpapers and carpets:

I am afraid you are having a dreadful time, and my fear is that you will worry too much. Rather than that I'll be happy with any sort of paper and any sort of carpet. Today I telegraphed to say that of the two papers sent I liked best the one with the least colour in it (25084), though it is not quite an ideal paper. Possibly you will have better luck at Hammersmith: if not, give it up, my dear, and choose this one, or any other you may like a little better.

As to carpets, we shall get a very good thing at H's and no dearer than we calculated. I'm glad you like the Wilton in shades of red: short of something very good from the East, I like it best. If I were in London, I am afraid I could do nothing to improve matters with the painters and the servants. What I want you to do is to come here on Saturday, and stay till Monday. I send you a list of trains.

In Yorkshire he pencils for the family several pages of diary from which I take a few phrases of a true country-lover on his solitary walks; but he could also enjoy companionship—he was, it will be remembered, one of Leslie Stephen's 'Tramps'.

Sunday. The sun blazed out and the clouds on all the hills began to lift: so out I went: at end of $\frac{3}{4}$ hour, back came the vast volume of blue-black cloud. I had for $\frac{1}{2}$ hour to go through a violent storm.

Monday. The most delicious spectacle of fleeting lights and shades. One bit of hill, with emerald mosses interspersed with rich brown heath, was more beautiful than any jewel.

Tuesday. Feeling sure of afternoon and evening, wrote an article for the *Pall Mall*. As soon as that was finished, skies clouded—black with murky underskirts of yellow. Nevertheless, I trudged off down the valley road. The clouds on the hills gave them a wild grandeur; and so my ten miles' trudge (if one can be said to trudge who goes at 3 miles an hour, not including an occasional pause to scan the country) gave me four hours of pleasure.

Wednesday. The same doubtful skies, but fully warranting a long venture.

Friday. For nearly 2 miles out, road steep, footwringing, execrable: like bed of hill-stream, little pony having quite enough to do to drag my portmanteau. Then on moor—four miles of it, nearly. Breath of moor like the breath of life. But ah, the jolting! Cart rude, road ruder; in the former and over the latter my twelve stone tossed about as 'twere no more than a bandbox.

Monday. Luncheon of bread and butter half an hour on bridge; then, through a stile, a most lovely walk through meadows and (for the most part) by side of river. In this walk I went through nearly a quarter of a mile of oats such as are rarely seen—they tickled my ears on either side of the path. Out all day, from 11 till past 8.

Tuesday. Through cross country field paths; very pretty views.

Wednesday. Thunder, rain and darkness all day. No stirring out.

One missive, written in the *St. James's* office, is about his share in the framing and supporting of a House of Commons resolution in which Sir Stafford Northcote was interested. But much of all his letters is about his daughters' health. Kate at Eastbourne, he fears, is 'pulled down very much', and needs 'every kind of warming comfort in food, clothing and sunshine'.

Pray don't worry about expenses just now. We are not paupers yet, and the best use of fifty pounds more or less is found when any of us is out of health. Stay or go elsewhere just as you think best for your health. It would be a vast pity to return for some little while yet, *I* think. The prime of the year is coming on, and the chances are that if Eastbourne is doing you good now it will do you more good by and by. Of course if you would like to change your quarters for a prettier county to go about in, that is another thing. Don't think of coal scuttles or anything of the sort till you are well again. If Jessie would like to buy the picture she fancies, let it be so by all means.

Once in a note from Brussels he is fearful that a cheque of his may not be honoured because it is made out with 'a new thin steel pen'—it has been seen that he preferred quills. 'I enclose Mr. Cooper's bill that you may see that the Peacock at Rowsley is a moderate bird enough: I expected that there would be several more pounds to pay, from the general style of things.' [It has a Duke for an owner and is still comfortable.] He feels 'brighter and cheerfuller, except when thinking of home or of my faults'. In one letter he says he is sorry that Jessy is troubled about her authorship but it 'should not turn out a disappointment'. At the *St. James's*, in his absence—the letters are a little out of order here, but the reader will remember that few are dated—'they are taking things much too easily—writing what is soonest said, and with least trouble; and neglecting points suggested to them which can't be worked out without some pains, or putting them in so feeble a way as to suggest that their importance is not understood.' One day his gossip is:

Mrs. Stanley's party was a fine one; plenty of good nature, and gaiety, and humanity in general. Besides the Prince Xtn and Princess, there were Lord and Lady E. (she, *not* a gay person, but, rather, like the mother of undertakers), Sir Frederick and Lady Roberts, Lady Constance Stanley, Lady Tweeddale, Lady Salisbury,

Sir W. Gregory (who was of Ceylon, you know) and Mr. Robert Bourke. The Princess gay even unto friskiness, and everybody very pleasant. Lady Tweeddale seems ill—very thin: but looking really beautiful.

Last night I dined where was Mr. Drummond—also looking ill, and not, poor man, beautiful at all: thence I went on to a grand musical party at Mr. Oppenheim's—all the world there, and some excellent singers, as costly and delightful as could be got. This evening I am going to be quiet at home, and am most glad of the prospect. Punch is quite affectionate again; the Virginian prodigiously vociferous. Punch, I think, has added a note or two to his repertory.

That engraving is rather a hack engraving, but what its original worth is, what the value of a good copy I don't know. You might ask, and, if you like it, buy it.

At Whitby—on his way to the moors—he says 'Southend is an Italian scene compared with it'. Of Lord Carnarvon's second gift of venison Maurice Drummond is to have some. Kate is told by her father that he would have been glad had she taken with her to the Crystal Palace 'a poor little maid' called Lucy. 'Lucy affected me when she was with us some time ago, and for the same reasons: her distressful gravity was striking enough then. I should not hesitate to let Mrs. W. know that you think the child very poorly and probably lonely and fretting.' In a paragraph on *Daniel Deronda* he says, 'How strained and false all that is about mother and son.' But, with his feeling heart, already concerned about Lucy, he is troubled about a real boy: 'I'm really mortified about little Dick. I like the boy, and shall be very sorry indeed if he thinks he is thrown over. However, when I come back we can make it right by a visit to the play, perhaps.' Here is a happy letter:

My dear Kate, and my dear Jessy, It does not seem right to thank you for your letters, received this morning, but it can't be wrong to say how thankful I am for them. Your love and goodness, the being what you are to me, are the sole unfailing blessings of my life: (boy included, of course.) Your affectionate and grateful Father.

And a nice note on which to end my extracts from a budget

which, in full, would have filled half a dozen times the space that has been occupied. It has been taken up in order not only to bring out, as I have said, significant traits in Greenwood's character, but to reflect something of the temperament, outlook, and conditions of the period.

CHAPTER XXXIV

Kate Greenwood on her grim Visit to the Coventry Patmores

HOW FAR CAN SHE BE TRUSTED? — 'A TERRIBLE MAN FOR A POET' — HOW MUCH MAY BE TOLD? — A PROBLEM OF DAUGHTERS

THE first letter I have of Kate's—to 'My dearest Jessy'—was written from Frant in the *Anti-Jacobin* period. She thinks lodgings at three guineas a week for father and herself 'too much'. 'Service rougher than in any lodgings I have ever been in; I may make Mrs. Drayton'—with a husband and five children under twelve—'improve in the matter of plates.' The landlady 'worries father and me with cotton sheets' and provides a looking glass in which 'I cannot see the back of my head'.

When father asked 'the funeral tablet mason which was a pretty walk he replied, "Through the churchyard to the cemetery!"' A pony carriage is hired and 'father drives it'. Kate had arrived 'very tired and ached so much all over that I could not get to sleep for a terrible time'. 'Father is very good and does all sorts of little things for me—brought my breakfast Friday and Saturday—but I shall get up in future, as, what with waiting for the tea to draw, it is nearly 10 o'clock before he appears.' 'Father delights in Eridge Park', the Marquess of Abergavenny's place. He has read *Jess* and *Soldiers Three*. She has been reading *Troublesome Daughters*.

To what extent Greenwood's daughters were 'troublesome' the reader must form his or her opinion. I have withdrawn from inspection no scrap of material on which a view may be based. There is a photograph of one only, Jessy, a comely girl. We have to come to some conclusion as to the young women's temperament, particularly the temperament of Kate, for I am about to give her impression of a visit to the home of Coventry Patmore, which is in another key from that in which he has been sometimes presented to us. How far can her impression be trusted? In the final chapter of this book, when we take leave of Kate, there will be found appreciative accounts of her by neighbours on which reliance may be placed. She was then in her nineties and a little odd, as any of us who chance to reach her age will no doubt be. But there is abundant testimony to her strength of character during the bombings, and those who knew her liked her. At the time of her visit to the Coventry Patmores, half a century before, there can be little doubt, however, that she was in poor health; we should now say neurasthenic. She speaks indeed of being met at the station with a garden chair pushed by a son and daughter of the poet. She was a little body, only four feet four—her brother was also short. As I have said, I have no photograph. Readers of the letters are well able to make the necessary allowances. The first letter is dated July 24, 1892. The house visited is the one at Lymington. From the beginning Kate did not approve of the poet:

Mrs. Patmore [the third wife] looks as before, Gertrude worn and haggard, a sort of *battered* look, difficult to describe. Piffie[1] much improved.

And Mr. Patmore much older, and his appearance not improved by his not having shaved for a couple of days. He was very glum and grumpy too. I don't think he made a definite observation once during dinner, did not come into the drawing room at all, tea being served in his study and those who wanted any were asked to go there for it, and we were expected to go there to bid him 'Good night'. Now a man need not invite visitors, but if he does I think he is bound to exercise common civility towards them, if he wants them to feel welcome.

We went to bed at 9.30, but from what I gather of the family ways, and from my own experience of last night, all one's sleep must be obtained between 1 o'clock and 7 o'clock. They have kindly in intention given me a room next to Mrs. Patmore's. Mr. Patmore comes to bed about 1 o'clock as a rule, I believe, and between 10 o'clock and that hour he stamped and banged into his wife's

[1] Who, realizing that his father had been married three times, said to him, 'Why, father, you're half as bad as Henry VIII!'

room four times. At 7 o'clock tea is taken in, and a succession of stamping and banging begins. Piffie makes more noise with his mother's door than could be made by any hall door in Argyll Road. It is not banging in the ordinary sense; it is a clanging that suggests a medieval castle, and shakes you in your bed.

I must say, I feel horribly tired today; I had scarcely two hours' sleep. I really think the bed linen was not quite aired,—I had my doubts at first, but by 12 o'clock I just ached all over, faceache both sides included, and I am very aching today. At three o'clock I wondered what was going to happen to me. However, I don't suppose it will be anything further now, so am no longer in a fright, and you need not worry at all.

I have been all round the garden this morning; part of it is very pretty indeed, and everything is flourishing. Since I came in I have been sitting with Mrs. Patmore in her room; she is not so well and is staying in bed until luncheon at least.

Will you send Charles to the post as early as you can, with a piece of soap? It can be easily done up. My face feels as if it had been varnished from the yellow soap in my room. Also, later, send me a soiled-linen bag; I forgot it. Sorry to bother you with these little parcels, but I really need both.

It is a lovely day, everybody complains of the heat, but a new place is never so warm at first to a stranger. I find it just comfortable.

It has been suggested that I should go out in the boat, but I told them I would rather not, that I liked a good rough tossing, but smooth rowing and river boating did not agree with me, which is literally true.

Two days later Kate is still complaining:

They don't like me to go into my room for a few minutes. If I rise to leave the room, I am asked where I am going and why? and cannot I do it down there and so on. The worst of it is I sleep so terribly badly until the middle of the night, nor keep long asleep. In the morning there is too much noise from 6 o'clock beneath my room. The Patmores are very kind, and I am quite conscious of that, but they are always moving you on. Whatever you are doing they want you to go and do something else. You sit in the conservatory two hours and leave it because you felt chilly. You are told it really could not have been chilly, and please come back at once, and they will put you in a place where they are sure it cannot be chilly,—then everybody in the house is told that 'wasn't it strange Miss Greenwood has been sitting in the conservatory and found it chilly?' As for reading a line, it is out of the question.[1] If Mrs. Patmore is not yet up I am asked to go and sit with her; if she is, she talks to me straight on—and if I chance to come into my room, she generally follows in a few minutes to fetch me down, or to ask some little question, or tell me something.

Tomorrow there is a Capuchin Brother coming to stay, of the kind who goes around barefoot.

Now we have an account of the visitor's bout with the poet:

Mr. Patmore did not behave at all well, I consider, to me, in his contemptuous ways of talking. I will tell you all that when I come home. He is a terrible man for a poet. Personally he cannot make me uncomfortable intellectually; he has no terrors—it would be a discredit to my upbringing if he had. He has a way of dismissing any question, or settling any subject, by some carelessly formed (we should call it childish at home) opinion, quite good enough for his womenkind; they just accept it as final.

I did so wish you could have seen all these women. The other evening when I said 'But Mr. Patmore I really don't see how you make that out?' even Miss B. — a very lively, ordinary, good-looking woman, 'about as old as other people'—looked as if she wished the floor would open and swallow her up. I quite enjoyed it—because any quick child could see that Mr. Patmore could have only one way out of his corner—backwards. He saw that in a moment, and ingeniously turned the subject over to the sentiment side of it, and I took that up at once and let him off having to confess he was wrong before his women-folk. He knew too that I had let him off, and he has been much nicer and more civil to me since. I was actually asked last night if I wouldn't 'come and talk?'. Whereat the girls stared at each other. A man has no right to assume that another man's daughters are fools.

Piffie is much improved in many ways and is a nice boy, but he

[1] On this question and on references to the boat, here and on a later page, she is in accord with what her father wrote in the previous chapter.

wants robuster companionship. They talk to him sometimes as if he was a baby, and he is ten. He is far too up and down in spirits to make one comfortable about him; his devotion to the gardener is quite comical.

Gertrude looks very ill to me. Something ought to be done about her I am sure. No woman or man looks like that without some grave cause I should say. But no notice is taken of her, and in fact the girls rarely seem to speak to Mr. or Mrs. Patmore, or to be spoken to. I think there must be some friction among the women. The two girls are always ready to stand up for each other. Gertrude was literally stamping with rage the other night outside the study door, because Mr. Patmore was keeping Bertha up to read to him. And Bertha is always putting in some plea for Gertrude—in that placid (tiresome) voice of hers.

Mrs. Patmore will not be happy until she gets me on board the steamer bound to Yarmouth and Alum Bay. I don't in the least care about it or want to go, and would much rather stay in the garden, but she means me to go, I can see.

Then Kate gets to her account of 'this place':

I did not like to say much at first because I thought Father would think I was a little perverse, and I might change my mind after a day or two. The situation I think simply hideous, and as for the 'view across the water', it requires one to swallow a lump of protest before one can answer to the continual demands as to its beauty. The one room (little drawing room) that has a fine view towards the Isle of Wight is always shuttered, and from the rest there is a *bit* of a view only, of mud chiefly with a lot of rotten boats, disused buildings of all sorts, ages and sizes, timber and rubbish, and a muddle of houses behind, absolutely not a spark of beauty about it, and as for the smell, I call it nasty. I wouldn't live here for any consideration: it would be much more convenient and quite as pretty in any of the river backwaters and building yards. The Patmores have really got a 'glamour' over them. Twenty hours a day you are asked by one or the other 'Isn't this a lovely view?' 'Don't you think that bit of water delightful, Miss Greenwood?' 'Isn't it a pretty garden?' 'Isn't this corner charming?' and so on.

12 o'clock. I have just a few minutes while taking off my bonnet. Before 10.15 I had been 'moved on' into two sitting rooms and out

on the road to Lymington. It really is very worrying to be so hustled about.

Piffie has got a cold, certainly does not look well, and was very feverish last night, I should not be greatly surprised if he has whooping-cough. They knew he felt ill last night, because he took all his 'bunnies' to bed which he has not done for a year.

The next letter tells of trouble at Argyll Road with the servants—we do not need that bit—but it seems that the Patmores have their frets also. Kate says:

Mrs. Patmore often comes into my room and waits for me to finish dressing or take off my outdoor things, and I thought once she looked vexed when I turned the key in my box before leaving the room—but it is really necessary according to her own showing. Last week or so a girl was staying here who takes very good photographs. All Mr. Patmore's were put away in a box to take home to develop, but when the box was opened the photographs had flown —were spoiled—because some of the servants had opened them and let in the light.

Gertrude and Bertha took me out to tea yesterday and to see the archery practice, next door, where the people were kind. A most taking place, with heaps of old china and good needlework and pretty things about.

I have had to get out of that boat business more times than I can count now.

The girls go about tea-partying. They are very kind when I have anything to do with them.

I found after I had put on my black and pink dress the other night that I never made the pocket.

Mrs. Patmore won't leave the two boys alone together in a room for a moment, for fear they should hurt themselves.

There is a letter the next day in which we hear of priests, whist, boating, and Austin Dobson:

Mrs. Patmore did not get up at all today, and I was sitting in her room all the afternoon. Tonight I was obliged to play whist again, though I begged to be excused.

Can you imagine me playing with a Capuchin friar, the parish priest and Mr. Patmore for 3d. points, that is 3/- gain or loss on every rubber? Father O'Connell (parish priest) and I lost the first rubber, and I saw the awful prospect of walking up to Father Cuthbert tomorrow morning when he is in his robes, and presenting him with 1/6 gambling debt. So I said to myself, 'A priest and a woman ought to beat a friar and a poet, and this rubber is going to be won'. And I am glad to say we did win in grand style to Mr. Patmore's disgust, and the parish priest went home no poorer. You know when I am flurried now, things go quite out of my mind, and whist is therefore more of an effort than I like, played seriously. It made my head fairly spin.

Would you believe that Father Cuthbert was taken out in the new boat today? Bertha is very indignant, admitted that it was too rough to be quite safe in the Solent.

Tell Father I heard a terrible tale of tea being upset on the wonderful drawing room carpet [evidently during a visit of his] but no names, none given, so I laid low and smiled to myself. I have not been out for any drives, Gertrude took me to Lymington in the chair, and we got a boy there to pull me about the town, and she took me next door to tea, and once along the road, but really I do not like her to do it; it is too much for her though she declares it is not. I generally have found her quite done up. I don't like this naturally, and would much rather potter round the garden.

Today she was out rowing all the morning, and over at Lymington for Mrs. Patmore all the afternoon, and when she came in I had quite a fidget with Mrs. Patmore about her dragging me up the hill in the chair. I really could not consent but anything like the Patmore insistence whether you like it or not I have never met. I did not feel up to being jolted about in the chair either, but even that was no good,—I should think a good hour was spent over it, but I had made up my mind I would not go, and did not give in. Mrs. Patmore, finding I would not allow Gertrude to tire herself further, insisted that Piffie! should do it, that Jane, the parlourmaid should do it, finally and quite seriously that Father Cuthbert should be asked. I felt quite angry at this and I think not without reason. Remember that I had plainly said I had rather not go because I did not feel up to it. I could never have conceived such persistent endeavour to have things a certain way in spite of one's feelings. It is the same twenty times a day. I have never been in leading strings of this kind, and I don't like it. I shall hope to get home on Saturday. Perhaps now Mrs.

Patmore is in bed they won't care for me to remain. The girls have their own little rounds of pleasures and visits, and must find me a nuisance—except when I play whist instead of them.

I am sorry about Father. I do wish he would go away for a while, that is what he wants. How is it that he has never sent me a single note? Such a thing has never happened when I have been away before.

The people are all very kind, but we live such different lives; mind, habits, occupations, interests, everything is so opposite there is absolutely no common ground, and I should think they would be relieved at my departure.

Piffie has been indifferent to me quite, until today, but suddenly he quite warmed up, and shewed me special favour—all his treasures, shutting everybody else out of the room—and being quite delightful in his odd way.

Terrific fuss, but coming home. Mr. Austin Dobson here for tonight.

All this might almost be from the speeches of a Jane Austen character, though one might feel that the picture was a little overdrawn. So is truth ever stranger than fiction. I do not see why what Kate has written should be discarded. Patmore himself, writing of his father, was sure that he would have been specially anxious that, in describing him, account should be taken of 'defects and merits'. He also said that it was impossible to see people truly 'unless you look a little on one side of them'. The sympathetic biographer of the poet, Champneys, on whom some suppressions were imposed, objected to 'distinctive features' being 'rubbed down'. Another biographer, Sir Edmund Gosse,[1] says Patmore's 'grim ghost will not rise to upbraid the biographer who strives to paint him exactly as he was'. One recalls Lewes's note in his life of Goethe on his unwillingness to 'slur over' points 'on which the poet may incur blame'. To take a woman's view, that joy of Victorian homes, Mrs. Gatty (*Parables from Nature*) a clergyman's daughter and a clergyman's wife, wrote, 'Let us pray to be preserved from the insincerity of memoirs'. In our own time Conan Doyle begged

[1] *Coventry Patmore* (Hodder & Stoughton).

that in biography there should be 'the frail human side as well as the other'. For an impartial account of the strange mixture of a mortal that Patmore was, the reader may turn to his great-grandson's well-written study *The Life and Times of Coventry Patmore* (Constable) published last year. The uxorious poet married, after *The Angel in the House*, a woman with whose financial resources he 'revelled' in a country estate (which he sold at a profit), and then a strange, sensuous-looking, managing friend of one of his daughters, and finally developed, in a friendship with a married poetess, Mrs. Alice Meynell, a 'passionate heat' which dismayed her. He wrote a book, *Sponsa Dei*, which friends got him to burn. One of the friends was Gerard Manley Hopkins, who was sorry afterwards, but had offered him the alternative of showing it to his spiritual director. Another friend was Greenwood, who 'never regretted counselling suppression'. An odd combination of true poetic power, sensibility, physical desire, religiosity, jingoism, unsparing judgements, and what Mr. Vulliamy calls bland egotism, he had the regard of men as downright and sincere as Carlyle.[1] As for the unsparing judgements, he said of Gladstone, in an Ode, 'his leprosy's so perfect that men call it clean'. He described democracy as 'a continually shifting aristocracy of money, impudence, animal energy and cunning'. He wrote that 'the world has always been the dunghill it is now'. Another sentence of his is, 'There are few more damnable heresies than the doctrine of the equality of men and women'. Again he says, 'the widely extended impatience of women under the present condition of things is nothing but an unconscious protest against the diminished manliness of men'.

As for Kate's representation of him, Mr. Derek Patmore (who is not old enough to have seen him) mentions—he tells me on

[1] 'There were few famous men in literature or art with whom he was not at one time or another closely intimate. Not one of these friendships survived. That with Tennyson ended in bitterness; that with Ruskin in disillusion; from Browning, Carlyle, and Rossetti he drifted apart. The one apparent exception is Patmore's friendship with Frederick Greenwood.'—*The Idea of Coventry Patmore*, Osbert Burdett (Humphrey Milford).

the authority of a description written by his grandfather—that at breakfast 'neither his wife nor his children dared to speak unless they were addressed first'. Mr. Patmore also states that the late Edward Garnett, whom I knew, gave him 'a similar description of the family circle'. Arthur Symons, writing in 1906,[1] says he was 'certainly an autocrat in the house'. Gosse, who wrote in the lifetime of the third Mrs. Patmore, said that Patmore 'was something of a Pasha', and that, away from home, 'at little parties collected to meet him at luncheon or dinner, he would sometimes scarcely say a word or would wither conversation by some paradox ending with a crackle or cough'. In a portrait of a family group, in which Patmore, the third Mrs. Patmore, the two daughters and Piffie appear, the poet seems to me to be the only person not under some degree of strain. 'His favourite daughter, who was devoted to him', writes Mr. Richard Church, basing himself, perhaps, on Mr. Derek Patmore, 'became twisted up in a turmoil of complicated emotion, from which she escaped only by taking the veil and dying young.' (For a Roman Catholic view, see *A Daughter of Coventry Patmore, Sister Mary Christina, S.H.C.J.*, by a Religious of that Society.) Gosse describes the house Kate stayed at as 'dowdy-looking, on a muddy point of land'.

In case my reference to the third Mrs. Patmore may seem harsh, I may say that Gerard Manley Hopkins said to one who was about to pay her a visit, 'You will like her very much', Mr. Frederick Page who knew her well reports. On the other hand, Mr. Derek Patmore writes to me: 'My grandmother, who was normally the kindest of women, was always bitter on the subject of Harriet. I am sure that her estimate was reliable. I myself met her in her old age and found her still beautiful but imperious. She was a hard woman. She was clever but she did not have the distinction of the other two Mrs. Patmore's.'

One may add that Coventry Patmore, for various reasons, was not a happy man in the last days of his life. That he could inspire great affection is beyond doubt. It is clear that Green-

[1] *Figures of Several Centuries* (Secker).

wood, for example, had a deep friendship for him, and there is no question, as Mr. Derek Patmore writes to me, that 'he could be unexpectedly sensitive and thoughtful'. Something of the poet's disposition is reflected in extracts from a letter to his third wife, written from the Meynells' house, at which he was staying: 'I am having a solitary morning, sitting alone in my room and meditating very much as I do at home. . . . Yesterday there were three literary men to dinner—not famous but fairly clever and quite gentlemen. But I do feel the average literary man a great bore. I spent much of my evening downstairs in my own room smoking. I had nothing to say, and felt that I might be thought sulking when I was only—as usual—stupidly silent and uninteresting'.[1]

Greenwood, in his masterly article on Patmore in *Blackwood*, speaks of his 'beautiful lines, brilliant similitudes, thoughts that engender thought'. 'The worst of them was', he says, 'that they signified the withdrawal of the writer's genius to regions where few could follow just when it had attained to its utmost capacity.' But that is very much what we find Greenwood saying in a letter to Patmore himself.

There survives one note only of Greenwood's on Patmore for which I have not already found a place. It says that 'Patmore had no general conversation; the only talk that gave him pleasure or that he was at home or adept in was intimate talk'. Patmore once wrote to his wife that Greenwood gave him 'the sensation of society'. I have a card: 'Of your Charity, Pray for the Repose of the Soul of Coventry Patmore, who departed this life November 26th, 1896, in the 74th Year of his Age, Fortified by the Rites of the Holy Church, R.I.P. "O Lord, I have loved the beauty of Thy house and the place where Thy glory dwelleth." "My covenant shall be in your flesh." '

As for Greenwood, we have now, from his family correspondence, some impressions of the situation of a widower father with rather unhappy, somewhat crochety daughters whose supposed ill health did not hinder them from surviving

[1] *The Life and Times of Coventry Patmore*, Derek Patmore (Constable).

him. It will have been noticed that he did his best in introducing them to his friends. Just how they got on with them we do not know, except in the case of the Patmores and a few others.

In June 1894, when their father was no longer an editor, Kate, at Ventnor, tells Jessy that 'father comes in to luncheon and tea only, and in consequence eats more than is good for him', and that they go 'the same old drive as before'. There is the grievous remark that the tired parent who has done so much for his daughters' happiness, 'will not see *our* business or pleasure point of view'. On October 12 Kate states that 'Father spent the day with me yesterday upon the balcony, literally the whole day from the time he came from the station until 4.30'. Three days later it is noted that 'Edgar has been amiable; he likes entire charge of coffee-making'. A poet has 'read to Father the preface of his book of verses' which had a reference to 'provincial liars'. These words, Greenwood urged, should be cut out. Someone else plagues him to write 'a rigmarole'. Jessy is not to 'tire herself; father prophesies all sorts of evil from doing so'. An American Colonel has lent an affectionate cat 'which licks your face or hands with its rough tongue'. Jessy is not to send Kate any more acid drops, but 'would it be possible, convenient and agreeable for you to buy a whisk'? It is to be 'silver-bound'.

In the last month of the year, from Glendower, Brittany Road, Hastings, Kate is 'pitying you all day' about moving, and adds: 'You see how humble I have grown; honestly so; I don't think there is much cocksureness about anything left in me'. The next day she is speaking of people who 'have not the ghost of an idea that one can have anything to do but sit in an easy chair and talk to them'; someone talked 'until 5.30, all the afternoon'.

There is a letter, written it is not clear where, which says

Father has been hard at work in the little room, and has just returned again to finish, but he did not hurry over his dinner.

He sat thinking, and I don't want to provoke a discussion at first going off. No doubt it will all come out presently. Why did father not bring his linen, or some of it? I have not told him yet, but he has not even a nightshirt for tonight—please post one the very first thing tomorrow if it be possible to do it with all your work, muddle and anxiety.

I don't feel worse in myself, but can't manage to swallow anything but liquids, and have been getting along with cocoa, soup, and rice pudding; a piece of bread will not go down. I tell you because you will find it out and then reproach me, but I have not kept anything back. I have been inhaling iodine which is comforting.

I have seen a house-parlourmaid who may do; at least she has no fringe to speak of (Cecilia has reduced hers, to her great improvement).

There is already a drawer full of Father's letters! It took me longer to collect them scattered all over the floor, and put them tidy than all his other belongings. It looks as if he does not trouble himself to secure anything but papers. He has taken to the American chair.

I am always thinking of you two poor things. Telegraph if you are in any difficulty that I can solve.

In her last letter she suggests that Edgar 'will have to economise to the very last'. Among her papers is a note from that somewhat enigmatic personality, Sir Morell Mackenzie, thanking Kate for a 'most beautiful present, too handsome for my consulting room you have been good enough to do for me; I am afraid your fingers must have often been very tired, and your eyes weary on my behalf'.

CHAPTER XXXV

Jessy's Authorship and the Family Inventions

The Moon Maiden AND *Nelly Blythe* — 'HONESTY IS THE SECOND BEST POLICY' — THE BARONESS BURDETT-COUTTS — DIFFICULTIES WITH LITERARY CHILDREN — THE 'PORTE-MIROIR PERFECTIONNÉ'

AMONG the letters which Messrs. Macmillan have courteously let me have to copy are the two following from Greenwood to that firm. The first reminds one of the letters which Thackeray wrote when he enclosed a piece by his daughter Anne to George Smith:

Sept. 9, 1886. One of my daughters [says Greenwood] has written off three fairy tales; for a little volume. I have read them with intent to be impartial to the point of sternness; and the result is that I should very much like to get them published. Today I send you one of them: the other two I have asked her to send; and if you will have them read, with a view to publication, I shall be much obliged to you. They come a little late for Xmas publication, I am afraid, whatever their value or prospects; but I should like very much to get them out.

Dec. 6. I assure you it was just because I thought my girl's stories *did* address themselves to young people that I hoped they would succeed. And Patmore and some other of my friends whom I can trust for telling me the truth as they see it, are of the same opinion. However, you may be right; but if you are, the little book will fail just where I hadn't a doubt it would succeed.

At first, I had a notion of asking some of my fellow Able Editors not to overlook the book, but on second thoughts it seemed to me that Jessy had better take her chance, and so I've not said a word about the book anywhere or to any one.

I should be glad if you would send a copy to Mrs. F. Pollock at 48 Great Cumberland Place, and I will think of a few more names by Thursday. For, my dear Macmillan, I propose to lunch with you at the Garrick on that day, according to your word.

'*The Moon Maiden and other Stories*, by Jessy Eleanor Greenwood', was published within the year (at £25 down or half profits). It was a small volume, but books could be produced quickly then. At an earlier date *Jane Eyre* seems to have come out two months after receipt of copy! Greenwood told Jessy he was 'very much gratified by it', and later on advised a second edition 'with five or six pretty, fanciful pictures'.

In the collection of letters which Messrs. Blackwood have been good enough to let me see I came on these two notes dated September 2 and 21, 1899, from Jessy about a less-fortunate book:

Dear Mr. Blackwood. My father advises me to ask you if you will kindly look at this little batch of manuscript? Manuscript however it is not, but type writing, which gives me all the more courage in asking you to read it. One little book of fairy stories I have published already, and it was pretty well received. This you will see is legendary, and romantic too. Yours truly, Jessy Greenwood.

Dear Mr. Blackwood. Thank you very much for your kind consideration of my manuscript. I am very sorry that it could not have your approval. Believe me, Yours truly, Jessy Greenwood.

A copy of Jessy's *Nelly Blythe* reposes in the Bodleian. It was published in two volumes, in one of the dreadful covers of the period, by the once well-known firm, Ward & Downey. According to the *Athenaeum* the book was 'a very pretty pastime for a summer day', to the *Spectator* 'pretty and refined', to the *Saturday Review* 'romance tempered by good sense', and to the *Academy* 'a very fair specimen of the circulating library novel'. *The Times* was civil, and the *Pall Mall*, for old times' sake, gave a quarter of a column at the head of a column, but its verdict was 'atrociously bad'. Even friend J. M. Barrie in the *British Weekly* could say no more than that 'the story is told in graceful English'. A manuscript called *Rupert of the Ruby Hills* was declined by Fisher Unwin, and Griffith Farran & Co. Cassell's *Little Folks* pronounced *Up the Path of Stars* to be too long, but 'would consider something shorter'.

Coming to the letters I have from Greenwood to Jessy there is one in which he speaks definitely about the Church:

Impossible that you can ever convince your friends, or even move them to a new line of thinking for ten consecutive minutes. I wonder whether Miss K. ever asked herself what the Church *is* wh. she identifies with Christ? How does she describe it, as it stands, as it looks, moves, and is? What figure does it take in her mind? If she makes any more of it than an ordered association of religious men, quite agreed on certain articles of faith, generally agreed upon others, but not agreed upon all, she must have a lively imagination and a misleading one. Of course she may add to that a belief in the unbroken association—of a chain of many links, each feebler than the one before it—with the Fathers, the Apostles, and through them with Christ himself: and that is something, a good deal perhaps; but a long way from the identity of the Bishops or any one Bishop, or Convocation, or the vicar or the curate, or the churchwardens, or the congregation, or any or every member of the congregation, with Jesus Christ. Yet that is what Miss K. must believe, if she only knew it.

He concludes, about some deal-top table, with an expression of alarm at his daughter's 'upholstery feats on ladders and contortionary stooping over and under all sorts of furniture'. There is a letter in which he mentions that he has taken Kate for a five hours' drive, and that he has been ill for a short time at the Savile Club. Of someone he says, 'Harum Scarum should be the motto of that family: with, for a change, Honesty is the second best policy'. He has missed seeing some rooms at the Baroness Burdett-Coutts's 'with lovely hangings':

The old lady was very gracious and one might almost say affectionate in her manner. Over our little whiskey and water she told me some of her early troubles on coming into the property—from her own ignorance and the character of people. She has another sort of trouble now, unless we mistake her sensitiveness. But she is fond of him, [her young husband] and in fear of making the good gentleman angry, or putting him out. I saw a very full example of that on Thursday evening.

The *Lexicon* copies [his '*Lover's Lexicon*'] came 2nd post—just before I write. I had not seen it before. It looks well, but why the printer has so arranged that half the outer margins are a quarter of an inch wider than the other half, puzzles me. A new stroke of originality in taste, perhaps. Look at the outer margins from the top of the book; and you will see a ridiculous sight.

He is dining with the Baroness in the evening, the next night at Lady Jeune's.

Jessy reports that Edgar 'contemplates doing more work for the *St. James's*, and is working steadily at German papers. Father was very pleased with the notice he sent in some days ago. We are to have another batch of books [for review] tomorrow morning, which means pretty quick work but not more than six will be needed I fancy.' Another day there is this bulletin on literary endeavours, the punctuation being the writer's:

My story has not been read by Father since I altered it, it has been in the drawer a week, and now I am going to take it out and send it off—he has depressed me considerably about it, one night we were talking of which magazine it should be sent to and he said there was the *Sunday at Home*, but he did not know if it was good enough for that. So I told him that if it wasn't good enough for the *Sunday at Home*, it wasn't worth while troubling to send it anywhere, that paper was not being so well edited as *Good Words* by any means. Edgar was very hot for *Good Words*, and Father said he would send us magazines to look at. He forgot the magazines but sent a packet of children's books, so I sent out for a *Leisure Hour* and *Good Words*. The *Leisure Hour* it will have to be, *Good Words* is several steps too high for me I think, Cassell has 'The Driver' and father wants to veto Cassells, at all events at first. I will send you the *Leisure Hour* notice to correspondents, it is not very favourable, and evidently I shall have to possess my soul in patience, but I can do that. Edgar is going to buy me a stout lawyer's envelope and then we are going to send it off.

Father says I might say something about my father the editor, but I incline to let it fail or succeed on its own merits, like other folks' efforts. Two magazines it might suit are published by Cassell's. With Cassell's and Smith and Elder cut off, one's chances are reduced, and Father is evidently not enchanted with the little story.

I did a review this morning which astonishes me, I really never thought myself capable of doing it. I hope it will be all right.

The gas rate was not called for. Now there is an alarming looking thing to do with rates, something over 12 pounds, a slip of paper, a church rate apparently, for 18/- and the water rate. Those nasty looking papers always make me suspicious.

'H.R.H. the Prince of Wales has sent us four pheasants and a hare', runs a paragraph in another note; 'the birds are extraordinarily fine I believe; they always are; and the hare is fine too.' And there is a glimpse of a dress reformer famous in her time:

Lady Harberton and the Lord were there, he was silent and bored, and I pitied him extremely. He seemed to have no one to talk to, she wore *the Garments*, black satin under a pale blue satin tunic coming to the knees, or rather below it. The Garment was frilled, much frilled. She put her foot on the fender, and I giggled internally. She looked like a gigantic black and blue cochin china hen. Some one felt a draught. Lady Harberton said, 'I am always *dressed* so I don't feel the changes of air'. The lady who was affected by changes of air had on a gown fitted close round the throat, and made of cream figured silk. She had no dual garment. She had I am very much afraid, stays! so she was not *dressed*.

All the time in the drawing-room I was in a fatiguing state of suppressed laughter, you never heard such comicalities. The unhappy mortal who felt draughts I heard talking enthusiastically of cabbages! and cauliflowers! The poetical effect these lovely things had upon her, and that perfect thing the Jerusalem artichoke suggested. Ah yes! Artichoke *so* perfect,—and a lot more.

Miss Jessy then discourses—according to her time, shall we say?—on Japanese pictures:

Mrs. Hart has some. Very curious, very novel, pretty coloured and all that, but as to beauty of form, correctness in drawing, close resemblance to nature, these were quite out of the question I should have thought, but no, I was all wrong. The enthusiasm about the drawing, and naturalness was simply ecstatic. It was in one instance too much for speech,—so bold! so!—a wave of the hand—*too* splendid.

Sir Julius and Lady Benedict were there. And the great lawyer and his wife, Russell. The wife was so bored, so sort of lost. I don't know what her great interest in life is: there was no opportunity of finding out—Lady Benedict seemed ready to be interested in anything and everything.

I wore my hair high, and Father was pleased with my appearance.

Next year we have mention of 'a grand question of a voyage to Australia under serious discussion'.

Edgar seemed very inclined for it, father also, and yesterday morning ways and means were carefully considered, with the result that Edgar thought he would start on the 15th January. But afterwards he changed his mind and thinks he will not go.

Edgar and I went to explore our old curiosity shop, and I was bold enough to buy a little water colour painting for father.

Some game came from Sandringham and I am just now going to send a couple of partridges to Mrs. de Morgan.

Father has dined out every day this week but one, and seems pretty sick of it.

You saw that some of our books were in yesterday. Edgar gave up some more this morning, and I have two not printed yet, I suppose yours are not all in either.

Then we are brought forward five years to 1892. Jessy says that 'Edgar and father are both out, and I cannot think of sending a letter unsealed or sealed with a button or suchlike'. (In a letter from her father I notice him saying, 'Request for sealing wax noted'.)

Father has not been feeling well. He has had nasty headaches and a cold. It is very disturbing to him, and very depressing. I wish he would go off to the moors for a nice refreshing little holiday. It is what he wants. He does not get enough exercise. His article in *Blackwood* came today. I have just been reading it. What a curious life it must be without any reading. I should hate it, but it suits some people I suppose.

And that is the last of Jessy's correspondence.

In all the letters of Kate and Jessy there is no reference to their mother. It may be added that neither is there a reference to any love-affair of their own, or to any men friends, or, indeed, any mention of what their generation called 'the tender passion'. But who knows that something may not have been destroyed—one knows what the propriety of the period was capable of.

Edgar's school correspondence is noteworthy for a note of father wearing 'a new billy-cock hat after his own design'. Father has also got 'a copy of Mr. Harry Furniss's new comic paper *Lika-Joko*, but the quantity of comicality supplied for the three pence is moderate'. The ex-*Punch* artist's paper with the appalling name had a short life.

It is of interest that on December 8, 1890, an application was made for a patent in the name of Edgar Francis Greenwood—which was not granted—for books to contain newspaper cuttings, &c. Messrs. Carpmaels & Ransford, chartered patent agents of Southampton Buildings, Chancery Lane, kindly looked up for me that, in the preceding April, 'on behalf of Mr. F. Greenwood', they obtained 'in the name of a Miss Kate Mansfield Greenwood', patent 5217/90 for 'an improved mirror support'. It was a device for 'supporting a hand mirror to the body by means of a bracket, enabling a lady to have both hands free to do her back hair and yet see what she is doing'. I have before me a *brevet d'invention* for her from a Paris firm respecting a *porte-miroir perfectionné.*

A number of later letters from Edgar show that he had a head on his shoulders. He eventually became a solicitor. He lost his life in a street accident in November 1932, a year or so after the death of Jessy.

THE SCENE CLOSES

CHAPTER XXXVI

At the End of the Day

'THE ILLUSTRATED LONDON NEWS' — GREENWOOD AND THE FAIRIES — HIS STAND OVER THE BOER WAR — THE ADVANTAGES OF HAVING A QUEEN — ANECDOTES OF QUEEN VICTORIA AS A YOUNG WOMAN — A LETTER FROM GENERAL GORDON

It has been convenient in the preceding chapters to keep the family letters together, and they give, towards the end, a somewhat affecting picture of Greenwood. But they carry the story of his life forward to a stage which outpaces the narrative. We now, therefore, go back a few years, and follow, for a short period, his busy writing life, when, after being in an editorial chair for so many years,[1] he had no longer a paper of his own. 'It is instructive to notice', writes Winston Churchill in his biography of his father, 'that Lord Randolph's conduct during the years that followed his resignation will bear a far more exacting scrutiny than the years of his good fortune.' No less may be said of Greenwood's labours and public and personal conduct in the remaining part of his life. That he missed his daily paper editing and, later on, his *Blackwood* 'Looker-On' there is no doubt. I remember, when I was a young journalist, interested in foreign affairs, benefiting by the letters I had several times a week from a veteran continental editor after his resignation of his post. He said he could not sleep until he had written to me a short leading article or editorial note!

Shortly after starting the *Anti-Jacobin*, Greenwood began a series of articles in the *Illustrated London News*. His salary from his own paper was probably moderate, and he was a worker.

[1] *Pall Mall* 1865–80, *St. James's* 1880–8, *Anti-Jacobin* 1891–2, not to speak of his early experience on the *Queen* and other publications, and the editorial work he did on *Cornhill*.

Writing on 'The Glories of the West'—the West End of London—he contrasts 'women growing taller and more beautiful in every generation' with East-enders' 'blurred features and stunted frames, the most painful of all painful sights in great cities'. (Two years before, he had written an article in the *Nineteenth Century* on 'Misery in Great Cities'.) A week later the title is 'In Redemption of Craigenputtock' and he begins: 'There are times when I envy the first-class misdemeanant the solitude of his cell in the fine air of Islington. Temptation whispers "Choose some mild and dubious offence, something that Advanced Opinion may applaud (little difficulty there!) and commit it, and take a first class misdemeanant's invictable repose for three months at the least.' Which recalls the fact that, only two years before, Stead, his successor, after Morley, at the *Pall Mall*, had served for three months as a first-class misdemeanant in Holloway. In a paper on 'Robust Writing' we are told that there has been enough of 'the spiritless "journalese" that has infected and dejected and impoverished every form of speech; robust thought is a crying want of the time, and robust English is so much of a rarity that blessed be he, say I, who speaks and writes it'. Discoursing on 'This Tight Little Island', Greenwood dwells on the good fortune we have had to back our national virtues. 'At many a crisis, at many a sharp turn, the luck of the country has been so conspicuous as to strike the dullest reader.' This good fortune is 'largely due to our much despised climate'. And our insularity surely, as Freeman pointed out long ago in his life of William the Conqueror.

There has been frequent evidence of Greenwood's interest in children. In 'Science as Dream-Dispeller', in the *Illustrated London News*, he tells a story which again puts in our minds his successor, Stead, with his *Books for the Bairns*. Greenwood had spent a few summer days in a country house 'set in a little park beautifully wild, and with two or three gentle and beautiful children among its inhabitants'.

Going out one morning early for a ramble, I was presently lost in a lovely little dell. Deep, irregular, studded with birch and thorn, it was profusely decked with gorse and bramble and fresh-springing fern, and, above all, with a lake of wild hyacinths, the tallest and the bluest that ever were seen.

As I paused to look about me in this pretty scene, I was discovered by the children, who came bounding down; but, seeing me intent, they became cautious and inquiring immediately. 'What is it?' said a little voice, in the tone of one who apprehends a mystery. This gave me my cue; so as the girl stole to one side and the boy to the other, 'Yes', said I, 'it is just such a place as they would visit! And there was a moon last night. Just such a place!' And so I went on, murmuring and peering about. 'What? what? Who? who?' from the little voices. 'Why, Oberon, Titania, and their fairy Court! Yes, now I see!' and I made for a tiny clear space of sward, expecting that the children would enter at once into the makebelieve. I was much disconcerted when they came slowly after me in a puzzled mood, with 'Who is Tania? What are fairies?' What are fairies! Surprise was instantly banished by a rushing desire to make the most of such an unequalled chance of opening the doors of fairyland, which was done amid a world of wonder; and soon we were all three marking where Oberon must have thrown himself down to rest, or where Titania's foot had bent some flowering weed. Such excitement there was, and who more glorious than the cause of it all?

When it was late for breakfast, in we went. Racing ahead the children burst in upon mamma through an open French window their breathless voices shouting, 'Oh, mamma, mamma! we've seen the fairy dance! And Tania and Obrion! And oh, mamma, mamma. . . .!' In the midst of the clamour, I came up, to be clothed with confusion by one reproving glance from the lady's eyes. And as soon as the children had gone from the room (not so wildly as they had entered) this is what I heard: 'I don't thank you. Of course, you did not know; but here I have been striving most carefully from the day they were born to keep all such debilitating superstitious nonsense out of my children's heads, and you have undone everything in a moment!'

Between February 15, 1904, and January 2, 1905, the editor of *Country Life* kindly tells me, Greenwood contributed a series of articles—'An International Epistle', 'A Re-Countrified England', 'Richard Jefferies', 'Mechanic Warfare', 'The Philosophy of War', 'Reading by Prescription', 'The British Army', 'The Ladies' Battle', 'To Literary Apprentices', 'Marriage and the Novelists', 'Sir William Harcourt', 'Bushido', 'Miss Whitwell', 'Some Mysteries of Modern Warfare', and 'The Tree of Knowledge'. His daughter Kate's poem in the paper appeared on October 1, 1910.

Some years after Greenwood's editorship of the *St. James's* and the *Anti-Jacobin*, he was concerned in a libel action in respect of letters from his unsatisfactory proprietor at the former paper, Steinkopf, which were published in the *St. James's* and *The Times*. As is explained in Scott Stevenson's *Life of Morell Mackenzie*,[1] the letters, which had to do with the English specialist's treatment of the cancerous throat of the Emperor Frederick, were made public by an accident: 'Greenwood brought an action for wrongful dismissal against the previous proprietor and the letters were read in court to show that it was intended that Greenwood should continue under Steinkopf. It was agreed between counsel that the passages relating to Morell Mackenzie should not be read, but somehow the reporter of *The Times* included them in his report.' Morell Mackenzie got £150 damages, with costs, against *The Times*.[2]

Greenwood not only returned to the pages of the *Pall Mall* occasionally, as we have seen in the letter to Craik, but to its successor the *Westminster*. J. A. Spender, its second editor, explains:[3]

> Holding strong views about the unwisdom of Unionist policy in South Africa, he courageously came out of his retirement and hinted to me that he was ready to write if I would give him the word. Needless to say, he had the word at once, and for four years or more he wrote steadily on South Africa and was sometimes lured into other themes. In spite of his advanced age he wrote as well as ever, and seemed to have lost none of the skill and subtlety with which he had held the previous generation of serious readers. I saw him often, and talk with him was always stimulating.

[1] *Morell Mackenzie, A Victorian Tragedy* (Heinemann, 1946).
[2] *The Times*, May 22, 23, 24, and 25, 1889.
[3] *The Public Life* (Cassell).

I remember that, at the *Westminster*, whenever we had an article by Greenwood, we were careful to put it on the contents bills—there were such things then. One of Greenwood's non-South African contributions was a warning against the Anglo-Japanese Alliance, which I also had on the bill, little realizing that one day I should be editing a periodical in Japan[1] and that a Japanese Prime Minister would write for me a *kakemono*, 'The Anglo-Japanese Alliance is the Will of Heaven'.

The late J. L. Hammond, the veteran publicist who formerly edited the *Speaker* (which was absorbed in the *Nation*, which was itself submerged in the *New Statesman*) and did, with his wife, such praiseworthy work in *The Village Labourer*, *The Town Labourer*, and other works, told me that he admired Greenwood 'very much for his stout opposition to the Boer War', in protesting against the needlessness and ingloriousness of which I resigned from the *Daily Chronicle* and, as I have mentioned, wrote two pamphlets.[2]

He was certainly an impressive figure. I am very glad you are writing about him. I well remember the impression made by his courage and independence at the time of the Boer War. In that struggle, and the sequel, public opinion had a great influence on events, both in checking and correcting abuses (the reform of the concentration camps is a notable example) and in enabling the Liberal Government in 1906 to treat the South Africa problem with statesmanlike courage and generosity. Greenwood, as a Conservative of great standing, who took his place among the critics of the Unionist Imperialist mood of those days, played an important part in creating that temper.[3]

[1] *The New East*, which I founded in Tokyo in July 1919, after more than a year in Japan, and edited 1917–19. See my book, *The Foundations of Japan: 6,000 miles in its Rural Districts as a Basis for a Sounder Knowledge of the Japanese People* (Murray).

[2] My main contentions have been borne out by Mr. Winston Churchill (in *My Early Life*), by the help given by General Botha and General Smuts in the first of the Great Wars, and by General Smuts in Commonwealth and international affairs.

[3] Hyndman says Greenwood told him this story of Chamberlain's 'disposition to see only what he wished to see'. Chamberlain, Harcourt, Morley, and Greenwood were dining at the Reform Club in May 1899 when matters

A letter from Meredith to Greenwood, when he was doing this work, signed 'Yours warmly' speaks of one article as 'the summary and exposition of a statesmen. Good for the country if the writer were publicly that and carried authority! It should be shot abroad in the form of pamphlets.' 'Ever warmly yours' is at the end of another note bidding Greenwood 'open-armed' to Box Hill.

As we have seen, Greenwood's uncertain health towards the end of his life often brought him depression of mind and made him pessimistic. In the autumn of 1902 Meredith is writing to Lady Ulrica Duncombe, 'On Thursday F. Greenwood comes, and I shall have another melancholy feast of forebodings.' Twelve years before, in the *Contemporary*, Greenwood, in an article 'Britain, *Fin de Siècle*', had predicted 'national troubles and perils before the end of the nineteenth century—domestic anarchy and *defeat* in a great war'! When he wrote on Charles Pearson's *National Life and Character*, which was so widely discussed and is now almost forgotten—I remember having some correspondence with the author—his title is, 'The Limbo of Progress'.

Stead said in the *Review of Reviews* what 'a great loss to journalism' it was when Greenwood ceased to be a daily-paper editor. As early as August 1890 the editor of the *Review of Reviews* notes that for fifteen years Greenwood had done service in prophesying that the nation's armaments 'had become so gigantic that war was imminent'. Greenwood thought war was not more than ten years' distant—and was not so far out.

in South Africa were approaching a serious crisis. The question of peace or war hung in the balance. Chamberlain could, and eventually did, decide which it should be. 'If', said he, 'I could be sure of public opinion behind me, I would have war in a fortnight.' The others expressed their disapproval of such a view and regarded a war against the Boers as a very dangerous and doubtful enterprise. 'Not at all', was the answer of the Secretary of State for the Colonies, 'the whole thing would be a matter of three months and would cost about £12,000,000.'—*The Record of an Adventurous Life*, H. M. Hyndman (Macmillan). (The war against the Boers lasted three years, cost, as I have said, £200 millions, an immense sum in those days, and brought in a new era of war-preparedness in the world.)

'Britain, *Fin de Siècle*, apart from the pervading pessimism, is very interesting and very good', Stead wrote. In the course of the *Contemporary* contribution, Greenwood pays a tribute to the qualities of his fellow Britons: 'Guidance they may lack, but, speaking for the people at large, they remain the same in enterprise, the same in courage, the same in hardihood, the same in love of country and pride of race. They have not lost their old, slow, sure-footed commonsense, at the call of anyone who knows how to appeal to it.'

The problems of the future include, he says—he is writing in the reign of Queen Victoria—the succession of the Prince of Wales to the throne:

> Ministerial government will become far more difficult when a king sits on the throne. Kings are men, and therefore targets for many a shaft of questioning suspicion and damaging innuendo that cannot be aimed at an equally blameless woman. The assumption when a queen reigns is that the sovereign trusts to her counsellors; when a king reigns that the sovereign has a will of his own, preferences, favouritisms, and 'pulls the wires', even though his hand is never seen in the direction of public affairs. The most fortunate thing for monarchy in England—which is the very prop and centre of stability for the whole empire—would be succession in the female line. Under the best of kings, it will probably be no more safe from assault in a proximate future than the House of Lords is now. Under a changed order of succession—which, I need not be told, is impossible—the monarchy would go tranquilly on as long as the country could reckon upon as much careful good sense, as much sweetness, kindness and honour in its Queen as may be found in thousands of English homes.

This is interesting to read at a time when the heir to the throne is a woman, and when across the North Sea, the reign of one Queen has followed another, and that Queen has daughters only. A contrary view to that expressed by Greenwood is to be found in Professor E. S. Beesly's *Queen Elizabeth.*[1]

In an account of Queen Victoria's jubilee which Greenwood

[1] Twelve English Statesmen series, p. 34 (Macmillan).

wrote for the *Melbourne Argus* he gets his image of celerity from 'the electric spark that goes round the earth in less than 40 minutes'. But his careful and particularly readable article has interest because in it he recalls gossip about his Sovereign which he had had from various 'ancient ladies'. 'It is no treason to say', he writes, 'that when the young Queen came to the throne she showed other aptitudes besides those which Melbourne, who saw her every day for four years, preferred to cherish.' She was a determined young person and, Greenwood was told, would pass the evening with her friends 'in a manner which is supposed to be originally and entirely bourgeois of the third class'.

'There was no lingering at the dinner table', said an octogenarian *grande dame*. 'Ladies and gentlemen alike, we were soon in the drawing-room. There was a round table for all, and about this table we arranged ourselves for the rest of the evening in chairs that compelled the upsitting attitude expected of us by the manners of the time. These chairs were placed before we entered, a sofa being drawn up for the Queen, and Lord Melbourne always sitting at the opposite side of the table facing Her Majesty. It was mostly very dull—conversation, little table games and so forth.'

One night Lord Melbourne fell asleep at the table, though with so much discretion that he still sat bolt upright. There was some consternation and a neighbourly hand stole out to rouse the Minister. But the Queen interposed with a quick gesture, saying softly and with a smile: 'Poor man, how tired he must be'. Her courtesies were always softer to him than anybody else. On all formal occasions her demeanour to him was much more that of a daughter than a sovereign. With reference to Melbourne's inveterate damns, according to my informant, one would slip out now and then within range of her hearing, but, punctilious as she was, she never took the least notice of these misdemeanours.

One of the girl-friends of the childhood of the Queen related that, before her marriage, 'she would sometimes lock the door and start a downright romping dance or a furious laughing shuttlecock game in kirtled petticoats'. Referring to the discontent with the Queen in 1865–6, at the long seclusion of her widowhood, the subject of the leading article in the first number

114 Beaufort St
Chelsea
9.8.80

My dear Mr Greenwood

I am truly sorry you have left Pall Mall Gaz^tt^. You will not forget what I said to you about the Coast of Red Sea.

I send you some extracts concerning death of the Shereef of Mecca, if you could send them to Lord Northbrook. I would be much obliged.

Yours sincerely

C. G. Gordon

of the *Pall Mall*, Greenwood says: 'The only really dangerous time was at the beginning of her reign when the Sovereign, a girl of twenty and unmarried, became the victim of a dreadful mistake and one of her maids of honour the prey of a most cruel scandal. The mistake was the mistake of persons about Her Majesty, by whom she was misled, a physician amongst the number.'[1]

Greenwood again stresses the view, which he pressed on more than one occasion in his leader writing, that, although, through many stages of national growth, the country has benefited by the Sovereign being a man, 'there comes a time when the sovereignty seems to prosper most in the hands of a woman, and many sound reasons why it should be so lie to hand'. Ministerial responsibility, he notes, 'takes a much sterner shape when a woman is on the throne'. Even these short extracts mark his care in the use of words, whether for publication or in a private letter.

It has not been known that Greenwood was on friendly terms with General Gordon, with whose mission to the Soudan his successor Stead had so much to do. One of Gordon's letters fills the opposite page.

There is also a pencilled map by Gordon showing the Soudan, Red Sea, Aden, and the territories then in dispute in Abyssinia, and bearing some notes of expenditures.

Among his magazine contributions Greenwood had an article in which he stressed 'the duty of all who do not believe in Christ to be better Christians than those who do'. Again, in a paper in the *Fortnightly*, he had 'A Conversation in a Balcony' (in Geneva) in which two characters talk of the mysteries of the Christian life. Writing in *Blackwood*, he urged doughtily that, during three generations, the life of the British people had reached 'loftier heights of spiritual growth'. There had been 'a new and remarkable growth of sentiment which might be called millennial. Compare the case of sentiment in every class a hundred years ago and now, and in every class will be seen much less of

[1] The allusion is to the baseless charge made against a Maid of Honour, Lady Flora Hastings, and the unprofessional conduct of Sir James Clark.

the selfishness, oafishness of wild life, and a far deeper sense of the obligations of common kindness. It is not an intellectual but a spiritual growth, which has only to go on unblighted and unchecked for two or three generations more—meanwhile spreading here and there in other lands—to substantiate the hopes of the religionists of humanity.' In what one publication called 'a prose poem', Greenwood had Religion on a rural church tower and Materialism on the top of a factory chimney accusing and defying one another.

W. E. Henley, writing to 'My dear Greenwood' in September 1889, on *Scots Observer* paper but from Ivy Lodge, Levendale, Musselburgh, says that 'everybody is delighted with an article of yours,[1] indeed it is one of the best things you have let me have'. He continues: 'Do you think this new turn of the [dockers'] strike—the action of John Burns and Ben Tillett'—on behalf of what I remember John calling 'the full round orb of the docker's tanner'—'worth a short article? You might wire me yes or no tomorrow morning, and write or not as it strikes you.'

Among Greenwood's papers I came on an undated, pencilled memo. containing the names and addresses of sixteen London doctors, including a woman doctor. But he may have made this in the interest of his daughters who were so often ailing. Among his friends, as we have noticed, was the eminent physician, Sir Richard Quain. A note from Quain runs: 'A thousand thanks my dear friend for your kind good wishes which I most heartily reciprocate for yourself and your dear Surroundings. I do indulge the hope that you are well—if not, remember there is balm in Gilead and a physician.'

[1] When it became the *National Observer* Greenwood wrote an article for the first number. Mr. John Connell, in his *W. E. Henley* (Constable), says that Henley, after dining with Greenwood, described him as 'an admirable host'. He seems to have written more than once for the *National Observer*, and in a letter on July 16, 1891, when the weekly was in a bad way financially, Henley says in a letter to Charles Whibley—it is quoted in Mr. John Connell's *W. E. Henley* (Constable): 'It is proposed (between ourselves) that Frederick Greenwood comes in as political editor, absorbs the *Anti-Jacobin* in us, and sinks £3,000 as well. It looks well enough on paper; but we shall see. Anyhow it is under serious consideration.' But nothing came of the plan.

CHAPTER XXXVII

The Man Himself

HIS AUTOBIOGRAPHY — A TALE OF A MOUSE — JOHN MORLEY'S TRIBUTE — GREENWOOD AS EDITOR — SHOULD IT BE MENTIONED?

I AM indebted to Mr. E. A. Constable of the B.B.C. for a story told him by a common acquaintance, the late P. Anderson Graham, editor of *Country Life*. Greenwood met in his club one day Lord Riddell, who died a few years ago, and in the course of conversation Riddell said to him, 'You know, I own a paper'. 'Oh, do you,' said Greenwood, 'what is it?' 'It's called the *News of the World*—I'll send you a copy', replied Riddell, and in due course did so. Next time they met Riddell said, 'Well, Greenwood, what did you think of my paper?' 'I looked at it', replied Greenwood, 'and then I put it in the wastepaper basket. And then I thought, "If I leave it there the cook may read it"—so I burned it!'

Why did not Greenwood write an account of his life? Robertson Nicoll notes that

> he was in some ways the proudest and most reticent of men. For years I laboured with him, endeavouring to induce him to write his autobiography. He gave very friendly and very prolonged consideration to the plan, and at one time, it seemed as if it were to take shape. He had a scheme of writing passages of his life to be published in a certain number of monthly parts. One was to be on Thackeray, another on Beaconsfield, another on the Suez Canal, another on Gladstone. I think they were to be twelve in all, at half-a-crown each. But though some fragments appeared in *Blackwood* he decided at last that he would not carry out his design.[1]

As for a book on his views on the journalistic life, for the younger members of his profession, if he was not to bequeath such a work, he did deliver, as I was to do also, a series of lectures at the School of Journalism, started in connexion with the City of London School on the Embankment.

[1] *A Bookman's Letters* (Hodder & Stoughton).

In my varied reading for this book I have met with the assertion that Greenwood applied for the editorship of *The Times* on the retirement of Delane in 1877. I have good authority for saying that this is untrue.[1] His good friend Kinnear[2] did think of him, however, in connexion with the *Quarterly Review*. 'When I saw the account of the vacancy [he wrote] I said to myself, "That's the place for Greenwood!" It has been recalled to me lately in the *Athenaeum* that there are a hundred men in the field. I don't the least know if you would like it—or how you stand with Murray—but *I* should say that in knowledge, tact, politics and every other particular, you were out of sight the best man he could get.' Someone else was appointed, and I have no reason to believe that Greenwood's name was considered.

In earlier chapters there have been many references to the bird and animal pets that Greenwood had in his house and to the interest he took in them. Mrs. Lusted, in whose affectionate care Greenwood's daughter Kate passed her last years, said to me that he 'was good with animals and tamed a mouse'. Her other memory of him was that 'he used to take cold sitz baths and could not abide noise on the stairs'!

Among scraps I have in Greenwood's handwriting is the following in pencil:

At seven o'clock the maid will knock;
Breakfast at eight, or bide your fate;
Rise then, my friend, at half past seven,
Or make your peace with outraged heaven!
Sunday, they say, 's a day of ease;
None of that nonsense if you please.

[1] Nor, by the way, is it true, as I have seen printed, that Dickens, whose editorship of the *Daily News* has been referred to in Chapter III, was ever a reporter for *The Times*. The writer was evidently thinking of the *Morning Chronicle*. But in the index to the Nonesuch edition of Dickens's 'Opera Omnia' there are many references to Dickens's letters to the editor in *The Times*. And some of that paper's police-court reporting was rather Dickensian and may have given rise to a belief that he was a member of the staff.

[2] J. Boyd Kinnear, who lived to be 90.

This is a memorandum on Clemenceau:

Intelligent, cool and resolute, marching slowly but firmly towards a goal known to himself alone. Sarcastic, painstaking, disdainful of successes without a purpose; a man who can wait his time but who will then march without hesitation. Skilful, calm, logical speech. Calm authority. Resolute countenance, erect figure, clear voice, sunken eyes, broad forehead increased the impression created by his sarcastic style.

It is always of interest to see the kind of passages a busy man takes the trouble to copy out from his reading. I come on the following extract from Jeremy Taylor made by Greenwood. It is on the fear of death:

Blindness is odious, and widowhood is sad, and destitution is without comfort, and persecution is full of trouble, and famine is intolerable, and tears are the sad ease of a sadder heart; but these are the evils of our life, not of our death.

Take away but the pomps of death, the disguises and solemn bugbears, the tinsel and the actings by candle-light, and proper and fantastic ceremonies, the minstrels and the noise-makers, the women and the weepers, the swoonings and the shriekings, the nurses and the physicians, the dark room and the ministers, the kindred and the watchers,—and then to die is easy, ready, and quitted from its troublesome circumstances. It is the same harmless thing that a poor shepherd suffered yesterday, or a maid servant today: and at the same time in which you die, in that very night a thousand creatures die with you,—some wise men and many fools: and the wisdom of the first will not quit him, and the folly of the latter does not make him unable to die.

When men will by all means avoid death, they are like those who at any hand resolve to be rich. The case may happen in which they will blaspheme, and dishonour Providence, or do a base action, or curse God and die; but in all cases they die miserable and insnared, and in no case do they die the less for it.

To be angry with God, to quarrel with the Divine providence by repining against an unalterable, a natural, an easy sentence, is an argument of a huge folly, and the parent of a great trouble. A man is base and foolish to no purpose; he throws away a vice to his own misery, and to no advantages of ease and pleasure. Fear keeps men in bondage all their life, saith St. Paul: but patience makes him his own man, and lord of his own interest and person. Therefore possess yourselves in patience, with reason and religion, and you shall die with ease.

There is also a passage on envy and on the man that 'always goes in a great company'.

In his *Recollections*,[1] John Morley, Greenwood's successor at the *Pall Mall*, wrote this high tribute to the man who has been called 'one of the ablest editors and journalists of his time'.[2]

I took charge of an evening print that had been raised to well-deserved prominence by the talents, industry, and zealous political sincerity of its first editor. Greenwood had a most ingenious pen, his judgements alike in politics and letters were independent without being flighty, the topics that interested and absorbed him were well chosen and thoroughly worked, and he attracted a staff of writers of ampler literary training than his own; but they owed much to the liveliness, gaiety, and clever pointed insight of an editor who, from his early days as a journeyman printer, had carried on a hard fight with the naked realities of life, and had learned to explore them with energetic and unquenched spirit. He soon began to do his best to encourage a vigorous all-round reaction against the Liberalism associated with Mill in one field and Gladstone in another. Hitherto he had taken it on trust as other people took it; but as things went on, as the incidental drawbacks of the creed came into view, a Tory instinct that has often quite as deep a root in born sons of toil as in nobility and gentry, revolted both against theories of liberty, equality, and fraternity, and against crusades of sentimental passion for turning the Turks bag and baggage out of Europe.

The testimony of that energetic London correspondent, Sir Henry Lucy, was that Greenwood was 'the ablest journalist of his day, in editorial gifts second only to, if not fully compeer with, Delane. This fact makes stranger the reflection that through a long and distinguished career he was never personally connected with, or chiefly responsible for, any commercially successful periodical. Personally and professionally his career passed along the highest levels of honour and capacity.' He also said that Greenwood's 'editorial skill and instinct were only equalled

[1] Macmillan. [2] Siegfried Sassoon.

by the perfect sincerity of his opinions and his absolute disinterestedness'. In Clement Shorter's *Victorian Literature* Greenwood is described as 'the most honoured journalist of the day'. The following eulogy was penned by an able journalist, Herbert Paul, writing in the *Speaker*:

> Few people realise what it is to produce every day, except for a week or two, throughout the year, an excellent English essay on the politics of the hour, containing much information, much criticism and one principal idea. Nobody has done that better than Mr. Greenwood, and his style was his own. He never used catchpenny phrases, or aimed at emphasis by repetition. Although, or perhaps because, he owed nothing to public schools and universities, he wrote with strong unhackneyed freshness and vigour. The secret of his success and the source of his influence may be found in the essential manliness of his character. And, after all, it is character that tells. Mere cleverness may excite a momentary enthusiasm. Gifts and accomplishments have their pecuniary value. They become, or their owner becomes, the fashion. But the fashion of this world passeth away. Somebody else does the trick better, and the first performer is forgotten. Devotion to great principles and to public duty—its effect, if slow is irresistible.

Mr. Frederick Page, editor of *Notes and Queries*, told me that Greenwood was a man he had 'always held in affection'. With this proviso I may mention that a friend of Mr. Page whose name he gave me, 'and George Saintsbury in writing', alleged that 'everybody's friendship with Greenwood ended in a quarrel'. Mr. Page said he was 'happy to believe this wasn't true'—much the same allegation, and with as little support, was made against Cobbett—and I have come on no evidence to establish it as true. But it is true, added Mr. Page, that 'Saintsbury asked the Oxford University Press to approach Greenwood for permission to reprint, in the seventeen-volume Thackeray which Saintsbury was editing for the O.U.P., his postscript (or whatever it should be called) to *Denis Duval*, as he and Greenwood were no longer on writing terms'.

'When I first met Greenwood', writes Robertson Nicoll in

A Bookman's Letters,[1] 'he was in his last days as editor of the *St. James's*, a figure full of dignity and authority'.

He had lived through more than twenty years' high and gallant journalism. During this long period he had exercised an admitted influence in politics and in literature. Wherever you had met him, you would have known him to be a remarkable and powerful man. As a talker, when he was at his best I never heard any one to compare with him. Greenwood spoke as he wrote, in a style full of trenchancy, clear, decided, pictorial, with a fair share and no more of surprises in diction. Greenwood was above all things independent. Mark Rutherford once remarked that Greenwood's leaders had this peculiarity, that they hardly ever failed to offend both Tories and Liberals. Greenwood was in style one of the most severe purists that ever existed. I do not believe that there was any writer on his staff whose work he did not skilfully emend. He belonged to the old school of editors who re-write the work of their authors and pay no attention to susceptibilities. Greenwood used his knife very freely.

Sir Sidney Low was candid about the position of the *St. James's*, to the editorship of which he was to succeed.

Although its circulation was what would be called contemptibly small, and its influence was out of all proportion to the number of copies sold, it was distinctly the organ of the 'governing classes', and it was read by them with a reverential attention which always surprised, and sometimes amused me. As its news service was never really good it depended almost entirely upon the strength and quality of its writing, and the character of its comments on men and affairs. Its leading article, to which Greenwood devoted an excessive amount of attention, had become one of the features of the London Press; and even in my own less robust hands, a single leader in the *St. James's* could sometimes do more to affect the course of legislation or the opinions of statesmen than a whole series of special articles and exciting news 'stories' in the huge and powerful journals of a later day.[2]

Sir Sidney Low's sister, Florence, who has been very kind

[1] Hodder & Stoughton.

[2] *A Memoir of Sir Sidney Low*, Desmond Chapman-Huston (Murray).

in searching her mind for memories of the *St. James's* in her brother's time, writes to me: 'Sidney always spoke of Greenwood as a man of great integrity who would never swerve from any position he had taken up and believed to be true. Because he was so uncompromising, he was understood to be difficult to work with'. Against this suggestion there may be borne in mind the long association of Sir Fitzjames Stephen and other contributors, and men, like Traill, who were on the office staff. 'Claudius Clear' (Robertson Nicoll) in the *British Weekly* has a note that Sir James Barrie and he (Nicoll) agreed that Greenwood was 'too proud' and said that 'in a world like this no one had a right to be proud, also no one should take offence too easily. Greenwood readily took offence, and in consequence was much alone for many years, and was estranged from many of his former friends.' But Nicoll has also written that Greenwood was 'the very soul of kindness'. A letter sent to his daughter Kate, when he died, from a man who had evidently been on the *St. James's* staff, speaks of him as 'the friend of every man who worked for him'. H. W. Massingham, no doubt on the basis of what he had heard from contributors to the *St. James's*, says, 'one of his greatest merits was the shrewd and kindly regard he always cast on newcomers'.

Except for a single sentence in the *Spectator* after his death,[1] these are the only printed criticisms of Greenwood I have come across. I have set down, without exception, every fact, incident, or statement throwing light on his character, temperament, and work which I have met with in the rows of books and in the volumes of daily, weekly, and monthly publications I have read or looked into. As for what has been written or said to me about him, I have neither suppressed nor softened anything.

Greenwood was in mid-career at the *St. James's* when Meredith wrote to him:

> I do not reply to reviews of my work favourable or the reverse. But the friendliness of your little note in the *St. James's* is out of the regions of criticism, and I may notice it to thank you. Innovators

[1] See page 439.

in any department have a tough struggle to get to the field through the hedge for a hearing. Mine has lasted about thirty-five years, and still I have only to appear for the bawlers to be in uproar. As I know the world I do not complain. I am sensible not the less of generous voices. We are at issue on politics. You are a man who can rise to pure ether while in the sweat of the fray.[1]

Some account of his bearing and looks early in life has been given. David Williamson, sent as a young man to interview him in his later years, writes to me that he was 'genial, shy, very courteous and old-fashioned, a handsome old man with rosy complexion and snow-white hair. His courtesy had a charm that fascinated you.' To quote Lucy again: 'No change of fortune altered his personal manner or bearing. He remained to the last the simple-mannered, unaffected, kindly-hearted gentleman.'

He had lived [writes Nicoll] through a most eminent career, during which he had mingled freely with the ruling spirits of his time. He had the air and manner of a grand gentleman. In this he closely resembled his friend Meredith. Both were singularly handsome men in their days of health, very erect and stately, most gracious in their manners, especially to women, but never failing in dignity. That a man of such aristocratic bearing and taste and aspect, a man so devoted to the highest standards of literature, should have emerged from Frederick Greenwood's first twenty-five years is amazing.

Mr. Frederick Page remembers a photograph on Mrs. Coventry Patmore's table showing 'a Victorian face of the type of J. A. Froude's, a grave face.' Mr. Hamilton Fyfe's mother spoke of him as 'rather shy and reserved'. Fyfe himself, a youngster of fifteen when he saw Greenwood, has told me that 'he had a venerable but lively air about him. His whiskers were belied by his bright, smiling eyes. He seemed to be in excellent, though not robust health. He took care of himself. Sometimes he would send out for three or four oranges and make his lunch off them. My boyish impression was that he was a wise, kindly old chap.' And that is surely a rather fine thing for any old man to have said of him.

[1] *Letters of George Meredith* (Constable).

It is odd that in all my reading about Greenwood, and in all the descriptions of him with which I have been favoured, I have not come upon any reference to the fact that, like some other men—more than is supposed—who have done a job of work in the world, he had only one eye. The wonderful centenarian, Mrs. Robinson, to whom I have referred in Chapter XI, told me that, when someone in the family mentioned this disability, she did not believe it; but she spoke to her father, Greenwood's brother-in-law, on the subject, and he told her that such was the fact. Both eyes looked the same, as the photographs show, but as far as seeing went, Greenwood had only one. And the present account of his life, now drawing to its close, is written by a biographer who for nearly thirty years has not found one idle eye much of a disadvantage.

Although Greenwood had always a look of self-possession, firmness, and distinction, the portraits which appeared in the newspapers when he was an elderly man show a rather sad face. (The negatives were destroyed in the bombings.) He had had not infrequent spells of physical weakness. His family circle was broken early when his wife, who seems to have been a little odd, parted from him. Some of his children died. His son, for whom he made sacrifices, did not, in his short term, have an opportunity of distinguishing himself. His daughters must often have been a care—did he say to himself, as Thackeray did twice over, 'No one comes to marry my girls'? On points of principle, for which he deserves the greatest credit, he lost successively the editorship of the *Pall Mall* and the *St. James's*, and, later on, while his interest in politics and social affairs was still keen and informed, he was unable to go on with the *Anti-Jacobin* or with the *Blackwood* causerie which he had so much satisfaction in doing. He had a considerable circle of appreciative friends, and the newspaper world had feelings of respect and regard for him; but a large public knew little of his distinguished service in maintaining journalism at a high standard of energy, ability, instruction, and disinterestedness, and in securing for his country the Suez Canal shares. And one is conscious in reading the end of the Blackwood correspondence, that, towards the close of his life, he had to do not a little task work. To the last, however, his writing was marked by independence, responsiveness, self-respect, and industry.

A reference he made to himself in print—in *Blackwood*, twelve years before he died—was a carefully-phrased acknowledgement that, 'with the rest of mankind, there had been griefs upon the road, hardships as well as error, and various kinds of wounding and robbery to endure, as well as too much matter of self-reproach'. 'Too much matter of self-reproach'—may one speculate on the precise weight and significance of these words? Do they mean more than many persons would intend in using them?[1] A biographer who would deal faithfully with his readers and the man he is writing about would be inadequate in discharging the duty he has assumed if he did not apply to Greenwood two well-known touchstones of character and temperament. Persons whose lives are brought by themselves into print and exposed to the judgement of their fellow mortals may ordinarily be valued, in no small measure, according to the way they behaved about money and the way they demeaned themselves, men with women, women with men. Concerning money, Greenwood was 'in action faithful and in honour clear'. With regard to the second test, we have seen that he was on terms of cordial friendship with not a few women; but there is no sign in the mass of correspondence I have read with care, that, in his often rather lonely life—he took most of his holidays alone—he had attachments of affection other than to his own daughters.

I have gathered, however—and in our day there is no call for the hush-hush favoured by an earlier generation, more habituated to make-believe—that, as his unfortunate married life drew to a close, his association with a particular woman led to criticisms from a relative, culminating in a breaking-off of friendship. There was a child, not his wife's, who grew up. As to the origin and duration of Greenwood's friendship with the mother, no

[1] Is he by any chance at all autobiographical in the first verse of the lines on page 120?

information is now available, and no fair judgement is possible.

Basil Champneys, Coventry Patmore's friend and biographer, knew Greenwood as a friend of Patmore and went to Greenwood's funeral. He saw there a mourner, unknown to the rest of the company, except that one of them explained her to Champneys as an illegitimate daughter of Greenwood. After the funeral the writer of a letter in one of the London papers described herself as Greenwood's adopted daughter. Wide inquiries have yielded no further particulars. That Greenwood, a widower with two daughters and a limited income, should add an adopted daughter to his family is as odd as that there should be no reference to her, apparently, in any of his hundreds of letters or in Kate's or Jessy's correspondence, and no knowledge of her among Kate's friends in her last days. There are thirteen lines about Greenwood in *Who's Who* of 1897, but there is no mention of his family. I have ascertained that he was among those who did not return the questionnaire sent out by that publication and that the entry was written by Douglas Sladen, then its editor.

Ought I to have mentioned this matter? The only reason for not being open, that the feelings of persons related to Greenwood might be hurt, does not serve. All his near connexions are dead. One of the nearest, who has 'read through very carefully several times' the three previous paragraphs and the present one, writes to me: 'I see no objection; a biography should be a fair statement of what is known about a man.' One may recall Benjamin Jowett's complaint to Sir Henry Taylor: 'The friends of so many people whose lives are written are always softening and improving—they are afraid of telling faults lest the public should exaggerate them. I have been told that an eminent scientific man, of whom more than one life has been written, twice attempted to commit suicide. Not a word of this occurs in either of the lives—the last man of whom you would have supposed it.' 'There are many who think it an act of piety to hide faults and failings,' wrote Dr. Johnson; 'we therefore see whole ranks of characters adorned with uniform panegyric, and not to be known from one another but by extrinsic and casual circumstances. If we owe regard to the dead, there is yet more respect to be paid to knowledge and to truth. . . . If a man proposes to write A Life he must represent it as it really was.' E. V. Lucas said of Charles Lamb's regrettable letter to Southey that while it does not show Elia at his best, it 'shows him as he was, and this is the only Lamb that is permanently interesting'. Can it be other than an impertinence in a biographer deliberately to refrain from showing 'as he was' the man whose whole character and disposition his readers are trusting him honestly to place before them? I have been incompetent in describing Greenwood and the work he did, if, as they come to the end of this book, they are not in a position to place the matter now recorded in its just relationship. No one disputes the unsocial character of illegitimacy. But on this subject is there not still a little hypocrisy and insincerity? Are the merit and quality of the poetry of Wordsworth lessened by the fact that the man who wrote an indignant sonnet against railways tried to invest £500 in railway shares, and that, in France, in his early twenties, he became the father of an illegitimate child?

FREDERICK GREENWOOD. A Cartoon from *Vanity Fair*

CHAPTER XXXVIII

The Great Occasion

THE DINNER WITH FIVE SUCCESSORS IN THE 'PALL MALL' EDITORSHIP — THE TRIBUTES — A FINE SPEECH — MORLEY AND BARRIE — A WORD ON JOSEPH CHAMBERLAIN

THE dinner to Greenwood, in his seventy-sixth year, suggested by Sir James Barrie, was marked in the *Westminster* by a sonnet by Mr. Hamilton Fyfe. Its author does not think much of it as verse, but it is sincere and testifies to the regard and respect in which the old editor's career and character were held by his colleagues:

As round some veteran scarred in many a fray
  Gather his younger comrades of the sword
  And from his mind with battle-memories stored
Draw forth the lessons of each hard-fought day,
So come we, first our debt of praise to pay,
  And next we seek some helpful, hopeful word
  To set high aims before us and afford
Encouragement upon our upward way.

Nestor, alike in wisdom and in years,
  Of all who daily write for daily bread;
    Statesman,—so statesmen named thee, and their friend;
Patriot, by none but noblest motives led—
  Teach us to show, when our days near their end,
    Such stainless honour as in thee appears.

Ample reports of the speeches appeared in *The Times* next day, and there are accounts of the gathering in articles in the *Speaker* and the *British Weekly*, and in the impressions of Herbert Paul and Robertson Nicoll recorded elsewhere. But neither at the British Museum nor at the Bodleian is there the brochure *Honouring Frederick Greenwood, being Speeches delivered in Praise of Him at a Dinner held on April 8, 1905. With an Introduction by*

C. K. Shorter.[1] The members of the committee were George Meredith, Thomas Hardy, Sir Edmund Gosse, Andrew Lang, Sir Douglas Straight (editor of the *Pall Mall* 1896–1909), J. A. Spender (editor of the *Westminster*), Clement Shorter (editor of *Illustrated London News*), and Arthur Spurgeon, of Cassell's. Hardy and Andrew Lang sent messages and E. V. Lucas brought a bunch of violets from Meredith, who wrote:

> Greenwood is not only a great Journalist; he has a Statesman's head. The National interests have always been urgently at his heart, and moved him to personal sacrifices in the maintaining of his view touching the country's welfare. John Morley in the chair assures me that we shall have a public appreciation of his work and quality. Often in disagreement, I yet can say of him that there has been no truer patriot in our time.
>
> Do not forget Greenwood's suggestion of the purchase of the Suez Canal Shares with which England has benefited so largely in every way.

A note from the Baroness Burdett-Coutts spoke of her 'dear and honoured friend'. Sir Henry Campbell Bannerman wrote that he had 'great admiration' for Greenwood's character, for his style, 'and sometimes for his opinions'.

John Morley was supported by, among other fellow Liberals, Lord Crewe, H. H. Asquith, Leonard Courtney, and Augustine Birrell. Not only the Commons but the judiciary, the bar, and all branches of journalism, what Morley called 'the leaders, the promoters, the inspirers of public opinion', were represented. But not a single member of the Balfour Cabinet was present. The diners, the list of whom occupies thirty lines in *The Times*, included four editors of the *Pall Mall* besides the chairman—W. T. Stead, Sir Edward Cook, Henry Cust, and Sir Douglas Straight—and Sir F. Carruthers Gould, cartoonist first of the *Pall Mall* and then of the *Westminster*, and J. A. Spender, editor

[1] 'Shorter, the type of literary man', Meredith once said, 'who would print a famous writer's blotting pad in a limited edition if he could get hold of it, though, according to his lights and limitations, he did his best to further the appreciation of good literature'.

of that second off-shoot of the *Pall Mall*, D. C. Lathbury (formerly editor of the *Guardian* and the *Pilot*), Edward Clodd, Maurice Hewlett, Sir Evelyn Wood, Rufus Isaacs (to be afterwards Lord Reading), Sir James Knowles (in whose hands the *Nineteenth Century* and what he had the wit to call, when the century ended, the *Nineteenth Century and After*, was a power), G. R. Sims ('Dagonet'), Charles Whibley of *Blackwood*, S. H. Jeyes (of the *St. James's*), Edmund Gosse, W. M. Meredith (George Meredith's son), Ernest Parke of the *Star*, and H. M. Hyndman of Greenwood's *Pall Mall*. It was, Lord Crewe told me, a 'very distinguished crowd, and I remember thinking Greenwood very agreeable; not at all pompous or dogmatic'. Many people who wished to join in the tribute to the man whom Morley, in his *Recollections*, calls 'one of the few clear-headed and stout-hearted publicists of his day', were unable to get tickets.

Part of the speech made by Morley has been quoted on page 206. In other passages he said that Greenwood had done 'splendid work' and shown 'a splendid example in the arduous, noble and the most responsible profession of journalism'. The fortunes of the *Pall Mall*, he said, 'made one giddy'!

Founded to promote Anti-Jacobin principles, it fell by stages into the hands of the Jacobins. Greenwood introduced new elements into journalism which had an uncommon mark. At starting the *Pall Mall*, he was surrounded by a phalanx of men in intelligent training and power of mind unsurpassed by any Englishmen of their generation. As months went on, Greenwood sank his shafts deeper, scaled eminences of survey upon the affairs of this nation and other nations, of which he saw the importance for the welfare of Great Britain. To all these elements he assimilated, he added a flavour of his own, his own humour, his own fancy, his own imagination, his own play of mind, his own versatility, his own fidelity, to all the other qualities [and this was spoken with 'immense force'] of a really sparkling brain. He showed an extraordinary aptitude for public affairs in their widest sense. He also showed extraordinary powers as a pugilistic controversialist—he had himself winced under his quarterstaff. He gave a sort of impetus, through his own native vigour and originality of mind and character, to journalism which it had not lost. As for the Suez Canal shares, the national exchequer received a considerable addition from that grave transaction.[1] He had shown in his work splendid and unstained disinterestedness. He had not been surpassed by any journalist in disinterestedness and devotion to great national objects.

As his mind went back, Morley recalled to his audience (one who was at the dinner wrote) his 'first editor, Douglas Cook of the *Saturday*, spoke admiringly of Delane, mentioned that Leonard Courtney (sitting near him) had been the only leader-writer whom he could trust without first reading his "copy", and referred twice to Richard Holt Hutton of the *Spectator*, "one of the rarest spirits of our time".'

Robertson Nicoll says Greenwood looked 'hale and vigorous when he rose, greatly moved, to reply'. 'An erect figure, the expression in which authority and benignity are so pleasantly blended, the keen eyes, the swift perception of every point in the situation are his still', wrote 'Claudius Clear', who marked 'how rare a gift of speech is his, no surprise to those who have heard his conversation, who have had the happiness of sitting at his feet as he narrates a story or estimates a character or gives a judgement'. Greenwood spoke in 'the brightest, raciest English', and in the course of what he said told the story of the shares, already reported from pages 199 to 234. He ended with a reference to Morley, as having been in the old days 'one of the very choicest' of his contributors, deprecated the praise that had been showered upon him and declared that the qualities and ideals to which the company was met to do honour could be found in fifty others, and that that accounted for a good deal in the power which journalism had attained.

Lord Crewe, writing to me, could not remember whether he himself spoke or not, but he did, delivering, I find, what was reported as being 'a very neat and graceful speech'. Then came

[1] But the *British Weekly* noted that in Morley's *Life of Gladstone* 'there is, so far as the index tells me, no reference to the purchase'. As we have seen, Gladstone opposed it.

Barrie, 'pure genius expressing one of his oldest and strongest affections', Nicoll said. Critics present had 'never heard anything like it; "the most delightful speech I ever listened to" said one of them.'

'Claudius Clear', in concluding his account, says 'the humblest journalist present must have carried away a fresh sense of the greatness and importance of journalistic work.' 'Greenwood did not choose journalism to make money out of it, but to guide aright the public mind. Like R. H. Hutton and Meredith Townsend, he has been satisfied to do his life's work as a journalist.'

And this observer found it 'gratifying and reassuring to hear five Liberal speakers, bearing such testimony to the merits of a staunch Conservative. Mr. Morley spoke with very noticeable severity on the absence of Cabinet Ministers.'[1]

After the dinner Nicoll, I learn from Mrs. Wyatt-Smith, who before her marriage was his secretary, described Greenwood as 'the prince of journalists'. An article by Herbert Paul in the *Speaker* traced the source of his influence.

> His knowledge of foreign politics is surpassed by few, if any, of his contemporaries, and he is the master of a pungent, incisive style. But the secret of his success and the source of his influence may be found in the essential manliness of his character. Gifts and accomplishments are narrated in a thousand articles. They are extolled on ten thousand platforms. They become, or their owner becomes, the fashion. But the fashion of this world passeth away. Somebody else does the trick better, and the first performer is forgotten. But devotion to great principles and to public duty has results, it may be less glittering, but far less transient. But Greenwood raised his profession by the singleness of his aim. Neither fear nor favour, neither affection nor illwill, would induce him to deviate from furthering what appeared to him the true interests of his country.

Paul wrote impartially because, as he said, he had never had the privilege of Greenwood's friendship, and for the greater part of his editorial reign he was writing on the other side in politics. 'Yet I never missed reading an article of his if I could help it,

[1] See pp. 230 and 435.

and I never read one without feeling proud that I, too, was a journalist.' He adds in the *Speaker* article pungently:

What struck me as I heard Greenwood tell the story was his public spirit, of which he seemed himself to be quite unconscious. He was not a rich man. He was in possession of a secret by which he might have made a fortune. His one idea was so to use it that England might derive from it the most national advantage. The millionaires whom Mr. Morley addressed in New York would, no doubt, think him a fool, and it is a simple fact that he has never founded a free

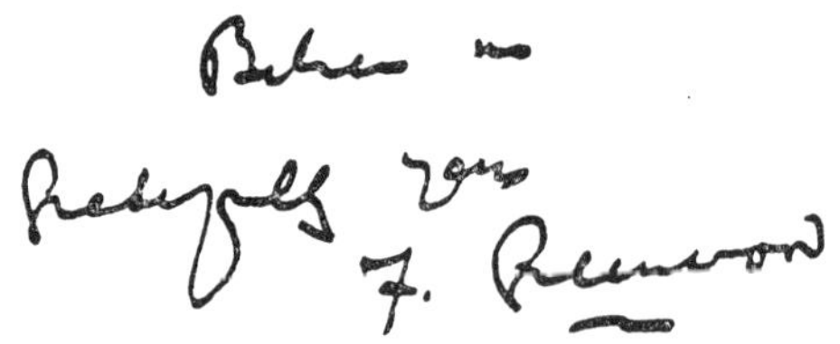

A late autograph.

library. What he founded was British influence in Egypt. Disraeli, who was no more a man of business than Greenwood, had, like him, the imagination which a really great emergency requires. We all remember the Biblical story of the poor man who by his wisdom delivered the city, 'yet no one remembered that same poor man'. Greenwood will not be forgotten. But when one thinks of him, and then tries to remember the names of Mr. Balfour's colleagues in the Cabinet, the solemn plausibilities of the world seem hollow mockeries indeed.

Next, quoting Beaconsfield's apophthegm, 'All great men have the same religion', Paul went on to say that opinion is not the source of real agreement:

Fighting with fair weapons implies a common standard, and inspires mutual respect. No one appreciated more highly the ability of Greenwood than Gladstone, whom for twenty years he hardly ceased to attack. Formidable indeed the attack was. Greenwood combined the unsparing analysis of a French sceptic in such curious harmony with the fervour of a Hebrew prophet that he almost seemed like a sort of Voltairean Carlyle. Gladstone did not disdain to enter the lists with his opponent. But he was no match for Greenwood with the pen.

In concluding this careful and penetrating sketch, which, as the work of a journalist of repute, it is good to salve from the files, Paul says

Greenwood had been a staunch Tory, but he was before all things an Englishman, and the policy of Chamberlain did not appear to him English. It may be that for that reason the Government boycotted the Trocadero. Greenwood's reputation, however, does not depend on any Government. The journalism to which he belonged, and which he adorned, had in it nothing vulgar or flashy or sensational. He and the powerful staff he gathered round him gave their readers good English, sound criticism, trustworthy news. If they never let the Liberal dogs have the best of it, they kept up that wholesome spirit of honourable emulation which is the salt of parties and the life of the Press.

And here, perhaps, an acute reader, with some recollection of the period, may say, the cat or one of the cats is out of the bag: the explanation of the absence of any leader of the Conservative party from the dinner is disclosed. Greenwood had dealt as sharply as cogently with Chamberlain over the South African business. The party side of Chamberlain, who was personally kind and charming, remembered; and it was not its way to let off a political opponent. From the strangers' gallery of the House of Commons, during an East Africa debate, the late Lord Lugard and I—he was but a captain then—were astonished to see the Colonial Secretary come back after dinner to pink a back bencher whom a bigger man would have forgotten or thought unworthy of his rapier.[1] And about the time of the Greenwood dinner the Prime Minister, Mr. Balfour, who found his balancing position on tariffs by no means easy, seemed to be careful not to do anything to create tension between Chamberlain and himself. Morley, who was personally on friendly terms with Chamberlain, would certainly not have spoken as sharply as he

[1] 'Chamberlain, with his almost painfully incisive delivery.'—*Viscount Cecil.*

did about the absence of any member of the Government from the dinner had he not felt that the circumstances warranted it.

In conclusion, it may be asked whether, when all is said and done, too much has been made, in considering the career of Greenwood, of the part he played in the buying of the shares. J. A. Spender, in referring to the dinner[1] said that what was in his mind during the evening was

> the inordinate stress which Greenwood and other speakers laid on the part he had played in the purchase of the shares. It was no doubt a useful and interesting part, but it would have been all in the day's work of even a subordinate Minister, and that it should be seriously regarded as the principal event in the life of a man who for fifty years had been giving his best to journalism and had influenced opinion as steadily as any man in his time, seemed to me a strange distortion of values. Greenwood's title to fame is not that he helped Disraeli to purchase the Suez Canal shares, but that he was a great editor and a very distinguished writer.

Hyndman takes much the same view:[2] 'No doubt', he writes, 'it was an extraordinary thing for an individual to bring about a State transaction which resulted in a market enhancement in the value of the shares bought, at his instance, of close upon £20,000,000 in his own lifetime; but the other work he did was in a higher sphere.'

This is all very well. But Spender and Hyndman miss the point. It is not that 'all in the day's work, a subordinate Government official' might have instigated the buying of the shares but that no such person did so, that no such person had the opportunity of doing so, that, but for Greenwood, Great Britain would have missed the chance of the purchase, that, until the

[1] *Life, Journalism and Politics* (Cassell).

[2] *The Record of an Adventurous Life*, H. M. Hyndman (Macmillan). Reference has been made on an earlier page to Bernard Shaw's picture of Hyndman. Mr. W. H. Robinson sends me an impression: 'I heard him speak, in 1908, I think, in the Guildhall at Bath, Lady Warwick in the chair. He wore a rather old-fashioned frock coat, looked as if he might be the Governor of the Bank of England. The contrast between his respectable appearance and his revolutionary language still makes me laugh. I doubt if anyone in the audience had ever heard of the Marx he spoke of. They listened stupefied. It was indeed a funny scene.'

period of air warfare and the arrival of the atomic age, our part-ownership of the shares was a factor in international policy, and that Greenwood's 'far-sighted stroke' (E. T. Cook's words) by which Disraeli profited so much in reputation was made with singular disinterestedness.

CHAPTER XXXIX

The Greenwoods Pass Away

THE JUDGEMENT OF THE LONDON PRESS — 'WITH A SINGLE EYE TO THE PUBLIC GOOD' — THE CIVIL LIST PENSIONS — THE BRAVE LAST DAYS OF KATE IN HER NINETIES

THE end of Greenwood's life came on December 14, 1909, at his house, 6 Border Crescent, Laurie Park, Sydenham. He was buried at Highgate cemetery four days later. His gravestone bears the inscription:

Frank son of Fred^{k} died June 27 1863 aged 10 years
Edward brother of Frank died May 7 1868
Catherine wife of Frederick Greenwood who died Oct. 28, 1900 aged 77 years.
Also in Affectionate Memory of Frederick Greenwood who died December 14 1909. Aged 79 years.
He used his great qualities of mind and judgement with a single eye to the Public Good.

The wreaths included a 'magnificent' one of red roses inscribed, 'In honour of a statesman of the pen and a true patriot, and in affectionate memory of an old and dear friend of the Baroness and myself.' The grave is reported to me to be 'in a very neglected state'.

The respect in which Greenwood was held by the leaders of the Press at the time of his death was shown in the way in which the news of his decease was received. 'A master of history has been removed from the world', said *The Times* in its large type; 'his influence on his time was greater than is known to the general public.' He was 'a journalist of genius', but his influence 'was not altogether the outcome of his journalistic work. His instinct for capacity in others was as unerring as his journalistic judgement.' The Suez Canal shares incident was 'proof of the weight and regard he had earned'. After reciting other incidents of his journalistic career, *The Times* noted that, at the end of his life, in his contributions to the *Pall Mall*, *Westminster*, and the leading reviews, he 'displayed always that gift of clarity which was his and the "quality of a really sparkling brain", to which Lord Morley bore estimate'. He was 'kindly and generous to all, ever helpful to the members of the profession which he influenced so powerfully'. His memory 'will long be held in honour. He impressed his personality on the discussions of his country and his time.' And in that 'he was a forerunner, for personality in journalism was more rare in England than in France till Greenwood made the *Pall Mall* a power. He wielded this power in the spirit of self-abnegation. He neither sought nor found personal reward. He used his great qualities of mind and judgement with a single eye to the public good.' And, as we have seen, the last sentence went on his tombstone.

The *Pall Mall*, not much of a paper in those days, discharged its duty to its first editor not unworthily. The *Westminster* bid him farewell as 'one of the greatest journalists England has ever produced'. The *Daily Telegraph* said that, as editor of the *Pall Mall*, Greenwood 'wielded a greater influence in politics than any other journalist. He not only maintained the best traditions of his profession; by his ability, honesty and sincerity he added lustre to it.'

At the end of three pages of its 'News of the Week' chronicle the *Spectator* spared sixteen lines in which to say that Greenwood was 'too uncompromising in his individualism to have a long following', but he had passed away 'in the enjoyment of the esteem of colleagues, men of letters and politicians of both parties'. There was no allusion in the note to the Suez Canal shares. Nor was the subject mentioned in a characteristic sniff in the *Saturday Review*. Greenwood, it said, 'had not anything in the nature of genius; he dwelt in the safer region'. But he 'had taste, discretion and a sense of responsibility'.

On August 10, 1910, eight months after the death of Greenwood, his services were tardily recognized by Downing Street. 'In consideration of the literary abilities and public services of their father, the late Mr. Frederick Greenwood, and of their inadequate means of support', a Civil List pension of £100 a year was given to his two daughters, Jessy and Kate, 'jointly and to the survivor'.[1] There were two protests. 'Looker-On', 'a political opponent', writing in the *Daily Mail*, regarded the amount of the annuity as 'most discreditable, shabby'. 'Being personally well acquainted with all the circumstances which led up to the acquisition of the Suez Canal shares', he said, 'it seems to me that a country which has benefited so enormously could well have afforded to show a little more generosity.' The other correspondent was Hyndman—was the first one Henry Oppenheim, or Charles Whibley, reviving the *Blackwood* pseudonym?—who wrote, 'I also saw the first steps taken for the acquisition of the shares. There is certainly at least one member of the Cabinet [Mr. Asquith] who knows all the facts as well as I do. An annuity of £100 a year to Mr. Greenwood's daughters is not a creditable return on the part of this nation.'

Greenwood had made his will on August 25, 1882. It is formal and appoints as his executrix his daughter Kate, who proved it on January 11, 1910. The value of the gross estate was £6,552 and of the personal estate £4,729.

The facts about Greenwood's financial position are stated in a letter which his eldest daughter wrote, a year later, to the *Melbourne Argus* in which she says:

> I read with amazement and distress that 'Mr. Greenwood's closing days were dependent upon the liberality of private friends'. The writer has been strangely misinformed, and I should fail in duty and respect towards my father's memory if I did not give the statement an unqualified denial. Mr. Greenwood never received pecuniary assistance from his friends. Those who knew him as he was, a singularly independent man, a proud man, will not need any assurance that such an arrangement as that suggested in your columns would have been impossible to him, even supposing necessity had arisen, and it did not arise.

[1] I am indebted for the precise facts to Sir Edward Bridges. On the death of Jessy, Somerset House wrote, I see, that 'it is not proposed to raise any claim for duty in respect of the cesser of her interest'.

A receipt for the rent of 6 Border Crescent, Sydenham, where Greenwood died shows that the rent was £25 a quarter.

Early in 1944 I tried to trace Greenwood's son and daughters. When I heard of a daughter living in Hastings a letter to the local paper brought me into touch with the late Mrs. Hill-Reid, who told me of Kate being still alive, and of the pluck she had shown under the bombings, and gave me extracts from some letters. Mrs. Hill-Reid had known Miss Greenwood for thirty years.

Kate says in one communication to her that one day she heard three big explosions, and 'it is wonderful how determined and brave people are', and, with her father's touch, 'the world has made a little mistake about us'. Later on, again choosing her words well, Kate writes of the 'enemy evening aircraft growling their way past on their dreadful business in London. It is a nightly distress, about two hours of it. They come by dozens and dozens.' In another letter—and the record is worth keeping for the next generation—she speaks of them 'coming regularly three or four times a day and pretty nearly at the same time. There is always one about lunch time, another at tea time, and the dozens that grunt their way over on the road to London at 7 p.m.; sometimes about 9.30 a.m. to worry the early shoppers.' Again she writes: 'I do feel unhappy and distressed when I think that I can never see England peaceful and prosperous again. All that will come, but beyond my time—I have just heard three bombs.' One thinks of her father's forebodings.

On November 13 she announces: 'I have to day passed into my ninetieth year.' 'I am not now able', she says, 'to cope with all that should be done. I have to use one eye only, which throws my sight out of the straight.' Although Miss Greenwood had reached such a great age I hoped I might be able to see her for a few minutes, but, writing in July 1945, Mrs. Hill-Reid said: 'She will not see anyone. She reads the paper but never writes letters now.' In a later letter Mrs. Hill-Reid wrote: 'When I last saw her she mentioned that her father was so young when she was born that they were always great friends, and at an hotel were taken for a young married couple. She never mentioned her mother at any time.' Mrs. Hill-Reid received the following letter, signed 'Yours affectionately', before the recluse had a stroke:

> It is most kind and forgiving of you to write to me again when I have been such a very bad correspondent for some months, not only to you but to all friends. I have almost, if not quite, ceased to write letters. Perhaps those who have passed their 93rd birthday, well towards 94, do get too tired after having done their various odd duties. I have had an uncomfortable month or so with a persistent cold, chiefly of the bronchial kind, which gives me bad nights. I hope you will both escape anything of that sort—life is tiresome enough even if one keeps free from winter ailments.

Among Kate's papers I notice a receipt, but as far back as 1894, for half a crown 'being your tribute to the Primrose League'.

> Miss Greenwood is dignified and proud [Mrs. Hill-Reid wrote to me]. She preferred to live alone. Most of her furniture has been in store for some years. She lived for a time in Sutherland Avenue, Bexhill. Her late sister, Miss Jessy, was more free and easy. I did not know the brother, but they were a devoted trio. A young aunt of Miss Greenwood lived with her for some years but in time she went blind. Miss Greenwood had lovely rings and other jewellery. I do not know that she has done anything to do justice to her able father's memory. A pity she has not written his biography. I wish you had taken up this matter years ago.

Later it was reported to me that the old lady was 'very comfortable and her mind clear, but she did not talk much and would see no one but her doctor'. And then Mrs. Hill-Reid got no news, and on March 3, 1946, I learnt from her that the last of the Greenwoods had 'passed peacefully away' at ninety-four and was to be buried 'in the family grave' at Hastings.

I ascertained in London that the pension had not been applied for since March 4 of the previous year; letters from the Treasury addressed to Miss Greenwood had been returned through the post. I understand that when Edgar died £1,500 came to Kate.

The income tax returns of Kate and Jessy for 1928–30 show that the income, less charges, of Kate was £128 and of Jessy £149. Besides their respective halves of their Civil List pension and the interest on the Egyptian Bonds they owned two houses called Eton Villas.

Among the odds and ends Kate had preserved were several photographs. One of them bore out Mrs. Triggs's recollection that Jessy 'was quite pretty when we knew her'. Kate had also saved a lot of invitation cards received by her father. In two, in the same month, 'the Comptroller of the Household is desired by Their Royal Highnesses the Prince and Princess of Wales to invite Mr. F. Greenwood to a Morning Party at Chiswick', 'Weather Permitting' being underlined. In an invitation from Lord and Lady Derby 'favour' is spelt without a 'u' in 'The favor of an answer is desired'. Among the At Home cards, one is 'to have the honour of meeting His Imperial Majesty the Emperor of Russia', two each are from the Duchess of Sutherland, Lady Salisbury, Lady Derby, Lady Granville, Lady Northcote, and Lady Beauchamp; several from Lady Waldegrave, four, with the addition of Miss Greenwood's name—one being 'to meet H.R.H. The Duchess of Teck'. A card from the Duke and Duchess of Albany is 'on the occasion of their daughter's wedding'. An invitation to the opening by the Queen of the Royal Courts of Justice on December 4, 1882, at which 'Levée Dress will be worn', is accompanied by particulars of the ceremonial which would occupy four pages in the type of this book. The Victorians took such things very seriously.

Kate had lived at the same address for twenty years—twelve years by herself. Then one day the good Mrs. Lusted, who had looked after her for eighteen years, found her in a faint and took her to her own home. Miss Greenwood's next-door neighbours in Lower Park Road, Mrs. Triggs and her sister Miss Pain, had been kind in sending in appetizing things and in other ways. I saw, on the wall half way up the stairs in their house, the worn place where they had knocked daily in order to make sure, by receiving a knock in response, that the old lady was all right.

Here is one of Kate's letters, beginning 'Dear Friends', written the last Christmas she was alive:

I am afraid the general outlook does not come up to expectations. Weather is miserable and news not comforting from any point of view. Tempers seem to be fraying wherever two or three are gathered together publicly and privately.

Thank you very much for the very nice things this morning. You know how I appreciate your great kindness. I do hope Mrs. Triggs' cold, if not gone is steadily going and that neither of you will have another such winter. I have had a horrid week myself, my long lasting head-cold invited trouble in my chest, so I have been coughing and wheezing in such a tiresome manner that I have had to put off my Christmas packets and parcels for New Year's Day. I simply cannot manage them at present.

Another year of it is now ending a long series. I wonder how 'the world at large', and our people in particular, will feel when we have to face another year of War, and a stiff, savage war too. Our leaders ought to have known German temperament better than they have shown in the last month or so, and cleared the ground as they went, but the Americans are anxious, determined to be first in Berlin. The poor Belgians! It is terrible for them: and all that horrid work to be done again!

All good wishes and to all the others if there are any more.

I intended to put this on the sill at tea-time, but it was so wet.

I have mentioned that Mrs. Hill-Reid never heard Miss Greenwood speak of her mother. Mrs. Triggs wrote to me: 'One might wonder whether she ever had a mother; she never spoke of her. My sister asked her if her mother died when she was young. She said "Yes". That is all we ever heard.' Mrs. Lusted told me that Miss Greenwood often spoke of her father. Having, as she told Mrs. Lusted, no one of her own to whom to bequeath what little she had, she left it to the faithful Lusteds.

Mrs. Triggs and Miss Pain, because I was writing about Miss Greenwood, generously insisted that I should have her portrait as a girl. The portrait of her father in the frontispiece was in the possession of Mrs. Lusted, who was good enough to let me buy it from her. To my great regret, I was prevented from getting down to Hastings until some time after Miss Greenwood's death, and the books and any other memorials of her father she possessed had been dispersed at a sale, and I could hear nothing of the buyers. But Miss Pain gave me her copy of Jessy's *Moon Maiden*, and Mr. Hayward, whom I met at Hastings, also insisted on my taking Greenwood's own copy of *Imagination in Dreams and their Study*.[1]

Mrs. Lusted, in speaking to me of Jessy Greenwood, said that 'she had a marvellous way with animals. It was uncanny. They would do anything for her; the mice used to lie down beside her. She was also kind and considerate and looked after Miss Kate, who was always considered the delicate one. Miss Kate was a dear old lady. Sometimes she used to speak of her "ghost", always with her, sometimes a man, sometimes an animal.' Mrs Lusted mentioned a kindness between Miss Jessy and someone she named to me, 'but she broke it off, though they remained friends'.

It seems clear, I think, that as Kate and Jessy got older their natures expanded. I have come on no note or memory of querulousness in their later years, and Kate in her last letter touching on public affairs showed herself in her outlook not a little her father's daughter.

Her sister Jessy had died on August 27, 1931, twenty-two years after her father, and was buried at Hastings. Edgar, who had not married, followed in twelve months and lies in his father's grave at Highgate. With the death of Kate, who was buried at Hastings, the family of Frederick Greenwood passed away.

[1] Bodley Head.

Envoy

AND now I come to the Editors of the *Pall Mall* after Greenwood, with all of whom I was acquainted. My respect and regard for John Morley was such that I once had the audacity, as a young man, to propose myself as his private secretary. I possess letters which he wrote from the editorial office to Stead.

Of Stead, who brought me up from Birmingham to Northumberland Street, I have, beyond my own memories, the memories of the surviving member of his family, his daughter Miss Estelle Stead, and of his son, the late John Stead, and large boxes of unpublished miscellaneous material from many friends and colleagues.

I was with Stead and his successor, Sir Edward Cook, and his successor (on the *Westminster*) J. A. Spender, for thirteen years.

I worked for a few months with a *Pall Mall* editor of fine parts, Harry Cust, who followed Cook, and I have been entrusted by his widow and by his cousin, Sir Ronald Storrs, with memories and papers regarding him and the journalism and the social life of the time.

J. L. Garvin, who was the last outstanding editor of the paper after Sir Douglas Straight, was appreciative enough of my *Countryman* not only to buy it but to bind it.

In my autobiographical volume on the further adventures of a remarkable newspaper, with editors and staff of quality, I bring the story to its end, and also tell what is of interest in the adventures of Greenwood's second *Gazette*, the *St. James's*, under the editorships of Sir Sidney Low, Hugh Chisholm, and Ronald McNeill, afterwards Lord Cushendun, to its vanishing also.

Possibly I may add a short account of my adventures in rural journalism and authorship in Essex after I retired from the *Daily Chronicle*, and of my experience in founding the *New East* in Tokyo and the *Countryman* in the Cotswolds in, if I may say so, something of the *Pall Mall* spirit.

If I have done well, as is fitting the story, it is that which I desired; but if slenderly and meanly, it is that which I could attain unto.

II MACCABEES XV. 38

APPENDIX I

'Rockney', George Meredith's Greenwood

As some of us have not been reading Meredith lately,[1] his reflection of Greenwood as 'Rockney' in *Celt and Saxon* is worth reproduction for the phrases in which the novelist has obviously his editor friend in mind. The novel was published a year after Greenwood's death. The following extract is condensed.

Among the patriotic of stout English substance, who blew in the trumpet of the country, and were not bards of Bull to celebrate his firmness and vindicate his shiftings, Richard Rockney takes front rank. A journalist altogether given up to his craft, he was a man of forethought besides being a trenchant writer, and he was profoundly not less than eminently, the lover of Great Britain. He was physician, spiritual director, man-at-arms.

There were occasions when distinguished officials and Parliamentary speakers received the impetus of Rockney's approval and not unhesitatingly he stepped behind them to bestow it. The act, in whatever fashion it may have been esteemed by the objects propelled, was a sign of his willingness to let the shadow of any man adopting his course obscure him, and of the simplicity of his attachment. . . .

His changes of view were not attributed to a fluctuating devotion; they passed out of the range of criticism upon inconsistency, notwithstanding that the commencement of his journalistic career smelt of sources entirely opposed to the conclusions upon which it broadened.

One secret of the belief in his love of his country was the readiness of Rockney's pen to support our nobler patriotic impulses, his relish of the bluff besides. His eye was on our commerce, on our courts of Law, on our streets and alleys, our army and navy, our colonies, the vaster than the island England, and still he would be busy picking up needles and threads in the island. Deeds of valour were noted by him, lapses of cowardice: how one man stood against a host for

[1] The works are published by Constable.

law or humanity, how crowds looked on at the beating of a woman, how a good fight was maintained in some sly ring between two of equal brawn: and manufacturers were warned of the consequences of their iniquities, Government was lashed for sleeping upon shaky ordinances, colonists were gibbeted for the maltreating of natives: the ring and fervour of the notes on daily events told of Rockney's hand upon the national heart—with a faint, an enforced, reluctant indication of our not being the men we were.

But after all, the main secret was his art of writing round English, instead of laborious latinized periods: and the secret of the art was his meaning what he said. It was the personal throb. The fire of a mind was translucent in Press columns where our public had been accustomed to the rhetoric of primed scribes. He did away with the Biscay billow of the leading article—Bull's favourite prose-bardic construction of sentences that roll to the antithetical climax, whose foamy top is offered and gulped as equivalent to an idea. Writing of such a kind as Rockney's was new to a land where the political opinions of Joint Stock Companies had rattled Jovian thunders obedient to the nod of Bull. Though not alone in working the change, he was the foremost. And he was not devoid of style. Fervidness is the core of style. He was a tough opponent for his betters in education, struck forcibly, fenced dexterously, was always alert for debate. He was a steam ram that drove straight at the bulky broadside of the enemy.

Premiers of parties might be Captains of the State for Rockney: Rockney was the premier's pilot, or woe to him. Woe to the country as well, if Rockney's directions for steering were unheeded. The refusal of the captain to go this way caused Rockney sincerely to discredit the sobriety of his intellect. It was a drunken captain. Or how if a traitorous?

Rockney could not be a mild sermoniser commenting on events. Rather no journalism at all for him! He thought the office of the ordinary daily preacher cow-like. His gadfly stung him to warn, dictate, prognosticate; he was the oracle and martyr of superior vision: and as in affairs of business and the weighing of men he was of singularly cool sagacity, hard on the downright, open to the humours of the distinct discrimination of things in their roughness, the knowledge of the firmly-based materialism of his nature caused him thoroughly to trust to his voice when he delivered it in ardour....

Great love creates forethoughtfulness, without which incessant journalism is a gabble. He was sure of his love, but who gave ear to his prescience? Few: the echo of the country now and then, the Government not often. And, dear me! those jog-trot sermonisers, mere commentators upon events, manage somehow to keep up the sale of their Journals: advertisements do not flow and ebb with them as under the influence of a capricious moon. . . .

In the season of prosperity Rockney lashed the old fellow with the crisis he was breeding for us; and when prostration ensued no English tongue was loftier in preaching dignity and the means of recovery. The country has gone the wrong road, but it may yet cross over to the right one, when it perceives that we were prophetic. . . .

Behind the plethoric lamp, now blown with the fleshpots, now gasping puffs of panic, he saw the well-minded valorous people, issue of glorious grandsires: a nation under monstrous defacement, stupefied by the contemplation of the mask: his vision was of the great of old, the possibly great in the graver strife ahead, respecters of life, despisers of death, the real English.

APPENDIX II

THE SUEZ CANAL SHARES

THE Company's board of directors consists of 32 members, each elected for 8 years, 16 French, 10 British, 1 American, 1 Dutch, and 4 Egyptian. The number of Egyptians is to be gradually raised to 7. The President and two vice-presidents are French. The third vice-president is British. The British members are Sir Harrison Hughes, Sir Alan G. Anderson, Major A. H. Bibby, Lord Cromer, Sir William Currie, Sir Hubert Heath Eves, Sir Ronald Fraser, Lord Hankey, Lord Rotherwick, and Sir Francis Verner Wylie.

Besides the new 7½-mile by-pass, the Canal is to be deepened by 20 inches over the whole of its length in order to allow the latest tankers, with a draught of 36 feet, to pass through, and to improve the steering of large vessels. The enlargement of one of the basins in Port Said harbour will permit the berthing of 18 ships 660 feet long, compared with nine 330 feet long as at present.

In the narratives of the Canal Shares purchase a little bit of history is omitted. Miss Edith M. Bigg-Wither tells me that her grandfather, Lieut.-General Sir John Stokes, K.C.B., a Near East expert, was consulted by Disraeli, and his advice was to buy. Sir John, to whom Disraeli paid a tribute in the House of Commons as 'a gentleman of very great ability', had represented Great Britain on the Danube Commission and in negotiations regarding the Suez Canal dues. When the purchase was decided upon Sir John went out to Egypt with Mr. Cave, and dealt with the Khedive and de Lesseps. He was one of the first three representatives of Great Britain on the Canal board. In the minutes of a meeting of the Conseil d'Administration on December 2, 1902, Prince Auguste d'Arenberg, in the chair, spoke, at the length of four pages of typed quarto, in warm praise of Sir John, to whom de Lesseps had referred in appreciative terms, and his words are followed with '*Très bien, très bien. Marques unanimes de profonde sympathie*'. I have seen a portrait of Sir John in uniform—'he is the very model of a modern major general'—and have also handled his Canal medal. (On one side are the words, in French, with emblematic figures 'French thrift prepares the way for world peace'; on the other, *Compagnie Universelle du Canal Maritime de Suez. Le 17 Novembre 1869. Le Canal Maritime a été ouvert à la grande navigation.*) It is of interest that our representative who succeeded Sir John on the Danube Commission was General Gordon, who perished in Khartoum, the friend of two editors of the *Pall Mall*, Greenwood and Stead.

Great Britain's shares having been halved in 1924, our present holding is 353,504 against the purchase of 176,602. The figures do not quite tally owing to a later purchase of 300 directors' qualifying shares, subsequently halved. Half were added to the holding, the other half being used as directors' qualifications.

The shares, which cost Great Britain £3,976,582, plus commission at 2½ per cent., are 225,940 *actions de capital* and 127,564 *actions de jouissance*. *Actions de capital* are quoted on the London Exchange at £125 per share, *actions de jouissance* in Paris at fr. 85,500 with the franc at 1,097. *Actions de capital* represent the share capital of the Company. They carry interest at 5 per cent. together with a variable dividend dependent on net profits. These shares are subject to redemption at par by annual drawings ending in 1968, when the Company's concession expires. In the place of the drawn *actions de capital*, shareholders are given *actions de jouissance* on which dividend, but not interest, is paid. A shareholder whose shares have been redeemed retains the right of voting at meetings; all that he surrenders in return for the par value of his shares is the statutory interest at 5 per cent. Founders' shares are allocated 10 per cent. of the total net profits of the Company each year. The number of *capital* shares is reduced yearly by redemption, with corresponding increase in *jouissance* holding.

Receipts in 1948 amounted to 19,935,442,100 francs, expenses to 6,107,826,595 francs. To the profit of 13,011,895,782 francs there is to be added 61,348,965 francs carried forward from the previous year, forming a total of 13,073,244,747 francs. The gross dividend was 7,000 francs. To this should be added, for capital shares, statutory interest which, for 1948, amounted to 975·57 francs.

INDEX